D0094274

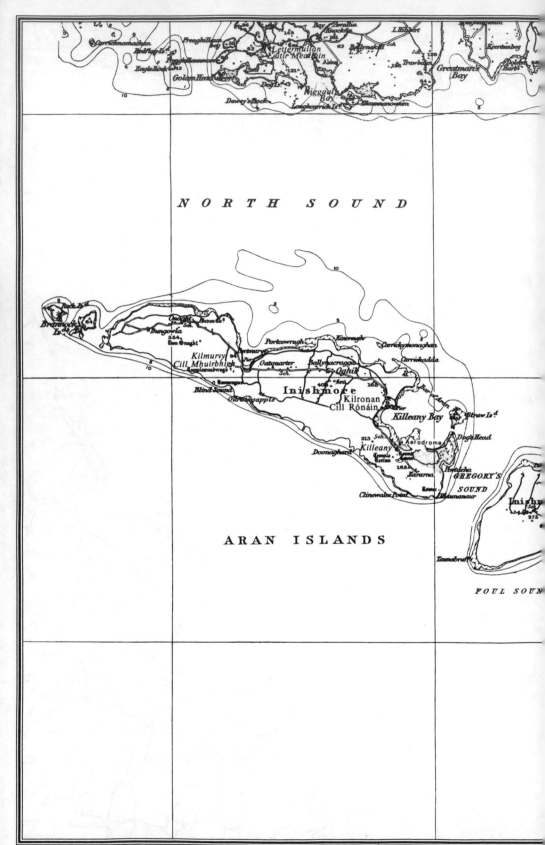

ARAN ISLANDS

AN ARAN READER

Do mhuintir Uí Eithir in Inis Oírr
For the Ó hEithir family in Inis Oírr:
Bríd, Deirdre, Ciarán, Lorcán agus Rút

AN ARAN READER

Edited by
Breandán and Ruairí Ó hEithir

The Lilliput Press

Copyright © The Lilliput Press Ltd

First published 1991 by
THE LILLIPUT PRESS LTD
62–63 Sitric Road, Arbour Hill, Dublin 7, Ireland

This paperback edition published 1999

A CIP record for this title is available from the British Library

ISBN 1 901866 28 9 *paper*

The Lilliput Press receives financial assistance from
An Chomhairle Ealaíon / The Arts Council of Ireland.

Set in 10 on 12 Garamond 3
by Koinonia Ltd of Parker St, Bury, England

Printed in Ireland by Betaprint of Dublin

Contents

Preface and Acknowledgments

All extracts have been reproduced in their original form. In the case of manuscript material it was decided not to correct or edit the text but to preserve it without alteration. Unless otherwise indicated, all translations from the Irish were by the editors.

Our thanks go to the following holders of copyright material: John J. O'Meara for his translation of *The History and Topography of Ireland* (Dublin 1982) by Giraldus Cambrensis; the Board of Trinity College, Dublin for the letters of the Reverend Alexander Synge, TCD MS. 8200; Faber & Faber Ltd for 'The Mirage of the Fisherman of Aran' by James Joyce from *The Critical Writings of James Joyce* (London 1959), edited by Ellsworth Mason and Richard Ellmann; the family of Thomas Mason for *The Islands of Ireland* (Dublin 1936) by Thomas H. Mason; the Department of Irish Folklore, University College, Dublin and the editor of *Béaloideas* for 'Aristotle and His Wife'; Peters Fraser & Dunlop for *Thy Neighbour's Wife* (London 1923) by Liam O'Flaherty; Wolfhound Press, 68 Mountjoy Square, Dublin 1 for *The Black Soul* (London 1936, Dublin 1981) and *Skerrett* (London 1932, Dublin 1977) by Liam O'Flaherty; Niamh Sheridan for selected poems and the extract from *Feamainn Bhealtaine* (Dublin 1961) by Máirtín Ó Direáin; The Goldsmith Press, Newbridge, Co. Kildare for the translations of poems by Máirtín Ó Direáin from *Tacar Dánta/Selected Poems* (Newbridge 1984), translated by Tomás Mac Síomóin and Douglas Sealy; Oxford University Press for 'Epitaph for Robert Flaherty' by Derek Mahon from *Poems 1962-1978* (Oxford 1979); The Gallery Press for 'Aran' by Derek Mahon from *Selected Poems* (Dublin 1991) and 'Leaving Inishmore' by Michael Longley from *Poems 1963-1983* (Dublin 1985); A. M. Heath and the estate of the late Richard Power for *Apple in the Treetop* (Dublin 1980) by Richard Power; Faber & Faber Ltd for 'Lovers on Aran' by Seamus Heaney from *Death of a Naturalist* (London 1966); Harcourt Brace Jovanovich for *Inis Beag* (London 1969) by John Messenger; Etienne Rynne for 'Dún Aengus – Fortress or Temple?'; The Lilliput Press for *The Rock Garden* (Mullingar 1984) by Leo Daly; Shevawn Lynam for 'A Change of Outlook'; The Calder Educational Trust, London for *Balcony of Europe* (John Calder Ltd, London and Riverrun Press, New York 1972) by Aidan Higgins; The Lilliput Press for *Stones of Aran* (Mullingar 1986) by Tim Robinson.

The editors and publisher have made every effort to trace copyright owners, and apologize for any inadvertent errors in or omissions from the list above.

We would also like to thank Gerry Long and the staff of the National Library, Dublin; the staff of the Rare Books Library and the Manuscript Library, Trinity College, Dublin; the Department of Irish Folklore, University College, Dublin; Peigin O'Sullivan and Muiris Mac Conghail. Special thanks are due to both Antony Farrell and Vincent Hurley, without whose inspiration and hard work this book would not have been possible.

Finally, I would like to acknowledge my debt to my father, Breandán Ó hEithir, who died suddenly before this book was completed. I wish to express my gratitude at having been able to work with him for the last three years and my sorrow at his not being here for the publication of *An Aran Reader*; I hope it is a fitting monument to his passionate and heartfelt love for the islands where he was born.

Ruairí Ó hEithir
July 1991

AN ARAN READER

Introduction

When viewed from the coast of Clare or Connemara at sunset, the three islands of Aran, resembling gigantic humpback whales of varying sizes, straddle the mouth of Galway Bay. They have been inhabited for four thousand years, probably without interruption, and the present community will carry its accumulated traditions into the twenty-first century.

The purpose of this anthology is to create a mosaic of island life and history in the words of those who came to know the place as strangers, as well as those who wrote of the life they experienced from childhood.

Some of the strangers – the word generally used in Aran for a tourist is the Irish word *strainséir*, a stranger – came with a purpose: antiquarians like O'Donovan and Petrie; botanists like Praeger and Colgan; linguists like Marstrander and Finck; cultural and revolutionary nationalists like Hyde and Pearse; writers like Synge, Joyce and Richard Power; film-makers like Flaherty and Mac Conghail; painters like Keating, Lambe, Rivers and McGonigle; an occasional mystic in search of the wisdom thought to exist on the fringes of continents like poor Antonin Artaud, founder of the Theatre of Cruelty, who saw his frightening vision of the horrors which were about to envelope Europe (at Dún Aonghasa in 1935) but could not pay his landlady; restless wanderers in search of their true vocations like Orson Welles; and the mildly curious like Tim Robinson, a Yorkshireman who came to look and stayed to learn Irish and restore the place-names to their original forms, thus putting the islands definitively on his magically detailed map.

As well as writing, creatively or autobiographically, about island life, the native writers also cast a gull's cold eye on some of the antics the strangers in their midst got up to. In one of his two best novels, *Skerrett*, Liam O'Flaherty dealt with the deadly rivalry between the parish priest of Aran and one of his schoolteachers during the early years of the twentieth century.

This very personal antagonism, which tore the community apart, was between two domineering and vain outsiders (one from Mayo, the other from Limerick) who sought to impose their differing views on the island

1

community. The author availed of an opportunity to step outside both these circles of conflict and give the complete outsider's view, through the mouth of an English coastguard, stationed unhappily on Inis Mór.

'It's my idea that the sooner we English get out of this country the better. Hand the lousy country over to the priests. Then the bloody Irish'll soon be sorry we left.'

Dealing with a later period in island history, the filming of *Man of Aran* in the early 1930s, Pat Mullen adds a wry footnote to that prediction when he tells of how the astute Robert Flaherty dispelled the misgivings of the parish priest of the day concerning the moral problems which might be created by the filming of the community he both ministered to and controlled. Flaherty contributed liberally to the pastor's Christmas collection.

Pat Mullen wrote exclusively in English, Liam and Tom O'Flaherty wrote mainly in that language but also produced some work in Irish. All three were bilingual. So too was the poet and essayist Máirtín Ó Direáin, who wrote exclusively in Irish. Ó Direáin was not as overtly political as the others, and his essays deal in a very personal way with childhood, life and death.

But what is striking about the work of all these Inis Mór writers is that it reflects a very strong sense of place and particularly of the continuity of life in Aran. History and lore leap off the pages. This is hardly surprising. The islands have been described as vast outdoor museums, with the inhabitants going about their daily work amid the exhibits.

For instance, a man from the village of Cill Mhuirbhigh who goes to one of his nearby fields to milk his cow casts his eye over a wide range of island history during his short walk. His village lies under the brooding presence of Aran's best-known monument, the pre-Christian fort Dún Aonghasa. Closer to the village stands Teampall Mac Duach, an eighth-century church dedicated to St Colmán Mac Duach. It stands in the grounds of Kilmurvey House, built in the early nineteenth century for Patrick O'Flaherty, magistrate and landlord, who compiled the first detailed census of the islands in 1821.

As he walks towards the seashore he passes the last house in the village: a larger than usual construction built originally as a second police barracks (there was another in Cill Rónáin five miles to the east) to deal with acute agrarian disorder in the 1880s. A short distance away, overlooking Cill Mhuirbhigh's dazzlingly white strand, is the little graveyard of Cnocán na mBan (The Women's Hillock). According to tradition, it was from this eminence that the O'Brien women sat and watched their men do battle with the 'Ferocious' O'Flahertys from Connemara on the beach below during the reign of Elizabeth I of England. That some such battle for control of the island did indeed take place was verified by the many cloven skulls recovered here during road-widening in the 1930s.

The little cemetery is dominated by a large Celtic cross that marks the grave of Patrick O'Flaherty and his descendants. It is described in the opening lines of Máirtín Ó Direáin's longest poem, 'Ó Mórna', based on the stormy lives of the O'Flahertys of Kilmurvey House.

In the distance is the village of Gort na gCapall (Field of the Horses), birthplace of Liam and Tom O'Flaherty and of their father, Michael, who organized the destruction of Patrick O'Flaherty's son's stock during the Land League agitation by driving them over a cliff at night; a chilling episode, described by his son Liam in his novel *Land*.

And above Cill Mhuirbhigh pier are the thatched cottages built specially by Robert Flaherty (who had no known Irish connections) for the filming of *Man of Aran*, the powerful but fundamentally spurious documentary that made Aran known internationally.

But why Aran? The question was put to me some years ago by the historian Leon Ó Broin. We were having breakfast together during the Merriman Summer School in Lahinch, County Clare, where my function was to conduct a morning seminar on the Aran Islands.

'Did you ever ask yourself why so many people find those three limestone rocks in the Atlantic so terribly interesting?'

The short answer is that Aran islanders now take that interest for granted and find their own interest stimulated by the attention of others. To be an Aran islander is to be someone special, part of a long and many-faceted tradition, growing up in a bilingual community with an intense interest in its own history, just that trifle removed from mainland life and, perhaps, as one recent writer on island life commented acidly, imagining oneself to be just a shade better than most.

When did this journey towards restrained narcissism begin? The very beginning is shrouded in mystery and in a deal of scholarly uncertainty. None can date the islands' stone fortresses with complete accuracy. Some say pre-Christian; others early Christian.

Other than their being a well-organized community capable of manipulating large blocks of limestone with great skill, nothing is known of the builders either; and where facts are absent theories abound. Interestingly there are almost no local legends connected with the seven surviving Aran forts, but visitors with fertile imaginations more than compensated for the absence of genuine folklore. Some of their fantasies are to be found in print but are scarcely worth reading.

The experts are also baffled by the purpose of these constructions. Were they meant to protect people under attack and provide shelter for their stock? If so, who were the attackers and where did they come from? Or were they, as one recent academic theorist has maintained, intended to glorify the builder and provide a suitable arena for ceremonials in his honour; with the focus on what was happening inside rather than outside the great circle of stone?

3

One could go on, for these forts have been fertile founts of myth, but their builders obviously possessed similar skills to those to which the modern dry stone walls of Aran bear witness.

Once the early Christian community arrived on the islands, verifiable facts survive alongside local legends about various saints – many of them marked by most unchristian sentiments and unsaintly behaviour.

Monasticism was brought to Aran by St Enda (Éinne or Éanna in Irish), the island's patron, who died in the settlement he founded at Cill Éinne in Inis Mór, about 520. He came from north Leinster and his little church, buried to the gables in sand, stands in Cill Éinne graveyard. Enda's system of monasticism consisted of prayer, fasting, vigil and work, and, judged solely by the remains that have withstood the assaults of Cromwellian and other invaders, its extent was vast.

The main settlements were at Cill Éinne and what is now called Na Seacht dTeampail (The Seven Churches), at the other end of Inis Mór. Other surviving churches, on all three islands, were clearly built by hermits. One of the smallest, oldest and most spectacular in its setting is Teampall Bheanáin (Benan's Church) near Cill Éinne.

Some of the churches and holy wells, named after various saints, are still places of pilgrimage. Caomhán (Kevin or Cavan) is the patron of Inis Oírr and on the eve of his feast-day people still hold a vigil in his little church in the island graveyard.

One of the later churches on Inis Mór, the fifteenth-century Teampall an Cheathrar Álainn (the Church of the Four Beautiful Saints), and the nearby holy well, have been immortalized by Synge in his play *The Well of the Saints*. The well is still a place of pilgrimage for people suffering from ailments of the eyes.

According to legend, many saints came to visit Aran because of its reputation as a centre of learning and holiness: it became known as Árainn na Naomh (Aran of the Saints). Among them was the ubiquitous Colmcille (Columba), at whose well 'stations' are still performed but who is said to have been sent packing by Éanna, portrayed as a stern and rather dictatorial man.

The sound between Inis Mór and Inis Meáin, Sunda Ghrióra, is named after St Gregory of the Golden Mouth. He is said to have died in Rome and been interred there, despite his wish to be buried in Aran. But his coffin rose out of the grave and floated across the sea to his nominated burial-place close to the sound.

Galway City prospered and grew as a garrison and busy sea-port, and the strategic importance of the islands which controlled all entrances to the bay increased. Various interests took possession of Aran, especially Inis Mór and Inis Oírr guarding the principal sounds, and exacted tribute from Galway. In time they were ousted by a more powerful faction. Because it was the only island to have a safe anchorage and natural harbour, Inis Mór – and particularly the villages of Cill Éinne and Cill Rónáin – also grew in size and importance.

When Queen Elizabeth I decided to bring the dissident Irish to heel and introduce direct rule, the islands were controlled by the O'Briens of Clare, one of whose many castles stands on the crest of Inis Oírr. Elizabeth encouraged the ambitious O'Flahertys to oust the troublesome O'Briens and then proceeded to cut the O'Flahertys down to size as well.

In 1587 she granted the islands by letters patent to John Rawson of Athlone and his heirs, on condition that they retained a posse of not less than twenty English soldiers on the islands. Apart from a brief period during the Cromwellian war, the islands were henceforth garrisoned by Crown forces until the Treaty of 1922.

The garrison was at its strongest after the end of the Cromwellian war, when Inis Mór was used for prisoners of war and most of the Catholic priests (who were ministering illegally at the time) rounded up in the west of Ireland. Arkyn Castle, overlooking Cill Éinne harbour, was extended with stones taken from the nearby Franciscan monastery and round tower.

The strength of the garrison and the number of prisoners varied, but by the beginning of the eighteenth century the garrison was reduced, and for the next two hundred years the islanders were left to the mercy of a series of rapacious landlords, their agents and the representatives of law and order who protected them.

These events affected the islands in various ways. Crown representatives were in direct contact with the islanders for hundreds of years, with the result that English became the language of the governing class which existed there at a surprisingly early stage for a place so remote. All official contact with the mainland was through Galway City, although it is thirty miles away, and continued to be for years after the first regular ferry service was established. This in turn meant that Cill Rónáin gradually became the island metropolis and the English language was in common use there before the end of the nineteenth century.

Indeed, Synge, who left Cill Rónáin for Inis Meáin after a short stay, wrote that the Irish language would shortly die out on Inis Mór. Synge and others who came to the same conclusion were wrong.

Although Inis Meáin is still the most thoroughly Irish-speaking island, Inis Mór and Inis Oírr are bilingual communities and the language is probably stronger in Cill Rónáin – christened 'Aran's Big Smoke' by Brendan Behan – today than when Synge arrived in 1898.

Not until the publication of two scientific studies, in 1955 and 1958, did the long-term effect of the English garrison on the Aran community become known. These scrutinized the physical characteristics and the blood groups of the islanders and found that both showed a strong English admixture. The popular newspapers of the day had great fun with the peripheral fact that the teeth of Aran children seemed to resemble those of their London Cockney counterparts. However, all the obviously English surnames that appeared in the 1821 census – such as Billet, Broughton, Simmers, Simpson, Wiggins, Nolly, Rochford and Brabson – have disappeared, though the surname Hernon, which is common in Inis Mór, is thought to date from the time of the Cromwellian occupation.

The Great Famine of the 1840s did not greatly affect Aran; the population of the three islands decreased from 3529 in 1841 to 3333 in 1851. But the two events that had the most marked impact on island life during the second half of the nineteenth century were the Land War and the efforts to establish an up-to-date fishing industry, for which the Congested Districts' Board must be given due credit.

The war for the land was as bitter in Aran as anywhere else in Ireland and various writers, including Synge, have described evictions and the violence and hatred they generated. Anyone who looks down from an aircraft on the pitifully scarce patches of good land scattered through the world of stone will immediately understand that land is of greater relative value in Aran than in the plains of Meath.

This struggle, and particularly the Land League itself as a national organization run by the people, politicized the islanders and brought them into direct contact with events on the mainland. The community remains passionately involved in party politics.

The great Celtic cross that overlooks Cill Rónáin harbour was erected by grateful islanders to the memory of Father Michael O'Donohue and sculpted by James Pearse, father of Patrick Pearse. Father O'Donohue was parish priest of Aran (the three islands make up a parish in the Archdiocese of Tuam) between 1881 and 1892, a time of hardship, hunger and epidemics of fever, when the traditional methods of fishing – with small nets or spillards, using the native currachs, or with lines from the cliffs – were no longer adequate in a changing world. In 1886 he is said to have sent his famous telegram to Dublin Castle: 'Send us boats or send us coffins.'

Boats did eventually come, piers were built and instructors brought in from the east coast. With the twentieth century came prosperity, particularly to Inis Mór and Cill Rónáin, as a world war created new markets and appetites. Tom O'Flaherty has written of the couple in the village who had trained their dog to go to the pub with a pound note in its collar and bring back a bottle of whiskey and the change. Post-war decline, which accelerated under the first native government, is well illustrated by the folk memory of a particular fisherman's death. He drowned while in harbour on the mainland but was taken home uncoffined as the crew did not have the price of a coffin between them, nor could they raise it.

6

But although fishing went into a long decline a tradition had been established and the industry remained strong enough to be revived to good effect in the mid-1950s. This revival was assisted in no small way by the semi-state fisheries board, Bord Iascaigh Mhara. The present Aran fleet is the backbone of the island economy and there is no shortage of skilled young fishermen whose ambition is to own their own trawlers. Predictions are difficult for an industry notorious for its fluctuating fortunes. If fishing thrives, so will the island community: if not, the community will find it difficult to maintain its present healthy condition.

The nineteenth century also saw an awakening of interest in antiquities, folklore and the Irish language. Aran had the advantage of being remote but accessible. Sailing boats could be hired in Galway City, where the Claddagh fleet was based, or visitors could cross over from Connemara in one of the hookers that ferried turf to the bogless islands.

The antiquarians set about repairing crumbling monuments and explaining their importance to local and national audiences. Their writings aroused others who found the thought of a community living among such treasures, preserving an ancient language and way of life, intoxicatingly romantic; at least when the weather was fine.

The publication of John Millington Synge's *The Aran Islands* in 1904 brought this primitive life to the attention of an even wider public. Synge left Inis Mór, which he found to be too modern and English-speaking, for the more inaccessible Inis Meáin. His book and his magnificent photographs provide a record of a way of life that was about to come to an end.

Aran repaid him by providing the plots for four of his most successful plays: *Riders to the Sea*, *The Well of the Saints*, *In the Shadow of the Glen* and *The Playboy of the Western World*. When he claimed credit for having directed Synge from Paris to the Aran Islands, W.B. Yeats seemed to have been unaware of the presence in Inis Mór, many years previously, of the playwright's uncle, the Rev. Alexander Synge. The record of that tenacious man's efforts to modernize fishing methods in Inis Mór, while trying to convert the people to Protestantism, is one of the most interesting contributions to this collection.

Like Synge, Patrick Pearse also chose Inis Meáin. Some say it was because he believed the English flag never flew over it: there were police and coastguards in Inis Mór and coastguards in Inis Oírr, whereas Inis Meáin had a limited form of home rule. Others say Pearse was attracted by the purity of the Irish and locally it was believed that the presence on the island of Eibhlín Nic Niocaill could have influenced his decision. She was subsequently drowned off the Great Blasket along with the son of Tomás Ó Criomhthain (author of *An tOileánach*, 'The Islandman'), who was attempting to save her.

At this stage it was considered desirable to establish branches of the Gaelic League on the islands. On its first elected committee in Inis Mór was the only

Protestant shopkeeper in Cill Rónáin, Richard Charde. Some years previously there had been serious tension in the village between the small Protestant community and the Catholic majority. It had its roots in agrarian rather than religious matters and was eventually resolved, but the Protestant community died out in the mid-1930s, and the parish church is now a ruin in the centre of Cill Rónáin.

Interest in Celtic studies was also intense on the Continent. The great Celticist Holger Pedersen encouraged his pupil Franz Finck from Marburg to go to Aran and study the Irish language. Finck spent two periods learning Irish in Inis Mór and published his two-volume *Die Araner Mundart* in Marburg in 1899.

He, like most other visitors to the island at the time, lodged with Mrs Costello in the Atlantic Hotel. It was here that Synge heard the soft murmur of Irish through the floorboards of his room on his first night in Aran. When Arthur Symons visited the islands with Yeats he was the next visitor to sleep in the bed that Finck had used, and he met one of Finck's teachers, who had also taught Synge during his short stay. It seemed as if the world and his wife were beating a path to the door of Mrs Costello's inn.

With the growth of the fishing industry and the presence on the islands of more and more government officials, police, coastguards, teachers, lighthouse-keepers, priests and fish buyers, communications with the mainland improved. The mainland meant Galway, for although all three islands imported turf from Connemara and Inis Oírr had a connection with nearby Clare, there was neither a harbour nor a town, other than Galway, substantial enough to serve the needs of a population of about 3000 in 1900.

The paddle-steamer *Citie of the Tribes* went into service in 1891, to be followed by the *Duras*, the *Dún Aengus* and the *Naomh Éanna*. Cill Rónáin post office was opened in 1897 and a telegraph service with the mainland, and later between the islands, commenced in 1902. Events in Aran were covered regularly by the Galway newspapers and some of the more dramatic incidents raised in the House of Commons. In spite of all this, Aran retained its romantic reputation as a place apart.

One man was to reinforce that reputation by introducing a community invented by himself to the international cinema audience. He came to Ireland to make a film about a primitive people, struggling against the raw forces of nature and hunting the basking shark for its oil. Robert Flaherty, an American-Canadian, went to Achill Island in Mayo, where sharks were hunted, but was disappointed with what he saw. Hearing of his presence in Ireland, a young Irish film-maker, Norris Davidson, who had been in Aran, persuaded Flaherty to go there and see for himself. The rest is film history.

Man of Aran did not create the stir in Aran that it did in other parts of the world, for the simple reason that it was not seen there until 1947. Its reputation had preceded it and when an enterprising showman imported an oil-powered generator and showed it in the community hall in Cill Rónáin, the audience loved it. Aside from its dramatic impact, it was admired for what it had already clearly achieved, and was seen as the best possible advertisement any island in the world could have asked for.

During the tourist season – between June and September – the film is shown twice weekly in Cill Rónáin community hall. Although the showings are for the benefit of visitors, some islanders boast of having seen the film scores of times. Nothing succeeds like success and all reservations about its artistic integrity may be safely left to Graham Greene. The islanders may have had to be taught how to harpoon the basking shark, the dubbed-in dialogue may indeed sound ridiculous, the camera may have avoided more of island life than it selected as a re-creation of that life, but nobody taught the crew of the currach how to row ashore through the ferocious breakers, in what is the film's outstanding scene.

Aran has taken a great leap into the modern world in the last half of the twentieth century. Diesel generators brought electricity and all the conveniences it powers, including television and technology's greatest gift to guest-house owners in remote places, the deep-freeze. Great storage tanks were built and water piped into the increasingly modern and state-subsidized houses. Roads were widened and tarred and were soon filled with mini-buses, cars and tractors. A fine post-primary school was opened in Cill Rónáin, but the children of Inis Meáin still have to go to the mainland for second-level education.

In 1970, as a result of a crusade launched by Colie Hernon of Cill Rónáin – long-serving coxwain of the Galway Bay lifeboat – the islands got an air service. Aer Arann now operates a daily service from Galway to the three islands throughout the year, and the original grass landing-strips have been replaced by tarmacadam. This service ended the frightening sense of isolation, particularly when sudden sickness struck in winter or during stormy weather, that caused many young, and not so young, islanders to leave. It was also seen as a reassuring vote of confidence in the future of the community, which numbered 1339 in 1986.

It is now time to give that community voice, in words written by both natives and strangers, remembering the old Aran saying: 'Baile Átha an Rí a bhí; Gaillimh atá; agus Árainn a bheas', 'Athenry was; Galway is; and Aran will be.'

Breandán Ó hEithir

9

I

Early Visitors

*The earliest allusions to the Aran Islands
give little insight into the life of the islands apart from the references in various annals
and legal documents to raids, occupation, natural disasters and other such occurrences.
Cambrensis's account in 1185 merely attributes to Aran a well-known tale told of many
remote, unseen islands, and even John Speed, that most accurate of seventeenth-century
cartographers, drew his map of Connacht with only two Aran Islands.*

*The account by Roderick O'Flaherty in 1684 marks the first survey of the islands
we have. His description of island monuments, mention of local legend, and details of the
flora and fauna prefigure the concerns of hosts of later visitors to the islands. His
accuracy and reliability can be contrasted with* Dineley's Tour in Ireland 1681,
*which briefly mentions the island 'where 'tis sayd the Inhabitants complaine of living too
long, and are faine to come out thence to dye'.*

*However, it was not O'Flaherty who drew the later visitors to the islands. Apart
from the visit by the famous naturalist Edward Lhwyd in 1700, not until the nineteenth
century did the first wave of visitors break on the islands, impelled by a national
reawakening of interest in history, archaeology and antiquarianism. And as great
luminaries of Irish scholarship such as Petrie, John T. O'Flaherty, O'Donovan,
Wakeman, Sir William Wilde and Samuel Ferguson examined and catalogued the
monuments and debated their origin and significance, many of them also left us with
fascinating descriptions of the islands themselves and the life of their inhabitants. The
amazing banquet held by the Ethnological Section of the British Association in the ruins
of Dún Aonghasa in 1857, attended by many of Ireland's leading scholars, might be
seen as marking Aran's 'coming-out' into the modern academic world.*

*The number of visitors, while still small, continued to grow up until the end of the
century and many committed to paper their impressions of the islands and their
inhabitants. In 1893 the most comprehensive account yet was published by the Royal
Irish Academy –* Haddon and Browne's Ethnography of the Aran Islands –
*detailing such aspects of island life as work, transport, clothing, folklore, family names
and language, as well as compiling copious notes on the bodily dimensions and characteristics of the islanders in an attempt to determine their racial origins. By this stage, the
Aran Islands had been firmly brought to the attention of all Ireland, if not the world.*

*A second group of nineteenth-century visitors came for very different reasons indeed.
In the 1820s a new wave of Protestant evangelical fervour made its presence felt
throughout Ireland. Remote as they might have been, the Aran Islands were not ignored.
After the early and largely ineffectual attempts of the London Hibernian Society to found
a school in Aran in 1826, the Islands and Coast Society was founded in 1833 to
concentrate its campaign on the more remote areas of Ireland. It had great difficulties in
getting clergymen to stay on Aran until 1851, when the Reverend Alexander Synge,
uncle of the playwright John Millington Synge, arrived to take up the fight. His
struggles, outlined in his letters to his brothers and in the columns of* The Galway
Vindicator, *show clearly the impact he had on island life and foreshadow the more bitter
confrontations of ensuing decades under his successor, the Reverend William Kilbride.*

Giraldus Cambrensis

Topographia Hiberniae (1220)

¶ *An island where human corpses exposed in the open do not putrefy*
There is an island in the sea west of Connacht which is said to have been
consecrated by Saint Brendan. In this island human corpses are not buried and
do not putrefy, but are placed in the open and remain without corruption. Here
men see with some wonder and recognize their grandfathers, great-grandfa-
thers and great-great-grandfathers and a long line of ancestors.

There is another remarkable thing about this island: while the whole of
Ireland is infested with mice, there is not a single mouse here. For no mouse is
bred here nor does one live if it be brought in. If by chance it is brought in, it
makes straight for the nearest point of the sea and throws itself in; and if it be
prevented, it dies on the spot.

From Gerald of Wales, *The History and Topography of Ireland* (1982), transl. John J.
O'Meara.

Roderick O'Flaherty

A *Chorographical Description of West or H-Iar Connaught* (1684)

The three Isles of Aran half barony, extending in length from west to east, have the barony of Moycullin on the north, Moyclea in Corcamro barony, and county of Clare, on the east, and the Cape of Kerryhead, far off in sight stretched out in the sea, on the south. They are fenced on the south side with very high cliffts, some three score, some four score and five score fathoms deep, against the Western Ocean's approach.

The soile is almost paved over with stones, soe as, in some places, nothing is to be seen but large stones with wide openings between them, where cattle break their legs. Scarce any other stones there but limestones, and marble fit for tomb-stones, chymney mantle trees, and high crosses. Among these stones is very sweet pasture, so that beefe, veale, mutton are better and earlier in season here, than elsewhere; and of late there is plenty of cheese and tillage mucking, and corn is the same with the sea side tract. In some places the plow goes. On the shore grows samphire in plenty, ring-root or sea-holy, and sea-cabbage. Here are Cornish choughs, with red legs and bills. Here are ayries of hawkes, and birds which never fly but over the sea; and, therefore, are used to be eaten on fasting-days: to catch which, people goe down, with ropes tyed abut them, into the caves of cliffts by night and with a candle light kill abundance of them. Here are severall wells and pooles, yet in extraordinary dry weather, people must turn their cattell out of the islands, and the corn failes. They have noe fuell but cow-dung dryed with the sun, unless they bring turf in from the western continent. They have *Cloghans*, a kind of building of stones layed one upon another, which are brought to a roof without any manner of mortar to cement them, some of which cabins will hold forty men on their floor; so antient that no body knows how long agoe any of them was made. Scarcity of wood and store of fit stones, without peradventure found out the first invention. There is a waste island on the south-west side, called Oilen-da-branoge, where they goe to slaughter seals yearly; and where there is abundance of samphire.

From the Isles of Aran and the west continent, often appears visible that inchanted island called O'Brasil, and in Irish Beg-ara or the Lesser Aran, set

From *A Chorographical Description of West or H-Iar Connaught* (1846), ed. J. Hardiman.

down in cards of navigation. Whether it be reall and firm land, kept hidden by speciall ordinance of God, as the terrestiall paradise, or else some illusion of airy clouds appearing on the surface of the sea, or the craft of evill spirits, is more than our judgements can sound out. There is, westward of Aran, in sight of the next continent of Balynahynsy barony, Skerde, a wild island of huge rocks, the receptacle of a deale of seales thereon yearly slaughtered. These rocks sometimes appear to be a great city far of, full of houses, castles, towers, and chimneys; sometimes full of blazing flames, smoak, and people running to and fro. Another day you would see nothing but a number of ships, with their sailes and riggings; then so many great stakes or reeks of corn and turf; and this not only on fair sun-shining dayes, whereby it might be thought the reflection of the sun-beamse on the vapours arising about it, had been the cause, but alsoe on dark and cloudy days happening. There is another like number of rocks, called Carrigmeacan, on the same coast, whereon the like apparitions are seen. But the inchanted island of O'Brasil is not alwayes visible, as those rocks are, nor these rocks have always those apparitions.

There is now living, Morogh O'Ley, who immagins he was himself personally on O'Brasil for two days, and saw out of it the iles of Aran, Golamhead, Irrosbeghill, and other places of the west continent he was acquainted with. The manner of it he relates, that being in Irrosainhagh, in the south side of the barony of Balynahinsy, about nine leagues from Galway by sea, in the month of Aprill, Anno Domini 1668, going alone from one village to another, in a melancholy humour, upon some discontent of his wife, he was encountered by two or three strangers, and forcibly carried by boat into O'Brasil, as such as were within it told him, and they could speak both English and Irish. He was ferried out hoodwink'd, in a boat, as he immagins, till he was left on the sea point by Galway; where he lay in a friend's house for some dayes after, being very desperately ill, and knowes not how he came to Galway then. But, by that means, about seaven or eight years after, he began to practise both chirurgery and phisick, and so continues ever since to practise, tho' he never studied nor practised either all his life time before, as all we that knew him since he was a boy can averr. [...]

The isles of Aran are fameous for the numerous multitude of saints there living of old and interred, or there trained in religious austerity, and propagating monasticall in other parts; venerable for many sacred churches, chappells, wells, crosses sepulchers and other holy reliques of saints, still there extant, as monuments of their piety, reverenced for many rare priviledges of sacred places therein, and the instant divine punishments inflicted on such as dare violate or prophane them; frequently visited by Christians in pilgrimage for devotion, acts of pennance, and miraculous virtues there wrought.

Ara-Mhor, the greatest and furthest to the west of them, contains twenty-four quarters of land, and is twenty-four miles in compass, wherein, on the south side, stands Dun-Engus, a large fortified place, on the brim of a high clifft, a hundred fathoms deep; being a great wall of bare stones without any mortar, in compass as big as a large castle bawn, with severall long stones on the outside, erected sloapwise about it against assaults. It is named of Engus

16

McAnathmore [Uathmore], of the reliques of the Belgmen in Ireland, here living about the birth-time of Christ. On the east side thereof, the island is somewhat soe low, that about the year 1640, upon an extraordinary inundation, the sea, overflowing that bank, went cross over the island, to the north-west. [...]

Giraldus Cambrensis was misinformed, to say that St Brendan was the chiefe patron of this island (St Brendan visited St Enna here once, passing to Kerry; and, another time, on his second adventure of navigation on the ocean). And that humane carcasses need no buriall on it, as free from putrefaction; which last was attributed to Inisgluaire on the sea of Irrosdownan, and there itself it is by experience found false. But what he alledges, that it did not breed rats, and that by chance, thither transported, they immediately dyed, I believe was true in his time; for that is the nature of all the rest of the territorie, except the districts of Galway town. [...]

The midle island of Aran containes eight quarters of land, where there is the like old fortification as in the great island, named from Connor Mac Huathmor, brother to Engus of Dun-Engus, as the tradition goes. Hallowed places in the isle are, our Blessed Lady's chappell; St Kenanack his chappell; a hallowed place called *atharla* Kenerge; and the chappell of Seactmicrigh, or the seven sons of a king. Tradition goes that St Kenanack was a king of Leinster's son, and Kenerg, a king of Leinster's daughter. Her well is there in a rock, and never becomes drie. In this island is a great deal of rabbets. Hence eastwards, to Tract-each, in the third island is another streight ship-road, called Bealagh-na-fearbag.

The third island of Aran, Inisoirthir, or the eastern Isle, soe called of its situation from the two other, contains four quarters of land, with a castle on a height. This island was also called of old Ara-Coemhan, of Saint Coeman of the antient Dal-Messincorb family, descended of the kings of Leinster, brother to St Coemgin, Abbot of Glindalough, and likely disciple to St Enna, as his brother was. He lies buried in this island, on the north side of the church dedicated to his name; where he is worshipped on the 3rd November. There is a marble stone over his tomb, with a square wall built around it, on a plain green field in prospect of the sea, where sick people used to lye over night, and recover health of God, for his sake. I have seen one greviously tormented by a thorn thrust into his eye, who by lying soe in St Coeman's burying place, had it miraculously taken out, without the least feeling of the patient; the mark whereof, in the corner of his eye, still remaines.

Samuel Lewis

A *Topographical Dictionary of Ireland* (1837)

ARRAN ISLANDS, a barony, in the county of Galway, a province of Connaught, 30 miles (W.S.W.) from Galway; containing 3191 inhabitants. This barony consists of a group of islands called the South Arran Isles, situated in the centre of the mouth of Galway bay stretching south-east and north-west from 52° to 53° (N.Lat.), and from 9°30' to 9°42' (W.Lon.); and comprising Arranmore or the Great Arran to the west, Ennismain or Innismain (called also the Middle Island), and Innishere or the Eastern island, which are thickly inhabited; also the small rocky isles called Straw Island, the Branach Isles, and Illane-Earhach or the Western Isle. They are supposed to be the remains of a high barrier of land separated at some remote period by the violence of the sea; and from evident appearances of their having been anciently overspread with wood, their retired situation, and the existence of druidical remains, to have been appropriated to the celebration of the religious rites of the early Irish, prior to the introduction of Christianity. The Firbolg tribes had possession of these islands at a very early period; and in the third century they were held, it is said, by the sept of Eogan More, King of Thomond. They subsequently became the residence of St Ibar, one of the missionaries sent to Ireland before the time of St Patrick; and in the 5th century the Great Island was given by Aengus, King of Cashel, to St Endeus or St Enda, who founded several monasteries, and built several churches, of which the principal was named after him Kill-Enda, now called Killeany. This island soon became celebrated for its number of holy men, and such was the fame of Enda for sanctity, that it was visited during his lifetime by St Kieran, St Brendan, and the celebrated Columbkill; it still bears the name of 'Arran of the Saints'. In 546 it was agreed between the kings of Munster and Connaught, whose territories were separated by the bay of Galway, that these islands should be independent of both, and pay tribute to neither. In 1081 the Great Island was ravaged by the Danes. The sept of Mac Tiege O'Brien were temporal lords of the islands from a very remote period, and the inhabitants of the English part of the town of Galway entered early into strict alliance and friendship with them; but this compact did not save the islands from being plundered and burnt by Sir John D'Arcy, Lord-

Justice of Ireland, who, in 1334, sailed round the western coast with a fleet of 56 vessels. In 1485 a monastery for Franciscans was founded in the Great Island, in which was also erected a famous abbey for Canons Regular. In the reign of Elizabeth the O'Briens were expelled by the sept of O'Flaherty, of the neighbouring mainland of Connaught; on which occasion the mayor and sheriffs of Galway sent a petition to the Queen in favour of the former, to whom, they state, they paid an additional tribute of wine, in consideration of their protection, and of their expenses in guarding the bay and harbour of Galway against pirates and coast plunderers. In consequence of this petition, a commission was issued, under which it appeared that the islands belonged of right to the crown; and in 1587 letters patent were granted, by which the Queen, instead of restoring them to the ancient proprietors, gave them to John Rawson, of Athlone, on condition of his keeping constantly on them 20 foot soldiers of the English nation. This property afterwards became vested in Sir Robert Lynch, of Galway; but the Clan Tieges still claimed it as their patrimony, and taking advantage of the troubles of 1641, prepared, with the assistance of Boetius Clanchy, the younger, a man of great property and influence in the county of Clare, to invade the islands; but the execution of their design was prevented by the timely interference of the Marquess of Clanricarde and the Earl of Thomond. In 1651, when the royal authority was fast declining, the Marquess of Clanricarde placed 200 musqueteers on these islands, under the command of Sir Robert Lynch; the fort of Ardkyn, in the Great Island, was soon after repaired and mounted with cannon; and by these means they held out against the parliamentary forces for nearly twelve months after the surrender of Galway. In December of that year, the Irish, defeated in every other quarter, landed here 700 men in boats from Iar Connaught and Inis Bophin; and on the 9th day of the following January, 1300 of the parliamentary infantry were shipped from the bay of Galway to attack them, and 600 more marched from the town to Iar Connaught, to be sent thence, if necessary, to their aid; but on the 13th the islands surrendered, on condition that quarter should be given to all within the fort, and that they should have six weeks allowed them to retire to Spain, or any other country then at peace with England. Sir Robert Lynch, the late proprietor, being declared a traitor, the property was forfeited and granted to Erasmus Smith, Esq., one of the most considerable of the London adventurers, from whom it was purchased by Richard Butler, fifth son of James, first Duke of Ormonde, who was created Earl of Arran in 1662, and to whom it was confirmed by royal patent under the Act of Settlement. On the surrender of Galway to the forces of Wm III, in 1691, Arran was again garrisoned and a barrack was erected, in which soldiers were quartered for many years. In 1693, the title of Earl of the Isles of Arran was conferred on Charles, brother of the second Duke of Ormonde, with whom it became extinct in 1758; it was revived in favour of Sir Arthur Gore, Bart., in 1762, and from him the title has descended to the present Earl. The islands are now the property of the Digby family, of whom the present head is the Rev. John Digby, of Landerstown, in the county of Kildare.

Their appearance, on approaching, is awfully impressive; the dark cliffs opposing to the billows that roll impetuously against them a perpendicular barrier, several hundred feet high, of rugged masses shelving abruptly towards the base, and perforated with various winding cavities worn by the violence of the waves. *Arranmore*, or the *Great Island*, which is the most northern of the three, is about 11 miles in length, and about 1³/₄ miles at its greatest breadth; and comprises the villages of Killeany, Kilmurvey, and Onought, and the hamlets of Icararn, Ballyneerega, Mannister, Cowruagh, Gortnagopple, Furnakurk, Cregacarean, Shran, and Bungowla. In the centre is a signal tower; and at Oaghill, on the summit, is a lighthouse, elevated 498 feet above the level of the sea at high water, and exhibiting a bright revolving light from 21 reflectors, which attains its greatest magnitude every three minutes, and may be seen from all points at a distance of 28 nautical miles, in clear weather. The island is bounded on the south and west by rocky cliffs, from 300 to 400 feet high; but on the north are low shelving rocks and sandy beaches; and the passage to the northward is called the North Sound, or entrance to the bay of Galway. There is only one safe harbour, called Killeaney or Arran bay: in the upper part of the bay is a small pier, erected by order of the late Fishery Board in 1822, which has eight feet of water. *Ennismain*, or the *Middle Island*, is separated from Arranmore by Gregory Sound, which is about four miles broad and navigable from shore to shore: it is of irregular form and about eight miles in circumference; and comprises the village of Maher and the hamlets of Moneenarouga, Lissheen, Ballindoon, and Kinavalla. The inhabitants are chiefly engaged in fishing and making kelp; they have a few row-boats and a number of canoes, or corachs, made of osiers and covered with pitched canvas. The northern point of this island is lofty and rugged, but terminates in a low sandy beach, and on several sides it is boldly perpendicular. *Innishere*, or the *Eastern Island*, is separated from Ennismain by a rocky and dangerous passage, called Foul Sound, which is about a league broad, with a ledge of rocks having on it six feet of water. It is about a mile and a half in length, three quarters of a mile in breadth, and four miles in circumference; and comprises the village of Temore, and the hamlets of Forumna, Castle, and Cleganough. The tillage is chiefly for potatoes, with a little rye; but the inhabitants live principally by fishing and making kelp, which is said to be the best brought to the Galway market. There is a signal tower on the island, and near it an old castle. To the west of Arranmore are the *Branach Isles*, two of which, about eight acres in extent, afford good pasturage, and the third is a perpendicular and barren rock of about two acres.

The surface of all the islands is barren rock, interspersed with numerous verdant and fertile spots. There are many springs and rivulets, but these afford in dry seasons a very inadequate supply of water, which is either brought from the main land for the use of the cattle, or the cattle are removed thither during the continuance of the drought. The best soils are near the shore and are sandy, with a mixture of rich loam: the prevailing crops are potatoes, rye and a small kind of black oats; the inhabitants raise also small quantities of barley and wheat, for which they apply an additional portion of sea-weed, their only manure; and they grow small quantities of flax; but the produce of their

20

harvests seldom exceeds what is required for their own consumption. The pasture land is appropriated to sheep and goats, and a few cows and horses, for which they also reserve some meadow: the mutton is of fine flavour and superior quality; but the most profitable stock is their breed of calves, much sought after by the Connaught graziers. The grasses are intermingled with a variety of medicinal and sweet herbs, among which the wild garlick is so abundant as to give a flavour to the butter. The plant called *Rineen*, or 'fairy flax', is much relied on for its medicinal virtues in almost all cases; the tormentil root serves in place of bark for tanning; and there is another plant which gives a fine blue dye, and is used in colouring the woollen cloth which the islanders manufacture for their own wear. The fisheries are a great source of profit, and in the whole employ about 120 boats; of these, 30 or 40 have sails and are from five to ten tons' burden; the rest are small row-boats and canoes, or corachs. The spring and beginning of the summer are the season for the spillard fishery; immense quantities of cod, ling, haddock, turbot, gurnet, mackerel, glassin, bream, and herring are taken here; and lobsters, crabs, cockles, and muscles [*sic*] are also found in abundance. The inhabitants rely chiefly on the herring fishery, which is very productive; and in April and May, many of them are employed in spearing the sun-fish, or basking shark, from the liver of which they extract considerable quantities of oil. Hares and rabbits abound in these islands, which are also frequented by plovers, gannets, pigeons, ducks, and other wild fowl; and the cliffs are the resort of numerous puffins, which are taken for the sake of their feathers by cragmen, who descend the cliffs at night by means of a rope fastened round the body, and are lowered by four or five of their companions. In one of the islands a very fine stratum of dove-coloured and black marble has been discovered; and from the various natural resources of this apparently barren district, the inhabitants are enabled to pay a rental of from £2000 to £3000 per annum to the proprietor. The most remarkable of the natural curiosities are the three caverns called the Puffing Holes, at the southern extremity of Arranmore; they communicate with the sea and have apertures in the surface of the cliff, about 20 perches from its brink, from which, during the prevalence of strong westerly winds, prodigious columns of water are projected to the height of a ship's mast.

The three islands form three parishes in the diocese of Tuam, and, in respect to their vicarages, are part of the union of Ballynakill, from the church of which they are 28 miles distant; the rectories are impropriate in the Digby family. The tithes amount to £47.19.10¾, of which £38.8. is payable to the impropriator, and £9.11.10¾ to the incumbent. In the R.C. divisions they form one parish, which is served by a clergyman resident at Oaghill, where a chapel, a neat slated building, has been recently erected. About 400 children are educated in four pay schools at Arranmore. There are still some very interesting remains not only of druidical antiquity, but also of the ancient churches and monasteries. The ruins of the old abbey of Kill-Enda are situated nearly at the eastern extremity of the largest island; and in the opposite direction are the ruins of seven churches, one of which, called Tempeil-Brecain, was probably dedicated to that saint. Near it is a holy well, and throughout the island are various others, and also numerous ancient crosses. In Ennismain are the ruins of two churches, dedicated to the Blessed Virgin; and in Innishere, anciently called Arran Coemhain, were three, namely, St Coemhain's or Kevin's, St Paul's, and Kill-i-Gradhandomhain, with the first of which was connected a monastery founded by St Fechin. The most remarkable of the primitive fortifications is Dun Aengus, situated on the summit of a great precipice overhanging the sea: it consists of three enclosures, the largest of which is encircled by a rampart of large stones standing on end; and there are one of similar size and others smaller. From the secluded situation of these islands, the language, manners, customs, and dress of the natives are peculiarly primitive; instances of longevity are remarkable. The shoes worn are simply a piece of raw cow hide, rather longer than the foot, and stitched close at the toes and heel with a piece of fishing line. The Irish language is commonly spoken, and being replete with primitive words, varies from the dialect of the natives of the mainland, but not so as to be unintelligible; a great portion of the inhabitants, however, speak good English. In the Great Island is a place called the Field of Skulls, from the number of human bones found in it, and thence supposed to have been the site of a battle fought during some intestine quarrel of the O'Briens.

Reports of the Islands and Coast Society

1843–50

'I am sure it will be gratifying to your Society to learn, that, though when I visited this Island nine or ten years ago, there was not a single native who would listen to the Gospel, there are now twenty-one persons who have been trained up in the appointed means of grace. At seven o'clock this afternoon we had divine worship and a lecture, which was well attended. In consequence of the great opposition given to every department of work here, the Schools are much hindered. That at K—— contains 25 children. The conduct of your master is, I believe, in all respects most exemplary, and the parents appear duly sensible of the benefit; as I am credibly informed, the most unworthy means have been used to induce the parents to withdraw their children, but in vain. I have more than once thought that an evening School might be tried in this locality with advantage.' [...]

In the last visit he was permitted to make to these Stations, some time previous to his death, Captain Forbes wrote as follows:

'I walked this day, after examining the School, to the village of the Seven Churches, where I witnessed one of the most affecting scenes I ever beheld. As I was about to enter the churchyard in this wild and picturesque quarter, the well known accents of the Irish cry, with which I had become familiar in Kerry, burst upon my ear with startling effect. This – said I to the Teacher who accompanied me – this is death. Oh what a heart-rending cry! I then saw a man and his family coming towards me, uttering the most bitter lamentations in Irish. The moment this was heard in the village, a number of the people from thence came forth to join them, and all flocked down to the grave which had been lately closed. It reminded me forcibly of that touching picture in John xi. xxxi. "The Jews, when they saw Mary, that she arose up hastily, and went out, followed her, saying, she goeth unto the grave to weep there." Some went on their knees, others prostrated themselves on the ground, while others sat down around the grave, where their lamentations continued for a long while. This was no scene got up to produce effect, it was true heart-felt sorrow indeed. The poor old father, as he wept over the remains of his "darling and beloved young

From *Annual Reports of the Islands and Coast Society*, 1843–50.

daughter" – expressions which he uttered again and again, in the most affecting tones of his native tongue – was a sight that no one could behold without sympathy: the big tears chasing one another down his aged and weatherbeaten features, while his eyes and clasped hands were raised, as if imploring help from above. We did not attempt to intrude on the sorrowing group, but sat down outside the graveyard until the lamentations should be over. I then learned that the young girl whom all seemed to unite in regretting, had been a most extraordinary child. That she had evinced the most remarkable love and obedience towards her parents, for whom she thought she could never do enough. They often felt it necessary to restrain her, lest her labours should be injurious to her health, and when her father gave her any little task to perform, she was in the habit, they said, of thanking him, and setting about it immediately. Though little more than thirteen years of age, she had undertaken to carry the seaweed from the shore to the little plot of ground around the father's cabin – the manure necessary to its cultivation – but to accomplish this, there was a toilsome cliff to ascend, and many massive rocks to be traversed. On Friday last, while bearing her burthen as usual, up the mountain side (it was a summer day) becoming fatigued, she stopped to rest her basket on the top of a dry stone wall, the rope which upheld it being bound across her breast and shoulders. It is supposed that while thus standing, enjoying the freshness of the sea breeze, indulging perhaps, in some fond thoughts of those parents and that loved home which she was never fated to behold again; her burthen slipped from the wall behind, its weight brought the rope from her chest across her throat, and in the course of the day, when the parents, alarmed at her continued absence came to seek her in the haunts of her innocent and useful toil, the poor frantic father found her in this position, quite dead. Well might he cry out, *mo inghean féin, mo inghean óg féin*, "My own, my own young daughter!" I felt as if this young creature, little instructed as she was, had left us an example that we might well follow with profit. This law of our God, "honour thy father and thy mother", had been written on her heart. I know not when I witnessed a more affecting scene. The aged and the young – the keen sorrow of heart – the wild and piercing cry in the Irish language – the deep sobs and bursts of grief, that told your own heart it was true, and made you feel and sympathize with those that wept. The situation of the place itself; the remains of the old churches; the vast number of the dead that are congregated there – how many, alas! without having ever heard of the salvation that is in Christ Jesus. The mighty ocean before me, its waves bursting with the noise of thunder on the shore, the surrounding scenery of the opposite coast, its mountains and islands, with the wild, half civilized, half clad natives of the village; all made upon me such an impression, as it would be impossible to describe. This is the village from which ——, his wife and seven children, have been turned out for receiving your Teachers, and hearing from them the words of everlasting life. He now with his poor family lives under a large rock, and is in much want, being persecuted both by priest and people, particularly as he has not gone to mass for some time.* I inquired here for a poor woman whom

*A few very humble dwellings have since been arranged, for this, and other persecuted families.

I had met with on my former visit to this Island, at the "blessed well". The Agent told me he had seen her since, and that she assured him she had given up all hopes of being cured *by the well*, she would henceforth – she said – seek and look for relief, where we had informed her it was alone to be found.'

[1846]

The Church which was mentioned in the last Report as being in progress, is now completed, and forms a striking object in approaching this group of Islands; and a congregation waits to assemble there to worship Him whom they desire to serve; but unhappily we again have to lament, that no Pastor has yet been found able and willing to undertake this important charge. It is a Mission which requires self-denial; but in the Church of Ireland that grace abounds, and we cannot attribute to a want of missionary zeal among her Ministers, that which we so deeply lament: it must be, that those who are competent to the task, find themselves called to places which seem to offer a wider field of usefulness; but this objection would vanish if they would visit the locality and judge for themselves. Besides a small, but interesting Protestant flock, now isolated and cut off from all the public ordinance of the Church, there is, during the summer months, a considerable recourse of tourists and bathers who would add to the congregation; beyond this circle are numbers enquiring and ready to be taught; while even among those who might altogether reject his pastoral instruction, a Minister would find in the inhabitants of an Island, abounding with capabilities never used, room for the exercise of all the talent, ingenuity, energy and devotedness of an Oberlin. Though as yet silent and unconsecrated, the erection of this beautiful edifice, sacred to the worship on which they have hitherto looked with contempt, seems already to have produced an effect on the minds of the natives, who now treat with respect those persons they had been taught to despise – formerly a walk round the largest Island, nineteen miles in circuit, without food, was the penance for communication with any of the Protestants or converts – this is entirely done away with. There are three tombs of Saints, objects of great veneration, and a prosperous voyage was supposed to be secured by lying three successive nights on one of these; this and many other superstitions of the place are now falling into disuse and disrepute.

As the mention of the Church, the only modern building of any value existing on any of the Irish Islands, although many of them abound with ruins of ancient architecture, necessarily marks the locality to all acquainted with the circumstances, it is considered prudent to withhold extracts from the journals of this place; and merely to state generally, that during the year 1846, two Teachers have been employed under the Coast and Island Society; that Schools have been regularly taught; the Scriptures read and explained to as many as would hear; that one large family of respectability have been added to the number of those who, renouncing the delusion of Romanism, are waiting to be farther instructed in the things of God; that the Converts have continued steadfast with the exception of one, who on account of incorrect conduct, has been separated from among them.

The Appendix will give ample information as to the temporal relief afforded by the Society, and the present circumstances and state of feeling on these Islands.

There is every reason to hope, that whenever it may please the Lord of the harvest to send a labourer into this field, there will be an abundant in-gathering: in the meantime let us do what we can. [...]

[1846 APPENDIX]

After a tedious sail of several hours we reached Arran on Wednesday; that night I slept in the 'Atlantic Hotel', a small whitewashed cottage on the beach, and the following day took up my quarters in Kilronan School-House, which is sufficiently comfortable for one not fastidious. The first thing which arrested my attention on sailing into the bay was the church, and I cannot express my feelings of exultation and joy on seeing this temple for the true worship of God, erected in an island, once known as 'Arran of the Saints', and where repose the remains of many worthies of our ancient Irish Church. The building is constructed of solid masonry, and is erected on an eminence between the village of Kilronan and the bay facing the Bay of Galway; our church is consequently the first object to strike the eye of a stranger; it will hold about 150 people. I would expect great good from the location in this island of a godly pastor, kind and firm, who would protect converts by his presence and influence. The aspect of the island is many degrees better than that of Lettermore, as the land is generally cultivated; yet there is much distress, as the new government measures have not yet come into operation. I have got permission to use their boiler, which I have placed in charge of the Society's Agent. This will do much good. Our boiler gives 200 quarts a day to the Arran poor. This morning early I went to the middle island in our Curragh or canvas boat, and decided on changing the Schoolmaster who is at present there. I have placed two most promising young women under your Agent's instruction, with a view to their being employed as teachers. Our visit to Arran has been, I think, most useful.

[1848]

In this populous Island an important Missionary work might have been accomplished, had it been possible to obtain a Minister of the Gospel of a Missionary spirit, who would have taken charge of the Society's interest in this place; but, unhappily, this has not been attainable, and the Church which has been lately erected has not yet been opened for Divine Worship, nor can it be hoped that the Missionary objects contemplated by the Society could possibly prosper, until it please God to provide the scattered flock of this populous Island with a Pastor after his own heart. Many faithful witnesses for the truth have been gathered from this locality; but in a region demanding so much self-denial and cut off from the enjoyment of civilized society, it is not to be wondered at if few are found willing to take charge of a few sheep in such a wilderness. A Clergyman, lately resident on the Island, reports an attendance of only twenty Children at the School; yet, he writes that the Irish language is held in such high estimation, that in reading the Burial Service in the Irish tongue, the people who were assembled round the grave joined audibly in it, and seemed to pay the greatest attention and respect.

The conduct of the Teacher is reported as in every respect correct, and many of the Islanders gladly receive and read the Tracts circulated among them. [...]

[1849]

In South Arran we have been happy to learn of the appointment of a clergyman considered by the Bishop of Tuam competent to afford religious instruction in the native tongue. The Church is now opened for Sabbath services. A Sunday and Daily Schools have long been in operation. A number of converts from the erroneous creed of Rome have been gathered out, but we lament to say that poverty and persecution attend this step in the most distressing manner, and unless the Superintendent be enabled to afford some employment to these poor people, when cast out from that to which they are accustomed; the present converts to the truth of the Gospel must fare like many that have, in years past, gone before them, and have to desert the Island, that they may not be forced to deny the faith. This is much to be lamented, as a very moderate assistance in boats and fishing-tackle would enable many heads of families to preserve themselves and their children from starvation while following the dictates of an awakened conscience. [...]

[1850]

During the past year the cause of truth has not been progressing in South Arran, while in the northern island of that name it has been going quietly but steadily forward. Over the impediments to improvement the Society has had no control, but the seed which has been sown among the population of that isle needs only the faithful, honest and zealous efforts of a godly minister to render it equally if not more prolific of good than Cape Clear. With two good school-houses and a church that needs only zeal and faithful proclamation of the Gospel to fill it, it is not possible that Arran can long remain, in this day of energetic activity, in a less hopeful condition than other isles with similar advantages. Many precious souls have been gathered from its thickly populated shores: three of the most faithful Teachers of the Society were there awakened from their popish errors; and if all the individuals, who have from time to time been aroused to care for their everlasting peace, were collected into a congregation, instead of being scattered by persecution and the desire for ministerial teaching which they were obliged to seek elsewhere, Arran would now display a flock of well instructed Protestants. The Committee have rejoiced to learn that the good Bishop of Tuam is making a new division of the district, by which the Isles of Arran will enjoy an independent provision for a minister; it is therefore earnestly hoped that the spiritual prospects of this interesting field of labour, on which the Island and Coast Society has expended so much for the last twelve or fourteen years, will become brighter and the mission be more firmly established. Faithful clerical superintendence they believe is absolutely necessary to the building up a flock, and inferior agency should only prepare the way for that desirable end.

Reverend Alexander Synge

Letters (1851–52)

My Dear John,

I received your letter today & as a boat is going in the morning I reply – I have not of course had any answer to the YI Advertisement yet – the next boat may bring some – All eyes here are turned towards the Atlantic in expectation of seeing the American packet – but if she sailled on the day named she must have had a long passage – the ninth day is up this afternoon & no sign of her – A Galway Pilot was down here last night waiting for her – he says if she does not come up today & she has not – he does not know what quantity of good things wont be spoilled in Galway – they had prepared a feast of no ordinary sort I hear for the Yankees – I hope she has not followed the Harry – In reply to Sr. James proposal I do not much like it – I would set the ground on the same terms as he has the other plots but I would not like to sell it out and out unless we sold all out together – I have been getting a small garden dug for turnips – but failled to get any quan[tity] in Galway – I am sending for some bonedust tomorrow – this is the first real warm sunny day we have – I have past most of my time making up a stock of sermons. I have two services on Sunday & I am to begin a Sunday School next S. the coastguards & 2 policemen are the chief of the protestants – but the others are as civil as need be – so far – I wish the schoolmaster was come that we might get the children into training – If you see Chaterton next week perhaps he or [?] Exorm could tell you something near the hire I ought to give for such a boat Exorm I am sure knows some thing about such things – I am still in the Inn but I think of moving next week to a cabin – clean & small – the worst thing about it is there is no view from it – & the Animals are all round it – beside I must get bedding – chairs, table etc delf pots kettles etc.– but I had twice to give up my quarters here this week for [?word illegible] police inspectors etc which is not very pleasent – & the house I am to have wont be done these two months – you must date your epistles for it may be more than a week before I get them – so Monday Tuesday etc wont do. [...] what wd be the cheapest way to get a paper of any sort I have not seen

From 'Letters of the Reverend Alexander Synge, June 1851–December 1852', TCD MS. 6200.

one since I came here – any on the Island are the priests or his sort – Glanmore
ones go to Derbyshire – some [?of] the newsmen in Dublin perhaps wd send
one cheap the 2' or 3' day some English one wd be best – will you ask some one
– wht does the Admiral do with his –?–

Ever your affte brother
Alex H. Synge

WEDNESDAY JULY 9TH 1851

Dear John,
[…] I went to Galway on Monday and back yesterday for a change & little fresh
meat wh[ich] I much wanted – I was not at all well the later part of the week
but the sail I think has brought me all right again. […] I never got any other
answer to my advertisment – I want a boat very badly. I heard of a decked
hooker near Westport & sent a message by one of the boatmen to the owner but
I cant say whether I will hear from him or no – the bad cooking & dirty things
& sour milk etc are some of the little inconveniences of my present abode the
screaming of the women & children sometimes is dreadful it quite addels my
head & it is too hot & close to shut the window – shd you happen to come to
Dunmore that week w[ould] you bring some small *cookery* book with you for
me for I must learn to make up some mess of some sort – meat is not to be had
& their bacon poisons me & the fish is not always to be had either. I d[id] not
get a fish today –

ever yr affte brother
Alex H Synge

THURSDAY JULY 17TH 1851, TO HIS BROTHER EDWARD

My Dear Edward,
I am just setting out in a boat laden with 'fish and potatoes' for Galway 30
miles East – 'en route' for Tuam to be Priested on Sunday next – here I am Lord
of all I survey – surrounded with dirt + ignorance – we have not got our
Schoolmaster yet but we expect him shortly. it is a very wretched Island. the
soil very scanty almost all a barren rock– we have a little church – 20 & 25
make our congregation mostly of the families of the coastguard I have 2
services each Sunday – I am at present living in a very small inn but intend next
week DV to move into a 'private' Lodging a house with a kitchen and two small
rooms overhead. I shall have one dirty little chap for my man Friday – who I
expect will always be where I don't want him to be + never to be had when he
is wanted however we must not be nice – it is very hard to make off a living here
some times fresh meat we never think of I have it once in 5 weeks – and the
chickens are scarce. it blew a little the last few days so we have no fresh fish and
must do with salt ones or half saved bacon – we have no market nearer than
Galway & no good boat to get there the hookers are all open & the passengers
& things often get wet thro' – nice service for flour, groceries, etc. They stay
away for a week at a time & we may do as we can until they choose to come back.
I want a vessel for my self woefully. I am a regular prisoner – I get on with the

people so far very well but how it will be when we begin to attack their bad ways & religion etc. I don't know. The proprietors of the Island are fitting up a house for me wh[ich] will be a very g[rea]t comfort when it is done. the noise and dirt of my present situation is very bad indeed – we have not a wheel machine cart or wheelbarrow on the Island the women carry everything on their backs – or else asses – Have you been to the Exhibition yet? do you think you will come over here? if you do I will run over and see it – but I have no one to take my place when I am absent they have no service – I will try to get over in Sept. if possible I [?would] like to see it very much – I have a good deal of time for reading and writing sermons – we have no good walks on the Island, the rocks are very sharp & no sandy beach either – shoes last no time – & as to black coats you can't have them – I came down in one but it soon ceased to be black. I never saw any thing turn brown faster –

May the Lord bless you and keep you and lift up the light of his countenance upon you – filling you with peace & joy in the Holy Spirit – which is the continual prayer on yr behalf from yr affte brother

Alex H. Synge

AUGUST 19TH 1851

My dear Edward,
It is a long time since I have heard from you, I believe our last letters crost on the road –

I am now living in a small house I have taken until my own is finished. It is very small. I have no one living in it but myself. I have a boy who comes in the morning & lights the fire etc. but he goes away in the evening I am my own cook very often – & always bake myself. The worst thing I am off for is fresh meat. this I seldom see. I have been three weeks without it & I suspect when winter sets I shall be often much longer – the days are passing very rapidly I suppose it is the constant preparing for Sunday that makes them go by so quickly but I think they never went so fast before – The sermon writing is the most difficult of all & takes up a great deal of time – then preaching it to a very small number makes it some thing harder I think.

Our School is daily increasing – I have succeeded in putting a stop [to] a ball match that used to go on here every Sunday. I attacked them very sharply the other Sunday & the next Monday the *priest* was the first to begin pulling down their wall tho' the rascal had seen them playing there 100 times before – but when I went to them and spoke about it he took it up at once. However it is well to put it down.– when will your ordination be held – will you come over after it? would you come here for a Sunday if so I wd be tempted to run over & see the Exhibition, have you seen it yet? We have the railway open to Galway now which facilitates our travell gtly – tho I have not been on it.

What a nice figure the Bishops cut last session I did not see yr Bishop's name mentioned – I have no news here – let me hear from you some time soon & believe me ever yr affte brother

Alex H. Synge

FEBRUARY 17TH 1852, TO HIS BROTHER JOHN

My dear John.

I think I must draw on you for 20£ again I have heard nothing from the Commissioners – I expected to have found a letter from them waiting my return – I have written to the Bishop's secretary on the subject but have not received the reply the Georgianna has not arrived yet when she does there will be an arrear of wages to be paid – also I [must] find some 5 or 6 pound for a new foresail the old one was blown away – the wind is right ahead and very strong the last few days but I expect her the first South wind. [...]

April will soon come when we ought to be prepared for the Sun Fish the men all talk very big about all she ought to catch of them. [...] Could you get me any where in Dublin from any shop or any of the Societies – Oh Education Kildare St Society or any other a dozen or two of large sheets with the alphabet printed on them in large letters that we can paste down on linen for it is utterly impossible to keep the little beasts in spelling books one week would not do – I could not find any at Glanmore reading sheets I have plenty but no readers – the priest cursed away finely last Sunday. He said three Devils had come to the Island & cursed all who spoke, saluted, visited, bought or sold to them or allowed them into their boats etc. [...]

FEBRUARY 29TH 1852

My dear John,

[...] I went last week to Boffin in the Georgianna to inspect & examine the school there we had fine weather all the time altho' a very heavy sea round Sline Head I like her sailing qualities very well so does her Captain we returned on Saturday She was christened by the Roundstone men 'the Jumpers boat' – how soon they found out what she was – We purpose getting nets & all tonight this week & next DV to begin the fishing will you order the same butcher to send me another cask of salt beef the last was very nice meat *a little too fat* – I have only two pieces left. I have nothing else to live on except fish & that only the last week, during the gales we got none.

MARCH 8TH 1852

My dear John,

Your note of the 5th has reached me with the second halves for 20£ [...] tell the Beak the Georgianna was quite staunch going around in her bottom and sides – any water she made she made thro' the deck but that was very little – I wish to know some *Salemaster* in *Dublin* – it is idle to talk of Galway I do not think we would be allowed to sell our fish there – we had a score of Galway boats lying all about us last week driven in from bad weather & I hear they threatened our men and said they would serve her as they did one before – but I do not think they will I hope not.

yr affte brother
Alex H Synge

But for yr beef & biscuits I might have starved the last month no eggs no butter little milk & fish.

[NO DATE]

My dear John,

Your letter as well as two from Miss B reached me this day so I start just now for Galway to try and reach the morning train for Dublin Miss B's last account was very indifferent – perhaps you will be in town shortly – I wrote to you last week in Dublin as I heard you had *been seen there* –

I was the week before last in Galway getting some repairs wh[ich] were necessary a very disagreeable weeks work it was The men were severely threatened last week on two occasions – some of the boats came quite close to them & just before coming up were observed to hide stones in their bosoms & pockets our men had to get their guns up but I suppose from seeing so many men & all well armed they passed on & did nothing. the young men are the worst & do not like giving up their old ways. I hope our men wont get frightened that is all I dread – they made a very good week of it as regards to fish – I write to let you [know] my movements I suppose I must return by [?] Friday night Francis says he will be in Tuam on the 20th for the fair –

Yr ever affte brother

A H. Synge

DECEMBER 26TH 1852

My dear John,

On Thursday yours of the 17th reached me. I think you got one from me since then – about bedding – I have not heard since – I have moved into the large house a wet and windy concern – it leaks like a sieve & rocks in the wind like a ship – we had a great storm the last three days – terrible last night at ? o'clock – I am uneasy about the Georgianna I sent her to Galway very early Friday with one of [the] Coastguardsmen whose daughter had fallen down a rock & very much hurt to the Infirmary in Galway – they were to have returned Friday but have not yet come in. [...] I am sending a process I received from the Claddagh men whose anchor we cut off to Galway to an Att[orne]y to defend. The Plaintiff summons Alex Cinque – I suppose I need not answer to such an appellation neither does he give any date when the alleged injury happened (or rather a *wrong* month and *no* day) so I suppose he will be cast – are there not law points against him.

33

THE GALWAY VINDICATOR

1852 & 1853

June 2nd 1852, Sat. p. 2

ATTACK ON MR SINGE'S TRAWLING BOAT

We deeply regret to find that a most determined and desperate attack was made on the trawling boat of the Rev. Mr Singe, near Costello Bay, on yesterday. The Rev. Gentleman with a crew of one boy and three Arran men, had been trawling in his yacht off Costello Bay, when a fleet of Claddagh boats bore down upon him, with the view of boarding his little craft. The crews of the attacking boats were armed with sunfish spears instead of boarding pikes, and stones instead of hand grenades, which latter missile they discharged to some effect. Mr Singe was struck on the arm with a large stone, and severely hurt; some of his men were also more or less injured; and one of the hookers came under the boom of the yacht and prepared to board, but was beaten off by Mr Singe, who presented a loaded musket at the foremost assailant, and threatened to shoot him if he advanced further. At this critical juncture, a breeze, luckily, sprang up, and the yacht, pursued by the whole fleet for a considerable distance, steered for the roadstead of Galway, where she safely arrived, with the loss of some of her nets, which they were unable to haul in, and had, consequently, to cut away.

Such lawless conduct as that now described is calculated to injure instead of serving our fishery, and must be put down with the strong arm of the Law. If men cannot be convinced by reason or friendly advice, to act honestly, they must be taught wisdom by a more stern monitor. It is the duty of every man who has the welfare of Galway at heart, to put down such illegal combinations.

April 13th 1853, Wed. p. 2

DISGRACEFUL OUTRAGE PERPETRATED BY THE CLADDAGH FISHERMEN

We regret to detail a disgraceful outrage lately perpetrated by the Claddagh fishermen. On Monday last the *Scots Grey* fishing boat, the property of Mr

From *The Galway Vindicator* 1852 & 1853.

Brown, while engaged in trawling in the bay, was pursued by a flotilla of Claddagh boats. When the crew on board the trawler perceived this hostile demonstration, they immediately sunk her trawl with the buoy attached. The Claddaghmen followed up the exploit by giving chase to the Rev. Mr Syng's boat, the crew of which also after letting down their trawls and attaching buoys, went off. The trawling gear of both vessels were destroyed, and, doubtless, but for their timely escape, the crews would have been massacred by those savages. A word of comment on the outrage we have detailed would be superfluous. Formerly we were favoured with the presence of one of her Majesty's sloops for the protection of our Fisheries. This protection has been withdrawn, and the consequence is that lawless violence can work its wicked will with perfect impunity. We entreat the authorities to take some measures to repress this system of organized terrorism, and prevent the future recurrence of outrages, so disgraceful to any community calling itself civilized, and believed to be living under the safeguard of the law.

April 16th 1853, Sat. p. 2

ASSAULT AND OUTRAGE

In a recent number of this journal we noted a malicious attack made by the Claddagh fishermen upon the trawling boats of the Rev. Mr Synge and Mr Browne, while fishing upon the high seas, near Arran [11th]. On Tuesday last [12th], the attack was followed up, but not with the same violence. With the view of bringing the perpetrators of the outrage to justice, the Rev. Mr Synge proceeded last night [15th] to the Claddagh Quay, for the purpose of identifying the owners of the several boats whose register numbers he had noted on the former occasions. But, being recognized by the Claddagh women, he was immediately assailed with stones and every available missile. Attempting to make his escape through the Fish Market, he was met by the denizens of that fragrant locality and was thus literally hemmed in by his assailants. No other means of escape being left he jumped into the river with the intention of fording it, but even there his pursuers continued the attack and it is difficult to say what might have been the result had not the police immediately come to his assistance. Gentle means having proved useless in dispersing the mob, the police had to charge with fixed baynots [*sic*], whereby we learn some persons were wounded. Seven of the rioters were arrested and several more can be identified. Even after the arrival of the police the violence of the mob was such that an additional reinforcement of the constabulary had to be summoned to the spot. Several of the police received slight injuries from the stones which were hurled.

The parties in custody were brought before the Magistrates today, but were remanded until Thursday next.

April 24th 1853, Wed. p. 2

STEAMER IN THE BAY

We are happy to state that our remonstrances have been at last attended to and that a steamer has been placed in the bay for the protection of the fisheries. It was not, however, until the late mischievous attack upon the trawling boats, and the riotous proceedings which followed at the Claddagh, had convinced our worthy Governors that longer delay might endanger the public safety, that this necessary protection was afforded. But, better late than never. The *Advice* steamer, a tender, we believe, to the *Ajax*, and commanded by Captain Balfour, has taken up her position in the Bay, and we hope that we have done with reporting 'riotous proceedings' and 'assaults upon the high seas'.

May 7th 1853, Sat. p. 2

ARREST OF CLADDAGH FISHERMEN

Yesterday the steamer *Advice* having on board J. B. Kernan, R. M. and Captain Richardson, Commander of the Coastguards, seized the crews of several of the boats which had been employed in the late attack on the Trawlers in the Bay. The prisoners, to the number of twenty-five, were brought on shore and conveyed to the county jail by a strong escort of police.

May 14th 1853, Sat. p. 2

GALWAY PETTY SESSIONS

[This concerns an attack made on the 16/4/53, the day after the Claddagh riot.] The prisoners being placed at the bar, the Clerk of the Peace read the informations of Robert Evans, master of the trawling boat *Georgiana*, to the effect that on the 16th April, informant had made informations before J. B. Kernan, Esq., R. M., describing an attack on the trawling boat *Georgiana*, belonging to the Rev. Mr Synge. Informant states that in the attack mentioned, about twenty boats had been engaged, that the assailants on board of them were armed with hatchets and spears, and that they threatened to kill informant and his crew unless the trawl, which was thrown out at the time, was instantly cut away. Informant fired a pistol over their heads with the hope of frightening them away, but, failing in producing the desired effect, he was at last obliged to cut away the trawl, which he has not recovered since, nor does he expect ever to be able to do so. Informant believes that they would have killed himself and his crew had he not acceded to their demands in cutting away the trawl. The numbers and names of the boats were all covered over, but he afterwards recognized 'No. 1' and that there were three persons on board whom he was able to identify. The information then went on to mention several other parties, whom, when arrested by the crew of the *Advice*, informant had identified as having been engaged in the attack.

The informations of John Donohue and Patrick Flaherty, the crew of the *Georgiana*, were also read, proving the attack and identifying several others of the prisoners.

Mr Kernan expressing the decision of the Bench said – This is the second time these informations have been read. They were sworn to on a former

36

occasion when each of you was identified as having been engaged in this lawless outrage. I have, therefore, no doubt on my mind of your guilt and it only remains for me, as I have been advised by the Law Officers of the Crown, to send you to the assizes, where you will have an opportunity of defending yourselves from the charges which has [sic] been brought against you. The Bench, however, have decided on admitting you to bail, yourselves in £30 and two sureties in £15 each. You should also be bound to keep the peace towards all her Majesty's subjects, yourselves in £20 and two securities in £15 each.

June 8th 1853, Wed. – [Meeting of Harbour Committee discusses situation of poverty-stricken Claddagh fishermen, suggestion they be assisted to commence trawling, Synge in favour, collection taken up to assist in this.]

June 22nd 1853, Wed. p. 2
We are happy to perceive that the resolution adopted by the Claddagh fishermen of trawling in the bay has been attended with the most beneficial results. The boats that had been fitted with trawling gear proceeded to sea on Monday, and returned yesterday evening with a large supply of fish – sole, red gurnet, etc. A meeting of the Claddagh fishermen fund was held on Monday last, on which occasion it was announced that his Excellency, the Lord Lieutenant, had contributed £10 towards the fund, with a promise of a further contribution of £10 for the same laudable object.

It is gratifying to see these men, instead of committing acts of lawless violence, and unsuccessfully endeavouring to prevent others from availing of the natural resources that Providence has bountifully bestowed, abandoning their unfounded prejudices, and peacefully entering upon a career of industrial occupation. While they persevere in this course, they deserve every aid and encouragement, and we hope the example of their success will induce the more turbulent members of that community to see the error of their ways, when they find that success crowns the efforts of the peaceful and industrious, and destitution and punishment are the certain doom of the lawless and refractory.

July 27th 1853, Wed. p. 2
Crown Court (before Chief Justice Lefroy). [List of 27 men] were placed at the bar and indicted for conspiracy against the Rev. Mr Sing, in order to prevent trawling in the Bay.

When the prisoners were called in to plead, Mr James O'Shaughnessy, Solicitor, said he appeared for all the prisoners who instructed him to enter a plea of guilty, and expressed their regret for what they did, and threw themselves on the mercy of the Court. He also intimated that the Crown did not wish to press for prosecution.

Chief Justice Lefroy then addressed the prisoners, and expressing his satisfaction that they now acknowledged the error they committed, and were determined not to transgress the laws in future, ordered them to stand out on their own recognizances.

The prisoners then left the court, loudly protesting their gratitude to the judge.

July 30th 1853, Sat. – [Rioters are discharged after Rev. Synge asks that the matter be dropped.]

George Petrie

The Islands of Aran (1822)

About thirty miles west of Galway, lie the three Aran Islands – Inishmore, Innishmain, and Innisheer, and our last extract shall be from the journal of Petrie's visit to these islands, which are so little known, but which present to the student of antiquity such unequalled opportunities for the study of pagan and Christian remains – the latter manifestly of the earliest periods.

Here are many gigantic forts of uncemented stone, the works of a by-gone race, rearing their ruined crests above the ocean, or crowning some central point, each surrounded by its walls of circumvallation, and in some cases with a chevaux-de-frise of upright stones. Here may be seen villages of bee-hive houses, stone-roofed or covered with clay; solitary uncemented dome-topped structures, the dwellings or oratories of some early ecclesiastics or hermits; churches of the rudest architecture, and others – such as those of Saint Benignus and Saint MacDuagh – startling in the cyclopean character of their masonry and their doorways, with groups of collegiate churches and other buildings, including the remains of the round tower of Saint Enda.

Of these singular islands, though previously described by O'Flaherty, Petrie may be said to be the discoverer – at least in an antiquarian point of view – and he bears witness to the character of the inhabitants, so long known as being that of a people kindly, pious, and peaceable. The old influences still hang about them; the old traditions of the time when the early saints of Ireland made holy their sea-girt and barren rocks; and for the last ten years, out of a population of three thousand three hundred, and with only one magistrate, the committals to prison have not annually averaged one per thousand of the people, and not one has been sent for trial at assizes or quarter sessions.

What an answer is this to those shallow and conceited writers, who maintain the necessary connexion between the amount of crime in Ireland and the prevalence of the Celtic race.

(William Stokes)

From William Stokes, *The Life and Labours in Art and Archaeology of George Petrie LL.D., M.R.I.A.* (1868).

ARAN — CHARACTER OF THE ISLANDERS

'The wild Irish are at this day known to be some of the veriest savages in the globe!!!' — *Pinkerton's History.*

I had heard so much of the virtues of the Aran islanders, of their primitive simplicity, their ingenuous manners, and their singular hospitality, that I could not help doubting the truth of a picture so pleasing and romantic, and felt anxious to ascertain, by personal observation, how far it might be real.

The result of much inquiry and attentive observation was a conviction, that though from recent circumstances the brightness of this picture should now be somewhat lessened, and that the Araners can no longer be considered the simple race unacquainted with crime, such as they were generally depicted, yet that enough still remains of their former virtues to show that the representations of them were but little, if anything, exaggerated.

The introduction, a few years since, of a number of persons into Aranmore for the purpose of erecting a lighthouse, has had an injurious effect on the character of the native inhabitants of the island. Their unsuspicious confidence and ready hospitality were frequently taken advantage of and abused, and their interesting qualities have consequently been in some degree diminished. Till that time robbery of any kind was wholly unknown in the island. 'Such was their honesty,' said one who has passed his life amongst them, 'that had a purse of gold been dropped in any part of the island, there would have been no uneasiness felt respecting its safety, as assuredly it would be found at the chapel on the Sunday or Holiday following, no instance having ever occurred of anything lost not being restored in that manner.' There is some reason to doubt that this would be so now. Several petty thefts have occurred, and though they have uniformly been attributed by the islanders to the strangers lately settled among them, it would perhaps be rash to conclude that they themselves have hitherto wholly escaped the vicious contagion. [...]

They are a brave and hardy race, industrious and enterprising; as is sufficiently evinced, not only by the daily increasing number of their fishing vessels — the barren rock which they are covering with soil and making productive — but still more by the frequency of their emigration from their beloved country and friends to a distant wilderness, led solely by the hope that their indefatigable labour may be employed there to the greater ultimate benefit of their families.

They are simple and innocent, but also thoughtful and intelligent, credulous, and, in matters of faith, what persons of a different creed would call superstitious; but being out of the reach of religious animosity, they are *as yet* strangers to bigotry and intolerance. Lying and drinking — the vices which Arthur Young considers as appertaining to the Irish character — form at least no part of it in Aran; for happily their common poverty holds out less temptation to the one or opportunity for the other. [...]

Would that I could convey to the mind of my reader even a faint outline of the character of our never-to-be-forgotten host! But as the most skilful artist finds beauty of form beyond his most laborious efforts to embody, so the beauty of character seems equally difficult for language to describe. [...]

Mr O'Flaherty is a native of Aran, and he has never been farther from his native rocks than to the city of Galway and the adjacent coast of Thomond. Even such journeys have never been entirely voluntary; and so deeply does absence from home afflict him with melancholy, that he appears on those occasions a man of quite different character to those who have seen him among the loved scenes of his philosophic musings. He is curious to see Dublin, but he has felt the pains of home-sickness so severely that he cannot trust himself upon a journey that would expose him so much to its severity.

What, then, reader, do you suppose such a man to be? A child, perhaps, or a rustic simpleton. A child he is in innocence and simplicity, but in wisdom and understanding he is most truly a man: nay, more, in manner of conduct a polished gentleman. [...]

Mr O'Flaherty may be justly denominated the *pater patriæ* of the Araners. He is the reconciler in all differences, the judge in all disputes, the adviser in all enterprises, and the friend in all things. A sound understanding and the kindest of hearts make him competent to be all those; and his decisions are never murmured against or his affection met by ingratitude. Of the love they bear him many instances might be adduced, but the following will be deemed sufficient, and too honourable both to them and him to be omitted.

In 1822 a great number of the islanders had determined to emigrate to America. A ship lay at anchor at Galway to convey them, and they proceeded thither accompanied by Mr O'Flaherty, to aid them to the last with friendship and advice. Several days elapsed before the vessel was ready to set sail, and Mr O'Flaherty still continued with them; but at last the hour to bid an everlasting adieu arrived. They must know the Araners that could fancy the scene that then ensued.

Men and women all surrounded him – the former with cheeks streaming with tears, and the latter uttering the most piercing lamentations – some hung on his neck, some got his hands or arms to kiss, while others threw themselves on the deck and embraced his knees.

It is no discredit that on such an occasion the object of so much affectionate regard was more than unmanned, and it was a long time before his health recovered the injury, or his face lost the sorrowful expression caused by the grief of that parting. [...]

I am unwilling to close this chapter without a short notice of two other persons of humbler rank in society with whom I became acquainted, and to whom I am beholden for some of the topographical information which these pages contain. One of these persons is an eccentric character named Tom O'Flaherty, who, with an originality somewhat Hibernian, combines the honourable practice of medicine, with the less reputable calling of a tailor, thus making himself doubly useful to the Araners, in healing their bodily complaints and protecting them from the inclemencies of the seasons. Tom himself is not an Araner. He came hither in the year after the memorable rebellion of 1798, in which, it is suspected, he was somewhat concerned, and, finding an

41

unoccupied theatre for the display of his varied talents, has continued exercising them ever since, to the perfect satisfaction of all ranks. Of the extent of
these talents, I, of course, cannot speak, but if the health and longevity of his
patients be considered as a criterion of his skill in his higher capacity, the
Araners have no reason to complain of the absence of a more regularly
instructed practitioner.

Tom is really what many doctors are not, a clever fellow. He has a sharp and
clear intellect, and a singularly retentive memory, stored with a variety of
information, historical, traditional, genealogical, and topographical, relative
to the west of Ireland. He has a romantic imagination, and is never happier, he
says, than when wandering about ancient ruins and among lakes and mountains. He is a great talker, a great lover of tobacco, and a great drinker – not a
great drunkard – for it would be very difficult to make him drunk, and a great
humourist, qualities which are all very Irish. A pint of whiskey he considers a
small daily allowance; and on a late occasion, while attending Mr O'Flaherty in
a typhus fever, he was limited to six glasses, he begged that the whiskey might
be given to him in two equal portions or drams, morning and evening, so that,
as he expressed it, 'he might feel the good of it'. [...]

It is not, however, for these qualities, but those of a better order which the
Doctor possesses, that I have introduced him to the reader's notice. He is
remarkable for humanity and active benevolence. In the spring of 1822, some
very bad cases of typhus fever occurred in the island, one of which was of a
stranger lately settled there. The islanders, who, like all the poor Irish, have a
deep terror of this frightful disease, fled from him; he was without money or
friends, and thus circumstanced he must have perished but for the courage and
humanity of Tom O'Flaherty. He first removed him, on his back, from the
infected house to a more airy situation – one of the old Irish stone houses –
which he had prepared for his reception. He then went to Mr O'Flaherty and
peremptorily demanded five shillings. 'For what purpose, Tom? is it to drink?'
said the other. 'No, trust me with it without asking any questions, I'll make no
bad use of it.' The money was obtained, and immediately sent off to Galway for
medicine for the sick man. With this assistance, in addition to his own
resource, he was enabled to bring the poor man successfully through the fever.
He visited him several times each day, sat with him, washed him, and
performed all the duties of a humane and skilful nurse. At the same time he
would never let either his own family or friends know that he was thus
employed, but gave them to understand that the man was dead, and would
always proceed from home in a different direction from that which led to the
place of the patient, and reach it unseen by a circuitous route; nor is it likely
that he would ever have undeceived them, if he had not had the pleasure of
bringing the man back to society whom he had thus rescued from the grave.

Excellent and entertaining Tom O'Flaherty! my fingers would deserve to
be parted from my hand if I neglected telling the tale of your courage and
benevolence!

Martin Haverty

Ethnological Excursion to the Aran Isles (1857)

From Dun Onaght the party crossed the island to the great cliffs on the ocean side, at one of which an exciting exhibition was prepared, which few of the party can ever expect to witness again. We had all heard how the inhabitants of Aran, and the Hebrides, and some other places, descend the dizzy ocean cliffs by means of ropes, in search of sea-fowls' eggs, and of the birds themselves for the sake of the feathers; and here our ethnologists were to be treated to a view of the appalling feat performed in the most perfect manner. Fifteen or twenty of the hardy islanders had brought their ropes, and when we had assembled at a point which might be called the horn of a crescent-shaped cliff, the rope was fastened round the middle of an old man, upwards of sixty years on the island, who boldly let himself over, whilst a dozen of his comrades payed out the rope from above. When he got down some few yards, this active and fearless old man, striking the rock with his foot, holding the rope with one hand, and preserving his balance with the other, flew, as it were, outwards and down-wards, his feet constantly moving like paddles in the air; and as the oscillations of the rope, which grew longer and longer as he descended, brought him towards the cliff, in imminent danger of being dashed to pieces, he struck out again with a bold and graceful movement, until at last, becoming smaller to our eyes as he descended, he reached the bottom. He took off the rope, which was then hauled up, when another and younger man, and after him a third who was a mere lad, performed the same perilous feat in a manner precisely similar. The old man then assumed the rope again, and was swung outwards by his companions below, and during the first long vibration of the living pendulum ascended about fifty feet. The process of striking the cliff was repeated each time he approached it on the ascent, until arriving within thirty feet of the brow of the precipice, he literally commenced to run up the face of it, his body projecting horizontally, supported and raised by the men above; and thus he reached the summit again. Within a few minutes the other men were also brought up in safety, amid the applause of all who beheld the exciting and

From *The Aran Isles; or a Report of the Excursion of the Ethnological Section of the British Association from Dublin to the Western Islands of Aran in September 1857* (1859).

novel exhibition. It should be added that, with the experienced men who performed those feats, there was really no danger to be apprehended. [...]

THE BANQUET IN DUN ÆNGUS

Dinner-hour having arrived, and all our company being assembled within the great Firbolgic fort of Dun Ængus, which was most judiciously selected by Mr Wilde as our banquetting-hall on the occasion, 'and order being, with some difficulty, restored in the ranks of the hungry savants, it was proposed, to the great joy of all, that the repast should commence without further delay.' The stewards commenced their duties; the hampers were unpacked; and the company were arranged in a spacious circle on the grass in the centre of the fort, separated from the overhanging brow of the terrific precipice by a wide, low ledge of limestone, which formed a sort of table, upon which a part of the viands were laid: the waves of the great Atlantic breaking all the while on the rocks below, yet, at such a distance beneath us that their roaring only sounded like the gentlest murmurs.

It was a glorious day, the sun being almost too warm, notwithstanding the ocean breeze which fanned us, and groups of the islanders looked on from the crumbling ruins around. With such scenery and such associations, cold would have been the bosom which did not feel a spark of enthusiasm within it. An abundant dinner, in serving which both the stewards and some of the *Vestal*'s crew exerted themselves in a most praiseworthy manner, and which was washed down with some excellent sherry, left nothing wanting to give effect to the impressions of the scene. The repast being disposed of, the party assembled on the grass near the platform of level rock which has been already mentioned, and, on the motion of Mr Wilde, the Provost of Trinity College was called on to preside, and took his seat on the rock. [...] Mr Wilde then came forward, and, addressing the President, said –

'So much, Gentlemen, as to how we came; – now as to whom we have brought. We have presiding over us the Rev. Dr MacDonnell, Provost of Trinity College, without whom our party would have wanted its most appropriate and honoured head. [...] Dr Petrie is here, the pioneer of philosophic antiquarian research in Ireland, the far-famed author of the *History of the Round Towers and the Ecclesiastical Architecture of Ireland*. [...] We have Dr O'Donovan here, who has done so much to advance our knowledge of these Islands. [...] We have here Eugene Curry, the chief brehon and lexicographer of Ireland at the present day – the true, the genuine Irishman, to whom the people, the history, and the language of his country are the breath of life. Let not his great erudition pass away without leaving the amplest record. [...] We have Dr Graves here, the Ogham decipherer, and Samuel Ferguson, who, to his valuable contributions to the science of the antiquary, has so happily blended the popular fascination of the poet. Gilbert is here, the historian of Dublin. Frederick William Burton is here, whose pencil has so exquisitely portrayed the living generation of the islands, and whose present visit, we may hope, will tell its own tale in his own happy way. [...] We have William Stokes here, whom I introduce, not as a doctor, but as an Irishman, whose cultivated and refined mind so fully appreciates all that is good and grand in nature, and whose liberal and warm heart throbs in responsive pulse with all that is good and great in his fellow-man. I am happy also to see here amongst us the Consul of France, the representative of that great country which has ever been foremost in encouraging art and science, and preserving the monuments of its national antiquities. He belongs to the same race as ourselves. There are many others here I need not name, without whom we should not have been so complete nor so happy as we are.

'Now why have I brought you here, and more particularly to the spot where I stand at this moment to address you? It is because, after all you have seen, I believe I now point to the stronghold prepared as the last standing-place of the Firbolg aborigines of Ireland, here to fight their last battle if driven to the western surge, or, as I have already pointed out to you, to take a fearful and eternal departure from the rocks they had contested foot by foot. Of that race we have no written knowledge. We can but make our conjectures by such light as recorded history has afforded us, reading it, comparing, and referring it to what they have left us in these litanies of stone. Here, perhaps, the sentinel on Dun Ængus, two thousand years ago, casting his glance on a summer eve over that vast expanse of Atlantic water that now rolls between us and America, brought up in fancy on the western horizon that far-famed island of O'Brazil, the tradition of which still lingers among these peasants now grouped around us. It has been one of my fondest hopes to render Aran an object of attraction, and an opposition shop, if I may so say, to Iona. Should I succeed in doing so, I shall feel myself amply repaid. And with reference to these stones, allow me to say a few words to the islanders. It is much to be deplored that these vast buildings are so rapidly going to destruction, not by the slow hand of time, for to time they almost bid defiance. The destruction we lament has been recent, and has befallen them from the hands of those who should preserve, not destroy them, as they have done in the pursuit of rabbits. Now, let me earnestly appeal to you, Islanders – will you not after this day, when you have seen that the interest felt in these old buildings brings so many strangers to your Island – and some, I tell you, have come many hundred miles – refrain from (for the paltry advantage of catching a few rabbits) bringing these walls to the state we see so many parts of them in? In an interested view of the matter you will be the gainers – strangers, in visiting the island, cause occupation and yield profit to many of you; and do not, for your own sake, destroy the things which bring strangers to visit you. Remember, above all, that these were the works of your own kindred, long, long dead; that they tell a history of them which you should be proud of, and that there is no other history of them but these walls, which are in your keeping. You have a great right to be proud of them; they are grand monuments of the brave men your forefathers were, and of how they laboured and how they fought to defend the land they left to you and to your children. Do you defend them in peace as they built and defended them in war, and let your children's children see strangers coming to honour them, as we have done today.' [...]

Professor Eugene Curry, being loudly called on, then came forward to deliver a speech in Irish to the islanders, who, being invited by the Provost and other gentlemen, gathered round in large numbers, and mingled with the company. He described the party of gentlemen who visited their island on that occasion, and who were assembled within those ancient walls, as comprising many most distinguished men, who had come not alone from Dublin and various other parts of Ireland, but from England and Scotland, to see that island, so celebrated in times of old, and which contained so many objects of the deepest interest. There were gentlemen there in the midst of them with true Irish hearts, and who loved everything that belonged to their dear old country – gentlemen of great learning, who devoted their time for many a year to study and to write about Ireland [cries in Irish of 'Musha, they're welcome']. They had been told by other gentlemen how wrong it was for them to destroy their ancient walls for the sake of hunting rabbits. It was little a few rabbit-skins were worth, and little did they know the damage which they committed in searching for them. Mr Curry appealed to them, in the names of their own great St Enda and St Brecan, whom they venerated, and whose ancient holy faith they still preserved, to respect and preserve the ancient remains of which their island boasted. Mr Curry's command of the language was such that he was able to address his Irish audience in their own Connaught idiom with as much facility as he would have done in that of his native Munster; although the peculiarities in pronunciation, &c., of the *spoken* language in the two provinces constitute a very marked dialectic distinction. His words appeared deeply to affect the poor people, who frequently and warmly applauded him.

Dr O'Donovan followed, describing the state in which he had found the ruins twenty years ago, and the great dilapidation that had since taken place. He also briefly addressed the islanders in Irish.

Paddy Mullin, the Guide, was then called on, and made a short speech in Irish, very much to the purpose. He reminded his fellow-islanders that for the sake of their honour as well as their interest, they should endeavour to preserve their ruins.

A musician, with a bagpipes, then played some merry tunes, and the banquet of Dun Ængus terminated with an Irish jig, in which the French Consul joined *con amore*.

T. J. Westropp

Notes on Connaught (1888)

On the morning of May 30th 1878 we started in a large six oared canoe from the village of Bealahaghline at the north end of the cliffs of Moher; as we passed Crab Island the breeze freshened and the sea boiled and foamed around the rocks throwing sheets of dazzling spray high into the air as we with some difficulty passed into the open sea. Connemara with its sharp blue peaks fringed the northern horizon while behind us lay the ramparts & pinnacles of Moher & the Clare coast cape behind cape as far as the eye could reach. As we got into the shallows behind Inishere the sea became like glass so that we could see the seaweed at the bottom the fishes flitting through its fronds like birds in a forest.

We reached Innishere by $2^{1}/_{2}$ [2.30 p.m.] on every side lay white & yellow sand undulating like the sea. Before us on a ridge of dark brown rocks stood a little village where we were to spend the night with certain kindly pilots named Joyce who even surrendered their only bed room to us & slept round their kitchen fire; beyond the village rose a massive castle and telegraph tower while on a high sand hill to our right appeared the ivied gable of an ancient church Kill Cavan or Tampool Cavan. This building is nearly buried in sand which has risen over the cultivated lands within the last thirty years though rent was still paid for these desolate fields in 1878 and no one thought of refusing payment.

The church consists of a nave & chancel the West door with lintel and inclined jambs outside it a wall encloses the saint's tomb where women still spend the night praying like Hannah for the gift of children. [...]

Next morning, May 31st, after the Doctor had held a leveé, a sad sight indeed though the people befriend each other & poverty is less friendless & neglected here than on the mainland, old people on the brink of the grave sick or hurt children & sadder still a fine young fellow of 18 wrecked by rapid consumption fearfully frequent in the islands from exposure & close intermarriage, he was past hope and doubtless a few weeks more laid him under the sand

From 'Notes on Connaught and Clare, especially Aran and Sligo', 1888, TCD. MS. 973.

and bleached bones of St Cavan's.

[...] as we crossed the Sound to Inishmaan we met a canoe whose crew after cautious signalling & questions came alongside & proved to have 12 little kegs of pottheen, it was fresh made & to me seemed liquid fire & turf smoke.

Innismaan appeared before us in bare rocky terraces it had no landing places so we coasted till a strip of sand appeared & backed our canoe through the surf, a wave lifting the nose high in the air & as the waters retreated we fled up the beach pursued by the next wave & found ourselves stumbling through shingle buried in masses of wild seakale in full flower of creamy white & diversified by wild blue columbines & pinks. A few cultivated fields occur between the shingle & the rocks which were scarped & scored & polished apparently by glacial action.

This island is an extremely primitive place we saw women grinding meal with querns & weaving the cloth which dyed red or brown forms the staple female dress; the men usually wear blue cloth clothes & scotch caps & 'pampooties' or raw hide shoes of untanned skin laced up the heel & instep, the wooden home made vessels are of the earliest type and very like the ones in the RIA museum. The customs here are very singular, the guileless youth of the sterner sex of the Islands have their marriages arranged by their parents & their most delicate duties taught them by knowledgeable old women; charms are painted over nearly every door & on the rafters, sores cured by cloths drawn through a pierced stone or ancient cross and, when we were there, there was only one other English speaking man on the Island which in stormy weather is often inaccessible for months at a time the natives being cut off from all help and assistance temporal & spiritual Mass being only celebrated once a fortnight in the best of weather by the priest or curate of Kilronan. [...]

So we left Innishmaan & thanks to the full tide, crossed the sandbar past the lighthouse & at 4½ p.m. reached Kilronan the capital of the islands, a large rather clean village with police & coastguard stations, Inn, post office & a neat protestant church, the Roman Catholic one being at Oghil in the centre of the Island. The village has a small pier & shallow harbour & is well sheltered by hills from the Western gales. We lodged at Costelloe McDara's Inn 'The Atlantic' Hotel, a poor clean place; our hostess gave birth to a son at that time so as her eldest son had several children of his own, the family must have been extensive. The village is called from Ronan, an unknown saint whose name appears cut on a pillar near a well behind the village. [...]

Kilmurvey is a poor fishing village of little note, behind it is the house of Mr O'Fflaherty, a representative of that class against whom the citizens of Galway prayed in their Litany 'from the bloodthirsty O'Fflaherties, Good Lord Deliver us' – he had been living on the mainland for some years & happened to return that day so the natives (who at this time did not consider a landlord an ex officio target) decorated all the avenue with paper flags & held races & games before the door. [...]

In Arran the natives often raise excellent vegetables in sand manured with seaweed & only a few feet deep – on enclosed patches of crag, the cabbages and potatoes are here of the sweetest flavour & best quality.

Sunday June 2nd

We at first intended to leave but changed our minds thereby seeing a curious sight the bay was full of hookers carrying cattle from the Saturday's market in Galway the animals in abject terror were tossed into the sea & swam splashing & bellowing to shore; then all the town, having moored the lightened hookers in the harbour retired to dress for chapel; suddenly a yell arose two children fell into the sea, one clung to a hooker & the other was fished out by an ancient mariner all the town turned out half dressed to look & laugh, when the mother in a state of semi nudity rushed weeping through the crowd & finding the child alive beat it & boxed it all along the pier either to teach it not to fall in again or to avenge the useless laceration of her maternal bosom. [...]

Beneath the cliffs north of Oghil stands the fine church of Temple Manistir Kieran where tradition says Collumkille remained for some years studying with Kieran the carpenter, here a boy sold us two crown pieces of Queen Elizabeth found in a neighbouring field. Two 'tarmons' or crosses stand east & SW of this church the first has a hole through it. Through this I hear the natives draw cloths to bind around sore or injured limbs, this is also done in parts of Clare & cloths are rubbed or pressed against the curious figures called sheelanagigs for various complaints of the country-women.

June 3rd

Next morning we hired a hooker called 'The Fancy of Aran' navigated by a cross old man & young McDara and through baffling calms & heavy rains strove to reach Kilkieran & were drifted into Birthagh buye Bay in Connemara thus ending a most pleasant tour in the sacred islands of celtic learning and religion.

(Origl. written Aug. 1878 Thos. Westropp.)

Haddon and Browne

Ethnography of the Aran Islands (1893)

PHYSICAL CHARACTERS

(a) the general physical character of the people is as follows:

Height – The men are mostly of a slight but athletic build; and though tall men occasionally are to be met with among them, they are, as a rule, considerably below the average Irish stature. The Aran average is 1645 mm. or about 5 feet 4³/₄ inches, that of 277 Irishmen is 1740 mm. or 5 feet 8¹/₂ inches.

Limbs – The span is less than the stature in a quarter of the cases measured, a rather unusual feature in adult males. The hands are rather small, but the forearm is often unusually long.

Head – The head is well shapen, rather long and narrow; but viewed from above the sides are not parallel, there being a slight parietal bulging.

The mean Cephalic Index, when reduced to the cranial standard, is 75·1, consequently the average head is, to a slight extent, mesaticephalic; although, as a matter of fact, the number measured is nearly evenly divided between mesaticephalic and dolichocephalic. The top of the head is well vaulted, so that the height above the ears is considerable.

The forehead is broad, upright, and very rarely receding; not very high in most cases. The superciliary ridges are not prominent.

Face – The face is long and oval, with well-marked features.

The eyes are rather small, close together; they are marked at the outer corners by transverse wrinkles. The irises are in the great majority of cases blue or blue-grey in colour.

The nose is sharp, narrow at the base, and slightly sinuous or aquiline in profile.

The lower lip is, in many cases, rather large and full.

The chin is well developed.

The cheek-bones are not prominent.

In quite a large proportion of cases the ears, though not large, stand well out from the head.

From *Ethnography of the Aran Islands*, Proceedings of the Royal Irish Academy (1893).

In many men, the length between the nose and the chin has the appearance of being decidedly great.

The complexion is clear and ruddy, and but seldom freckled. On the whole, the people are decidedly good-looking.

Hair – The hair is brown in colour; in most cases of a light shade and accompanied by a light and often reddish beard. As a rule, the hair on the face is moderately well developed.

Sight and Hearing – The sight and hearing of the people are, as a rule, exceedingly keen, especially the former. The range and distinctness of the vision is astonishing, as we have had occasion to know; and we are informed by Dr Kean that, on a clear day, any of the men whose eyesight is average can, with the naked eye, make out a small sailing boat at Black Head, 20 miles away, before he can see it with a good binocular.

Certain characteristics appear to be somewhat local. For example, the hair appears to be darker in the neighbourhood of Killeany, at the south-eastern end of Aranmore; and the large, aquiline nose seems to be most common at Oghil and Oat-quarter in the middle of the same island.

Repeated inquiries tended to show that the natives of the Middle and South Islands are considered by those of the North Island to be somewhat more burly in build, and darker in colour, than those of the North Island, and they certainly are better fishermen. Our statistics, however, tend to show that the Inishmaan men are somewhat lighter than the Aranmore men. One of us, a couple of years ago, had the opportunity of seeing most of the men from the three islands collected together at Kilronan, on the North Island, as well as a fair sprinkling of Connemara men. The latter were distinguishable at a glance by their dress, and certainly they had a different build from the Aranites, and were darker in colour. The men from the Middle and South Islands appeared, as stated above, to be distinguishable from the Inishmore men. The occasion of the gathering was a regatta in which the crews from the Middle and South Islands beat those from the North Island in the Curragh races. One Aranmore man was heard to say in extenuation of the defeat: – 'It was only to be expected that them islanders would beat, as they have to go about in canoes so much'! ...

The South Island was visited in 1852 by a late President of the Academy, Sir Samuel Ferguson. In his interesting sketch of the island (1853) he says (p. 90): – 'The patches of vegetable soil which occur here and there over this rugged tract, are carefully enclosed, and generally planted with potatoes. The soil is light and sandy, but, owing to the absorption of heat by the rock, peculiarly warm and kindly; and the islanders here have had the singular good fortune never to have been visited by the potato blight; never to have had a death from destitution; and never to have sent a pauper to the poorhouse. They are a handsome, courteous, and amiable people. Whatever may be said of the advantages of a mixture of races, I cannot discern anything save what makes in favour of these people of the pure ancient stock, when I compare them with the mixed population of districts on the mainland. The most refined gentleman might live among them in familiar intercourse, and never be offended by a gross or sordid sentiment. This delicacy of feeling is reflected in their figures,

51

the hands and feet being small in proportion to the stature, and the gesture erect and graceful. The population consists principally of the three families or tribes of O'Flaherty, Joyce, and Conneely. [...] "Our island is clean – there are no worms here," were the repeated expressions of my companion. [...] To see the careful way in which the most has been made of every spot available for the growth of produce, might correct the impression so generally entertained and so studiously encouraged, that the native Irish are a thriftless people. Here, where they have been left to themselves, notwithstanding the natural sterility of their islands, they are certainly a very superior population – physically, morally, and even economically – to those of many of the mixed and planted districts.

'This practice of forming artificial fields by the transport of earth recalled the old tradition of the Fir-Volgic origin of the early inhabitants of Aran. [...] These Fir-Volg, according to their own account, were Thracians, who had been enslaved in Greece, and there employed in carrying earth in leather bags to form the artificial terrace-gardens of Bœotia. If any portion of the existing population of Ireland can with propriety be termed Celts, they are this race' (p. 91).

FOLK NAMES

In reply to our request, Sergeant Wm. Law, of the Royal Irish Constabulary, has kindly made a list of the names which occur among the Aran islanders. In his letter he writes:–

'I forward a list of the surnames of the people of these islands. The frequency of the names as shown on the list is strictly accurate.

'I have omitted a few names such as those of Johnston, Chard, Kilbride and a few others of more ancient appearance on the islands.

'I carefully went over the Christian names of above 250 families with the result as shown on No. 2 list. I give all the Christian names used here, so that you might see if we have any pagan ones amongst us.'

These lists contain 61 surnames belonging to 458 individuals and 61 Christian names, of which 37 are those of males and 24 those of females. The Christian names are those of 1314 individuals.

We cordially thank Sergeant Law for the trouble he had taken in so carefully compiling these interesting lists.

FAMILY-LIFE AND CUSTOMS

The family usually consists of six or seven children; they go to school as soon as they can walk, and about four or five years of age they attend regularly. The children now attend better than formerly, as the priests enforce attendance. We understand that the children are intelligent, and make fair progress. They stay at school till they are fourteen or fifteen, and till seventeen if they get monitorships.

The children very early help their parents in various ways, such as weeding potato fields, helping in putting the kelp out to dry, and carrying water for the house and for the cattle.

LIST OF SURNAMES OF THE INHABITANTS OF ARAN ISLANDS, GALWAY BAY

Surname	Approximate frequency	Surname	Approximate frequency
Beaty,	1	Joyce,	17
Brabson,	1	Kean,	5
Burke,	5	Kelly,	4
Concannon,	5	Kilmartin,[8]	1
Conneely,[1]	61	Kennedy,	1
Cooke,	5	Kenny,	1
Curlin,	8	King,	1
Coleman,	1	Keilly,	1
Costello,	8	Kyne,	2
Crampton,	1	Lee,	2
Davoran,	1	Leonard,	3
Derrane,[2]	57	Maher,	7
Dillane,	4	McDonagh,	27
Donohoe,	11	Millane,	6
Duignan,	3	McNally,	1
Faherty,[3]	78	Mulkerrin,	4
Fallon,	3	Mullin,	20
Fahy,	1	Murray,	2
Flaherty,[4]	80	Naughton,	3
Fitzpatrick,[5]	5	O'Brien,	5
Flanagan,	1	O'Donnell,	20
Folan,	18	O'Rourke,	2
Gauly,[6]	1	Powel,	14
Garvey,	1	Quinn,	2
Gillan,[7]	3	Ryder,[9]	1
Gill,	6	Scofield,	1
Gould,	1	Sharry,[10]	2
Griffin,	9	Toole,	4
Hardy,	1	Wallace,	3
Hernon,	11	Walsh,	4
Hogan,	1		

[1] This name is found over the three islands.
[2] This name is confined (with exception of two families) to the large island.
[3] Distributed over the three islands.
[4] Distributed over the three islands.
[5] Originally from the King's County.
[6] Originally from Dublin.
[7] Originally from the North.
[8] From County Clare.
[9] Originally from Boffin Isle.
[10] Originally from County Clare.

LIST OF CHRISTIAN NAMES OF PEOPLE ON ARAN ISLANDS,
SHOWING THE FREQUENCY WITH WHICH THE NAMES OCCUR

(a)
Males

Christian Names	Frequency of occurrence	Christian Names	Frequency of occurrence
Andrew,	3	Matthew,	1
Ambros,	1	Martin,	48
Anthony,	4	McDara,	8
Bartly,	34	Michael,	105
Bryan,	4	Morgan,	8
Coleman,	24	Myles,	1
Daniel,	1	Patrick,	113
Denis,	2	Peter,	31
Edward,	19	Philip,	1
Edmond,	1	Roger,	2
Francis,	2	Robert,	1
George,	1	Simon,	5
Hugh,	1	Stephen,	11
Hubard,	1	Thady,	1
James,	7	Thomas,	61
John,	101	Timothy,	1
Joseph,	18	Walter,	1
Lawrence,	2	William,	9
Mark,	1		

(b)
Females

Christian Names	Frequency of occurrence	Christian Names	Frequency of occurrence
Agnes,	6	Hannah,	3
Alice,	1	Judith,	2
Anne,	51	Julia,	10
Barbara,	28	Margaret,	62
Bridget,	95	Maria,	6
Catherine,	62	Mary,	165
Celia,	1	Norah,	3
Debby,	1	Nappy,	2
Delia,	12	Sally,	1
Ellen,	16	Sarah,	6
Elizabeth,	1	Sabina,	1
Honor,	27	Winifred,	8

If a girl is not married by the time she is twenty years of age she will probably emigrate to America, but the boys are generally much older than the girls when they emigrate.

There is no courting or love-making, nor do the young people ever walk together. The marriages are arranged for; as a rule the lad has his father's consent and may be accompanied by him when he goes to ask for the girl. It seems that most, if not all, the marriages take place immediately before Lent. Sometimes a young man may suddenly, a day or two before the beginning of Lent, decide upon marrying, and, after seeing what his father will do for him, he goes to the house where there is a suitable girl and asks her to marry him. If she refuses he might go straight on to another; and a man has been known to ask a third girl in the same evening before he was accepted. The marriage might take place immediately, and the couple would live happy ever after. Girls marry quite young, seventeen is a common age and some are married at fifteen.

The eldest son generally inherits the house and the bulk of the property, and he lives with his parents when he is married. Often however, when the latter get old the property is made over to the young people, and the old folks stay on in the house.

According to Miss Banim:– 'A strange custom prevails upon a marriage here: the bride's fortune goes to portion off the old couple – the husband's father and mother – in lieu of their giving over the little plot of land to the son and his wife, or perhaps they again portion off a daughter with the same money' (p. 147).

The dead are 'waked' on the night before the funeral, and this is an occasion for the consumption of a considerable amount of whiskey.

There are certain spots where the procession stops on the road to the cemetery, and there it is usual to raise a small memorial heap of stones or even only a single stone. In the North Island there are quite a number (about two dozen) of unique road-side monuments erected at these resting-places. The oldest of these were erected by the Fitzpatrick family in 1709, and the most recent is dated 1875.

There is no keening while going to the burial ground, but only when the latter is reached.

Wakes are held, not only upon those who die on the islands, but also on the absent dead in America or elsewhere. The neighbours gather at the house, candles are lighted, and everything proceeds as if the corpse were present.

CLOTHING

The dress of both sexes is for the most part homemade, being largely composed of homespun, either uncoloured or of speckled brown, or blue grey, or bright red colour. The people appear not only to be warmly clad, but as a rule to be over-clothed.

As previously mentioned the girls and women card and spin the wool, the wool is worth eightpence per pound. The cards are bought in Galway, and the spinning wheel is of the pattern which is common throughout the west coast. A large fly-wheel is supported on a form, at the other end of which is an upright board which supports the spindle. The wheel is turned by hand. The whole machine is of rough workmanship and is homemade. Some women will hire other women to come to their houses to do their spinning for them at the rate of eightpence per pound. All the yarn is woven in the islands by professional weavers who charge fourpence per yard for the plain and fivepence for the coloured flannel. The flannel or yarn is dyed by the women. Dr Kean informs us that formerly the wool used to be dyed a black of a very fast nature by steeping it in a decoction made from some plants which he has never been able to identify and, then boiling it in an 'ink', as they used to term it, composed of the black liquid from bog holes, which was imported from Connemara for the purpose. This method has been given up for some years since the introduction of the dyes of commerce. Those most in use now are madder and indigo. O'Flaherty writes (1824), p. 133:— 'There is a native vegetable, the name of which I now forget, which gives a fine blue dye, much used in colouring the wool which the islanders manufacture for their wearing.'

The men wear a shirt of dark flannel procured from Galway, and over this a jacket or sleeved waistcoat (bawneen) of white homespun nearly as thick as a blanket; outside of which is worn a waistcoat made of grey-blue or brown flannel, in many cases it is bound with a dark braid. Of this waistcoat there are two patterns, one with large collar flaps buttoned back on the shoulders, and the other buttoned up to the neck with a simple turnback collar without flaps. The latter pattern, though sometimes worn by the men, is for the most part worn by boys. The trousers are of white or grey homespun and are worn loose and rather short, ending well above the ankles, and are slit down the outer side of the calf for the lower four inches. The feet are clothed in blue woollen stockings with white upper bands and toes. These are knitted by the women. They also wear a homemade broad blue bonnet of the 'Tam o'Shanter' type with a chequered head-band, or a broad-brimmed soft hat which is imported. Up to the age of about twelve the boys wear a long frock of red homespun coming well below the knees and buttoned up the back, otherwise they are clothed like the men.

The women wear only one cotton undergarment, and bodice, and several heavy petticoats; the outermost is usually of a bright red colour. They often wear a white jacket like a man's. Frequently a woman will be seen wearing a petticoat over her head as a shawl; but more usually an imported tartan shawl is worn, the red patterns, as Stuart, Grant, and McNab, being the favourite. In many cases a red kerchief is worn on the head, but caps, hats, or bonnets are not worn. O'Flaherty (1824 p. 138) says:— 'The female headdress is completely the old *Baraid* of the Irish.'

Both sexes wear sandals made of raw cowhide, the hair being outside, the edges of the piece of hide are caught up with string, with which they are tied on over the instep. They are admirably adapted for climbing and running over the rocks and loose stones. Some of the men, however, are now taking to wearing leather boots. These sandals are precisely similar to the 'rivlins' of the western and northern islands of Scotland. In Aran they are now called 'pampooties'; the origin of this term is obscure (cf. Wilde, 1861, p. 281). A curious point about them is, that they have to be wetted with water before being put on, and that while in wear they must be kept damp in order to preserve their flexibility.

In a footnote on p. 96 of O'Flaherty's *H-Iar Connaught*, Hardiman says:- 'It is observed that the people of Aran, who wear seal-skin pumps, or "pampooties", are never afflicted with gout. They affirm that a piece of the skin worn on the person cures and keeps away the cholic.' A pair of pampooties will last about three months, and the cost of the skin is from 6d. to about 1s. 2d. per pair.

DWELLINGS

The houses of the better class consist of three rooms, a central kitchen, and a bedroom at each end; but many houses have only a single bedroom. The following description applies to a typical Aran house:– the walls are built of irregular stones and may be placed together with or without mortar, sometimes the whole is whitewashed. There are always two outside doors opposite one another in the kitchen. At a funeral the corpse is always carried out through the back door. The fireplace may be on the right- or left-hand side-wall of the kitchen; it is a large recess, in the centre of which there is always a peat fire burning; and there is often a seat on each side of this, within the fireplace. A hook ('crook') hangs down over the fire for the suspension of the cooking-pot. Very often there is a small pen by the side of the fire, this is the pigstye, it is circumscribed by long, low slabs of limestone, and the entrance is closed by a board. The pigs are very clean both in their bodies and habits. The kitchen floor may be the bare rock, or clay, or it is very rarely boarded.

The doors into the bedrooms are at the front door-end of the party-walls. The bed is a 'tent-bed', that is, with boarded ends and a pitched roof. It lies along the back wall of the bedroom, the head of the bed usually being towards the party wall. The bedrooms are sometimes boarded.

The peat is often stored on boards above the beams ('couples'). Sometimes there is a loft over a bedroom and opening into the kitchen, in which the peat is stored, or the boys of the house may sleep in a loft.

The houses vary in size; a kitchen would be about 14 ft. long by 10 ft. deep, and a bedroom about 8 or 9 ft. wide, and as long as the breadth of the house.

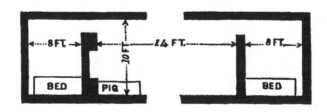

The roof is thatched with rye-straw; scraw (or sheets of grass-turf) are first laid on the rafters; the thatch is not fastened on to this with rods, or scallops as they are called in some parts of Ireland, but it is tied on by straw ropes, which are formed into a kind of net, and the ends are pegged into the walls of the house and over the edges of the gables. The latter may be made with straight edges, but very often they are left as a series of steps, in which case the horizontal straw-ropes are carried round in the angles of the stones. The houses are lightly thatched every year – or at least every two years – the new thatch being laid over the old. Nearly every house has a small out-house or shed, in which the potatoes are stored. Horses and cattle are never put under shelter.

II

Literary Revival

*B*y the end of the nineteenth century the *Aran Islands were well established in the public imagination as a remote and primitive place and were so used as settings for various novels. However, apart from Lady Emily Lawless's novel* Grania *(1892), which W. B. Yeats and Arthur Symons read on the boat during their trip to Aran, the picture of the islands given in these works bears little resemblance to reality. The novels range from Lever's* Luttrell of Aran *(1865), in which the Aran Islands and Aranmore are blended with copious helpings of the author's imagination, to* The Martins of Cro' Martin *(1856), with its memorable description of the Joyce family in their wigwam-shaped cabin on the Brannock Islands off the tip of Inis Mór.*

To other people, however, the islands symbolized a different set of values. As interest in the Irish language, folklore and associated matters grew rapidly towards the end of the century, so the more remote areas of Ireland and the Aran Islands in particular came to be seen as the purest repositories of the true Gaelic tradition. The first visitors were noted European linguists and Celticists like Holger Pedersen and Franz Finck. Heinrich Zimmer visited Inis Mór in 1880 and addressed a crowd in Cill Rónáin demanding lower rents, advising them to stick together to protect their rights and land.

These foreign visitors were followed by a succession of individuals who represented the burgeoning Anglo-Irish Literary Revival movement. Mary Banim (a Revival precursor), Lady Augusta Gregory, W.B. Yeats, Arthur Symons, Anna MacManus (Ethna Carbery) and, of course, John Millington Synge, all made their way as if on pilgrimage and wrote of their experiences in different ways. While Symons described the actual visit, Lady Gregory collected a large amount of folklore on the islands. Synge returned to the islands again and in his work The Aran Islands *inspired the hosts of visitors that were to descend on the islands over subsequent decades.*

On a slightly different tack came Patrick Pearse in 1898. Conradh na Gaeilge (The Gaelic League) had been established in 1893 to preserve and strengthen the Irish language, and branches were set up all around the country. In his article from Fáinne an Lae *(written in a rather stilted, didactic style), Pearse describes how the branch in Aran came to be set up and the reaction of the islanders to it. From this point onwards the Aran Islands, like the Blaskets and other remote Irish-speaking areas, became a popular destination for all language enthusiasts.*

In many ways this period definitively fixed an image of Aran that would be perceived by the outside world thereafter. The Aran Islands became an outpost of Irish tradition, a simple, primitive place embodying all that was good of Irish culture and language, a place to be revered and preserved. This picture, of course, owed much to the personal views and motives of those who painted it. In reality, the last decades of the nineteenth century on the Aran Islands were marked by poverty and hardship, with tension and violence between Catholic and Protestant, tenant and landlord's agent. Only in the writings of Synge do we find any impression of the frequent assaults, maiming of horses and cattle, boycotts, victimizations, evictions and allegations of forced conversions that arose constantly in the history of the period.

61

The strength of Synge's portrayal has been particularly enduring and still shapes the expectations of today's visitors. It was, of course, reinforced by that other great depiction of island life, the documentary film Man of Aran, *whose director, Robert Flaherty, said that Synge had taught him what to see. Against this, the frank, often scathing realism of the novels of Liam O'Flaherty could have little effect.*

Emily Lawless

Grania, The Story of an Island

Hardly had the smaller boat pushed away from the larger one and regained its former place before the little girl upon the ballast scrambled hastily down from her perch, mounted the deck, and went up to the boy as he stood there astonished, furious, red to the roots of his hair with anger and indignant surprise.

She had been watching the struggle between him and Shan Daly with breathless interest. She hated Shan with all the hate of her fierce little heart. She loved Murdough. He was their nearest neighbour, her playfellow, her big brother – not that they were of any kin to one another – her hero, after a fashion. She adored him as a small schoolboy adores a bigger one, and like that small schoolboy, laid herself open to be daily and hourly snubbed by the object of her adoration.

'Is it hurt you are, Murdough? Murdough dheelish, is it hurt you are? Speak Murdougheen, speak to me! Did the beast stick you? Speak, I say!' she asked in quick, eager Irish, pouring out a profusion of those tender diminutives for which our duller English affords such a meagre and a poverty-stricken equivalent.

But the boy was too angry, too profoundly insulted by the whole foregoing scene, especially the end of it, to make any response. He pushed her from him instead with a quick, angry gesture, and continued to stare at the sea and the other boat with an air of immeasurable offence.

The little girl did not seem to mind. She kept pressing herself closely against him for a minute or two longer, with all the loving, not-to-be-repulsed pertinacity of an affectionate kitten. Then, finding that he took no notice of these attentions, left him, and trotted back to her former perch, clambering over the big stones with an agility born of practice, and having dived into a recess hidden away between a couple of loose boards, presently found what she was in search of, and, scrambling back, came close to him and thrust the object silently into his hands.

It was only a bit of bread, perfectly stale, dry bread, but then it was baker's bread, not griddle, and as such accounted a high delicacy upon Inishmaan, only to be procured when a boat went to the mainland, and even then only by the

From *Grania, The Story of an Island* (1892).

more wealthy of its citizens, such as Con O'Malley, who had a fancy for such exotic dainties, and found an eternal diet of potatoes and oatmeal porridge, even if varied by a bit of cabbage and stringy bacon upon Sundays and saints' days, apt at times to pall.

It seemed as if even this treasured offering would not at first propitiate the angry boy. He even went so far as to make a gesture with his hand as if upon the point of flinging it away from him into the sea. Some internal monitor probably made him refrain from this last act of desperation, for it was getting late, and a long time since he had eaten anything. He stood still, however, a picture of sullen irresolution: his good-looking, blunt featured, thoroughly Irish face lowering, his upper-lip thrust forward, his hands, one of them with the piece of bread in it, hanging from his side. A sharper voice than Grania's came, however, to arouse him.

'*Monnum oan d'youl! Monnum oan d'youl!*' ('My soul from the devil!') Con O'Malley shouted angrily from the curragh. 'Go to her helm this minute, ma bouchaleen, or it will be the worse for you! Is it on to the Inishscattery rocks you'd have us be driving?'

Murdough Blake started; then, with another angry pout, crossed the deck of the hooker, and went to take up his place beside the helm, upon the same spot on which Con O'Malley himself had stood a few minutes before. The big boat was almost immovable; still, the Atlantic is never exactly a toy to play with, and it was necessary for some hand to be upon the helm in case of a sudden capricious change of wind, or unlooked-for squall arising. Little Grania did not go back to her former place upon the ballast, but, trotting after him, scrambled nimbly on to the narrow, almost knife-like edge of the hooker, twisting her small pampootie-clad feet round a rope, so as to get a better purchase and be able to balance herself.

The afternoon was closing in quickly now. Clouds had gathered thickly to northward. The naked stone-strewn country between Spiddal and Cashla, the wild, almost unvisited, wholly roadless region beyond Greatman's Bay, were all lost to sight in dull, purplish-brown shadows. Around the boat the water, however, was still grey and luminous, and the sky above it clear, but the distance was filled with racing, hurrying streaks of darker water; while from time to time sudden flurries of wind broke up the hitherto perfect reflections.

Usually, when these two companions were alone together, a chattering went on, or, to be accurate, an incessant monologue; for Murdough Blake already possessed one of the more distinctive gifts of his countrymen, and his tongue had a power of building up castles in the air – castles in which he himself, of course, was chief actor, owner, lord, general person of importance – castles which would sometimes mount up, tier above tier, higher and higher, tottering dizzily before the dazzled eyes of his small companion, till even her admiration, her capacity for belief, failed to follow them longer.

Neither of them knew a single word of English, for the schoolmaster had not in those days even casually visited Inishmaan, which is still, at the moment I write, the most retrograde spot, probably, within the four seas. The loss was none to them, however, for they were unaware of it. No one about them spoke

English, and had they spoken it, nay, used it habitually, it would have been less an aid probably than a hindrance to these architectural glories. To-day, however, Murdough was in no mood to exhibit any of his usual rhetorical feats. He was thoroughly out of temper. His vanity had been badly mauled, not so much by Shan Daly's attack upon him – for, like everyone in and around Inishmaan, he despised Shan Daly – as by the fashion in which Con O'Malley had cut short his own explanations. This had touched it to the quick: and Murdough Blake's vanity was already a serious possession, not one to be wounded with impunity. Con being out of reach, and too high in any case for reprisals, he paid back his wrongs, as most of us do, in snubs upon the person nearest at hand. The *tête-à-tête*, therefore, was a silent one. From time to time the hooker would give a friendly, encouraging croak as if to suggest a topic, sloping now a little to the right, now to the left, as the soft air began to be invaded by fresher currents coming in from the Atlantic – wild nurse, mother, and grandmother of storms, calm enough just then, but with the potentiality of, Heaven only knows how many, unborn tempests for ever and for ever brooding within her restless old breast.

Occasionally Murdoch would take a bite out of the slice of white bread, but carelessly, and with a nonchalant air, as much as to say that he would just as soon have been doing anything else. Whenever he did this, little Grania would watch him from the ledge upon which she had perched herself, her big dark eyes glistening with satisfaction as the mouthful disappeared down his throat. Now and then too she would turn for a moment towards the curragh, and as she did so and as her eye caught sight of Shan Daly's slouching figure a gleam of intense rage would sweep across the little brown face, the soft upper lip wrinkling and curling expressively as one may see a small dog's lips curl when it longs to bite. Ill would it have fared with Shan-à-veehonee or Shan-à-gaddy ('Shan the thief') – which was another of his local names – had her power to punish him been equal to her wish to do so. Her hates and her loves ranged at present over a ridiculously narrow compass, but they were not at all ridiculous in their intensity. It was a small vessel, but there was an astonishing amount of latent heat, of latent possibilities, alike for good and ill, in it. [...]

Leaning there, idly scanning the grey masses overhead, with floating, carroty beard, loose-lipped mouth, indeterminate other features, and eternal frieze coat dangling by a single button, this big, good-tempered-looking Con O'Malley of Inishmaan might have passed, in the eyes of an observer on the look-out for types, as the very picture and ideal of the typical Connaught peasant – if there are such things as typical peasants, or, indeed, any other varieties of human beings, a point that might be debated. As a matter of fact, he was not in the least, however, what we mean when we talk of a typical man, for he had at least one strongly-marked trait which is even proverbially rare amongst men of his race and class – so rare, indeed, that it has been said to be undiscoverable amongst them. His first marriage – an event which took place thirty years back while he was still barely twenty – had been of the usual *mariage de convenance* variety, settled between his own parents and the parent of his bride, with a careful, nay, punctilious, heed to the relative number of cows, turkeys, feather-beds, boneens, black pots and the like, producible upon either side, but as regards the probable liking or compatibility of the youthful couple absolutely no heed whatsoever. Con O'Malley and Honor O'Shea (as in western fashion she was called to the hour of her death) had, all the same, been a fairly affectionate couple, judged by the current standard, and she, at any rate, had never dreamt of anything being lacking in this respect. Sundry children had been born to them, of whom only one, a daughter, at the present time survived. Then, after some eighteen years of married life, Honor O'Shea had died, and Con O'Malley had mourned her with a commendable show of woe and, no doubt, a fair share of its inner reality also. He was by that time close upon forty, so that the fires of love, if they were ever going to be kindled, might have been fairly supposed to have shown some signs of their presence. Not at all. It was not until several years later that they suddenly sprang into furious existence. An accident set them alight, as, but for such an accident, they would in all probability have slumbered on in his breast, unsuspected and unguessed at, even by himself, till the day of his death.

It was a girl from the 'Continent,' as the islanders call the mainland, who set the spark to that long-slumbering tinder – a girl from Maam in the Joyce country, high up in the mountains of Connemara – a Joyce herself by name, a tall, wild-eyed, magnificently handsome creature, with an unmistakable dash of Spanish blood in her veins. Con had seen her for the first time at old Malachy O'Flaherty's wake, a festivity at which – Malachy having been the last of the real, original O'Flaherties of Aranmore – nearly every man in the three islands had mustered, as well as a considerable sprinkling of more or less remotely connected Joyces and O'Flaherties from the opposite coast. Whole barrels of whisky had been broached, and the drinking, dancing, and doings generally had been quite in accordance with the best of the old traditions.

Amongst the women gathered together on this celebrated occasion, Delia Joyce, of Maam in Connemara, had borne away the palm, as a Queen's yacht might have borne it away amongst an assembly of hookers and canal barges. Not a young man present on the spot – little as most of them were apt to be troubled with such perturbations – but felt a dim, unexplained trouble awake in his breast as the young woman from Maam swept past him, or danced with measured, stately steps down the centre of the stone floor; her red petticoat slightly kilted above her ankles, her head thrown back, her great, dark, slumberous eyes sweeping round the room, as she looked demurely from one strange face to another. Upon Con O'Malley – not amongst the category of young men – the effect was the most marked, most instantaneous, most overwhelming of all! Delia Joyce, as everyone in the room discovered in ten minutes, had no fortune, and, therefore, obviously was no match. She was the orphan niece of a man who had seven living children of his own. She had not a cow, a gridiron, a penny-piece, an inch of land, not a possession of any sort in the world.

Regardless of this utterly damning fact, regardless of his own age, regardless of the outrage inflicted upon public opinion, regardless of everything and everybody, Con O'Malley fell hopelessly in love with her; clung to her skirts like a leech the whole evening; followed her the next day as she was about to step on board her curragh for the mainland, carried her, in short, bodily off her feet by the sheer vehemence of his love-making. He was still a good-looking man at the time; not bent or slouching, but well set up; a 'warm' man, 'well come' and 'well-to-do'; a man whose pleadings no woman – short, that is, of a bailiff's or a farmer's daughter – would disdain to listen to.

Delia Joyce coyly but gladly consented to respond to his ardour. It was a genuine love-match on both sides – that rarest of rare phenomena in peasant Ireland. That it would, as a matter of course, and for that very reason, turn out disastrously was the opinion, loudly expressed, of every experienced matron, not in Inishmaan alone, but for forty miles around that melancholy island. A 'Black stranger,' a 'Foreigner,' a girl 'from the Continent,' not related to anyone or belonging to the place! worse than all, a girl without a penny-piece, without a stool or a feather-bed to add to the establishment! There was not a woman, young or old, living on the three islands but felt a sense of intense personal degradation whenever the miserable affair was so much as alluded to before her!

Marriages, however, are queer things, and the less we prophesy about them the less likely we are perhaps to prove conspicuously wrong. So it was in this case. A happier, more admittedly successful marriage there never was or could be, save, indeed, in one important and lamentable respect, and that was that it came to an end only too soon. About a year after the marriage little Grania was born, two years after it a boy; then, within a few days of one another, the mother and the baby both died. From that day Con O'Malley was a changed man. He displayed no overwhelming or picturesque grief. He left the weeping and howling at the funeral, as was proper, to the professional mourners hired upon that occasion. He did not wear crape on his hat – the last for the excellent reason that Denny O'Shaughnessy made none, and Denny O'Shaughnessy was much the most fashionable of the weavers upon Inishmaan. He did not mope, he did not mourn, he did not do anything in particular. But from the day of his wife's death he went to the dogs, steadily and relentlessly – to the dogs, that is, so far as it is going to the dogs to take no further interest in anything, including your own concerns. He did not even do this in any very eminent or extravagant fashion: simply became on a par with the most shiftless and thriftless of his neighbours, instead of being rather noticeably a contrast to them in these respects. Bit by bit, too, the 'Cruskeen Beg,' which had hitherto regarded him as only a very distant and unsatisfactory acquaintance, began to know him better. He still managed to keep the hooker afloat, but what it and his farm brought him in nearly all found its way across the counter of it or some kindred shebeen, and how Honor O'Malley contrived to keep herself and the small Grania, not to speak of a tribe of pensioners and hangers-on, upon the margin left was a marvel to all who were acquainted with the family. Nine years this process had been going on, and it was going on still, and, as the nature of things is, more and more rapidly of late. Poor Con O'Malley! He was not in the least a bad man; nay, he was distinctly a good man: kindly, religious, faithful, affectionate, generous – a goodly list surely of the virtues? But he had set his foot upon a very bad road, one which, all over the world, but especially in Ireland, there is rarely, or never, any turning back upon.

Lady Gregory

Seers and Healers

OLD DERUANE

Old Deruane lived in the middle island of Aran, Inishmaan, where I have stayed more than once. He was one of the evening visitors to the cottage I stayed in, when the fishers had come home and had eaten, and the fire was stirred and flashed on the dried mackerel and conger eels hanging over the wide hearth, and the little vessel of cod oil had a fresh wick put in it and lighted. The men would sit in a half-circle on the floor, passing the lighted pipe from one to another; the women would find some work with yarn or wheel. The talk often turned on the fallen angels or the dead, for the dwellers in those islands have not been moulded in that dogma which while making belief in the after-life an essential, makes belief in the shadow-visit of a spirit yearning after those it loved a vanity, a failing of the great essential, common sense, and sets down one who believes in such things as what Burton calls in his Anatomy 'a melancholy dizzard'.

I was told by Old Deruane:

I was born and bred in the North Island, and ten old fathers of mine are buried there.

I can speak English, because I went to earn in England in the hard times, and I was for five quarters in a country town called Manchester; and I have threescore and fifteen years.

I knew two fine young women were brought away after childbirth, and they were seen after in the North Island going about with *them*. One of them I saw myself there, one time I was out late at night going to the east village. I saw her pattern walking on the north side of the wall, on the road near me, but she said nothing. And my body began to shake and I was going to get to the south side of the wall, to put it between us; but then I said, 'Where is God?' and I walked on and passed her, and she looked aside at me but she didn't speak. And I heard her after me for a good while, but I never looked back, for it's best not to look back at them. [...]

I saw them playing ball one day when the slip you landed at was being made, and I went down to watch the work. There were hundreds of them in the field at the top of it, about three feet all, and little caps on them; but the men that were working there, they couldn't see them. And one morning I went

From *Visions and Beliefs in the West of Ireland* (1920).

down to the well to leave my pampooties in it to soak – it was a Sabbath morning and I was going to Mass – and the pampooties were hard, and wore away my feet, and I left them there. And when I came back in a few minutes they were gone, and I looked in every cleft, but I couldn't find them. And when I was going away, I felt *them* about me, and coming between my two sticks that I was walking with. And I stopped and looked down and said, 'I know you're there,' and then I said, '*Gentlemen*, I know you're here about me,' and when I said that word they went away. [...]

One time I was out putting seed in the ground, and the ridges all ready and the seaweed spread in them; and it was a fine day, but I heard a storm in the air, and then I knew by signs that it was they were coming. And they came into the field and tossed the seaweed and the seed about, and I spoke to them civil and then they went into a neighbour's field, and from that down to the sea, and there they turned into a ship, the grandest that ever I saw.

There was a man was passing by that Sheoguey place below, fishing in his curragh, and when they were about a mile out they saw a ship coming towards them, and when they looked again, instead of having three masts she had none, and just when they were going to take up the curragh to bring it ashore, a great wave came and turned it upside down. And the man that owned her got such a fright that he couldn't walk, and the other two had to hold him under the arms to bring him home. And he went to his bed, and within a week after, he was dead. [...]

I'm going to rise out of the cures and not to do much more of them, for *they* have given me a touch here in the right leg, so that it's the same as dead. And a woman of my village that does cures, she is after being struck with a pain in the hand.

Down by the path at the top of the slip from there to the hill, that's the way they go most nights, hundreds and thousands of them. There are two old men in the island got a beating from them; one of them told me himself and brought me out on the ground, that I'd see where it was. He was out in a small field, and was after binding up the grass, and the sky got very black over him and very dark. And he was thrown down on the ground, and got a great beating, but he could see nothing at all. He had done nothing to vex them, just minding his business in the field.

And the other was an old man too, and he was out on the roads, and they threw him there and beat him that he was out of his mind for a time.

One night sleeping in that little cabin of mine, I heard them ride past, and I could hear by the feet of the horses that there was a long line of them.

This is a story was going about twenty years ago. There was a curate in the island, and one day he got a call to the other island for the next day. And in the evening he told the servant maid that attended him to clean his boots good and very good, for he'd be meeting good people where he was going. And she said, 'I will, Holy Father, and if you'll give me your hand and word to marry me for nothing, I'll clean them grand.' And he said 'I will; whenever you get a comrade I'll marry you for nothing, I give you my hand and word.' So she had the boots grand for him in the morning. Well, she got a sickness after, and after seven months going by, she was buried. And six months after that, the curate was in his parlour one night and the moon shining, and he saw a boy and a girl outside the house, and they came to the window, and he knew it was the servant girl that was buried. And she said, 'I have a comrade now, and I came for you to marry us as you gave your word.' And he said, 'I'll hold to my word since I gave it,' and he married them then and there, and they went away again.

Nathaniel Colgan

Witchcraft in the Aran Islands

I was on hands and knees one morning, poring over a promising stretch of sandy pasture near the sea at Killeany, Aranmore, in search of the rare Milk Vetch (*Astragalus hypoglottis*), a species peculiar in Ireland to these islands, when I was startled by this remark, which came from one of the knot of puzzled Killeany-men who had gathered round me to watch my doings with embarrassing patience:

'That's a very dangerous thing you're about; I've known a man killed that way.' At first I thought the speaker, a grave, middle-aged man, meant to warn me against injury from some poisonous plant, but on close cross-questioning, it became evident that he was a firm believer in disease-transference by witchcraft.

His story was shortly this. Some years ago a friend of his, a man named Flanagan, living in the neighbourhood of Oghil, in Aranmore, lay sick of an incurable disease. He had been 'given over' by the doctors, and, face to face with death, his fears, after a long struggle, got the better of his religion, and he made up his mind to call in the services of a *cailleach*, who lived away in Onaght, at the other end of the island. This hag was well known to have the power of transferring mortal sickness from the patient, wicked enough to employ her, to some healthy subject, who would sicken and die, as an unconscious substitute. This was her method, evidently a combination of a plant-spell with the *gettatura*, or evil eye. When fully empowered by her patient, whose honest intention to profit by the unholy remedy was indispensable to its successful working, the *cailleach* would go out into some field close by a public road, and setting herself on her knees, just as I was kneeling then, she would pluck an herb from the ground, looking out on the road as she did so. The first passer-by she might cast her eye on, while in the act of plucking the herb, no matter who it was, even her own father or mother, would take the sick man's disease, and die of it in twenty-four hours, the patient mending as the victim sickened and died. My informant had known the *cailleach* well, but had only heard for certain of one case, the case of his friend Flanagan, where she had worked a cure in this way. The name of the man she

From *Journal of the Royal Society of Antiquaries of Ireland* (1895).

had killed to save Flanagan's life was O'Flaherty, and he had known him, too. [...] Unfortunately he could not tell me what the mystic plant was, though he was sure it was not the Milk Vetch, which I had the good fortune to find before we parted. More unfortunate still, the *cailleach* and Flanagan, as he told me, were both dead.

Mary Banim

The Arran Isles

Four years ago I made my first acquaintance with the Arran Isles, and that acquaintance has left a happy memory that can never fade.

From time to time an antiquarian has described the marvellous historic, or pre-historic forts, the druidical remains, the numerous ruins of early Christian architecture, all of which make these islands a very paradise for archaeologists. Historians have written of the 'Islands of Saints,' where Christianity was established even in the days of St Patrick, and to whose shores came all the great saints of that age, to learn lessons of wisdom and holiness from the lips and from the life of the blessed Enda. Botanists have spoken in glowing terms of the beauties and the variety of flowers, plants, and herbs to be found in Arran; while, on the other hand, agriculturists and politicians – notably, amongst the latter, that trenchant writer, Mr Labouchere – have written of the utter desolation and barrenness of those little spots out in the wide ocean, where no land exists save here and there a patch made by the unceasing labour of the people who call these out-of-the-way deserts 'home' – aye, and love them as home.

Then, too, I had been told by those who knew them, of a people the most genuinely Irish, in language and customs, of our race still left in the West of Ireland: a simple, primitive, but highly-intelligent people, full of the old kindly ways, that have such an irresistible attraction for anyone whose heart longs for the kind looks, bright, cheerful words, and thoughtful, friendly acts that have such a charm when shown in the simple, unstudied way that proves them genuine. Surely, a little while amongst such people, away from the selfish world, must do one more good, morally, than a course of the finest sermons from the most eloquent preachers in the world, and more good, physically, than a sojourn at the most fashionable watering-place in the kingdom.

But beyond all these powerful inducements to visit Arran was one the strongest of all to me. From the days when I first read that book of books, 'Robinson Crusoe,' I had longed to taste life on an *almost* desert island – to taste a mitigated Robinson Crusoe life. Of course, I know from the study of maps that Great Britain and Ireland are surrounded by water, but, for all the reality

From *Here and There Through Ireland* (reissued from 1896 *Weekly Freeman*).

there is about the matter, they might as well be continents, for from no given point in either country can the oceans be seen all around and be reached on all sides in a day's walk. That is my idea of a genuine island, and that is what I know I could have in Arran, with, besides, complete isolation and loneliness if I wanted them (*i.e.* was in a bad temper), or, again, plenty of human beings to associate with when in good humour. Some friends I already had on the island, whose kind nature I knew would never allow me really to feel loneliness, and I have all my life been too accustomed to our Irish peasantry not to know well the easy road straight to their warm hearts.

It was therefore in high glee at the prospect of a holiday in my favourite way that I despatched a business-like note to –

'THE PROPRIETOR,
'Atlantic Hotel,
'Arran Isles,
'Galway,'

and that I found myself, a few days later, with a friend on the quay in Galway, asking at the boat-office for tickets for the Arran Isles. For days the question had been – would the weather be fine? That, on such occasions, is the chief consideration, for there is this charm about these excursions to the Isles, – except in very fine weather you can't get in, and then it is a chance if you get out again (the natives never say 'land on Arran,' or 'leave Arran' – it is invariably 'come in' or 'go out'). Therefore there is always a delightful uncertainty in a visit to these islands, and this uncertainty was part of the excitement for days before that named for the starting of the 'splendid steamer, the City of the Tribes'. [...]

As we neared Arran that bright August day I saw the islands at their very best – yet what a strange sight! Right up from the ocean rose, in front of us, a world of stone – one vast rock, nine miles long and about two miles in width, with low rocks and sandy beaches on the north shore, where is the only safe harbour, and where stands, facing this harbour, the village of Kilronan, possessing one house – the Atlantic Hotel – actually of two stories; all the rest neat, low cottages. On the south and west the cliffs rise from three to four hundred feet above the waves.

The scene, as we neared the little pier, was a curious one. The decks of the steamer, packed with a crowd of very ordinary pleasure seekers in ordinary European costume, all gazing eagerly, wonderingly, and intently on a little gathering of men and boys on the pier; these, in costume and appearance, were as foreign-looking as if we were suddenly transported into the midst of the African in place of the Irish desert. On the extreme end of the pier were gathered about forty men and boys, and while the vessel was being got alongside I had time to take a good look at the group. The men were clad in white flannel suits of short, loose jacket and trousers; their head-covering, a round, grey woollen cap, made with the crown flat and a little wider than the red and white tartan band which fits it to the head; on the feet 'pampootys' (I spell the word by sound), or sandals made of one strip of raw cowhide, stitched at the toe and heel with a bit of fishing line; another piece of string is run half

74

way round at the top of the foot at one side, a second string goes an equal distance at the heel to the other side, and these strings being drawn round the foot while the hide is supple, the sandals form perfectly to the shape of the feet, making, with the brown or prettily mottled hair on the outer side, a sandal such as was worn, perhaps, in the days of Cain and Abel, and which is certainly as simple, and yet as pretty a foot covering as one could wish to see. They are necessary to the people of Arran, who have to spend their whole lives walking on the rocks and springing from crag to crag; so the pampootys are worn by every man, woman and child. I have been told that to the use of these sandals is to be attributed the light and graceful carriage of the islanders.

As I looked at the people on shore I thought I had never seen finer or nobler-looking men – most of them tall, slight, and graceful, with skin almost as dark as that of Arabs; curling hair, regular features, brilliant dark grey eyes, and a quiet, self-possessed, refined carriage, as they, in their turn, surveyed the strangers. Sitting on the edge of the pier and darting here and there amongst the men were a number of boys carrying for sale pampootys and large bunches of the beautiful maiden-hair fern which grows in the chinks of the rocks. The bigger lads were dressed like the men, while the little Arran boys, up to twelve, wear red petticoats like their mothers and sisters. In fact it appeared to me to be an article of faith in the West, but especially in Arran (and I have not the least doubt the parents are quite right), that the longer the little boys are kept little girls the better men will they grow up. These dark-skinned and dark-eyed little fellows, in pretty cowhide sandals, red petticoats, white homespun jackets and woollen caps, look exactly like young Arabs. Their very way of surrounding me as I stood on shore had something of Eastern quietness and politeness, and they patiently waited that I might examine and carefully weigh the relative merits of brown or brown and white pampootys, before finally deciding on one all brown and one sweetly mottled.

The little quay which leads from the landing-place in Arran pier to the principal village, Kilronan, is built along one side of the harbour. Here I saw, for the first time, the canoes, or corrachs, still so much in use along the west coast of Ireland. One of these, rowed by a young lad, was bounding o'er the water as if it scarcely touched the surface, so light and easy was the movement; another, turned up on land for repairs, showed the whole simple construction of these boats, which alone can live on the stormy waves of the western seas. The frame is simply a skeleton of cane, or wickerwork, outside of which is stretched a well-tarred canvas; a pair of oars completes the primitive vessel in which these hardy fishermen put out in a sea which would in a few minutes swamp the finest boat of ordinary build. But the corrachs are so light, and the western fishermen so skilful in their management, that accidents are almost unknown, and if a boatman but says it is safe to venture out with him, there is no danger whatever to a person who has nerve enough to remain quiet. I was told by a gentleman that his terror of the Arran seas was such that a few years ago, while urgent business made it necessary that he should go to the islands, his dread of the danger to be incurred kept him for months unable to face the ordeal. Since that time he has acquired such perfect confidence in the boatmen's skill, and so secure does he feel with them, that, once an Arran boatman tells him there is no danger, he could lie down and sleep in that cobweb canoe in the midst of waves that would dash a ship to pieces, but over the crests of which the light corrach bounds safely as a sea-bird. Indeed, the management of these frail boats is an art apparently founded on a careful study of the manner in which a sea-fowl turns itself to the breakers, now letting itself rise to the crest of the wave, now gliding gently down, and so safely skimming over billows that seem every moment to threaten its destruction.

The corrach, as we see it to-day, in the western islands, is built in almost the same primitive fashion known for ages on those coasts. More than three thousand years ago the Firbolgs, we are told, rebelling under the yoke of slavery in Greece, seized upon some ships belonging to their tyrants; some of the oppressed race, who had been forced to dig the earth and carry clay in leather bags upon their backs – made boats of the leather wallets, and in these ships and boats the Firbolgs sailed until they landed on the coasts of Ireland. It is supposed that the corrachs in use to-day scarcely differ in construction from those in which these early colonists came over the waves from the south. [...]

The bell calling passengers to return on board had rung three times before the tourists reluctantly began to obey its summons, and we turned our steps to the Atlantic Hotel to see what accommodation had been provided for us.

At the hotel door we were met by the landlady, a rather comely little woman, with fair, wavy hair, and dressed in the ordinary dress of an Irish peasant matron. No letter had been received from me (I saw it arrive when I had been some days on the island), but I need not have been so anxious lest the rush of tourists should leave us to seek beds in one of the ancient forts. I was shown up to a little bedroom, not very luxuriantly furnished, but bright and cheerful, and as fresh as plenty of good air coming in through the open window from the sea below could make it.

Before our hostess left us we got a first taste of the charming Robinson Crusoe unsophisticatedness, for, having informed Mrs Macdara that we meant to spend a week or two as her guests, I naturally inquired the weekly tariff of the hotel. The reply quite took away my breath. 'Why, then, saxe a wan of me knows, Miss; sure, we'll think about it, an' in the meantime I'll bring you a cup of tea – we can settle the rest anytime.' When it came to the 'settling' point the manner of arrangement was equally unlike the outer world. 'Well, then,' said our hostess, 'would you think (naming a most moderate sum) too much?' 'Ah then, dear knows it's enough!' interposed a daughter standing by, in a tone that clearly implied she considered it quite too much.

Not caring to go strolling about until the crowd of excursionists – who could, at most, only be allowed three hours on the island – should have left in the 'Cittie of the Tribes,' I sat down at my open window to enjoy the air, the scene, and the novelty of all that surrounded me. Scarcely a single Arran woman was to be seen going about, though one would have supposed that they would flock around to watch the unusual sight of some three hundred tourists, many of whom were sure to be in the height of fashion. But no; the women and girls kept discreetly and quietly within doors and did not 'demean' themselves by going about staring and gaping. From my window I looked right down on the pretty harbour, where two or three hookers lay beside the wharf; some half-dozen corrachs were drawn up on the beach, while one or two flew lightly over the wavelets of the incoming tide; the 'Cittie of the Tribes' was still at anchor at the very farthest point of the wharf, beyond which stretched the wide, blue bay, with the lighthouse on its little island, and the Clare coast rose dim and shadowy through a soft haze.

On taking a good look round my little chamber, I received a shock which made me for a moment think of using my return ticket and going straight back to Galway. Now, before coming out, I had seriously considered over a fashionable item of my travelling suit. In the first place, I well knew that in a walk of five or six miles over the stony hills of Arran I must of necessity cross about four hundred stone walls, and I naturally concluded that in the continual getting over or squeezing through tiny loopholes in these stone walls a 'Dress-Improver' (ladies will understand) would be neither graceful nor convenient. Then, I was going amongst simple, innocent, uncorrupted young island maidens: was I to bring to their shores such a horrible corrupter of grace and simplicity into the midst of such pastoral innocence of all the vagaries of fashion? Never! I could never forgive myself if, a week after my arrival, I saw the graceful, modest shawls and skirts of the peasant maidens bulged out in the fashions of not four years ago; perhaps overhear a young sister whisper softly the other as they came out of chapel: 'I'll go on a little before, asthore; do you see if my dress-improver is straight.'

I courageously drew one – two – three – four bars of steel from out the folds of my costume, and locked them in a trunk, and felt so free and untrammelled once the deed was done that I have never seen the things since. What, then, must have been the shock I felt when, taking note of all the belongings of my room in the primitive (very primitive) hotel of Arranmore, I beheld, hanging behind the door, a feminine costume with the unmistakable bulge out in its skirt, and saw the well-known rows that marked the bars of steel.

I still cherish my childhood's Crusoe, with the hero pictured on the cover, his face wearing the look of horror brought there at the sight of one footprint on the sand. This must have been something of my expression as I still gazed on what had given me such a shock for, the door opening, a young girl coming timidly in, stood looking at me for a moment. 'Oh! I was afraid you might want something,' she said, so gently and softly, with such an unmistakably kind look in the grey eyes, that – seeing this girl, at all events, had none of the fashionable thing about her – I made up my mind to stay, and at once set to work to make friends with Mary and to inquire all about the ways and means of seeing every spot on Arran, and to plan endless excursions of the kind I like best of any in the world.

The steamer, with its freight of mainlanders, being now well out in the bay, we set forth to take a first look around. The pier ended a few yards to the right, the sea was in front, and to the left were two roads branching off – one led up the village, and the second turned down behind the hotel and led away by a white strand to the south of the island.

Choosing to round the harbour, we found that, near the end, there was a road to the left branching off by a long shingly beach, where the waves stole in softly and quietly, making a pleasant little stir and rattle amongst the stones, the sea looking a lovely azure under the cloudless August sky, every boat on the surface reflected sharply in the water below. To the south, the middle island stretched along, seeming like a foreshore to the bold cliffs and headlands of the county Clare. To the north, I looked across to Connemara, and it is perhaps from Arran that one has the most exquisite view of Ireland's loveliest mountains, the Twelve Pins of Binabola. On such an evening, when the August sun is brilliant, yet low enough in the sky to strike right across at the mountains, the air has that rarefied clearness in which every object appears as if cut out, so distinctly is each defined against the sky.

On and on we strolled by the seashore, alternately watching the charmed fairyland across the water, or looking around the strange – land I cannot call it, but strange stone country in which we found ourselves. The naked rock shelves upwards almost at once from the eastern side; stone – stone – stone everywhere, except in one spot where a few low trees, just above this beach, surround the Parsonage and the little Protestant Church. With one exception, the parson is, I should say, the rich man of the island. He has an income of £125 per annum from the Church Temporalities, and £45 from the Irish Church Missions, but his life must be a sadly lonely one, his congregation consisting of an occasional coastguardman or policeman, while the people of the islands are all Catholics.

Rounding a point, we came on an old man, a kelp-burner, attending to his smoking pile of kelp, and who, in response to my salutation, 'Bail o Dia ort' (may be translated 'God bless the work'), cordially invited us to rest, and, as we sat on a stone beside him, chatted away about his work, the gathering of the seaweed, its drying and burning, and described the hardships of collecting it in cold and wet, those gathering the weed often standing up to the waist in water. The old man told us that it takes from twelve to fourteen tons of seaweed to make one ton of kelp; he spoke of the many weary hours and days and weeks necessary to prepare even one ton, and then – all this time and labour considered – of the poor price to be had in general in return for so much hard work. Some years ago kelp brought the maker as much as £7 per ton; now, owing to competition from Scotland and France, the price to be got is, on an average, but £2 10s. the ton, though sometimes the poor man gets a better price, as if to induce him to go on with the work in the hope of this chance. So, for the chance, as well as on the principle that 'half a loaf is better than no bread,' the people work on making the kelp, which is purchased for various uses, principally for the procuring of iodine, which is extracted from it.

Our old friend was a fair specimen of the Arran Islander: tall and erect, a very thoughtful and intelligent face, with regular, well-cut, Celtic features and clear, dark grey eyes, which looked the more striking from having the eyebrows still black while the hair was snowy white. His manner, a quiet, friendly kindliness – polite, respectful, and self-respecting at the same time. He wore the usual very simple, but becoming and substantial Arran costume, which I have already described.

After a good long chat with the old man, and having exchanged, in the beautiful old Irish fashion (long may it reign! as we say) a mutual 'a blessing be with thee', we turned homewards, gathering on the way a large bouquet of golden pansies, only a size smaller than the same species which we cultivate so extensively in our gardens; these I never found in any part of the island except in this, 'The Frenchman's Beach,' so called from the wreck, many years ago, of a French vessel whose crew was lost in this bay, none but dead bodies ever reaching the strand.

As we passed into the hotel I caught sight, through a doorway on my left, of a glorious old Irish fireplace in the kitchen. The bright blaze and the sight of the women grouped around were irresistible; I asked if we might, without disturbing them, sit by the fire for a while. 'Oh! heartily welcome, avourneen.' Mrs Macdara's apron was instantly in use to dust chairs and put them in the cosiest side of the immense fireplace, a fireplace so wide that it accommodated a guest at each side, besides some cooking utensils, while a splendid turf fire on the hearth blazed up and kept the big kettle (suspended over it by a long iron bar) boiling comfortably for the tea. Little cupboards, here and there in the wall, likewise held stores of small objects, and a flitch or two of home-made bacon made the old fireplace quite an establishment in itself. Beside it the stand of the spinning-wheel served as a form until the winter evenings should come, when the wheel would be mounted, the spindle put in, the carders set to work and the busy spinner be the centre figure in the warm, firelit kitchen, while the immense balls of yarn, spun last winter and now hanging up on the wall, would be taken down and knitted into stockings for the family, or dyed and prepared for the weaver to weave into flannel, frieze, or blankets. For nearly every article of clothing is made at home on the islands, and, though heavy and rather coarse to the touch of those accustomed to the finely dressed (and adulterated) English manufactured goods, the stuffs thus made at home are far warmer and more durable, and also healthier than any others, as nothing but pure wool and vegetable dyes are used.

To return to our kitchen – a genuine Irish kitchen, such as one sees with the peasants of the comfortable class, with its dresser full of delft and adorned by two pairs of tall thin brass candlesticks. On the long form sat, in solemn silence since our entrance, a son of the house, trying vainly to still a perpetual-motion baby, the property of the eldest girl, a fine-looking young woman who had married a policeman and was soon to bid good-bye to her family and island home. Another daughter was busy making bread at the kitchen table, while the youngest of all, a little black-eyed, merry-looking child, was preparing the pot-oven for the baking of the bread. My friend Mary came and went on household errands, while the vanithee (woman of the house) stood leaning against the dresser, her arms folded, and chatted away, taking in, I could see, what each of us was like and what we were made of, as shrewdly as could any woman of the world.

An elderly man, from whom I saw the son and daughters all took their Celtic eyes and features, came in, and, after a kindly welcome to the strangers, spoke in Irish to his family. When he left, I could not but note the innate good breeding that made the good woman at once translate for us what had been said in, unfortunately, almost an unknown tongue to me. Indeed, whilst among those simple island people, born and bred so far from the world and its conventionalities, I met with many a like instance of refined nature, quick perception of the fitness of things, and an inborn knowledge of what is becoming, correct, and polite, that one often finds sorely wanting in very pretentious members of society.

Having arranged that we would make our first grand excursion in the morning, we spent an hour at our open window, trying to realize that we were really and truly not only on a genuine island, but on the most out-of-the-way, most interesting, and least well-known island on the entire Irish coast. The evening scene was a pretty one and full of life. Just under the window was the end of the pier and the spot for unloading the turf, for there is no firing of any kind to be found on Arran – all has to be brought from the mainland. This being the season for laying in the winter's supply, there was a constant coming and going of men, women, and children with donkeys and panniers from the distant parts of the island, to where the busy crew of the hooker worked away incessantly, throwing the black sods of turf up on land. Coming along, either walking leisurely (all go leisurely here, where are none of the bustle and rush of the world of trains and trams and stock exchanges, and big fortune-makings – and breakings) beside the donkeys or seated behind the panniers, many of the women looked strangely like their own Eastern ancestresses: the sandalled feet, Venetian red petticoat, and, with many of them, bawneen, or white flannel jacket, worn covering the head, forehead, and body in truly Eastern style, have a curiously foreign effect. These women continued coming and going with their loads of turf until dusk. On the low wall outside the house, on blocks of timber, and on the broken wall above the beach, the men sat quietly chatting and smoking; a dozen little children came down for a play, and I never tired of hearing one sweet little voice that constantly kept up a call after 'Michaleen, Michaleen' (little Michael).

And so the evening shadows fell, and I heard but indistinctly the murmur of the men's grave voices, the calls of the children, the lapping of the anchored boats, the sough of the tide against the stones, in the great quiet that stole over all – a wide quiet, that seemed to spread itself over the whole air and earth and sea – such only, it seemed, as could come upon a spot far away from the world, and I felt that at last I was upon a real island, and that island Arainn-na-naimbh. [...]

Continuing our walk, the road led us on under the stony hill, where, at long intervals, could be seen the tiny patches of ground made by the hard toil of the people. Naturally, there is not a spot of earth on any of these islands; but the law of their owners, since the English gained possession of them, has been to exact from every tenant that a certain portion of the rock shall be broken up, sea-sand and seaweed carried up, load by load, by the men and women, and thus gradually accumulated on the spot partially cleared of the upper crust of stone; but when this little patch of land is made, it is appraised by him who says he owns the stones, and the maker henceforth has the privilege of paying a smart rent for what the labour of his own and his children's hands has made. Of course these little spots of earth are but shallow layers on a solid stone foundation, so that a dry season means the total failure of the crop of potatoes or oats – almost the only crops grown. At the best of times it is just barely possible to meet the rent with the help of the kelp and fish, which at best do not bring in very much, but when the potatoes fail, every available penny is swallowed up by the rent; often it cannot be met at all, and then famine and eviction are the fate of the islanders.

A marvellous sight are the broad tables of solid flag that border the highway, and as we look up at the bare, shining hills of limestone, and see nothing but sand and stone and sea, as far as the eye can reach, we find it almost impossible to realize that over three hundred human beings live on these island deserts, and, until quite recently, when the Land Commissioners made some much needed reductions in the rents, paid £3,000 per annum for permission to inhabit the place and use the bits of land they themselves had made.

With the exception of the landlord, and perhaps of his agent, all who see the place are of the same opinion as Mr Labouchere, one of the cleverest of English journalists. Here are that gentleman's words, taken from 'Truth':

'I give it as my deliberate opinion that the inhabitants of Arranmore ought, in justice, to pay no rent whatever. There is nothing in Arran of any value at all which has not been fished up out of the sea by the poor people. The island is as much theirs as if they had made it with their own hands. With their own hands they have, most truly and literally, made it, so far as it is a place capable of supporting human life. They ought to stand absolutely rent free. I declare, if I were an Arran fisherman, I would sooner throw my rent into the Atlantic Ocean than pay it to any landlord whatever.'

One of the vast flags has been turned to account for the pleasure of the children, and makes a level and unbroken floor for a fine racket-court, where a number of truants from school were having a game as we passed, our guide suggesting that the little lads should pose for a sketch, which she thought would be a very pretty one. Here too, along either side of the road, are memorial crosses erected on this, the way to the cemetery, by the different families whose relatives lie in the burial-ground about a mile and a half further on. These monuments are almost exactly similar to those to be found in Brittany, and are here very numerous. A square pillar, surmounted by a smaller square erection, in the face of which are inserted two slabs bearing the names of the persons to whose memory they are erected; the whole surmounted by a cross on which is, in some cases, a rudely carved Crucifixion. The monuments are in groups – sometimes three, sometimes six or more, and near them are cairns, or heaps of stones, piled up by those accompanying a funeral, each person at the funeral adding a stone to the heap. I think the idea a beautiful one, of thus bearing in mind, by the daily sight of these monuments, the friends gone before. There is nothing saddening in being reminded that we shall one day rejoin those we have loved, nor is there anything depressing about the wayside crosses: they are out in broad sunshine; the bay sparkles behind them, and thousands of ferns and flowers beautify them and hide the hard, stern rocks on all sides. I stood on

one flag beside a group of crosses and counted thirty different plants in full
bloom, growing in wild luxuriance from out every crevice around my feet. If
the islanders were only ethereal enough to be able to live on flowers, they could
never know want – but, graceful and charming though they be, flowers will
only fill the eye, and, from a practical point of view, the contrast between the
plenteousness of hanging brambles, lace-like ferns, and bright blossoms, and
the smallness and scarcity of the little patches of potatoes and corn, must at
times strike sadly on the hearts of poor fathers and mothers with eight or ten
little children to be fed every day. [...]

After a sojourn long enough to really know something of the Arran
peasantry, we left with genuine regret and a feeling of intense longing to return
and pass a longer time amongst a people and scenes never to be forgotten.

They are a gentle people, but deeply, quickly sensitive, with the keen
insight into character, and also the passionate feelings all such people possess in
a high degree. Quick to love, when met in honest kindness; quick to shrink
back and turn away, wounded and hurt, if they encounter rudeness or distrust.
'Ah, sure!' said a pretty Arran girl, explaining a grievance that had led to
unpleasantness with some visitors to the island, 'God knows we love to be kind
and civil to all but who'd blame us to turn away, an', maybe, give a hot word,
if we're spoke to like dogs?' Indeed, the Arraners' intuitive politeness and
appreciation of the same quality in others is very great, and, while they will not
easily force themselves upon one, it is evident that it delights them to be of
service – nothing is a trouble; they are hospitable, too, and we never rested,
even for a short space, near a village that someone did not hasten away to milk
the cow and offer a drink of fresh milk – a hospitality no one should refuse to
accept in Ireland. As is natural from the circumstances of their life, the
Islanders are a thoughtful race, and it would surprise many a cultured person
could he sit an hour with some old fisherman and con over with him, who
perhaps has rarely left his sea-girt home, all the deep and wise views of life, of
religion, of character, that old man could unfold. Although not, strictly
speaking, a very literate class, the natives of these islands are highly intelligent,
and have their full share of that almost universal aptitude for learning so
remarkable in the Irish. For years the Arraners were badly in want of schools,
for the owner of the islands refused to grant building sites until about five years
ago, when the late Lord Carnarvon, astonished at such a state of things, wrote
to the landlord and actually shamed him into granting sites. Being bi-lingual,
the present generation has a great advantage, for the knowledge of a second
language is one of the best helps one can have in the study of English, while it
aids in developing the intellect. If the School Board could secure teachers
having a really good knowledge of Irish it would be a double advantage, as they
would take an interest in promoting the study of the latter language amongst
the Irish-speaking children of the West and South, to whom alone we can look
for retaining our native tongue as a genuine living language.

One thing I remarked in Arran which struck me as very singular – that is
the want of music amongst the Islanders. As far as I could learn, this art – so
Irish – is almost unknown there. Rarely I heard a song, and then but a curious,

wild 'croonaun,' like the moaning of the wind at sea, but I never heard a musical instrument. Yet, in speaking, the voices of the natives are very soft and low and such as ought to be musical. Occasionally, at a wedding or some such festival, songs are sung, but I could not learn that even a wedding feast is a hilarious meeting. A strange custom prevails upon a marriage here: the bride's fortune goes to portion off the old couple – the husband's father and mother – in lieu of their giving over the little plot of 'land' (save the mark!) to the son and his wife, or perhaps they again portion off a daughter with the same money.

In appearance the natives of Arran are a fine and pleasing-looking race; the women and girls modest and gentle, without any trace of awkwardness in manner, and full of kindliness, as we frequently experienced; the men bold and hardy fishermen, who will venture out in their corrachs in wild seas that would terrify a landsman to think of. Indeed their pastors have to exercise no small courage in going from island to island in their ministrations, for, as the Arran fishermen have a tradition that no boat in which a priest is can be lost, they will man the priest's corrach on a Sunday in winter when any boat but one carrying a clergyman must inevitably be lost, and it sometimes happens that it is on the crest of a wave the soggarth is landed on the Middle or the Eastern Island.

One who has not lived long and intimately amongst these Islanders cannot speak from his own knowledge of more than such salient traits of character or manner as must catch the attention at once; but those who know them well have told of their earnest piety, their honesty, their sobriety, their affection for and gratitude to those who befriend them, and their passionate attachment to their island home. Of their industry and love of independence I can speak from my own knowledge: I was in Arran at a time when great distress yet prevailed after the famine of 1885 – a small, scandalously small sum had been given by Government for relief works, and a little harbour was to be made. The sum allowed of the employment of but one out of each family proved to be in dire necessity, that one to receive one shilling a day – six shillings a week for perhaps ten in family. I saw the poor men besieging the priest, the gentleman in charge of the works – even beseeching us to intercede for them for work – no matter how hard, but employment of any kind, to save their little children from beggary. Even women begged for men's work, ready to toil knee deep in the sea if they could but get honest employment. It was no fit labour for women, yet one fine young girl came weeping and praying so earnestly that it was impossible to refuse her, and, when work had been assigned to her, she joyfully toiled as hard as anyone, carrying huge stones and doing all required of a strong man, all that she might get that pittance with which to support her little orphan brothers and sisters – for the father and mother were dead.

Ethna Carbery

'On Inisheer'

On Inisheer, on Inisheer,
In the Spring-tide of the year,
You sought me, in your eyes love's rapture burning;
And for the words you said,
Above my drooping head,
My heart flew to you on the wings of yearning.

On Inisheer, on Inisheer,
I had never known a fear,
Nor a sorrow, nor a sigh to mar my laughter;
Until that saddest day,
When my true love sailed away,
And the sun grew dim, and darkness followed after.

Why did you go, oh love,
Ere the primrose peeped above
The scanty grass bleached with the wind salt-bitter?
Here, by a cabin fire,
Each with our heart's desire,
Had not the peace of home for us been fitter?

Than you to pine afar
Under the Southern Star,
And I to pine by Keevin's ruined altar,
Watching the cliffs of Clare
Fade in the evening air,
Telling my beads for you in tones that falter;

Or by the holy well,
Where as the darkness fell,

From *The Four Winds of Eirinn* (1902).

And out of dark the tender dawn came flowing
In seas of silver light,
You prayed the livelong night
That Christ would bless and guard you in your going.

Some day He keeps in store
You will return, *a-stor*,
Your curragh down our foaming current speeding
From the welcome of your clan,
On the rocks of Inishmaan,
To heal my wound of longing, ever bleeding.

On Inisheer, on Inisheer,
Love, I shall wait you here,
My radiant web of dreams through grey hours weaving,
Until, the red gold won,
And all your wandering done,
You take me to your heart and end my grieving.

Arthur Symons

The Islands of Aran

It was on the morning of Wednesday, August 5, 1896, that a party of four, of whom I alone was not an Irishman, got into Tom Joyce's hooker at Cashla Bay, on the coast of Galway, and set sail for the largest of the three islands of Aran, Inishmore by name, that is Large Island. The hooker, a half-decked, cutter-rigged fishing-boat of seventeen tons, had come over for us from Aran, and we set out with a light breeze, which presently dropped and left us almost becalmed under a very hot sun for nearly an hour, where we were passed by a white butterfly that was making straight for the open sea. We were nearly four hours in crossing, and we had time to read all that needed reading of *Grania*, Miss Emily Lawless's novel, which is supposed to be the classic of the islands, and to study our maps and to catch one mackerel. [...]

The butterfly, I hope, had reached land before us; but only a few sea-birds came out to welcome us as we drew near Inishmore, the Large Island, which is nine miles long and a mile and a half broad. I gazed at the long line of the island, growing more distinct every moment; first, a grey outline, flat at the sea's edge, and rising up beyond in irregular, rocky hills, terrace above terrace; then, against this grey outline, white houses began to detach themselves, the sharp line of the pier cutting into the curve of the harbour; and then, at last, the figures of men and women moving across the land. Nothing is more mysterious, more disquieting, than one's first glimpse of an island, and all I had heard of these islands, of their peace in the heart of the storm, was not a little mysterious and disquieting. I knew that they contained the oldest ruins and that their life of the present was the most primitive life of any part of Ireland; I knew that they were rarely visited by the tourist, almost never by any but the local tourist; that they were difficult to reach, sometimes more difficult to leave, for the uncertainty of weather in that uncertain region of the Atlantic had been known to detain some of the rare travellers there for days, was it not for weeks? Here one was absolutely at the mercy of the elements, which might at any moment become unfriendly, which, indeed, one seemed to have but apprehended in a pause of their eternal enmity. And we seemed also to be venturing among an unknown people, who, even if they spoke our own

From Arthur Symons, *Cities and Sea-Coasts and Islands* (1897).

language, were further away from us, more foreign than people who spoke an unknown language and lived beyond other seas.

As we walked along the pier towards the three whitewashed cottages which form the Atlantic Hotel, at which we were to stay, a strange being sprang towards us, with a curiously beast-like stealthiness and animation; it was a crazy man, bare-footed and blear-eyed, who held out his hand and sang out at us in a high, chanting voice, and in what sounded rather a tone of command than of entreaty, 'Give me a penny, sir! Give me a penny, sir!' We dropped something into his hat, and he went away over the rocks, laughing loudly to himself, and repeating some words that he had heard us say. We passed a few fishermen and some bare-footed children, who looked at us curiously, but without moving, and were met at the door of the middle cottage by a little, fat old woman with a round body and a round face, wearing a white cap tied over her ears. The Atlantic Hotel is a very primitive hotel; it had last been slept in by some priests from the mainland, who had come on their holiday with bicycles; and before that by a German philologist who was learning Irish. [...]

I remember no dreams that night, but I was told that I had talked in my sleep, and I was willing to believe it. In the morning, not too early, we set out on an outside car (that rocking and most comfortable vehicle, which I prefer to everything but a gondola) for the Seven Churches and Dun Aengus, along the only beaten road in the island. The weather, as we started, was grey and misty, threatening rain, and we could but just see the base-line of the Clare mountains across the grey and discoloured waters of the bay. At the Seven Churches we were joined by a peasant, who diligently showed us the ruined walls of Teampull Brecan, with its slab inscribed in Gaelic with the words, 'Pray for the two canons'; the stone of the 'VII. Romani'; St Brecan's headstone, carved with Gaelic letters; the carved cross and the headstone of St Brecan's bed. More peasants joined us, and some children, who fixed on us their usual placid and tolerant gaze, in which curiosity contended with an indolent air of contentment. In all these people I noticed the same discreet manners that had already pleased me; and once, as we were sitting on a tombstone in the interior of one of the churches, eating the sandwiches that we had brought for luncheon, a man, who had entered the doorway, drew back instantly, seeing us taking a meal. [...]

It was about four in the afternoon when we came to the village of Kilmurvey, upon the seashore and, leaving our car, began to climb the hill leading to Dun Aengus. Passing two outer ramparts, now much broken, one of them seeming to end suddenly in the midst of a *chevaux de frise* of pillar-like stones thrust endways into the earth, we entered the central fort by a lintelled doorway, set in the side of a stone wall of the same Cyclopean architecture as Dun Onaght, 18 feet high on the outside, and with two adhering inner walls, each lower in height, 12 feet 9 inches in thickness. This fort is 150 feet north and south and 140 feet east and west, and on the east side the circular wall ends suddenly on the very edge of a cliff going down 300 feet to the sea. [...] The Atlantic lies endlessly out towards the sunrise, beating, on the south, upon the brown and towering rock of the cliffs of Moher, rising up nearly a sheer thousand feet. The whole grey and desolate island, flowering into barren stone, stretches out on the other side, where the circle of the water washes from Galway Bay into the Atlantic. Looking out over all that emptiness of sea, one imagines the long-oared galleys of the ravaging kings who had lived there, some hundreds of years before the birth of Christ; and the emptiness of the fortress filled with long-haired warriors, coming back from the galleys with captured slaves, and cattle, and the spoil of citadels. We know from the Bardic writers that a civilization, similar to that of the Homeric poems, lived on in Ireland almost to the time of the coming of St Patrick; and it was something also of the sensation of Homer – the walls of Troy, the heroes, and that 'face that launched a thousand ships' – which came to me as we stood upon these unconquerable walls, to which a generation of men had been as a moth's flight and a hundred years as a generation of men.

Coming back from Dun Aengus, one of our party insisted on walking; and we had not been long indoors when he came in with a singular person whom he had picked up on the way, a professional story-teller, who had for three weeks been teaching Irish to the German philologist who had preceded us on the island. He was half blind and of wild appearance; a small and hairy man, all gesture, and as if set on springs, who spoke somewhat broken English in a roar. He lamented that we could understand no Irish, but, even in English, he had many things to tell, most of which he gave as but 'talk', making it very clear that we were not to suppose him to vouch for them. His own family, he told us, was said to be descended from the roons, or seals, but that certainly was 'talk'; and a witch had, only nine months back, been driven out of the island by the priest; and there were many who said they had seen fairies, but for his part he had never seen them. But with this he began to swear on the name of God and the saints, rising from his chair and lifting up his hands, that what he was going to tell us was the truth; and then he told how a man had once come into his house and admired his young child, who was lying there in his bed, and had not said 'God bless you!' (without which to admire is to envy and to bring under the power of the fairies), and that night, and for many following nights, he had wakened and heard a sound of fighting, and one night had lit a candle, but to no avail, and another night had gathered up the blanket and tried to fling it over the head of whoever might be there, but had caught no one; only in the morning, going to a box in which fish were kept, he had found blood in the box; and at this he rose again, and again swore on the name of God and the saints that he was telling us only the truth, and true it was that the child had died and as for the man who had ill-wished him, 'I could point him out any day,' he said fiercely. And then, with many other stories of the doings of fairies and priests (for he was very religious), and of the 'Dane' who had come to the island to learn Irish ('and he knew all the languages, the Proosy, and the Roosy, and the Span, and the Grig'), he told us how Satan, being led by pride to equal himself with God, looked into the glass in which God only should look, and when Satan looked into the glass, 'Hell was made in a minute.'

Next morning we were to leave early, and at nine o'clock we were rowed out to the hooker, which lifted sail in a good breeze, and upon a somewhat pitching sea, for the second island, Inishmaan, that is, the Middle Island, which is three miles long and a mile and a half broad. [...]

In the village we were joined by some more men and children; and a number of women, wearing the same red clothes that we had seen on the larger island, and looking at us with perhaps scarcely so shy a curiosity (for they were almost too unused to strangers to have adopted a manner of shyness), came out to their doors and looked up at us out of the darkness of many interiors, from where they sat on the ground knitting or carding wool. We passed the chapel, a very modern-looking building, made out of an ancient church, and turned in for a moment to the cottage where the priest sleeps when he comes over from Inishmore on Saturday night to say early mass on Sunday morning before going on to Inisheer for the second mass. We saw his little white room, very quaint and neat; and the woman of the house, speaking only Irish, motioned us to sit down, and could hardly be prevented from laying out plates and glasses for us upon the table. As we got a little through the more populous part of the village, we saw ahead of us, down a broad lane, a very handsome girl, holding the end of a long ribbon, decorated with a green bough, across the road. Other girls and some older women were standing by, and, when we came up, the handsome girl, with the low forehead and the sombre blue eyes, cried out laughingly, in her scanty English, 'Cash, cash!' We paid toll, as the custom is, and got her blessing; and went on our way, leaving the path, and climbing many stone walls, until we came to the great fort of Dun Conor on the hill, the largest of the ancient forts of Aran.

Dun Conor is 227 feet north and south and 115 feet east and west, with walls in three sections, 20 feet high on the outside and 18 feet 7 inches thick. We climbed to the top and walked around the wall, where the wind blowing in from the sea beat so hard upon us that we could scarcely keep our footing. From this height we could see all over the island lying out beneath us, grey, and broken into squares by the walled fields; the brown thatch of the village, the smoke coming up from the chimneys, here and there a red shawl or skirt, the grey sand by the sea and the grey sea all round. As we stood on the wall many peasants came slowly about us, climbing up on all sides, and some stood together just inside the entrance, and two or three girls sat down on the other side of the arena, knitting. Presently an old man, scarcely leaning on the stick which he carried in his hand, came towards us, and began slowly to climb the steps. 'It is my father,' said one of the men; 'he is the oldest man on the island; he was born in 1812.' The old man climbed slowly up to where we stood; a mild old man, with a pale face, carefully shaved, and a firm mouth, who spoke the best English that we had heard there. 'If any gentleman has committed a crime,' said the oldest man on the island, 'we'll hide him. There was a man killed his father, and he came over here, and we hid him for two months, and he got away safe to America.'

As we came down from the fort the old man came with us, and I and another, walking ahead, lingered for some time with the old man by a stone stile. 'Have you ever seen the fairies?' said my friend, and a quaint smile flickered over the old man's face, and with many ohs! and grave gestures he told us that he had never seen them, but that he had heard them crying in the fort by night; and one night, as he was going along with his dog, just at the spot where we were then standing, the dog had suddenly rushed at something or some one, and had rushed round and round him, but he could see nothing, though it was bright moonlight, and so light that he could have seen a rat; and he had followed across several fields, and again the dog had rushed at the thing, and had seemed to be beaten off, and had come back covered with sweat, and panting, but he could see nothing. And there was a man once, he knew the man, and could point him out, who had been out in his boat (and he motioned with his stick to a certain spot on the water), and a sea fairy had seized hold of his boat and tried to come into it; but he had gone quickly on shore, and the thing, which looked like a man, had turned back into the sea. And there had been a man once on the island who used to talk with the fairies; and you could hear him going along the roads by night swearing and talking with the fairies. 'And have you ever heard,' said my friend, 'of the seals, the roons, turning into men?' 'And indeed,' said the oldest man on the island, smiling, 'I'm a roon, for I'm one of the family they say comes from the roons.' 'And have you ever heard,' said my friend, 'of men going back into the sea and turning roons again?' 'I never heard that,' said the oldest man on the island reflectively, seeming to ponder over the probability of the occurrence; 'no,' he repeated after a pause, 'I never heard that.'

We came back to the village by the road we had come, and passed again the handsome girl who had taken toll; she was sitting by the roadside knitting, and looked at us sidelong as we passed, with an almost imperceptible smile in her eyes. We wandered for some time a little vaguely, the amiability of the islanders leading them to bring us in search of various ruins which we imagined to exist, and which they did not like to tell us were not in existence. I found the people on this island even more charming, because a little simpler, more untouched by civilization, than those on the larger island. They were of necessity a little lonelier, for if few people come to Inishmore, how many have ever spent a night on Inishmaan? Inishmore has its hotel, but there is no hotel on Inishmaan; there is indeed one public-house, but there is not even a policeman, so sober, so law-abiding are these islanders. It is true that I succeeded, with some difficulty, and under cover of some mystery, in securing, what I had long wished to taste, a bottle of poteen or illicit whisky. But the brewing of poteen is, after all, almost romantic in its way, with that queer, sophistical romance of the contraband. That was not the romance I associated with this most peaceful of islands as we walked along the sand on the seashore, passing the kelp-burners, who were collecting long brown trails of seaweed. More than anything I had ever seen, this seashore gave me the sensation of the mystery and the calm of all the islands one has ever dreamed of, all the fortunate islands that have ever been saved out of the disturbing sea; this delicate pearl-grey sand, the deeper grey of the stones, the more luminous grey of the water, and so consoling an air as of immortal twilight and the peace of its dreams.

I had been in no haste to leave Inishmore, but I was still more loth to leave

Inishmaan; and I think that it was with reluctance on the part of all of us that we made our way to the curragh, which was waiting for us in the water. The islanders waved their caps, and called many good blessings after us as we were rowed back to the hooker, which again lifted sail and set out for the third and smallest island, Inisheer, that is, the South Island.

We set out confidently, but when we had got out of shelter of the shore, the hooker began to rise and fall with some violence; and by the time we had come within landing distance of Inisheer the waves were dashing upon us with so great an energy that it was impossible to drop anchor, and our skipper advised us not to try to get to land. [...]

It was now about a quarter past one, and we set out for Ballyvaughan with the wind fair behind us. The hooker rode well, and the waves but rarely came over the windward side as she lay over towards her sail, taking leap after leap through the white-edged furrows of the grey water. For two hours and a half we skirted the Clare coast, which came to me, and disappeared from me, as the gunwale dipped or rose on the leeward side. The islands were blotted out behind us long before we had turned the sheer corner of Black Head, the ultimate edge of Ireland, and at last we came round the headland into quieter water, and so, after a short time, into a little harbour of Ballyvaughan, where we set foot on land again, and drove for hours along the Clare coast and inland into Galway, under that sunset of gold fire and white spray, back to Tillyra Castle, where I felt the ground once more solid under my feet.

Summer, 1896

Patrick Pearse

A Visit to Inis Mór and Inis Meáin, August 1898

One evening I walked to the cliffs and, when I came home, I saw a young man sitting at the fire. I soon found out that he was Tomás 'ac Conceannainn. He stood up and, like Napper Tandy, 'took me by the hand' and believe me he shook it hard. We drew up to the fire and started talking.

The next day we went down to the beach. We sat on the shingle and had a long chat about the Irish language and everything to do with it.

'Do you think, Pádraig,' said Tomás 'seeing that we're here, we could set up a branch of Conradh na Gaeilge here in Aran?'

'Of course, I do,' I said. 'Isn't it a shame there isn't already a branch? Let's get the work going in the name of God!'

'Are you willing?' he said.

'Why wouldn't I be?' I said.

Up we got and went to Páidín's house. We sat down at the table to write a letter to the secretary in Dublin.

'Hang on, Tomás' I said; 'shouldn't we go west to Cill Rónáin first and see the priest?'

'You are right, Pádraig,' he said. We stood up and left the room.

'Is there any currach going west, Páidín?' said Tomás.

'There isn't,' said Páidín, 'not a single currach. They're all out fishing.'

'Upon my soul,' said Tomás, 'if there isn't a currach we'll have to swim there through the sea.'

'God forbid!' said Páidín.

Off we went to the beach then. We found one currach there. We got in, Páidín and two others helping us. The sea was rough but the oarsmen worked hard and in an hour we landed at Cill Rónáin. We went to the priest and found him willing. We sent a telegram to the secretary in Dublin after that and another to the Irish language enthusiasts in Galway. We got a car then and went west to Fearann a' Choirce. We weren't long in the car when it started raining – and great heavy rain it was too, believe me. Máirtín Neile has a proverb 'a rainy day is a wet day' and it's true for him. It's no lie to say that it was wet that day and that we were wet also. I never saw such a downpour and

From *Fáinne an Lae*. Translated from the Irish.

I think I never will again. We went to Dáithí O Ceallacháin and to Séamus Mac Cárthaigh – they are schoolteachers. The next day we went out on the car again. We went east to Cill Éinne first and then we went west to the Seacht dTeampaill. I think we saw every single person in Aran that day and they were very willing to start the work, both young and old. It didn't stop raining all day. We had a meeting that evening – it was Friday – to get things ready for Sunday.

On the morning of the next day we went east to Inis Meáin to change and tidy our clothes. Coming back we met the steamer and who was on board but Stiofán Bairéad! We brought him back with us. We stayed up that night until four o'clock. The next day we had a big meeting in the schoolhouse. People came from Inis Meáin, Inis Oírr and Galway. I think there were at least seven hundred people gathered there. Father Muircheartach was in the chair. We had talk and chat and speeches without a single word of English. Aran of the Saints found its soul that day and it'll be a long time, with God's help, before it is lost again. We set up a branch of An Conradh and may that branch last forever! [...]

I spent a day and a month in Aran and in all that time spoke only Irish to the people of the islands. That pleased them very much. The people of Aran are not at all ashamed of speaking Irish. I'm not saying they wouldn't also like to have English. They would indeed and that's no cause of shame. I'm not saying that the children of Cill Rónáin don't have too much English. I know they do. But everywhere else throughout the islands there's only Irish. I often spoke to little boys and girls who hadn't a word of English. They only had Irish. I think there is no sound to be heard on the face of the earth as sweet as the Irish language coming from a child's mouth. Aren't they lovely, those children, God bless them?

Will the Irish language ever die in Aran? I think not. Now that they have set up a branch, people will be interested in Irish, it will be taught to the young and soon they will be able to read and write it. It will not be allowed to decline but will be supported until Aran will again be a university and a torch of knowledge for all the people of Ireland as she was in the old times. That is my wish tonight; and it is also my wish that we might all have Irish as sweet and as fluent as that of the people of Aran of the Saints.

Fáinne an Lae

1898

It is pleasant after this to turn to the Atlantic sea board and to think of Arran. Over seven hundred of the islanders attended the meeting to found a branch of the League. The speeches, resolutions, and all the proceedings were in Irish. All have joined the League, and many are enrolled in the classes, fifty books having been despatched. It is prophesied for Arran that 'there will not be in Ireland nor in any other place under the sun' a branch better than that just founded.

The instantaneous results which sometimes follow from a successful and enthusiastic meeting are wonderful. This fact was strikingly emphasised in Kilronan on Sunday week after the meeting at which the new branch was established. The children who before used English habitually, could be heard on the streets speaking Irish, and it was plainly evident that they felt much pride in their ability to do so. As the Inishmheadhoin and Inis-siar delegations were preparing to leave some twenty urchins came down to the shore, talking away with great ease and fluency in the native tongue. One thoughtless little *garsún* made use of an English word. He was immediately pounced upon by his comrade, and the little *Sasanach* had to promise that he would not be guilty of such an offence again.

It was a sight never to be forgotten to see the stalwart islanders in their unique and picturesque costume gathering in groups and discussing in voluble idiomatic Irish all that had been said and done at the meeting. They seemed for the first time to have realised the fearful results which the loss of their national language would imply, and resolved that should Irish ever die out in Ireland, its last stronghold would be Arran. Thank God, however, such a disaster has now been made an impossibility.

The fleets of Inismheadhoin and Inis-siar consisted of about a dozen *corachs*, and much good humoured rivalry was exhibited in the race home. Many and witty were the repartees in the native tongue that passed from boat to boat. The addresses they had just listened to seemed not only to have fired the

From *Fáinne an Lae* (1898).

94

imaginations of the oarsmen, but to have excited them to unusual physical exertion. The records to Inismheadhoin and Inis-siar were broken by fifteen and ten minutes respectively. The Inismheadhoin and Inis-siar men appeared somewhat jealous of their more fortunate neighbours, and will not rest satisfied until flourishing branches are in operation on all three islands.

Spread of the Movement
New Branch established in Arran

One of the most hopeful signs of the movement is the rapidity with which branches are being established in the Irish-speaking districts. On Sunday, 7th inst., another move in this direction was made. It has long been the ambition of the League to establish a branch in Ara-na-naovh.

The fact that some of the most earnest workers of the movement are at present spending a holiday there has been availed of to put the work in motion. The hearty co-operation of the respected parish priest, Father Murtagh Farragher, and of his energetic curate, Father Michael Kenelly, was at first secured, and it was announced from the altar in the three islands that a public meeting to establish a branch of the Gaelic League would be held at Kilronan, on Sunday afternoon at three o'clock. The use of the spacious schoolroom at Kilronan, which is capable of holding four hundred persons, was kindly given by Father Farragher. Long before the appointed hour, not only was the schoolroom crowded to suffocation, but the door was completely blocked up, and the crowd extended far into the yard. There must have been at least seven hundred present. The fact of an excursion being given by the Galway Bay Steamboat Co., was availed of by the Galway Branch to send a large and representative delegation.

Large delegations were also present from Inismheadhoin and Inis-siar, headed by Mr Michael Coonan, N.T., and Mr Costello, respectively.

The chair was taken by Father Farragher. [...]

The Central Gaelic League was represented by Messrs Thomas Concannon of Mexico, S. J. Barrett, Treasurer; and P. H. Pearse.

A feature of the meeting was the fact that the proceedings were conducted exclusively in Irish, as the audience was entirely Irish-speaking.

The Rev. Chairman said that he had addressed many meetings of various kinds and with various objects, but he had never attended any meeting that afforded him greater pleasure than that over which he now had the honour of presiding. Irish, he was proud to say, was his mother tongue, and from his infancy he had not only constantly used the language, but had always encouraged others to do so. He was proud to see such a splendid gathering there that day. The branch was now to be established under most auspicious circumstances, all that was necessary was to keep the ball rolling when once it was started. They might count on his most hearty co-operation in pushing forward the good work by every means in his power. He had great pleasure in calling on Mr Concannon to propose the resolutions.

Mr Thomas Concannon, Mexico, who was received with loud applause, said that after so many years sojourn in foreign lands, he was proud to see so many old familiar faces again, and prouder still to see them on such an occasion. A good beginning was half the work, and a good beginning they had already made. The Gaelic League now not only extended its branches throughout Ireland, but had also branches in England and Scotland, whilst there was a flourishing branch in every city in America, most of these latter he had himself visited. It gave him great pleasure to find that his native Arran was falling into line with the Irish race the world over. They should now put their shoulders manfully to the wheel. If they did that, then, with God's help, they would see the day when the sweet Irish tongue would be again spoken on the hills and in the valleys, at the fair, and in the market, in every corner of Ireland. Mr Concannon moved a series of resolutions which, together with his speech, will appear next week. [...]

Mr P. H. Pearse, Central Gaelic League, next addressed the meeting. He referred to the pain with which he noticed that whilst Irish was the language of the grown people of Kilronan, a marked and growing tendency to use English was visible in the children. He did not wish by any means to banish English, but he maintained that it was the duty of parents to speak the native language to their children and to make it the language of the fireside. English they could afterwards learn at the school, and they would then have both Irish and English, whereas now they have neither one nor the other. [...]

Mr O'Callaghan, N.T., delivered a scathing indictment of the National School system as worked in the Irish-speaking districts, maintaining that where Irish is the home language of the people it should be taught simultaneously with English from the time the child first enters the school.

John Millington Synge

The Aran Islands

Two recent attempts to carry out evictions on the island came to nothing, for each time a sudden storm rose, by, it is said, the power of a native witch, when the steamer was approaching, and made it impossible to land.

This morning, however, broke beneath a clear sky of June, and when I came into the open air the sea and rocks were shining with wonderful brilliancy. Groups of men, dressed in their holiday clothes, were standing about, talking with anger and fear, yet showing a lurking satisfaction at the thought of the dramatic pageant that was to break the silence of the seas.

About half-past nine the steamer came in sight, on the narrow line of sea-horizon that is seen in the centre of the bay, and immediately a last effort was made to hide the cows and sheep of the families that were most in debt.

Till this year no one on the island would consent to act as bailiff, so that it was impossible to identify the cattle of the defaulters. Now, however, a man of the name of Patrick has sold his honour, and the effort of concealment is practically futile.

This falling away from the ancient loyalty of the island has caused intense indignation, and early yesterday morning, while I was dreaming on the Dun, this letter was nailed on the doorpost of the chapel:—

'Patrick, the devil, a revolver is waiting for you. If you are missed with the first shot, there will be five more that will hit you.

'Any man that will talk with you, or work with you, or drink a pint of porter in your shop, will be done with the same way as yourself.'

As the steamer drew near I moved down with the men to watch the arrival, though no one went further than about a mile from the shore.

Two curaghs from Kilronan with a man who was to give help in identifying the cottages, the doctor, and the relieving officer, were drifting with the tide, unwilling to come to land without the support of the larger party. When the anchor had been thrown it gave me a strange throb of pain to see the boats being lowered, and the sunshine gleaming on the rifles and helmets of the constabulary who crowded into them.

Once on shore the men were formed in close marching order, a word was

From J. M. Synge, *The Aran Islands* (1907).

97

given, and the heavy rhythm of their boots came up over the rocks. We were collected in two straggling bands on either side of the roadway, and a few moments later the body of magnificent armed men passed close to us, followed by a low rabble, who had been brought to act as drivers for the sheriff.

After my weeks spent among primitive men this glimpse of the newer types of humanity was not reassuring. Yet these mechanical police, with the commonplace agents and sheriffs, and the rabble they had hired, represented aptly enough the civilization for which the homes of the island were to be desecrated.

A stop was made at one of the first cottages in the village, and the day's work began. Here, however, and at the next cottage, a compromise was made, as some relatives came up at the last moment and lent the money that was needed to gain a respite.

In another case a girl was ill in the house, so the doctor interposed, and the people were allowed to remain after a merely formal eviction. About midday, however, a house was reached where there was no pretext for mercy, and no money could be procured. At a sign from the sheriff the work of carrying out the beds and utensils was begun in the middle of a crowd of natives who looked on in absolute silence, broken only by the wild imprecations of the woman of the house. She belonged to one of the most primitive families on the island, and she shook with uncontrollable fury as she saw the strange armed men who spoke a language she could not understand driving her from the hearth she had brooded on for thirty years. For these people the outrage to the hearth is the supreme catastrophe. They live here in a world of grey, where there are wild rains and mists every week in the year, and their warm chimney corners, filled with children and young girls, grow into the consciousness of each family in a way it is not easy to understand in more civilized places.

The outrage to a tomb in China probably gives no greater shock to the Chinese than the outrage to a hearth in Inishmaan gives to the people.

When the few trifles had been carried out, and the door blocked with stones, the old woman sat down by the threshold and covered her head with her shawl.

Five or six other women who lived close by sat down in a circle round her, with mute sympathy. Then the crowd moved on with the police to another cottage where the same scene was to take place, and left the group of desolate women sitting by the hovel.

There were still no clouds in the sky, and the heat was intense. The police when not in motion lay sweating and gasping under the walls with their tunics unbuttoned. They were not attractive, and I kept comparing them with the islandmen, who walked up and down as cool and fresh-looking as the sea-gulls.

When the last eviction had been carried out a division was made: half the party went off with the bailiff to search the inner plain of the island for the cattle that had been hidden in the morning, the other half remained on the village road to guard some pigs that had already been taken possession of.

After a while two of these pigs escaped from the drivers and began a wild race up and down the narrow road. The people shrieked and howled to increase

98

their terror, and at last some of them became so excited that the police thought it time to interfere. They drew up in double line opposite the mouth of a blind laneway where the animals had been shut up. A moment later the shrieking began again in the west and the two pigs came in sight, rushing down the middle of the road with the drivers behind them.

They reached the line of the police. There was a slight scuffle, and then the pigs continued their mad rush to the east, leaving three policemen lying in the dust.

The satisfaction of the people was immense. They shrieked and hugged each other with delight, and it is likely that they will hand down these animals for generations in the tradition of the island.

Two hours later the other party returned, driving three lean cows before them, and a start was made for the slip. At the public-house the policemen were given a drink while the dense crowd that was following waited in the lane. The island bull happened to be in a field close by, and he became wildly excited at the sight of the cows and of the strangely dressed men. Two young islanders sidled up to me in a moment or two as I was resting on a wall, and one of them whispered in my ear –

'Do you think they could take fines of us if we let out the bull on them?'

In face of the crowd of women and children, I could only say it was probable, and they slunk off.

At the slip there was a good deal of bargaining, which ended in all the cattle being given back to their owners. It was plainly of no use to take them away, as they were worth nothing. [...]

While the curaghs are out I am left with a few women and very old men who cannot row. One of these old men, whom I often talk with, has some fame as a bone-setter, and is said to have done remarkable cures, both here and on the mainland. Stories are told of how he has been taken off by the quality in their carriages through the hills of Connemara, to treat their sons and daughters, and come home with his pockets full of money.

Another old man, the oldest on the island, is fond of telling me anecdotes – not folk-tales – of things that have happened here in his lifetime.

He often tells me about a Connaught man who killed his father with the blow of a spade when he was in passion, and then fled to this island and threw himself on the mercy of some of the natives with whom he was said to be related. They hid him in a hole – which the old man has shown me – and kept him safe for weeks, though the police came and searched for him, and he could hear their boots grinding on the stones over his head. In spite of a reward which was offered the island was incorruptible, and after much trouble the man was safely shipped to America.

This impulse to protect the criminal is universal in the west. It seems partly due to the association between justice and the hated English jurisdiction, but more directly to the primitive feeling of these people, who are never criminals yet always capable of crime, that a man will not do wrong unless he is under the influence of a passion which is as irresponsible as a storm on the sea.

If a man has killed his father, and is already sick and broken with remorse, they can see no reason why he should be dragged away and killed by the law.

Such a man, they say, will be quiet all the rest of his life, and if you suggest that punishment is needed as an example, they ask, 'Would any one kill his father if he was able to help it?'

Some time ago, before the introduction of police, all the people of the islands were as innocent as the people here remain to this day. I have heard that at that time the ruling proprietor and magistrate of the north island used to give any man who had done wrong a letter to a jailer in Galway, and send him off by himself to serve a term of imprisonment.

As there was no steamer, the ill-doer was given a passage in some chance hooker to the nearest point on the mainland. Then he walked for many miles along a desolate shore till he reached the town. When his time had been put through, he crawled back along the same route, feeble and emaciated, and had often to wait many weeks before he could regain the island. Such at least is the story.

It seems absurd to apply the same laws to these people and to the criminal classes of a city. The most intelligent man on Inishmaan has often spoken to me of his contempt of the law, and of the increase of crime the police have brought to Aranmor. On this island, he says, if men have a little difference, or a little fight, their friends take care it does not go too far, and in a little time it is forgotten. In Kilronan there is a band of men paid to make out cases for themselves; the moment a blow is struck they come down and arrest the man who gave it. The other man he quarrelled with has to give evidence against him; whole families come down to the court and swear against each other till they become bitter enemies. If there is a conviction the man who is convicted never forgives. He waits his time, and before the year is out there is a cross summons, which the other man in turn never forgives. The feud continues to grow, till a dispute about the colour of a man's hair may end in a murder, after a year's forcing by the law. The mere fact that it is impossible to get reliable evidence in the island – not because the people are dishonest, but because they think the claim of kinship more sacred than the claims of abstract truth – turns the whole system of sworn evidence into a demoralizing farce, and it is easy to believe that law dealings on this false basis must lead to every sort of injustice.

While I am discussing these questions with the old men the curaghs begin to come in with cargoes of salt, and flour, and porter.

To-day a stir was made by the return of a native who had spent five years in New York. He came on shore with half a dozen people who had been shopping on the mainland, and walked up and down on the slip in his neat suit, looking strangely foreign to his birthplace, while his old mother of eighty-five ran about on the slippery seaweed, half crazy with delight, telling every one the news.

When the curaghs were in their places the men crowded round him to bid him welcome. He shook hands with them readily enough, but with no smile of recognition.

He is said to be dying. [...]

A branch of the Gaelic League has been started here since my last visit, and every Sunday afternoon three little girls walk through the village ringing a shrill hand-bell, as a signal that the women's meeting is to be held, – here it would be useless to fix an hour, as the hours are not recognized.

Soon afterwards bands of girls – of all ages from five to twenty-five – begin to troop down to the schoolhouse in their reddest Sunday petticoats. It is remarkable that these young women are willing to spend their one afternoon of freedom in laborious studies of orthography for no reason but a vague reverence for the Gaelic. It is true that they owe this reverence, or most of it, to the influence of some recent visitors, yet the fact that they feel such an influence so keenly is itself of interest.

In the older generation that did not come under the influence of the recent language movement, I do not see any particular affection for Gaelic. Whenever they are able, they speak English to their children, to render them more capable of making their way in life. Even the young men sometimes say to me –

'There's very hard English on you, and I wish to God that I had the like of it.'

The women are the great conservative force in this matter of the language. They learn a little English in school and from their parents, but they rarely have occasion to speak with any one who is not a native of the islands, so their knowledge of the foreign tongue remains rudimentary. In my cottage I have never heard a word of English from the women except when they were speaking to the pigs or to the dogs, or when the girl was reading a letter in English. Women, however, with a more assertive temperament, who have had, apparently, the same opportunities, often attain a considerable fluency, as is the case with one, a relative of the old woman of the house, who often visits here.

In the boys' school, where I sometimes look in, the children surprise me by their knowledge of English, though they always speak in Irish among themselves. The school itself is a comfortless building in a terribly bleak position. In cold weather the children arrive in the morning with a sod of turf tied up with their books, a simple toll which keeps the fire well supplied, yet, I believe a more modern method is soon to be introduced. [...]

My voyage from the middle island was wild. The morning was so stormy, that in ordinary circumstances I would not have attempted the passage, but as I had arranged to travel with a curagh that was coming over for the Parish Priest – who is to hold stations on Inishmaan – I did not like to draw back.

I went out in the morning and walked up to the cliffs as usual. Several men I fell in with shook their heads when I told them I was going away, and said they doubted if a curagh could cross the sound with the sea that was in it.

When I went back to the cottage I found the Curate had just come across from the south island, and had had a worse passage than any he had yet experienced.

The tide was to turn at two o'clock, and after that it was thought the sea would be calmer, as the wind and the waves would be running from the same point. We sat about in the kitchen all the morning, with men coming in every few minutes to give their opinion whether a passage should be attempted, and at what points the sea was likely to be at its worst.

At last it was decided we should go, and I started for the pier in a wild shower of rain with the wind howling in the walls. The schoolmaster and a priest who was to have gone with me came out as I was passing through the village and advised me not to make the passage; but my crew had gone on towards the sea, and I thought it better to go after them. The eldest son of the family was coming with me, and I considered that the old man, who knew the waves better than I did, would not send out his son if there was more than reasonable danger.

I found my crew waiting for me under a high wall below the village, and we went on together. The island had never seemed so desolate. Looking out over the black limestone through the driving rain to the gulf of struggling waves, an indescribable feeling of dejection came over me.

The old man gave me his view of the use of fear.

'A man who is not afraid of the sea will soon be drownded,' he said, 'for he will be going out on a day he shouldn't. But we do be afraid of the sea, and we do only be drownded now and again.'

A little crowd of neighbours had collected lower down to see me off, and as we crossed the sandhills we had to shout to each other to be heard above the wind.

The crew carried down the curagh and then stood under the lee of the pier tying on their hats with string and drawing on their oilskins.

They tested the braces of the oars, and the oar pins, and everything in the curagh with a care I had not yet seen them give to anything, then my bag was lifted in, and we were ready. Besides the four men of the crew a man was going with us who wanted a passage to this island. As he was scrambling into the bow, an old man stood forward from the crowd.

'Don't take that man with you,' he said. 'Last week they were taking him to Clare and the whole of them were near drownded. Another day he went to Inisheer and they broke three ribs of the curagh, and they coming back. There is not the like of him for ill-luck in the three islands.'

'The divil choke your old gob,' said the man, 'you will be talking.'

We set off. It was a four-oared curagh, and I was given the last seat so as to leave the stern for the man who was steering with an oar, worked at right angles to the others by an extra thole-pin in the stern gunnel.

When we had gone about a hundred yards they ran up a bit of a sail in the bow and the pace became extraordinarily rapid.

The shower had passed over and the wind had fallen, but large, magnificently brilliant waves were rolling down on us at right angles to our course.

Every instant the steersman whirled us round with a sudden stroke of his oar, the prow reared up and then fell into the next furrow with a crash, throwing up masses of spray. As it did so, the stern in its turn was thrown up, and both the steersman, who let go his oar and clung with both hands to the gunnel, and myself, were lifted high up above the sea.

The wave passed, we regained our course and rowed violently for a few

102

yards, when the same manoeuvre had to be repeated. As we worked out into the sound we began to meet another class of waves, that could be seen for some distance towering above the rest.

When one of these came in sight, the first effort was to get beyond its reach. The steersman began crying out in Gaelic 'Siubhal, siubhal' ('Run, run'), and sometimes, when the mass was gliding towards us with horrible speed, his voice rose to a shriek. Then the rowers themselves took up the cry, and the curagh seemed to leap and quiver with the frantic terror of a beast till the wave passed behind it or fell with a crash beside the stern.

It was in this racing with the waves that our chief danger lay. If the wave could be avoided, it was better to do so, but if it overtook us while we were trying to escape, and caught us on the broadside, our destruction was certain. I could see the steersman quivering with the excitement of his task, for any error in his judgment would have swamped us.

We had one narrow escape. A wave appeared high above the rest, and there was the usual moment of intense exertion. It was of no use, and in an instant the wave seemed to be hurling itself upon us. With a yell of rage the steersman struggled with his oar to bring our prow to meet it. He had almost succeeded, when there was a crash and rush of water round us. I felt as if I had been struck upon the back with knotted ropes. White foam gurgled round my knees and eyes. The curagh reared up, swaying and trembling for a moment, and then fell safely into the furrow.

This was our worst moment, though more than once, when several waves came so closely together that we had no time to regain control of the canoe between them, we had some dangerous work. Our lives depended upon the skill and courage of the men, as the life of the rider or swimmer is often in his own hands, and the excitement of the struggle was too great to allow time for fear.

I enjoyed the passage. Down in this shallow trough of canvas that bent and trembled with the motion of the men, I had a far more intimate feeling of the glory and power of the waves than I have ever known in a steamer. [...]

The young man has been buried, and his funeral was one of the strangest scenes I have met with. People could be seen going down to his house from early in the day, yet when I went there with the old man about the middle of the afternoon, the coffin was still lying in front of the door, with the men and women of the family standing round beating it, and keening over it, in a great crowd of people. A little later every one knelt down and a last prayer was said. Then the cousins of the dead man got ready two oars and some pieces of rope – the men of his own family seemed too broken with grief to know what they were doing – the coffin was tied up, and the procession began. The old women walked close behind the coffin, and I happened to take a place just after them, among the first of the men. The rough lane to the graveyard slopes away towards the east, and the crowd of women going down before me in their red dresses, cloaked with red petticoats, with the waistband that is held round the head just seen from behind, had a strange effect, to which the white coffin and the unity of colour gave a nearly cloistral quietness.

This time the graveyard was filled with withered grass and bracken instead of the early ferns that were to be seen everywhere at the other funeral I have spoken of, and the grief of the people was of a different kind, as they had come to bury a young man who had died in his first manhood, instead of an old woman of eighty. For this reason the keen lost a part of its formal nature, and was recited as the expression of intense personal grief by the young men and women of the man's own family.

When the coffin had been laid down, near the grave that was to be opened, two long switches were cut out from the brambles among the rocks, and the length and breadth of the coffin were marked on them. Then the men began their work, clearing off stones and thin layers of earth, and breaking up an old coffin that was in the place into which the new one had to be lowered. When a number of blackened boards and pieces of bone had been thrown up with the clay, a skull was lifted out, and placed upon a gravestone. Immediately the old woman, the mother of the dead man, took it up in her hands, and carried it away by herself. Then she sat down and put it in her lap – it was the skull of her own mother – and began keening and shrieking over it with the wildest lamentation.

As the pile of mouldering clay got higher beside the grave a heavy smell began to rise from it, and the men hurried with their work, measuring the hole repeatedly with the two rods of bramble. When it was nearly deep enough the old woman got up and came back to the coffin, and began to beat on it, holding the skull in her left hand. This last moment of grief was the most terrible of all. The young women were nearly lying among the stones, worn out with their passion of grief, yet raising themselves every few moments to beat with magnificent gestures on the boards of the coffin. The young men were worn out also, and their voices cracked continually in the wail of the keen.

When everything was ready the sheet was unpinned from the coffin, and it was lowered into its place. Then an old man took a wooden vessel with holy water in it, and a wisp of bracken, and the people crowded round him while he splashed the water over them. They seemed eager to get as much of it as possible, more than one old woman crying out with a humorous voice –

'Tabhair dham braon eile, a Mhourteen.' ('Give me another drop, Martin.')

When the grave was half filled in, I wandered round towards the north watching two seals that were chasing each other near the surf. I reached the Sandy Head as the light began to fail, and found some of the men I knew best fishing there with a sort of drag-net. It is a tedious process, and I sat for a long time on the sand watching the net being put out, and then drawn in again by eight men working together with a slow rhythmical movement.

As they talked to me and gave me a little poteen and a little bread when they thought I was hungry, I could not help feeling that I was talking with men who were under a judgment of death. I knew that every one of them would be drowned in the sea in a few years and battered naked on the rocks, or would die in his own cottage and be buried with another fearful scene in the graveyard I had come from.

III

The Strangers

The early decades of the twentieth century saw a number of writers and travellers attracted by the lure of these remote islands. Many of their accounts, some more sympathetic than others, shed little new light on the life of the islands but in all we find hints of the peculiar magnetism of the place and the long-lasting impression it made on those who visited it.

James Joyce was already familiar with the Aran Islands through the writings of Synge and from his wife's Galway background. In 1912 he came back to Ireland from Trieste where he was living and visited the West with Nora Barnacle. They sailed out to Inis Mór in August and, upon his return to Italy, he wrote an article about the island (in Italian) for Il Piccolo della Sera, Trieste's main newspaper.

B.N. Hedderman spent many years as the public health nurse on Inis Oírr and Inis Meáin. In her little-known book she describes the isolation and hardship of island life, both for herself and the islanders, and, while at times appearing patronizing, she brings home clearly the vulnerability of the people to accident and disease. This vulnerability remained until Aer Arann was set up in 1970 and the building of airstrips on the islands began.

Visitors continued to see the islands as quaint and primitive outposts. In the accounts of both Alice Dease and Somerville and Ross (Edith Somerville and Violet Martin) we sense a view filtered through the prejudices and preconceptions of the authors. Later, Thomas Mason, in his fascinating book, The Islands of Ireland (1936), shows an openness and sympathy which differs sharply from these patrician airs. Others in thrall to a certain vision of the islands included the English artist Elizabeth Rivers and her adopted friend Lady Clare Vyvyan, their books entitled, respectively, Stranger in Aran (1946) and On Timeless Shores (1957).

In 1927 An Cumann le Béaloideas Éireann (later the Irish Folklore Commission) was formed. Dedicated and hard-working collectors, both full-time and part-time, were employed by the Commission to gather together a vast amount of folklore of all types from almost every part of the country at a period when such knowledge was fast disappearing. Just such a collector was Seosamh Ó Flannagáin, a primary-school teacher on Inis Mór. He drowned tragically in 1939 while returning from pilgrimage in Connemara. The story 'Aristotle and His Wife', recorded from Pádraic Ó Maoláin in Bun Gabhla, the most westerly point of Inis Mór, is well-known throughout Europe.

James Joyce

The Mirage of the Fisherman of Aran. England's Safety Valve in Case of War[*]

Galway, 2 September

The little ship carrying a small load of travellers moves away from the quay under the watchful eyes of the Scottish agent absorbed in a private fantasy of calculation. It leaves the little port of Galway and enters open water, leaving behind on its right the village of Claddagh, a cluster of huts outside the walls of the city. A cluster of huts, and yet a kingdom. Up until a few years ago the village elected its own king, had its own mode of dress, passed its own laws, and lived to itself. The wedding rings of the inhabitants are still decorated with the king's crest: two joined hands supporting a crowned heart.

We set out for Aranmor, the holy island that sleeps like a great shark on the grey waters of the Atlantic Ocean, which the islanders call the Old Sea. Beneath the waters of this bay and along its coast lie the wrecks of a squadron of the unfortunate Spanish Armada. After their defeat in the English Channel, the ships set sail for the North, where the storms and the waves scattered them. The citizens of Galway, remembering the long friendship between Spain and Ireland, hid the fugitives from the vengeance of the English garrison and gave the shipwrecked a decent burial, wrapping their bodies in white linen cloth.

The waters have repented. Every year on the day before the Feast of the Assumption, when the herring fishing begins, the waters of the bay are blessed. A flotilla of fishing boats departs from Claddagh preceded by a flagship, on whose deck stands a Dominican friar. When they reach an appropriate place the flotilla stops, the fishermen kneel down and uncover themselves, and the friar, muttering prayers of exorcism, shakes his aspergill on the sea, and divides the dark air in the form of a cross.

A border of white sand on the right indicates the place where the new transatlantic port is, perhaps, destined to rise. My companion spreads out a large map on which the projected lines curve, ramify, and cross each other from Galway to the great Canadian ports. The voyage from Europe to America will take less than three days, according to the figures. From Galway, the last port in Europe, to Saint John, Newfoundland, a steamship will take two days and

---

*Translated from the Italian of 'Il Miraggio del Pescatore di Aran. La Valvola dell'Inghilterra in Caso di Guerra', *Il Piccolo della Sera*, Trieste, 5 September 1912.

sixteen hours, and from Galway to Halifax, the first port in Canada, three days and ten hours. The text of the booklet attached to the map bristles with figures, estimates of cost, and oceanographic pictures. The writer makes a warm appeal to the British admiralty, to the railway societies, to the Chambers of Commerce, to the Irish population. The new port would be a safety valve for England in case of war. From Canada, the granary and warehouse of the United Kingdom, great cargos of grain would enter the Irish port, thus avoiding the dangers of navigation in Saint George's Channel and the enemy fleets. In time of peace, the new line would be the shortest way between one continent and the other. A large part of the goods and passengers which are now landed at Liverpool would in the future land at Galway, proceeding directly to London, via Dublin and Holyhead. The old decadent city would rise again. From the new world, wealth and vital energy would run through this new artery of an Ireland drained of blood. Again, after about ten centuries, the mirage which blinded the poor fisherman of Aran, follower and emulator of St Brendan, appears in the distance, vague and tremulous on the mirror of the ocean.

Christopher Columbus, as everyone knows, is honoured by posterity because he was the last to discover America. A thousand years before the Genoese navigator was derided at Salamanca, Saint Brendan weighed anchor for the unknown world from the bare shore which our ship is approaching; and, after crossing the ocean, landed on the coast of Florida. The island at that time was wooded and fertile. At the edge of the woods he found the hermitage of Irish monks which had been established in the fourth century after Christ by Enda, a saint of royal blood. From this hermitage came Finnian, later Bishop of Lucca. Here lived and dreamed the visionary Saint Fursa, described in the hagiographic calendar of Ireland as the precursor of Dante Alighieri. A medieval copy of the Visions of Fursa depicts the voyage of the saint from hell to heaven, from the gloomy valley of the four fires among the bands of devils up through the universe to the divine light reflected from innumerable angels' wings. This vision would have served as a model for the poet of the *Divine Comedy*, who, like Columbus, is honoured by posterity because he was the last to visit and describe the three regions of the soul.

On the shore of the bay fragile little boats of stretched canvas are drawn up to dry. Four islanders come nimbly down to the sea over rocks covered with purple and rust-coloured seaweed, like that seen in the shops of herb-sellers in Galway. The fisherman of Aran has sure feet. He wears a rough sandal of untanned cowhide, without heels, open at the arch, and tied with rawhide laces.* He dresses in wool as thick as felt and wears a big black hat with a wide brim.

We stop in one of the steep little streets, uncertain. An islander, who speaks an English all his own, says good morning, adding that it has been a horrible summer, praise be to God. The phrase, which at first seems one of the

*Pampooties. 'The tramper Synge is looking for you ... He's out in pampooties to murder you.' *Ulysses,* p. 197 (188).

usual Irish blunders, rather comes from the innermost depths of human resignation. The man who said it bears a princely name, that of the O'Flaherties, a name which the young Oscar Wilde proudly had printed on the title page of his first book. But time and the wind have razed to the ground the bygone civilization to which he belongs – the sacred druids of his island, the territory ruled by his ancestors, the language, and perhaps even the name, of that hermit of Aran who was called the dove of the church.* Around the stunted shrubs which grow on the hills of the island his imagination has woven legends and tales which reveal the depths of his psyche. And under his apparent simplicity he retains a slight trace of scepticism, and of humour. He looks away when he has spoken and lets the eager enthusiast jot down in his notebook the astounding fact that yonder hawthorn tree was the little tree from which Joseph of Arimathea cut his walking stick.

An old lady comes toward us and invites us to enter her house. She places on the table an enormous tea pot, a small loaf of bread, and some salted butter. The islander, who is her son, sits near the fireplace and answers the questions of my companion in an embarrassed and humble manner. He doesn't know how old he is, but he says that he will soon be old. He doesn't know why he hasn't taken a wife, perhaps because there are no women for him. My companion goes on to ask why there are no women for him, and the islander, removing his hat from his head, sinks his face in the soft wool, confused and smiling. Aran, it is said, is the strangest place in the world. A poor place, but no matter how poor it is, when my companion tries to pay, the old lady rejects the money almost angrily and asks us if we are trying to dishonour her house.

A fine and steady drizzle falls from the grey clouds. The rainy mist comes in from the West, while the little ship calls desperately for the laggards. The island disappears little by little, wrapped in a smoky veil. Three Danish sailors sitting stationary on the ridge of the slope also disappear. They were out in the ocean for the summer fishing and made a stop at Aran. Silent and melancholy, they seem to be thinking of the Danish hordes who burned the city of Galway in the eighth century, of the Irish lands which are included in the dowries of the girls of Denmark, according to legend, and which they dream of reconquering. On the islands and on the sea falls the rain. It rains as it can rain only in Ireland. Under the forecastle, where a girl is noisily making love to one of the crew, holding him on her knees, we again open the map. In the twilight the names of the ports cannot be distinguished, but the line that leaves Galway and ramifies and spreads out recalls the motto placed near the crest of his native city by a mystic and perhaps even prophetic head of a monastery:

> *Quasi lilium germinans germinabit,*
> *et quasi terebinthus extendans ramos suos.***

* St Columkill.
** It will grow like a sprouting lily, stretching out its branches like the terebinth tree.

B. N. Hedderman

Glimpses of My Life in Aran

On a dark squally evening, a curragh was seen fighting her way with very slow progress for Inishmain. I had been called with all possible speed to see a patient who abused my advice before, remaining obdurate, refusing to go to hospital or see a doctor, until now uræmic poisoning had set in. It was too late.

There was a stiff breeze always preceding the showers, and it was remarked by the Inishere people, who seemed to have a keener realization of the danger involved than the others, that despite the stillness in the intervals, the sea was disturbed, and they expressed strong disapproval at our crossing while showers were hovering near.

They were astonished that I evinced no fear and concluded that such indifference sprang from little knowledge of the sea, and they openly rebuked me, calling my courage folly. However, their counsel did not prevail. We were quickly launched; but certainly, to see our three-oared Lilliputian craft at that moment leave the strand, propelled with the slender equipment of a few sticks and a sail large enough to capsize her, would strike the onlooker unaccustomed to such sights as an act of daring boldness.

Yet it is the only means these islanders possess of obtaining help in any emergency, however urgent; hesitation to respond did not occur to me; I came prepared to be of use, to make every sacrifice for a work I professed to hold so dear. Starting, we had hoped to reach the other island before the shower, and a few minutes took us off from the shelter of the cliffs, when, hoisting the sail, we sped into the sound.

Casting a look before me, I saw that never-failing obstacle, a wall of surf on the slip, wave upon wave tumbling in upon it, recalling a previous adventure, but not a word of fear escaped my lips.

I calmed down every emotion, as nervousness would encumber the men at this critical time, so that every vestige of my feeling was mercifully hidden. With extreme anxiety they looked out for the coming squall, tortured perhaps by fear, but seemingly devoid of any. If they were afraid, they carefully concealed the fact. Their exertions were inspiring, if not heroic – one of them a mere boy – hastening in the face of such danger to carry, as they thought, aid

From *Glimpses of My Life in Aran*, Part I (1917).

to a dying friend. This – one of the most beautiful traits in human nature – I have always remarked is a special characteristic of the Inishmain people.

Half our journey still remained to be made; but the clouds had gathered – there was blackness in the west. It was coming nearer and nearer, the wind was beginning to blow, and there was tumult around us as we rattled along. The rain would soon come in torrents. At once there was a hush, a silence, as of a warning from an intervening power. Our sail was lowered, and in an instant, with one vengeful sweep, an ice-cold breaker dashed relentlessly in upon me. With savage swiftness the shower burst down. Peeping from beneath the hood that somewhat obscured my vision, it was terrible to witness the rush of the waves threatening to overwhelm us, and almost simultaneously there was a crash; one of the thole-pins had yielded to the straining power of the rower. He reeled a little, but the vigilance of the others instantly resisted, and he quickly regained his balance.

The boat groaned at every pull, the oars becoming almost entangled in the encircling foam that surrounded us for some minutes. Should it last much longer, where was our hope of refuge? A rush backwards to Inishere to an equal danger on the rocks, or onward on our track with the sea rolling in tremendous heights before us – which was the most desperate?

One of the men hesitated, uncertain whether to go on or toss about for a while. At this there was a volley of protest from his companions, and he vainly besought them to rest on the oars; but they still kept straining away. Here was a test of skill and endurance.

It is impossible to exaggerate the many dangers these Aran people undergo – not once or twice and then no more, but every day of their lives. I have never ceased to marvel at the indomitable spirit they display under circumstances, so Viking-like that one is forced to doubt if they are the real posterity of the landfaring Firbolgs!

When the shower had spent its force, the rowers dashed violently shore-wards, where we were soon safely piloted, and whence gleamed a sort of torchlight followed by a small procession of the islanders intensely excited; and soon a friendly voice hailed us 'Isteack lib go Zapaid!' (Come, come, quick.) With scrupulous care we were hauled high and dry on the slip, thus ending a very perilous passage, with a sigh of relief and a fervent hope that the next would prove less dangerous. [...]

The following incident occurred in a cottage – the only one of its kind in the Island. In other days it had been used as an outhouse, a kind of rough store for hoarding everything, and it was half a ruin when Peter and his bride took possession of it.

The walls in many parts were bulging with moisture and its every corner spoke of dilapidation. The roof too was in holes for want of sufficient thatch. There was no chimney – nothing but a few rude boards nailed together in triangular fashion leading to a fireplace of bare cold stone. The window was a single pane, quite immovable, so that very little fresh air ever penetrated to the interior.

It could readily be distinguished from the more clean and comparatively comfortable dwellings tenanted by the neighbours, and it appeared to be the only one not legislated for under the Public Health Acts. The one room with its earthen floor, and a loft to which the children ascended by means of a ladder, provided all the space a family of eight could obtain.

And now I will briefly describe the plight in which I found myself one winter in such an atmosphere.

Let nurses with aseptic knowledge imagine what it must be to come to a home like this in the early hours of the morning, with a stiff gale blowing, so that medical help was an impossibility. The patient lying on the floor, well-nigh exhausted with P.P.H., no fire or other convenience at hand; water as scarce as wine; no basin or table, but a large stool on which were placed a few mugs; the indispensable kettle coated with fallen soot. Antiseptic precautions indeed!

The above is not wholly descriptive of the desolation in which I found the patient; her surroundings were even worse. Her husband, who was mentally defective, had called me only a few minutes before, and her condition, when I arrived, was too alarming for words.

On entering, the first note that struck the ear was the intermittent wail of a last year's infant, who became clamorous at my appearance. I found the patient prostrate on the damp floor. I rushed towards the corner where there was a bed to prepare for her. When I was quietly attempting to lift her from the pool in which she was placed, the husband made an advance, angrily remonstrating. I made no answer to this unusual protest, and with all the strength I could muster managed to raise her, he meanwhile marching up and down in quite a paroxysm of rage as his orders had no effect on me.

'It is best for you to prepare a fire,' I said; but he took no notice of my commands, and stood gazing at me, and started to ask questions at this precious moment when every muscle and fibre of one's body were strained to the utmost in the effort to revive the poor patient, who had been into three successive swoons, the result of the fatigue she had undergone.

'Give her a drop of poteen,' he said in Irish.

'No!' I replied, explaining the ill-effects of giving stimulants to a hæmorrhage patient, and how it was likely to act on her heart; but regardless of the caution I had given, he managed, while my attention was directed elsewhere, to vanish from view, eventually returning, bearing a dark-coloured bottle which he held to the patient's lips. She had somewhat recovered by now, and resolutely refused to touch it without my knowledge. I endeavoured to persuade him that it was of no use, and ordered him to prepare tea instead; he persisted in saying the other woman always gave poteen. I said decidedly it must not be given, when immediately he dashed the bottle from his hands, flinging it with the precious liquid on the floor almost at his wife's feet. We were both obliged to inhale the fumes of the horrid stuff until morning.

I was dreading every minute a recurrence of the bleeding, as her lax and placid condition gave grave occasion for anxiety. It moved me almost to tears to watch the poor woman bear her trouble alone. She had no person in the world except myself on whom she could depend with any confidence, and who would sympathize with her forlorn state.

The husband, unheeding the situation in which his wife was placed, continued his questions, standing with dilated pupils focused in my direction at every turn, sometimes asking strange questions about people and events I had never known or heard of. It was trying to hear his babbling, and but for my own reserve of nervous energy the patient would have been left alone, for the husband behaved like a maniac that night.

Though the patient felt her need of things so much, she whispered to me in Gaelic, 'I will be better when next you come.' I went away, wondering would she become a mother for the ninth time. Peter had been an inmate of a lunatic asylum for some time before this.

MICK

Old Anna lived alone during her son Mick's sojourn in a lunatic asylum; but one day he suddenly arrived, to her great discomfiture, for she had hoped his detention there would last until infirmity would end her own remaining days.

In early manhood Mick developed a craze for emigration, and went to America. He had been a good son until, falling under the influence of evil companions, he became intemperate. This deadened any good impulse in him and led to melancholia, until at length he manifested symptoms of mania, necessitating a return to the land of his birth. He was speedily shipped back and transferred to the asylum and, after a while, from the latter institution to his native crags and wilds.

For some time before this, I was accustomed to pay daily visits to Anna, as her failing strength left her unable to move about much, and now, under the new order, I managed with a little tact to make Mick feel no repugnance for me.

I saw his inclination for reading, and was fortunately able to keep him supplied with papers. It was impossible also not to feel a deep sympathy for his mental affliction and his mother's lone condition, and so I visited them regularly.

In appearance Mick might be taken for a Nihilist, but his skin was more pallid and waxy looking. The conditions under which the poor fellow lived were sufficient to create emaciation in even a stronger person. His little habitation was of the rudest beehive construction, and contained, I am sure, half a century's products of combustion, retaining dust and earth in every crevice; and as the neighbours were not permitted to enter, it was like an anchorite's hut.

He often roamed round the Island at midnight, sometimes bare-headed and in shirt-sleeves, occasionally substituting a long black coat for a shorter one in which there was a large rent. His eccentric manner and dress attracted the children who raised a hue and cry at his approach; his hat was a kind of turban, and he never appeared abroad without a large cane.

As the days slipped by, Anna improved; meanwhile Mick had prevented any person from entering the house, and I was the only intruder permitted. He had a special aversion for those about him; but as I had to leave the Island often, I was unable to learn the actual cause of the hatred he showed. However, one day, as I was hastening along a craggy pathway, a little girl rushed my way, exclaiming in breathless accents, 'Mick is killing somebody.'

Hurrying on, I drew near the old house, and as I approached, the poor woman's wail met my ear. I listened, and heard a weak voice calling; then, stooping down and peeping through the little aperture which served as a window by the dim light I could barely discern Mick, dashing wildly about, muttering something, and evidently seized with some fresh cause for his fury.

It occurred to me instantly that if I procured a book it might soothe him, so I found one a few doors away, and taking my courage in both hands I ventured to enter. Nobody else would, although a number of people were assembled out of mere curiosity.

I tapped gently at the door. It yielded, and I stood facing Mick, to whom I presented the book. Instantly his prattling ceased. He received it with a slight nod, a token of recognition peculiar to himself, while I sought his mother on the dismal pallet on which she lay. An old rusty hoop – the fire-tongs ready for action – lay on a box beside her, and she was weeping dolefully. I asked the reason, and she signalled 'Hush' and pointed to Mick, who watched us keenly.

I saw at the moment his face was again becoming convulsed. He was a terrible looking figure – his skin now a pale green, and his whole body stiffened with madness. He fenced about the dim old fireplace, dancing on the few embers that lingered there; then, clenching his hands tightly, boxed some fancied opponent represented by an old paper photograph that was attached to the wall. He was evidently looking for the iron hoop, which I had thrown beneath the bed far out of hand's reach; but Mick's plans were not to be frustrated so readily. He groped about in a search for some other weapon, still talking and humming to himself, until his eye rested on a rusty little hatchet. Catching it up, flinging it from side to side in childlike fashion, he went to his mother's bed rather slowly and held it over her, at the same time demanding money. He rushed back again, still talking, and finally attacked a big musty chest that stood beside the wall, smashing it without mercy. I protested at the violence his mother's only piece of furniture was subjected to; he made no further reply, but with one fierce dash retreated into a hole behind the fireplace, from which he emerged shortly afterwards, wending his way towards the beach.

I sat down then at Anna's bedside in a more composed frame of mind and listened to her tale.

It appeared that the morning had brought a mail from her other distant son enclosing a pound, which Mick demanded, intending to confiscate it for drink, this fact giving occasion for the struggle in which I found the poor woman engaged. He was in the act of committing the note to the flames when I appeared, but I did not know what the missive contained until afterwards; this was the exciting cause of his frantic movements.

I knew there was no peace in store for Anna that night, at least until Mick's passion had somewhat abated, and I arranged with a woman to remain with her; but this person's husband objected, because he thought Mick was insane, so I resolved to stay myself, at any rate until I saw his mood on returning. Anna was trembling in terror, and I myself was suffering from the chill of that mud-cold atmosphere.

Upon his return I heard Mick talking as he walked in, but in a much lower key. He came to Anna's bed, and had no idea of my presence there. It was dark, but his whole aspect was altered. He spoke and, affecting a startled air of surprise at seeing me, relapsed into a sort of saddened depression. The next minute I saw that Mick's paroxysm was over, and that something akin to remorse was settling down upon him. I saw him turn to his mother as he said in Irish, 'Go Bfoirid Dia ort!' (God help you).

I hastened homewards without disturbing the peace of a yet unawakened island, and sought a much-deserved rest. Mick is again an inmate of the asylum, and poor Anna is where the weary are at rest.

THE GRAMOPHONE

There is a little village in the Middle Island called 'The Moor', and, because of its (comparatively) greater size, it is regarded by the islanders as most up-to-date and consequently as the capital. Indeed, those who reside there declare that they are never without dried fish – a distinction of quite an important nature, for too often a lack of this necessary article of food makes itself felt in bad weather when no boat can venture out.

It is also the proudest boast of 'The Moor' men that the tourist likes to linger there, though it is difficult to believe that its cobbled pathways and dreary appearance could appeal to anyone, and the general impression produced on the visitor must be one of dullness and desolation. It is called 'Blaithcliath' to denote its importance, because a Dublin student once stayed there.

The peaceful serenity of this old-world village was unexpectedly disturbed one mellow afternoon in the autumn when our gramophone arrived. It had been noticed that a box had been deposited with unusual care on the slip, so well secured that the boatmen who surveyed it exchanged glances, wondering what it could contain. I sometimes visit this landing-place, particularly on fine days, when there is a groundswell, to watch the difficulty experienced by the men landing. On this particular occasion they called me forward, and I at once assumed wondrous importance as the person to whom this unusual package was addressed. As soon as it was announced that the box contained a gramophone the scene became one of excitement and wonder.

The news spread like a prairie fire. A crowd gathered round peeping over each other's shoulders to see what was going on, and by the time the contents were unpacked fully a hundred people were squatting round, sitting on the bare ground, to witness the opening ceremony. The parts were carefully examined to see if we could arrange to piece them together. But, alas! we had no knowledge of the mechanism, nor was there any tradesman in the place who was any wiser. However, fortunately for us, there was a young graduate from Oxford visiting the islands, and he quickly consented to see what he could do. Eventually he succeeded, and suddenly the music started. The expression on the faces of the onlookers was indeed a sight to remember – the children in raptures, the old women enchanted, the men hardly believing their ears, and for a few minutes all other thoughts were laid aside. The question no one could answer was, where were the men and women hiding whose voices sounded so sweetly? They could not be seen. One woman suggested the spirits of the Firbolgs – Pagan ancestors – which tradition associated with the Duns (forts) to be found in Inishmain. In the rush and general bustle going on, the men forgot to prepare the nets, and all work was temporarily suspended. They continued exclaiming in Gaelic that 'somewhere there must be a person or there could not be a voice,' and the effect produced on them was really wonderful.

The day following a very pleasing incident occurred. A woman who had been ill with nervous trouble for many weeks previously, heard of the mysterious music. She asked me to let her hear it. Of course I consented. It acted like a charm. The spell was instantaneous. She, too, forgot her trouble, and the sad, worn face, on which suffering had left its mark, at once lighted up with hope and pleasure. Often afterwards I invited her to come and hear the music, and her visits were invariably followed by happy results.

I had no idea before that the Islanders had such a passion for music and song. One evening all the old men had assembled at one of the cottages. Among the records was a hornpipe. Directly the first bar was played, six of the men stood up in a line some distance apart from each other: all somehow procured short sticks, and at the first note, feet, arms and sticks commenced to keep time, each fellow swaying his body first to the right and then to the left. Scarcely any noise was heard, as they can move quite silently on the pampooties or cowhide shoes which they wear, the quiet being broken only by the clanking sound of the sticks as they clashed. Such a display was altogether foreign to me, but the motley crowd that looked on seemed in no way puzzled at the extraordinary motion of the performers. The pleasure of listening to the instrument and the generosity of the donor, Mrs Brian Wilson, are not likely to be quickly forgotten in the Island of Inishmain for life in such a spot is indeed shorn of most of its joys. [...]

One of the chief difficulties in connection with nursing, in fact the greatest obstacle I had to surmount in the early days, was the native aversion to doctors, as well as everything associated with medicine in any form. Outside their own contracted ideas of popular remedies, they were disposed to regard everything medical as a fad or something to be easily dispensed with. I have seen men and women submit with the greatest resignation to unnecessary suffering rather than seek timely aid, even when influenza was rampant in the country, and most of the people in the Island were stricken down with it. To assure them that it did not protect against itself like scarlatina, but, on the contrary, predisposed them to subsequent attacks, would be simply useless; they were so regardless of consequences that I saw one man, despising the severity of his own acute symptoms, actually going fishing. Small wonder, then, that he returned home at night with a congested lung, to be followed by fourteen days of acute illness, with a weakening of the respiratory tract as his future legacy. '*Tuil Dé*', meaning 'God's will,' met one at every turn. They are convinced that because influenza is supposed to be due to an external atmospheric condition no notice should be taken of it. '*Fuast,*' meaning a cold, is the term used by the Islanders to denote the presence of this treacherous and insidious infection.

The Dispensary they regarded as a kind of guillotine or death-trap – a tribunal from which, if they entered, they were never to emerge. Most of these fears are now in part dispelled, and the hostility towards the Dispensary is rapidly diminishing, the result of observing the large amount of suffering it has been the means of removing.

The advocates of these customs do not, and will not, give way without a struggle, so that nursing work in the early days was from some points of view a very thankless task. There were Island 'Gamps' to be reckoned with, as well as objections from others who did not believe in the efficacy of new methods, and who looked upon the nurse as a propagandist for 'doctors' bottles', as they curtly described anything I advised from that source. [...]

It is rare to have an appeal for help immediately after an accident in the South Island. It is only when the people's own remedies and decoctions fail that professional assistance is sought. I remember shortly after my arrival passing one of the villages, when an old woman hailed me. She had received a wound, '*loc*', as she termed the accident. In response to her request I looked at the part, and found a contused cut a few inches in extent, with much damage to tissue. It was not a recent occurrence, and was directly over the arch of the foot and around the os calcis, and the skin was very much discoloured. Dirt was actually rubbed into the bruised and torn part, with, I suppose, micro-organisms innumerable. The wound had been caused by a loose stone. These same stones are a real plague of the Island – they are here, there, and everywhere!

There was little chance of healing this by first intention. It was many days old, and inflammation, with severe throbbing, had already set in. It required immediate antiseptic treatment, and I set off to procure what was necessary. In the meantime a neighbour interfered and prescribed, and when I returned I found the entire leg enveloped in some composition that, judging from the odour which it exhaled, would have required the skill of an analyst to detect all its ingredients.

I departed at once in pursuit of more pressing duties, but had scarcely reached my lodging when a messenger came for me from the old lady. It was with some difficulty I removed the dreadful poultice from her leg, and applied a soothing antiseptic lotion with lint and cotton-wool held in place by a bandage. At the same time, in order to keep the lint I had immersed in the fluid in safe custody, I told her that it was poison, and at the bare mention of the dreaded word, '*mim*', as she called it, she grew more interested and never uttered a word. I did not revisit her until the following day, when I found her entirely disappointed with the treatment and with the dressing removed. She had again resorted to somebody else's method of cure. This time it was a compound of dock leaves blended with snails. On beholding her very much irritated leg, I remonstrated, fearing gangrene in so old a patient. She quickly retorted that I had used a big blue bottle to poison her, and it took fully an hour of reasoning in defence of antiseptic principles to assure her of the danger involved in her experiments. After a lengthy pleading on behalf of the poor foot, I was again permitted to use my own cure, which proved indeed a soothing balsam, dispersing the inflammation and irritation. A few days later showed marked improvement, and the patient then greeted me in a more friendly spirit. There is hope, I think, that many of these curious customs based on such utter ignorance will one day be unknown. [...]

Then came an epidemic of whooping-cough. A golden-haired little girl was one of the first to be attacked. I went in not expecting to find anything seriously wrong; but the mother remarked how very different from her former self the child looked. I said that her grave condition had caused the change; everything about the case was symptomatic of bronchial pneumonia, and I pointed out how the greatest care and skill must be exercised in nursing her if she was to be kept alive. To my surprise, the mother said sadly but emphatically, 'She is gone; she has been taken by the fairies.' Indeed, she went further and explained that the 'good people' had substituted for her child 'that object', pointing to the poor little patient on the bed.

After persuading her in vain to try some heat and other remedies, I had to call the father, who was much more rational. Later, one of the Island 'Gamps' entered, a rather clever woman in her own way, and tossing her tangled tresses disdainfully while she watched my efforts to help the child, said quite audibly, in Gaelic, ''Tis little good your cure will do.' Shortly afterwards the embarrassed breathing became less difficult and the temperature fell.

It was, however, many weeks before the mother could believe, as she thought, that her child had been restored by the fairies. At the commencement of the pneumonia they had not the vaguest intention of treating her for a natural illness, believing her as lost to this planet as was Spenser's fairy boy. [...]

Though the material outlook of the Aran Islanders has changed within the last few years, it is pitiful that the superstitious spirit still survives to such a degree that the causation of any disease that attacks them is looked upon as the immediate result of the 'evil eye' influence, and is often followed by serious and destructive effects on their health and homes. How these very absurd ideas and customs gained entrance in Islands said to be the dwelling-place of multitudes of saints, is not easy to say; but they exist, and fire and sword would not eradicate them. They enter into the daily life of the people; old and young believe in them, and they persist in attributing all sorts of happenings to that prevailing influence, the 'evil eye'. No disease is ever traced to the usual physical causes. It is always, 'He is not well since So-and-so met him on the rocks.'

Directly an infant is ushered into the world, the first person entering the lying-in chamber must spit upon the new-born, then on the mother, and finally on the nurse, doctor, or attendant who happens to be present. This is not done with a view to expelling either the cocci or bacilli family, but as a life-long preservative for the child and its parents. Remonstrance or disapproval of this repulsive habit is not effective – the people will protest against interference and extol its virtue as a potent charm.

At no time is superstition encouraged so readily as when acute disease sets in. I have seen lives ruined and lost that might have been saved, if only means could be found to dispel this black ignorance when sudden illness attacks the young and healthy. The first resort is the saliva cure, and should the person accused of casting the spell resent the insinuation and not be friendly disposed in that special direction, the patient's progress and relief from suffering are supposed to be hindered until he enters the sick-room and saturates the bed-clothes with this filthy secretion.

Alice Dease

A Western Island

Whatever the extent of the island's benefits will be, certainly English rule, as shown to us on session day, is carried out under difficulties.

The court, a room about fifteen feet square, was crammed with eager listeners, and it was only through the intervention of a huge and kindly policeman that we were able to make our way at all. Once inside we were told to seat ourselves on stools within the railing which enclosed the two magistrates, one local and one imported, the people they were examining, and the interpreter.

'Do you understand English?' was the first question, asked of an old man with a beard like a venerable goat.

'Not one word, your worship,' rolled out the answer, which called forth an excusable exclamation from the magistrate who was trying to get through two hours' work in the short hour allowed him by the steamer on which he had to return to the mainland.

The goat-like offender's words could not be taken as literally true; nevertheless, though scarcely any of the islanders, except the very old women, 'have no English', few if any of them could undertake in a foreign tongue the special pleading needful in the cases of trespass – where no boundary marks are visible – or of assault, following on the arrival of a fresh supply of porter, which principally occupy the bench.

The case of the day was one of the latter. Even the windows were blocked with eager faces when it was brought up for hearing.

'Was the language – that was uttered – upon this occasion, of a nature – calculated to prove defamatory to the – young lady's – good character?' The bland stipendiary examined the solitary witness himself.

'I'm sure I couldn't say, your honour,' came the answer, without hesitation.

'Bad scran to him and his English!' We were close behind the interpreter, so had the benefit even of his asides.

'Was it bad, ugly names he was calling her?' He put the amended form of question aloud.

This threw more light upon the case, and the witness replied with

From *Down West and Other Sketches of Irish Life* (1914).

precipitation, for understanding, he was now only too anxious to tell us all he knew.

'Troth an' he did that right enough, your honour. He called her a – '

But the magistrate too was roused, and quickly he interposed.

'Thank you, thank you,' he cried, motioning to the man to stop. 'It is quite unnecessary for you to repeat the words he used.'

The fate of what had once been a cuckoo-clock next occupied the attention of the bench. The mangled remains, gathered up in a woman's apron, were laid before the magistrates, and the accuser and accused were called to have their say.

Bartle Costelloe began by denying the offence, but being put on oath, he changed his plea, and said if he did give the clock a tip, in any case it was no good.

'It was good enough for you yourself to send into Galway for four pennyworth o' copper wire to make a pendulum,' interrupted the owner, angrily.

''Twas no good, your worship,' repeated Bartle, unmoved. ''Twas moth-eaten, that it was, an' you'd want to warm it at the fire e'er ever you'd make it go.'

Then came Colman Flagherty's statement.

'It was me own clock, your worship, that's before you now, an' isn't it a show after him? 'Twas a wag, that's what it was, an' doesn't Bartle come in, an' it hangin' on the wall. "What's the bright face thing?" says he. "What is it but me wag o' the wall," says I. An' with that he went for it, me darlin' bright face coo-coo an' he pegged it on the floor, an' kicked it round the kitchen. "Bartle," says I, "you'll pay for this." "When I have to pay for it," says he, "I'll kick the stuffin' out of it." He did indeed your worship, an' worse, savin' your honour's favour, "I'll kick the devil out of it," says he. An' with that he sets to, an' he kicked it, back body an' sides, an' makes bits of the lovely face an' glass of it. Not a hand did he leave on it, no, nor an arm neither.'

Finally the magistrates decided to impose a fine, with compensation for the clock.

'Have you the money to pay?' the offender was asked.

'Musha, devil a penny, not till the kelp boat comes in,' replied Bartle, unconcernedly. 'I must introud upon your honour for it, until then.'

'Nothing of the kind,' retorted the magistrate, testily. 'If you can't pay you must go to jail for a week.'

We thought the sentence somewhat severe, but the magistrates knew their people best. From a dozen pockets and more, including that of the clock owner himself, came the sum required, in coppers and sixpences. So the fine was paid, and the magistrate steamed back to Galway without his prisoner. Ten days later the boat came from Glasgow to take away the kelp, and Bartle Costelloe was the owner of ready money. Then the loan was repaid to the last farthing, probably with the interest of a glass of whiskey for each one concerned.

Business at the public-houses, however, was slack during our stay, and from an old man in a lone cottage across the island we learnt the reason.

'I haven't been into town this long time,' he told us. 'We had a mission here, this while back.' As 'the town' consisted of a public-house and half a dozen cottages we were able to put our own connection between these apparently irrelevant sentences.

'Did many take the pledge?' we asked.

'Many! you may be talkin'. Didn't we all take it?' The remembrance was seemingly not altogether a happy one.

'Did they take it for long?'

'Some did and some didn't. I took it for life. I usually does take it for life,' he added, candidly.

Somerville and Ross

An Outpost of Ireland

There was some delay in departure, owing partly to a genial sympathy with the unpunctual, partly to a question of precedence among a pig family in the process of embarkation. The captain, a large clerical man in a soft felt hat, bore it with the equanimity of one who has learned in many journeys between Galway and Aran what is the full significance of the devils having entered into the swine. The boat moved out at length into the gleaming breadth of the bay; slowly the grey town grouped itself in its low-lying corner, the spires rose, waist-deep in roofs, and the heavy tower of St Nicholas bore its associations of seven hundred years in the brilliant youth of the spring sunlight. [...]

The steamer plodded on at her ten miles an hour, the pig families below uttered no more than an occasional yell of fractiousness or dolour, and a party of Aran women sat and conversed under their red shawls with that unflagging zest and seemingly inexhaustible supply of material that may well be the envy of the cultured.

It was eight o'clock when the anchor was let go in Kilronan Bay, opposite the principal village of the principal island, while the changeless sunshine shone on shallow green water, on dazzling whitewashed cottages, on dark hills and valleys of grey stone. Round the steamer flocked battered punts and tarred canvas corraghs with their bows high out of the water; tanned faces, puckered by the sunlight, stared up from them, and in a storm of Irish the process of disembarking began – the phrase but feebly expresses the spectacle of a kitchen table lowered from the deck and laid on its back in a corragh, or the feat of placing an old woman sitting in the table with a gander in her lap. The corragh has no keel, and a sneeze is rightly believed to be fatal to its equilibrium, but an Aran old woman and an Aran gander can rush in where Sir Isaac Newton might fear to tread. [...]

A hostelry of two whitewashed stories and a thatched roof faced the pier, and we went thither in search of a car, ordered some days before. The door was open, admitting a flood of sunshine to a narrow passage, on one side of which was a kitchen, on the other a sitting-room, with a wall paper of drab trellis-

From *Some Irish Yesterdays* (1906).

work starred with balls of Reckitt's blue – so it seemed, at least, to eyes blinded by outer glare. It contained chiefly the smell of apples and sour bread proper to rooms of its class, such as in the Isles of Aran seemed impossibly conventional. Train-oil and sealskins would have shed a fitter perfume. Having invoked the household in vain, I essayed the kitchen, where an old man in shirt-sleeves was in the act of eating his breakfast. He regarded me, not without aversion, and continued to share an egg with a child of three years old who stood intent and dirty-faced at his elbow. I waited till a precarious teaspoonful had been lowered into the wide open mouth, and made my inquiry about the car.

'They're out since five o'clock looking for the horse.' Another spoonful of egg trembled in the balance, and entered the speaker's mouth, not without disaster.

I averted my eyes, and asked where the horse was usually kept.

'He does be out on the rocks.' The spoon was pointed out of the window, somewhat peevishly. Looking in the direction indicated, we saw the arid shore of the bay, where, instead of sands, grey stone in platforms and pavements met the blue and glittering tide. From the shore the country rose in haggard slopes of grey stone with rifts of green; cresting the height, one of Aran's many ruined oratories lifted a naked gable in the deep of the sky. A narrow road followed the bend of the bay, glaring white for two shelterless miles; no living thing was visible; the pursuit of the horse must be raging on the other side of the island. It continued for another hour, with what episodes of crag and crevasse can scarcely be imagined; finally a dejected and shaggy captive was led in and was thrust into the shafts of a car.

The drive that followed is not easily forgotten. There were moments when the car seemed to open at all its joints, as if falling asunder from exhaustion; and the shafts swayed and swung like twin bowsprits, the wheels creaked ominously, and one tyre left an undulating line in the gritty dust of the road. On either side spread floors of stone, on which sat parliaments of boulders; we passed a stone platform so large and so level that the addition of three walls has made a creditable ball-alley of it. The walls are said to have been built with money given for the relief of distress in Aran; if so, relief money has often been worse spent in the West of Ireland. The road kept in touch with the coast, the car mounted to higher ground, with the shafts pointing heavenward on either side of the horse's touzled mane. Pale green fields and pale tracts of sand mitigated the tyranny of rock, as the island sloped south-eastward into the rich and wide azure of the sea. A village straggled along the shore, the chief mass of the low white houses clustered round a fragment of bastion and buttress that tells of the days when Cromwell's arm was long enough to grasp even Aran and build a stronghold there, what time the iron entered into the soul of Galway.

Life at the Lodge on the hill during the ten days that followed had aspects that were wholly ideal, and aspects that were unreservedly scullion. The chief windows faced north-east, framing a splendid outlook across a plain of sea to where the Connemara mountains have pitched their tents in a jagged line, pale in the torpid heat of morning, dark at evening against some lengthening creek

125

of sunset. When, at some ten of the clock the rooms in the lonely house had passed from gloaming to darkness, and the paraffin lamp glared smokily at the semi-grand piano and the horsehair sofa, the wild and noble outline of Connemara was still sharp, the gleam behind it still a harbourage for the daylight.

The more elementary needs of the establishment were coped with by a henchwoman from the village below, a middle-aged and taciturn widow, wearing a red checked shawl over her broad chest, a smaller red shawl over her head, an excessively short red homespun skirt, and pampooties. In the early hours of the summer morning her step, muffled in cowhide, traversed the house weightily; in due time followed the entrance of the stable bucket, borne with a slow stride that showed to admiration the grey woollen ankles under the short skirt: her eye rested askance, and not without saturnine humour, upon the weakling of a later civilization who still lay in bed. As the bucket was set down a deep and serious voice uttered the monosyllable 'bath', as colourlessly as the bleat of a sheep, and, with the exit of her sallow face and dreamy blue eyes, the strange, arduous, trifling day began.

Breakfast was not its least achievement, prepared by our own hands at a turf fire that added an aroma of its own to the coffee, and delicately flavoured the hot milk. Owing to a scarcity of saucepans the eggs must be boiled in a portly iron pot and fished from its depths with the tongs, and through all, and impeding all, went the flushed pertinacity of the amateur toast-maker. Dinner was a more serious affair, a strenuous triumph of mind over matter and over the Widow Holloran, a daily despair, by reason of potatoes whose hearts remained harder than Pharaoh's, and chiefly by reason of the dearth of pie-dishes.

'Why wouldn't ye ax Miss O'Regan down in the town for the loan of a pie-dish? Sure she's full up of pie-dishes.' This remarkable information came from Mrs Holloran, but was not acted upon.

After twenty four hours of the ministry of the Widow Holloran, we found the conclusion forced upon us that the Simple Life was far more complicated, and infinitely more exacting than the normal existence of the worldling. To us, nurturing a sulky flame in a gloomy pile of turf, the truly Simple Life resolved itself into two words: good servants. Even the least of Miss Gerraghty's nieces would have been a Godsend; the thought of mutton chops, procurable at any instant, all but brought a dimness to the eye that foresaw a dinner – the third in succession – of American bacon and eggs that tasted of fish. It was in one of the long May twilights that we were waited upon by the man who had, on the hearthrug of Marino Cottage's Front Sitting-room, offered us mutton, sweet as sugar. This time he offered not mutton, but sheep; he produced a sort of subscription list, and invited us to put down our names for any piece we might prefer of an animal which was at the moment nibbling the dainty grass among the boulders. We subscribed, with a shudder which was, as it proved, super-fluous. The subscription list did not fill, and two days afterwards we were told that the matter had fallen through, and if we wanted 'butcher's mate' we must telegraph to Galway. [...]

The ridge of the island runs in table lands of rock, dropping in cliffs to the sea along its south-western face. These heights are level deserts of stone, streaked with soft grass where the yellow vetch blazes and a myriad wild roses lay their petals against the boulders. Yet even these handmaids of the rock are not the tenderest of its surprises. Look down the slits and fissures as you step across them on a May day, and you will see fronds of maiden hair climbing out of the darkness and warm mud below. A month later they will be strong and tall above the surface; the clots of foam may often strike them when, below their platform, the piled-up Atlantic rolls its vastness to the attack, with the cruel green of the up-drawn wave, with the hurl of the pent tons against crag and cliff. But for us, on that May morning, land and sea lay in rapt accord, and the breast of the brimming tide was laid to the breast of the cliff, with a low and broken voice of joy. The walk here became finally and definitely a steeplechase, and those not bred in Galway had better think twice before attempting an Aran stone wall; indeed, when five feet of ponderous and trembling stone lattice work has to be dealt with, the native himself will probably adopt the simpl course of throwing it down, building it up again or not, according to th dictates of conscience. If the explorer survives two hours of this exercise, he wi have reached the fort of Dun Ængus, built in days when Christianity, climbing sunrise, was as yet far below the Irish horizon. Of its kind, it reputed to be as perfect as anything in Europe, but it is an unlovely kind. Thr invertebrate walls of loose stones, eighteen feet high and fifteen feet thic sprawl in a triple horseshoe to the edge of a cliff, which, with its sheer drop three hundred feet to the sea, completes the line of defence. The innermost the three ramparts encloses a windy plateau where, in times of siege, t Firbolg Prince Ængus, son of Huamor, probably enjoyed the society of all t cattle in the island, and of an indefinite number of wives. The outermc rampart girdles eleven acres of rocky hillside, and here the unwearied sava, labour constructed a chevaux-de-frise by wedging slabs and splinters of sto into every crevice. Hardly now, in the intelligent calm of sight-seeing, can t invader make a way through the ankle-breaking confusion, where, in t gloaming centuries before St Patrick, bloody hands clutched the limestoi edges in the death stagger, and matted heads crashed dizzily down, unrecorded death and courage and despair. [...]

With its barbaric novelties of colour, its wild, red-clad women, its backgroun of grey rock, its glare of sunshine, Aran should be a place known to painter but at the first sight of even the sketch book the village street becomes a deser the mothers, spitting to avert the 'bad eye', snatch their children into the houses, and bang their doors. The old women vanish from the door steps, th boys take to the rocks. As it is the creed of Aran that any one that has h 'likeness dhrew out' will die within the year, it seems unfeeling to urge th matter upon them. Here and there the mission shilling makes its convert; a old woman braced herself to the risk on the excellent ground that she woul probably die before the year was out, and might as well make the most of he chances. She found the idea highly humorous, and so did several of the neighbour:

Our departure from Aran was not out of keeping with the general run of events there. Struggling with painting materials, plants of maidenhair fern, and the usual oversights and overflows of packing, scantily enveloped in newspaper, we made our way on foot from the Lodge to the bay below it, a distance of some two or three hundred yards, and there embarked, attended to the boat by Mrs Holloran and her next of kin – in other words, a crowd of some twenty deeply interested persons. We had shoved off and were moving out towards the steamer over the transparent green deeps of the bay, when I remembered the little boy who had driven our portmanteaux down to the beach in a donkey cart, and I flung a shilling to one of the next-of-kin in settlement of the obligation. We saw the emissary present the tribute.

'He'll not take it!' was shouted from the shore.

I protested at the full pitch of my voice to the effect that he must not allow his magnanimity to interfere with his just dues, that I was very glad to give it to him.

'He'll take three!' travelled to us like a cannon ball across the translucent water.

Nothing travelled back. Nothing, that is, except the Galway steamer, which presently flapped its paddles into the falling tide, and took us away to regions where we ourselves were natives, and viewed the tourist with a proper hauteur.

Meditating on those May days, winnowed now of their husk of culinary difficulties, they seem the most purely lonely, the most crowded with impressions, that could befall. Habituated to the stillness of West Galway life, these stillnesses were vast and expressive beyond any previous experience of mine; in the shadeless brilliance, the bare greyness, I breathed a foreign and tingling air. The people's profoundly self-centred existence has 'no thoroughfare' written across it; lying on the warm rocks, they see Ireland stretched silent, enigmatic, apart from them, and are content that it is so. Their poverty is known to many, their way of thought to a few; they remain motionless on the edge of Europe, with the dust of the saints beneath their feet.

Pádraic Ó Maoláin

Aristotle and His Wife

Aristotle was very wise and very intelligent but he didn't like women at all. He hated them so much he wouldn't let any of them near him to look after him. A man minded his house for him, cooked for him and did everything he needed. A woman used to come by the house and herself and the boy often spoke together, talking about Aristotle and the hatred he had for women. Finally, they decided between them that they would play a trick on him so he would have to marry. The boy used to bring him his breakfast in bed every morning and they decided between them that the woman would put the boy's clothes on and go into him with the breakfast, and when the boy had got her in, he would close the door on her and she would start crying and shouting, saying that Aristotle was keeping her in and he would run and bring back a lawman.

The next morning the woman went in dressed in men's clothes and she went to the side of Aristotle's bed with his breakfast. The boy locked the door outside and ran to look for a lawman. She started shouting inside, saying that she was being kept by Aristotle against her will. It wasn't long until the lawman came and she got her story in first. The lawman's verdict was that Aristotle would have to marry her or she would have a strong case against him in court. Sooner than have it brought to law, Aristotle agreed to marry her but said he would have the right to send her away from him if ever he found fault with her. She agreed to that but added to the bargain herself that whenever he sent her away from him that she would be allowed to take away with her any three loads she wanted when she went. That bargain was agreed between them and they got married.

Things continued like that for a while afterwards until they had a child. It wasn't long after that Aristotle began to hate her, and he also suspected that she and the boy were too friendly. Finally he spoke to the boy and told him he would put him to death but that he would give him three chances to save his life. He told him to come to him the next morning, at sunrise, wearing his shoes and socks and not wearing them, his hat on his head and not on his head at the same time.

The boy thought he was finished, but despite that he went to the woman

Published in *Béaloideas III* (1932). Translated from the Irish.

and told her what the master had said to him. The woman advised him and explained to him how he could do as he was ordered. The next morning, at sunrise, he knocked on the door of Aristotle's room. He was ordered to come into the room. In he went, a sock on one foot, the other up as far as his ankle, one shoe hanging loose, the other shoe in his hand and his hat hanging off one ear. Aristotle got up and looked at him closely. He saw his get-up and said: 'You win today but be here tomorrow morning at sunrise wearing your clothes and not wearing them!'

The boy went off and got the woman's advice again. She again explained to him how he could work it and, the next day, at sunrise, he presented himself to Aristotle. He had one arm in his shirt, the rest of the shirt hanging off him, the other arm in his waistcoat and his coat drawn up over his shoulders without any arm in it. He had one leg in his trousers and the rest dragging after him. Aristotle got out of bed and saw him. 'You win today, my lad' he said 'but be here for me tomorrow morning riding and not riding!'

The boy went off then, sadly, because he thought he was finished now more than ever, because he didn't know how in the world he could be riding and not riding. He went to the woman anyway and told her the story. She advised him to go up a nearby mountain and bring back the strongest billy-goat he could find there. The boy went off and brought back a billy-goat as big as a small donkey. He put reins and a saddle on him and got up on its back. When he chose to he could put his feet on the ground and when he drew up his legs, he was just like a horse rider. In he went to the door of Aristotle's room the next morning, at sunrise, and knocked on the door. 'I'm here as you ordered, master' he said. Aristotle came out to look at him. 'I am riding' he said, drawing up his legs, 'and I'm not riding' he said, placing his feet on the ground and taking his weight off the billy-goat's back. 'You win' said Aristotle, 'my blessing to you but my curse on the mouth that taught you! It's not your fault but my wife who is giving you advice, but I'll soon settle her!'

He went to his wife straight away and ordered her to clear out as quickly as she could, that he wouldn't put up with her any longer. 'I'll do that' she said 'but remember the bargain we had – any day you sent me away I would have permission to take away with me any three loads I chose.' 'That'll do' said Aristotle, 'in you go and take your three loads and clear off out of my sight!' She took the child with her as the first load and put it in a safe place. That upset Aristotle a lot because he was very fond of the child. She came the second time and took all that she could carry of gold and silver, clothes and everything else she wanted. She went in the third time and she looked up and down all around the house for a while, pretending that she was looking for something. Aristotle was standing in the middle of the floor and she marched up to him. 'Oh' she said, 'I don't see anything else in the house I'd rather have than you. Here, hop up on my back.' 'If that's how things are' he said 'wouldn't you be as well off bringing back the two loads you took out? We'd be better off staying where we are rather than going anywhere else and maybe we'll get on better from now on.'

Thomas Mason

The Aran Islands

We disembarked at Kilronan, the chief village of the largest island, Inishmore, and proceeded towards the village of Killeany where we judged by observation, as we approached on the steamer, that we might get a suitable camping-ground. We pitched our tent near the stump of an ancient round tower in a field that gave promise of a secure hold for the guy-ropes, for we knew from experience that the wind from the west can be devastating to small tents.

We slept well and arose about 7 a.m. When we emerged from the tent we were astonished to find a number of the inhabitants grouped at a short distance in a semicircle around the tent. This occurred for several mornings and we felt bashful in carrying out our toilet to such a gallery. We could not understand the reason for this performance and it was only when we had been resident for some days that we discovered the cause. We were camping, quite unconsciously, on holy ground and the locals believed that we would be 'dead in the morning.' As we survived they concluded that we must be saints and thereafter we were welcome everywhere. This is the only occasion on which I have been mistaken for a saint, although once before, in the dusk, I was credited with being a fairy.

The islanders had never seen a tent. One man told us that he had once seen a tent at Milltown Races in County Clare, 'but', said he, 'it wasn't a little tent like yours, it was a big tent where they sold drink.' One woman expressed her alarm and horror at gentlemen like us sleeping in such a flimsy contraption and exclaimed, 'Great God Almighty, does your mother not be afraid of your catching cold?'[...]

The Aran Islands are a storehouse of great archaeological and antiquarian interest. The remains embrace the prehistoric, early Christian and medieval periods. Perhaps the most interesting objects are the forts which are supposed to date from about the beginning of the Christian era. They are all built of loose stones without mortar; some are circular or oval, others, known as cliff forts, are built across headlands where the steep cliffs render them secure from attack on the seaward side. The most imposing of the cliff forts is Dun Aengus on

From *The Islands of Ireland* (1936).

Inishmore which has been described as 'the most magnificent barbaric monument now extant in Europe.' Approaching from the village of Kilmurvey the ground rapidly rises, for here the island is only about three-quarters of a mile wide, and one soon arrives at the first line of defence, a wall enclosing a large area with further defences inside, the most formidable being a *chevaux de frise* about fifty feet wide formed of large stones set upright in the ground. It is no easy job to traverse this barrier even in a leisurely manner. When the attackers had passed through the *chevaux de frise* they had still to surmount another rampart about twelve feet high and finally the citadel wall, which is eighteen feet high. The inner faces of the walls have platforms of a lower height than the external surface on which the defenders took their stand.

The entrances through the different defences never faced in a straight line, so that they could not be rushed, and the doorway in the last wall is less than five feet high and only three and a half feet wide. All the defences are on rising ground, and when one takes into account the primitive methods of warfare of these early times this wonderful fort would appear to be impregnable; and it would need to be so, as there was no possibility of escape for the defenders if it were taken. A sheer cliff is its boundary and defence on the western side.

In none of these forts could I find any trace of a water supply, so they must only have been used as a place for retirement at night when the cattle could be driven inside the outer walls, or as a place of temporary refuge during a sudden raid.

On one occasion when I passed through the doorway into the central open space of the fort I was astonished to see a man fishing. He was sitting with his feet dangling over the edge of the cliff, which is undercut and at this point three hundred feet high. I went forward and lay down flat, peering over the edge, and I was puzzled to know how he could feel a bite at the end of such a long thick line that was vibrated by the wind. The explanation, 'When I do see the line moving into the rocks at the bottom I know there is a fish on it,' solved the mystery.

As he spoke the line moved rapidly and he proceeded to pull it up and landed two bream. Before I left he had half-filled the creel with large fish averaging about four pounds each.

The sinker was a large stone weighing several pounds. When he was ready to throw out his line again he warned me and I lay flat. Whirling about fifteen feet of line around his head, the weight of the stone soon gave it an almost incredible velocity. I was fascinated, and when the line had left his hand and reached the surface of the water I was surprised to see how close it was to the rocks at the base of the cliff. I offered him a fill of tobacco which he accepted and whilst filling his pipe he tied the line to one of his feet, which appeared to me a dangerous proceeding. I remarked, 'If you caught a conger eel now, he would pull you in,' to which the reply, 'He would so, sir,' seemed to partake of that spirit of fatalism so common in Ireland and exemplified in the expression 'It was to be,' commonly used after the occurrence of some calamity. [...]

On my latest visit to Inishmore I went as the guest of Mr Robert Flaherty, who was then engaged in the production of his wonderful film, *Man of Aran*. It was very enjoyable as I renewed old friendships and made new acquaintances.

Pat Mullen, who was Mr Flaherty's chief of staff for local affairs, had spent some years in the USA, but few of the other islanders had ever previously seen the movies. One man said that he would not believe anything he saw on the screen because he once saw a man fall out of a fifth-story window and bounce back again and 'that wasn't possible'. Another, speaking of Mr Flaherty, said, 'I don't know where he gets all the money; ye'd think he was digging it out of the sand.'

The whole of Mr Flaherty's establishment was invited to a wedding, and as I had never been at an Aran wedding I availed myself of the opportunity. The procession from church was headed by several outside cars followed by a number of ponies, each of which carried two men. The cars drove at a furious pace and everybody was loudly cheering and wildly waving handkerchiefs or scarves.

The bride was a small woman who had been to America and, having saved some money, had come home for a holiday. She was dressed in a blue costume, thin stockings and light shoes; she wore a necklace, and her appearance was in strong contrast to that of the other women. It is hard to realise how she could remain contented with life in a cottage on the island, but such marriages frequently occur and always turn out well. The bridegroom was a magnificent specimen of manhood. He possessed a cottage and some land, and as the bride had some money the match was an eminently suitable one. Match-making is undertaken on the island by friends of the families or by the parents, and hard bargains are driven before consent is given. I heard of one case where a young woman inherited a cottage and some good land from a relative. The bride was well endowed but the 'boy's' parents – all men are called boys until they are married – either had not enough cash or would not give the requisite amount. The haggling went on for a long time with no definite result. Meantime a well-to-do neighbour, seeing the hitch in the negotiations, went to Galway and sent a cable to his son in America. He was afraid to be seen sending the cable from Aran for fear the news might leak out and cause gossip. The son was home in less than three weeks, his father paid the requisite amount and the young people were married shortly afterwards.

One would imagine that marriages arranged in this fashion would not turn out well, but the fact is that one seldom hears of unhappy unions. No divorce is possible in the Irish Free State and although this has a bearing on the matter it is not the sole reason.

These simple peasants have to work hard, they accept all the responsibilities of life, and in the daily round and common task they learn a spirit of give and take which ultimately, when the children arrive, ripens into an affection which survives all their vicissitudes and binds the family life with ties which are very strong and beautiful.

But to return to our wedding party: on our way to the reception I had an interesting conversation with a fellow passenger on the car. We were talking about modern life, and my friend, an island man who had been in the USA, wound up the discussion by stating: 'The successful business man is an idiot,' and, pointing to the ground, 'the nearer a man is to that the happier he is.' These are profound truths, which in the fever of modern life are often not realised until it is too late – 'for what is a man profited if he shall gain the whole world and lose his own soul?'

When we arrived at the cottage the place was thronged; refreshments consisting of strong tea, another more potent liquid, and cake and currant bread were dispensed by the bride and groom in one of the smaller rooms. In the living-room music and dancing were kept up for about five hours and then a number of the guests went to a wake which was being held in another house about a mile away.

I left early and walked home. I was afraid to wait for the car as I knew the other passengers were going to the wake, and, although I am a teetotaller, I had not the moral courage to offend the relatives by refusing the liquid refreshments which I knew would be pressed on me.

The wake lasted for two days and nights. The deceased was an old woman, and one man, describing the wake to me afterwards, said: 'They speeded her well on her journey.' Since then a 'mission' has been held on the island and spirits are absolutely forbidden at wakes. I hope the reform will last. [...]

I had the good luck to be staying on Inishmaan immediately previous to the great spring fair in Galway to which the islanders send their live stock. Some of the buyers came from Galway in order to forestall the fair, but the islandmen are shrewd judges, and if they are not offered what they consider to be a good price they accompany their cattle on the steamer to Galway where their beasts always command top price.

When a deadlock is reached in the bargaining a third party tries to close the deal by compromise. I remember 'listening in' to a deal which was not successful. When all efforts had failed to bridge the difference between the price demanded and the price offered by the buyer, the third party said to one of the principals: 'Ye are too hard altogether,' to which the latter replied: 'Hard! Is it me that's hard? The softest part of him is his teeth.'

The day of the shipping of the cattle is the great day of the year. All ordinary work ceases, even the children do not attend school, and for hours previous to the arrival of the steamer there is a bustle and excitement quite foreign to the usual tranquillity of the island life. Down the single road of the island come numbers of pigs and cattle. The former are generally in charge of small boys who drive them down to the slip where men are waiting who, having tied their feet together, carry them on their backs to the currachs, the whole process being accompanied by an unearthly squealing from the unfortunate pigs. When the currach is loaded it has to be rowed about a mile and a half to a position where the steamer will anchor.

There is no harbour on the island and the cattle have to be shipped from a strand. I had no difficulty in finding my way, for the route was thronged with women carrying enormous loads. The creels on their backs contained, in addition to food for their husbands who were making the journey to Galway a best suit of clothes, spare socks, drawers, etc. On top of the creels were tied sacks of wool and frequently a small hand-basket containing eggs and butter was also carried.

When I arrived on the strand the scene was extraordinary. One was reminded of the cattle hostings about which one reads in early Irish literature.

The steamer had not yet arrived and the women in their red skirts and different coloured shawls were sitting on the creels; the men were standing apart in groups, there were innumerable cattle and an occasional horse was to be seen. The whole population seemed to be gathered on the large strand, the children rejoicing in their freedom from school, and men who had no beasts to ship had come to help their neighbours to control the cattle, for sometimes, terrified by the noise and shouting, they run amuck. I was warned of the danger, and it was not an idle warning, for I saw a man thrown fifteen feet through the air by a terrified heifer.

When the steamer arrived the real work of the day began. A long rope was tied around the head of the animal and other ropes were fastened in a loop around its body. It was hustled by shouting men and barking dogs to the edge of the sea. Sometimes it refused to budge and the men had to drag or push it; terrified, it rushed wildly into the sea and was pulled into deep water by the rope fastened to its head, the end of which was held by a man in the stern of a currach. The cattle made no attempt to swim and the nostrils were kept over the water by the man in the currach, who, leaning over the stern, clasped his arms round the neck of the beast.

On arrival at the steamer an iron hook was lowered which the man in the currach placed in the loop of the rope fastened about the body. In order to fasten the hook the man in the currach had to release his hold of the animal's head, when it invariably sinks for a few moments. This is a critical time as, if the job is bungled, the beast may drown. When the unfortunate animal is raised from the sea and dumped in the vessel, sometimes it is so exhausted that it is unable to stand, and on one occasion a bull which had struggled fiercely dropped dead.

Frequently the animal refuses to enter the sea and lies down on the strand. When this occurs the men drag it to the edge of the water, and it invariably dashes into the water when a wave breaks over its nostrils.

The whole operation constitutes a great hardship to both men and beasts. The men do not think of themselves, but they are concerned about their cattle. As one man remarked to me, ''Tis a great hardship on the poor beasts, but we can't help it. What can we do? Sure we have no harbour.' The noise throughout the performance is terrific, everybody is shouting in Irish, the dogs are barking and the excitement is intense.

IV

Aran Writers

*F*or many years before the appearance of
Liam O'Flaherty's first novel, Thy Neighbour's Wife, *in 1923 the people of Aran
were used to being written about by visiting journalists, scholars and antiquarians. But
'creative' writings were the most controversial.*

News from Dublin of the riots that greeted the first Abbey Theatre production of
The Playboy of the Western World *would merely have reminded the islanders of
Synge's stay on Inis Meáin, his uncle Alexander's adventures while serving as rector on
Inis Mór and the true story on which the play was very loosely based. But the* Playboy
*and the riots were like the sound of distant gunfire. The play was not seen by the people
of Inis Meáin until performed in the local community hall by Galway's Druid theatre
company in October 1982, and they loved it.*

Thy Neighbour's Wife *was different. Here was an islander (Willie Mhaidhc,
as he was known locally) writing about the seamier side of life in a work in which most
characters, from the parish priest to the more colourful eccentrics, were instantly
recognizable. The Catholic clergy particularly resented the way they were portrayed and
exerted pressure on those of the author's relatives who still lived on Inis Mór. The roving
author continued his sniping from a safe distance and returned home occasionally to
collect more ammunition.*

*Liam O'Flaherty and his brother Tom owed a lot to their teacher, David
O'Callaghan. He taught them to write their native Irish as well as the compulsory
English, organized Liam's secondary education at Rockwell College in Tipperary and
almost secured Tom a place in Summerhill College, Sligo, through the generosity of Sir
Roger Casement, who was impressed by the boy's intelligence when he visited the school in
Fearann an Choirce.* Skerrett, *one of Liam O'Flaherty's best novels, was based on
David O'Callaghan's feud with the parish priest and school manager, Canon Murty
Farragher.*

*Tom went to America and became a radical socialist journalist. His health failed
and he returned to Ireland to write sketches of island life, in English, and some short
stories, in Irish, before his death.*

*Pat Mullen also emigrated at an early age and was converted to socialism in
America. He appears thinly disguised in* Thy Neighbour's Wife. *Aside from his
writings he became one of Inis Mór's best-known inhabitants and Robert Flaherty's
right-hand man and chronicler of the making of* Man of Aran.

*Máirtín Ó Direáin, on the other hand, was shy and apolitical, and left Inis Mór
as a boy to work in the post office in Galway. He devoted his life to poetry, exclusively
in his mother-tongue, and wrote a handful of essays, published under the title* Feamainn
Bhealtaine *('May Seaweed').*

*The sea, in all its moods and manifestations, plays a major role in the writings of
islanders. It also influenced the American writer and journalist, James Brendan
Connolly, whose parents emigrated to Boston from the village of Mainistir, Inis Mór, in
about 1870. His stories about sailors and fishermen off the north-east coast of America
were very popular at the turn of the century. However, he is now best remembered as the
first winner of a modern Olympic gold medal at the revived games in Athens in 1896.
His prowess in the triple jump proved more enduring than his hundreds of sea stories.*

Liam O'Flaherty

WINTER

In winter all things die. So roared the sea around the shores of Inverara. To the
west beyond Rooruck it was black with dim fountains of white foam rising here
and there as a wave formed and came towering to the beach. To the north,
between Inverara and the mainland, it was white, like the waters of a mountain
torrent, white with wide strips of green as if it had got sick and vomited. To the
south it was black with a belt of white along the shore beneath the cliffs, where
the breakers lashed the rocks. To the east beyond Kilmillick, where the north
and south met in the narrow channel athwart the Head of Crom, it was a
seething cauldron, hissing like a wounded snake. And around Rooruck it
roared in mad delight.

Winter had come. The sea was wrecking all that had generated in spring,
flowered in summer and borne fruit in autumn. It tore huge rocks from its
bosom and sent them rumbling through the deep. It hurled weeds shorewards
in a tumbling mass. They lined the beaches in mounds mixed with sand and
the carcasses of dogfish. It struck the cliffs monstrous blows that shook them
and sent the rockbirds screaming from their clefts. They soared wildly out,
their eyes searching the foam for fish.

In winter all things die. So shrieked the wind coming over the sea from the
west. It rose from the sea and whirled upwards over the land. It mounted the
wall of boulders that protected Rooruck on the west. It skirted the Hill of Fate
that guarded Rooruck on the south. It swept eastwards, flying straight in its
fury between earth and sky, blasting the earth. The grass was plucked up by the
roots. Sheep fled bleating, seeking shelter among the crags. Horses neighed
and ran in terror, their nostrils red. The goats wandering on the cliffs snorted
and ran eastwards to the hollow beyond Coillnamken. The fowls in the crops
cackled and hid their heads among their feathers. Dogs howled. Pigs grunted
and then huddled close together in their straw, whining. Old men sitting by
the fires in their cabins shivered and felt that their death was near.

In winter all things die. The rain carried on the wind fell in great black
drops that pattered on the crags and rose again in a blue mist. It came from the

From *The Black Soul* (1924).

140

darkened sky sparse and scattered as if the clouds had been disembowelled in mid-air and only fragments of them had reached the earth terrified. There was no moon. It was hidden by the torn clouds. And the stars shone dimly in twos and threes, scattered over the firmament.

Thy Neighbour's Wife I

All's well that ends well, and Inverara ended in Kilmurrage and Kilmurrage ended in the Pier, which was a fine place – the finest place in Inverara. It stretched out into the waters of the little bay of Kilmurrage, like a spear-head casting defiance at the whole world. It was finely built, all ferro-concrete, with iron ladders down the sides, and iron bitts for mooring purposes, and a promenade and a big warehouse belonging to the steamship company. There was a refreshment room set up in a corner of the warehouse, just as one might see at a big railway station in Dublin, where one could get a cup of coffee, steaming hot, in the cold weather, with four large slices of home-made bread, with a raisin here and there, from Mrs Devaney for the small sum of threepence; and in summer, when the weather was hot, there was a real Italian woman from the Big Town on the Mainland, selling lemonade and ice cream wafers – not one of these second-hand Italian people, who talk good English and dress just the same as everybody else, but a dark-faced woman with a multi-coloured shawl around her neck, and knowing only enough English to make the proper change for a sixpence, and to make the lemonade, so weak that 'it wouldn't knock down a flea', as Johnny Grealish said.

It was a fine place, the finest place in Inverara. In winter perhaps it was dreary, when there were no fishing boats, or turf boats from the mainland, or tourists, but in summer during the 'season' in Inverara, it was the gayest place on earth, at least so they said in Inverara.

And Inverara was proud of the Pier. Kilmurrage in particular, being the legitimate proprietor of the Pier, stuck up its head at the rest of the world. Though without the Pier Kilmurrage was a poor place. It couldn't exactly be called a town and yet it was larger than a village, and it was the capital of Inverara. But a town, in order to be a town, must have streets, and Kilmurrage had no streets, properly speaking. It started off well enough, presumably with the intention of having streets, up at the schoolmaster's house on its western outskirts, but it soon gave up the endeavour. After coming down in a straight line, with six houses on each side, as far as the police barracks, it suddenly ended. Possibly there was some old law against streets in Kilmurrage and that the police deliberately stopped the movement, though the RIC barracks itself did not look very law-abiding. The badge that hung over the door, the harp with a crown over it, had fallen all to one side, as if it were drunk and disorderly. Some said it was that way, as an advertisement for drunkenness, so that the police could get something to do and get a chance of promotion. But

From *Thy Neighbour's Wife* (1923).

the police themselves were a sufficient advertisement for drunkenness without the harp. But that's away from the point.

The street stopped at the police barracks, and beyond the police barracks there was nothing for some dozen yards but a potato garden and the ruins of a large wooden hut that an enterprising gentleman from the Big Town on the Mainland had erected to do duty as a Cinema Theatre. The enterprise was of course a failure, for the theatre was wrecked during the first performance, owing to Pat Farelly coming in drunk, and being under the impression that the murder of the heroine by the villain was real, and being a chivalrous gentleman, brandished his stick and led a mass attack on the screen. So there was the hut, never been used since, rotting in the sun, a monument to the prowess of Farelly.

Then came a row of labourers' cottages, right across the ruins of the cinema, and this row of cottages ended in Mulligan's public-house, a building that would have ruined the most respectable street, for there were empty porter barrels always lying outside in the roadway, in everybody's way, and people sitting on them drinking porter, and stopping everything that passed to have a talk. Then came the court-house and the dispensary, jumbled up in a corner, behind the new house that a shopkeeper had built as a residence for the curate, though the curate had never used it. It was too big, and he could neither afford to pay the rent nor the upkeep on the small sum that the parish priest allowed him. So the big house had the blinds drawn on it all the time, in summer and winter. A miserable-looking place, almost as miserable as the court-house, its neighbour, which was hardly ever used either, because the police were generally too drunk to bring anybody to court, and even if they did bring forward a case of trespass or assault and battery, 'it was the divil itsel' ov a job to git the magisthrate to come and thry it,' as Sergeant Donagan was fond of saying over his pint in Mulligan's.

This brought Kilmurrage as far as the Hill, and after that it would be impossible to describe it. Taking the court-house as the centre, it branched off in all directions, going a few yards in a straight line, and then ending suddenly in a potato patch, or a cul-de-sac, or a wooden hoarding, or the new store that Jim Shanaghan was building at the back of the Post Office. It ran around corners like a man trying to get away from the police, and it was as crooked as a drunken man in a gale of wind. It had seven different street levels, which was a great achievement for a small town like it. The lowest level was reached by the residence of the Protestant minister, a beautiful place surrounded by trees, in a glen, and the highest level was reached by the parochial house, where Fr O'Reilly the parish priest lived. The natives of Kilmurrage, being ninety-nine and a half per cent Catholic, reasoned from this contrast that the Protestant vicar was down in the hollow because he was well on the road to Hell, and the parish priest was on a height because he was well on the road to Heaven.

However, all's well that ends well, and Kilmurrage ended in the Pier. A wide, level, pretty limestone road stretched from the town to the Pier, along the shore of the harbour, and on a steamer day, when the *Duncairn* came on her thrice-a-week trips, weather and other circumstances permitting, from the Big

Town on the Mainland, that road was crowded by an endless stream of people going down to the Pier. The steamer days were the most important days in the life of Kilmurrage, and even in the life of Inverara, and on those days everybody who was not bedridden, or extremely busy, came to the Pier to await the arrival of the steamer, to do their business or just to hear the news and have a look at the new-comers.

In the summer time there was always somebody of importance coming on the *Duncairn*. One day it would be Fr So and So, coming to preach a mission to the young on temperance or some such popular subject. Another day it would be an official from the Congested Districts Board, coming to find out what the islanders could be induced to pay for the land, or whether they could be induced to pay anything at all. Another day it would be a committee from the Geographical Society, coming to examine the ancient ruins. Another day it would be an organizer from the United Irish League, come to 'rally Inverara to a man behind the Home Rule Programme'. Another day it would be a party of Gaelic League propagandists in kilts and spectacles and long hair, Smiths and Joneses and Hodges and von Strakers, urging the islanders to cultivate 'the language of the ancient Gael, which they had inherited from their proud forefathers'. Another day it would be somebody coming from the United States, or the District Inspector of Police, or the naval officer coming to examine the coastguards. There was always somebody coming.

A stream of people would wander down to the Pier an hour or more before the steamer's arrival. Groups of young girls, without their hats, would skip along arm in arm, laughing and talking. Cissy might expect a new hat from the Big Town on the Mainland, or Mary might expect her sister home from the convent, or Susie might expect her older brother, who was away in a college in Dublin 'going to be a priest for the foreign mission'. The shopkeepers and the publicans had to be down on the Pier, so that they could quarrel with the captain and the steamship company's agent, about paying the freight, and about whether their goods were entered correctly on the ship's manifest, and stand around, making a fuss while their goods were unloaded, so that nobody could steal anything, though nobody ever stole anything in Inverara, except a commercial traveller, who once stole fifty pounds from the till of Mrs Moroney's public-house, while Mrs Moroney was at the door talking to a neighbour.

Then the Protestant minister and his wife came down there. The wife, a pretty up-to-date kind of a woman, with a perky nose and a painted face, looked far more respectable than her husband, the vicar. The vicar was a sleepy individual, always wandering around talking to himself and reading Greek literature. They said that he was a brilliant man at college but that residence in Inverara had turned his intellect into incipient idiocy, and if the stories told about him were even in part true, the idiocy instead of being incipient was highly developed. Before his marriage he had lived alone in the vicarage, without any servants, and the place, under his sole control, had gone to rack and ruin; to such an extent that a carpenter who had gone to mend a staircase found the vicar lying on his back on a couch reading the *Wasps* of Aristophanes, while two hounds and a donkey shared with him the room. Of course, it might be asked how did the carpenter know that he was reading the *Wasps* of Aristophanes? And the fact that Mr Blake told the story, in the first place, and could not remember the name of the carpenter, although there were only two in the whole of Inverara, does not render the story very credible. There was also the story that he, the vicar, told John Sweeney that a mountain in India was three hundred and twenty-seven feet higher than the moon, but he might have said that to make fun of Sweeney, who was a religious maniac. Still the vicar was a silly fellow, a very silly fellow.

The hotel-keepers came to the Pier also, and the agent of the Glasgow merchants who bought the kelp, and everybody, in fact, who on any pretext whatsoever could claim to have business with the steamer *Duncairn*. The schoolmasters and the schoolmistresses were there, in a compact group, away from the rest of the people, as befitted people of their intellectual importance, talking about their schools, and the good looks of the inspectors, and the clergy and the shameless way the British Government and the National Board of Education paid their school teachers. They were very careful to keep apart from the common or garden islanders from the west of Inverara, 'the natives', as Mrs Cassidy the doctor's wife called them, who stood around in the background sheepishly, in their rawhide pampootees and thick homespun garments, looking down at the fishing boats, scratching their heads and spitting zealously, while they discussed the weather, fishing, and the price of pigs.

But all these people merged into the background when compared with Fr O'Reilly, the parish priest, and the most important man in Inverara. His was always the position of importance on the Pier, standing out in front, down at the far end, where the *Duncairn* came alongside, with the principal people around him, talking. On steamer days, when he stood down at the end of the Pier, he looked like a well-bred English country gentleman, and many people said he greatly resembled a fox-hunting squire, standing on his hearthrug before a roaring log fire, with fox-terriers scattered around the room, and the local gentry singing 'Tally ho! Tally ho!' or whatever they do sing. He was a tall man and well built, except for the prominence of his waistcoat at the fifth button, where it bulged into a rotund point, and made him look slightly, very slightly of course, like a cask with head, arms and legs attached to it. Apart from that, he was a fine-looking man. His head was firmly placed on his shoulders and always thrown back at a decorative angle, showing his firm jaw, piercing blue eyes and broad forehead to perfection. His hair had turned grey, but it was a greyness that suited the rest of him, a greyness that could be associated with a well-fed body, and the due respect given to fifty-one years of age, by a parish priest who knew that his reputation for sanctity was secure, as secure as his bank account, which ran well into four figures sterling. His rosy cheeks showed that he had good health. His fleshiness, which was not too apparent, showed that he had a good appetite, and the reddish tinge in his nose, and the pimple on the tip of it, showed according to his enemies that he was a 'little fond of the bottle'.

Whether he was or not, he was a clever man, the cleverest man in Inverara.

The people said he was the best man that ever came to the island since Fr
McBride, who had built the Pier. They claimed that it was due to his efforts
that the Congested Districts Board purchased the land from the landlord,
though of course it was the Land League agitation did that. Then they pointed
to the fishing industry with tears in their eyes. There it was 'on a sound
business footing' (to use Fr O'Reilly's own words) and it was all due to Fr
O'Reilly. He got the harbour blessed by the archbishop, and he got a committee of the Board of Fisheries to do something with the fishing grounds,
plant seeds there or something (nobody knew definitely what the committee
did beyond drinking whisky in Shaughnessy's hotel). Whether as a result of the
archbishop's blessing, or the planting of seeds by the Board of Fisheries, there
were good catches of fish every year since.

Further, Fr O'Reilly allowed the fishermen to break the Sabbath when
there was a glut of fish. So he was popular, extremely popular. He was popular
with the fishermen, with the 'natives', with the business men of Kilmurrage,
with the officials of the Congested Districts Board, with the officers of the law
– in fact, with everybody.

Of course he had enemies. Everybody has enemies, even in Inverara. And
those enemies of Fr O'Reilly claimed that 'he made a good thing out of
Inverara'. They pointed to the fact that when he came to Inverara he was as poor
as a church mouse, only a few years ordained, with a large circle of poor
relations hanging on to his coat tails, so to speak. And he was now a wealthy
man, measuring wealth of course by Inverara standards. He had married his
sister Ellen to Charles Bodkin the Government contractor, who was a man of
good social position, and a man who had a pull with 'the Government'. Of
course, the marriage was in a way unfortunate, since Bodkin died within a year
after his marriage, and his will showed that he left only a mass of debts, and his
estate outside Kilmurrage had to be sold by auction, but Fr O'Reilly saved
something out of it. Then there was the house that the islanders built for him,
as a mark of their appreciation. It was the finest house in Inverara, fitted out
with all the modern conveniences, even with electric light. However, the
electric light was a failure, being a hotch-potch affair, that went out when it
was most wanted, just like the night when the archbishop was dining at the
parochial house, during confirmation time, and they had to finish the dinner
with candlelight.

It was said too that Fr O'Reilly got considerable sums from the Government officials for his services in bringing the islanders to heel in the matter of
payment of rents. But the large sums that he received legitimately would make
it very improbable that he would descend to low means for the purpose of
swelling his bank account. If he accepted money from the publicans in return
for keeping the sale of potheen within reasonable limits, it was the reward of
just efforts, and why should not a priest be rewarded for so doing as well as a
policeman? And who had a better right to reward him than the publicans who
profited by these acts? But there it is. Evil-minded people like John Carmody,
who came back from the United States a Socialist and an agnostic, were always
in search of some scandal to cast a blemish on the fair fame of the parish priest.

Fr O'Reilly was the most important man in Inverara and what was more he was a coming man. His star was in the ascendant. He had just married his niece Lily to Mr McSherry, who had just come back from South America, 'rotten with money'. He had loads of it. He had built a great new house at Coill Namhan on the American plan, with a flat roof, and had brought an architect all the way from England to plan it. Ten thousand pounds it had cost, every penny of it, even though he had most of the materials for building, stone and sand, on the land he had bought, just beside the site of the house. And now he had married Fr O'Reilly's niece.

Of course Mr McSherry was fifty-five if he was a year, and the niece, Lily O'Reilly, was only a young girl of twenty-one, just after leaving the National University in Dublin, but what could the poor girl expect. It was hard enough for the poor girl to get wealth without expecting youth into the bargain they said in Inverara, for Lily had absolutely nothing of her own, not a stitch of clothes to her back they said, and her uncle had paid for her schooling, and maintained her since her mother died when Lily was a little girl of ten.

So here was Fr O'Reilly, fifty-one, the most important man in Inverara and bound to be bishop one day, as soon as Bishop Donnelly, a doddering old man, died and made room for a successor. Here he was standing on the edge of the Pier at Kilmurrage, on Saturday the 22nd of June, with the *Duncairn* puffing along towards the Pier, waiting for the arrival of his niece and her husband, back from their honeymoon trip on the Continent. Fr O'Reilly spread his legs wider that day. His look was more dominant than usual. He was crustier and more condescending in his answers to the drivel, with which the Protestant vicar was trying to engage his attention, about the decline of classical education in the Irish schools.

The *Duncairn* drew alongside. The captain on the bridge shouted to the mate on the fo'c'sle head. The company's agent on the Pier, a long lanky fellow, with boots three sizes too big for him, and a moustache that got mixed up with his tongue when he tried to talk, bustled around telling everybody to get out of 'the bloomin' way'. A line was cast ashore. The steamer was made fast. There were calls from the Pier to those aboard the ship. Handkerchiefs were waved. The women giggled. The captain, a handsome fellow with a fair moustache, puffed out his chest and smirked at everybody, in an endeavour to make the most of that moment of importance of coming alongside. Then the gangway was fixed into position and the passengers began to come ashore. Young pigs began to shriek in the hold. A swarm of men and boys struggled over the side and began to hustle around the cargo, and finally Mr McSherry and his wife appeared from the cabin and walked on to the deck.

*

SPRING

Winter died with a melancholy roar of all the elements. For three days storm-driven rain fell furiously on Inverara, while the exhausted sea writhed in the death agony of its winter madness. Then the sun rose in an arc of shimmering light south of the Head of Crom. It shot out its myriad tentacles over the sea and land. It sent out a heatless invigorating light. The sea danced, rippling, and hummed a tune like the sound of insects breathing on a weed-covered rock, as it tossed against the cliffs. Inverara, washed by the rain and torn by the wind, cracked in every pore noiselessly as it began to move. The dew on the crags glittered and then died, sucked into the sun. Each tuft of withered grass that had lain during the long winter between the crevices of the crags, bitten by the frost, shivered. Green sprouts began to crawl up through the withered ones. In the bare green plains above the beach at Coillnamhan the grasses began to wave their pointed heads spasmodically. Like blind men they clawed the air, seeking a way to the sun and warmth. The worms, dizzy after their winter's sleep, their heads swaying drunkenly on the coil of their bodies, squirmed in the cold light. The birds chirped as they flitted hither and thither trying to find a mate and a nesting-place. The larks rose with the bleak dawn, stammering as they leaped from the earth, as if their music, frozen by winter, was being melted in their throats by the joyous light. Their voices rang out clear and defiant as they soared high over Inverara. The heralds of spring and life, they sounded the reveille to the earth below.

'Spring has come. Up, you laggards. Your sleep is o'er.' So whispered the wind, coming in fast, hissing rushes from the sea. It was no gentle, languorous wind. It was sharp and biting. It beat the earth with thin steel rods. It throbbed with energy. It hardened the muscles. It sent the blood rushing from the heart to the limbs. It made the teeth chatter. It aroused passion. It was full of cold lust. It poured into every crevice of the crags, catching everything in its harsh grip. It poured into every cabin to rouse the people. It made the horses neigh and gallop, as it tore the shaggy winter hair from their backs. It was the lashing wind of spring.

The back of the sea was covered with wrinkles as if it were shrinking from the cold caress of the wind. And, spurred by the wind, it struck the cliff mighty blows gently, like a giant who is building with heavy instruments. It rolled banks of yellow and brown and black seaweed to the beaches to fertilize the earth. Its broad bosom was covered with low ridges, as it heaved itself towards the land, driven by the wind, white thin lines dividing green swathes of water. It hurried, ceaselessly building on the ruins of winter. Its never-ending sound carried all over Inverara, like the panting breath of nature building spring. Every living thing in Inverara breathed its strong smell that was carried on the wind. It loosened stiff limbs and poured iron into blood that had thinned in winter.

Life, life, life, and the labour of strong hands in Inverara in spring. From dawn to dark the people hurried, excitedly opening the earth to sow. At dawn they came from their cabins, their noses shining with frost, slapping their lean hands under their armpits, their blue eyes hungry with energy. They ran through the smoking dew for their horses. From dawn to dark their horses trotted, neighing, their steel shoes ringing on the smooth stones. Through rain and driven sleet the people worked. Cows gave birth to calves, and the crooning of women milking in the evening mingled dreamily with the joyous carolling of the birds. Yellow lambs staggered by their mothers' sides as they made their first trembling journeys in life. Lean goats were hiding their newborn kids in the crevices among the crags. Everything moved hungrily for life. Even the grey limestone crags seemed to move as the sun sucked the dew from their backs. Smoke rose everywhere, as if nature perspired conceiving life.

Thy Neighbour's Wife II

In Inverara they called an athletic sports a race meeting, probably out of respect for the first recorded race that was ever contested in the island in the year AD 457 on the 17th of April (which fell on a Monday that year, according to the testimony of old Mary O'Reilly of Kimillick, the oldest woman in Inverara, and who was suspected of relationship with the occult on account of her age). It is recorded that in that year, St Patrick, representing Christianity, contested the possession of the island with a Druid, representing the reigning deity, Crom Dubh. They chose a peaceful way (and therefore novel way in those days, as in these) of contesting the supremacy and 'to find a basis of agreement', as Mr de Valera would say. They decided to race from opposite ends of the island, and whoever was the first to arrive at the centre was the victor. The Druid, a gentleman called Brian of the Silver Tongue, a name which proved that soothsayers and politicians had attained their present-day characteristics even in the distant past, mounted a fleet charger at the west end of the island and galloped eastwards half an hour before the appointed time. St Patrick, being at that period a poor man, mounted a donkey, and, being also honest, he did not start until the proper time. But honesty was the best policy, and St Patrick won. The charger of the Druid was struck dead by a stroke of fire from heaven half a mile to the west of the central point, and the Druid himself went up in a blue flame, so that St Patrick on his donkey won at a slow walk.

Since the 17th of April, AD 457, until the 29th of June of the year with which this story is concerned, many races had been contested in Inverara and various feasts had been celebrated, but none to equal the sports that were now about to take place. The Inverara sports was the official designation given to the event by the Gaelic Athletic Association, but besides being a sports, the event was also a regatta, a bazaar, a tournament, and a religious festival combined. For the 29th of June had been celebrated in Inverara as the annual festival since the Fir Bolgs built the first fortress, and since the knowledge of Crom Dubh first reached the prehistoric inhabitants. But in later years the annual festival had degenerated into an annual debauch for the men and an annual source of revenue for the doctor, owing to the numbers of people who became ill, following that day, as a result of eating too many sweet things and drinking too much whisky. But this year the event had again attained importance, for the Gaelic Athletic Association had stretched forth its regenerating hand to 'win Inverara for the Gaelic Revival', as the secretary of the County Board would say.

The secretary of the County Board had done his best to make the sports a success from the Gaelic point of view. By sunset on Friday the Sports field, Mr Dignum's largest meadow to the west of the Pier, was arranged for the footraces, the long jump, the high jump, casting the hammer, etc. A platform had been erected in the centre of the field for the dancing. An old hulk had been stationed in the harbour as a turning-point in the boat-race. Everything was shipshape by nightfall. Then the alien element who had arrived from the mainland contributed their share to make the event look like an Eastern bazaar. Being debarred from the sports field by the rules of the GAA, they pitched their tents along the road leading from the town to the Pier during Friday night, and the publicans, who were also banned from the field, followed suit with their drinking-booths, so that when the first rays of the morning sun poured across the bay on Kilmurrage, a long line of white canvas stretched from the town to the Pier, glistening in the sun. The booths of the publicans gazed shamelessly at the sun, with two empty porter barrels as supports at their doors, ready to smile at their clients with their seductive roundness, ready to lure the thirsty islanders into the gloomy recesses beneath the canvas, where Mulligan's assistant or Mrs Moroney's assistant would hand out frothy pints of porter and glistening tumblers of whisky to slake the thirst and set the blood tingling. The booths of the foreign elements stared shamelessly at the sun, with the flaps of their tents thrown back to show that they had nothing to hide from the gaze of even the most innocent, disclosing strings of rosary beads in black and red and grey and green and amber, in glass and wood and ivory, exposed to the admiration and cupidity of the religious and devout, with heart-shaped Agnus Deis in blocks of six on worsted cushions, with crucifixes of wood and crucifixes of iron and crucifixes of tin, gilt with gold, with statues of saints canonized last year and canonized a thousand years ago, while the vendors stood within, with their semitic faces smiling blandly, to show the universality of religion and the all-conquering influence of coin of the realm. There were the fruit-stalls staring at the morning sun and the confectioners' stalls and the lucky-bag stalls, and right opposite the end of the Pier stood the most ornate booth of all, where the gipsy fortune-teller had installed herself, ready to peer into the future or the past at a moment's notice. [...]

At eleven o'clock, as sharp as the prospectus, the *Duncairn* snorted her way alongside the Pier, blowing her whistle more shrilly than usual in honour of the occasion, and loaded from stem to stern and from the keel to the bridge with passengers.

There were passengers stowed in the hold like cargo. They were on the hurricane deck, packed close together like immigrants coming into Ellis Island, New York. There were some even stowed away among the boilers in the stokehold, having been refused a passage by the steamship company, lest they might be prosecuted for exceeding the ship's capacity. There was the Brian Boru Pipers' Band in a position of honour on the saloon deck, with the Temperance Band close behind them. There were scores of young ladies in grey tweed skirts and grey coats and without any hats, and scores of young men in grey tweed suits and without any hats, advertisements, like the secretary of the County Board of home industry and the Gaelic Revival, in clothes. There were men in kilts, with rimless glasses and morose expressions, advertisements of the Gaelic Revival in art and literature. There were young men in military-looking suits and with military demeanour, advertisements of the Gaelic Revival in the ancient military prowess of the Gael. And mingled with them and about them were scores and scores of ordinary people, male and female, who had not reached the high state of culture of the Revived Gael, but who had their Post Office savings in their pockets, and showed in their happy faces that they had come determined to enjoy themselves, if not like Revived Gaels, at least like ordinary people of universal nationality, who feel that life is short and the world made to be laughed at and enjoyed, even though it be to the detriment of the dead soul of a nation.

But even at this moment of historic importance, this landmark in the history of Inverara, Fr O'Reilly stood out as the most important man in Inverara. He stood on the bridge beside the captain, and around him were assembled three canons, a county court judge, and two members of Parliament. It was to Fr O'Reilly that hats were raised; it was Fr O'Reilly who received a cheer when he stepped ashore on to the Pier, accompanied by his important people. It was then that the Pipers' Band struck up 'O'Donnell Abu', and followed by the Temperance Band and by the concourse of people, and preceded by Fr O'Reilly, the important people, and the small boys, led the way to the sports field to open the sports.

The Pipers' Band halted with a final shrieking blast from the pipes in front of the platform in the centre of the sports field. Fr O'Reilly, accompanied by the three canons, the county court judge, and the two members of Parliament, proceeded to open the sports with a speech suitable to the occasion, laying stress on the glories of the past of Inverara, and the still greater glories of the future, expressing his confidence that the natives of Inverara would that day live up to the greatness of their past, and show the rest of Ireland that Inverara's manhood was as stalwart as it was supposed to be. And then, since he had a habit of turning everything to political account, he proceeded to introduce the three canons and the members of Parliament, as men who were of widespread fame in the struggle for national liberty (taking care to omit the judge, who was a virulent Unionist). Then the three canons and the two members of Parliament began to talk volubly on their own achievements and on their own and their country's prospects, until O'Malley and the secretary of the County Board, vexed at being thus pushed into the background, and disgusted with this performance, which they understood to be a vile clerical intrigue for the purpose of deflecting the forward march of the nation, peremptorily told Fr O'Reilly that it was time to begin, and Fr O'Reilly interrupted the last canon in his remarks and declared the sports open. [...]

He walked through the crowd to the open space where the 'two hundred yards open' was about to be contested. At the far end of the course six men were waiting in a line, crouched with the tips of their fingers touching the ground, waiting for the starter to fire his revolver. Two of them being natives of Kilmurrage, and doing their best to imitate the customs of the mainland, were dressed in tights, green tights, significant of their nationalist fervour. The remaining four were peasants from the west of the island. Being prevented by poverty from being able to purchase a suit of tights, or possibly being too modest to appear in public wearing such scanty clothing, they had merely discarded their heavy over-garments and stood in their grey flannel trousers, rolled up above their knees, with their grey flannel shirts opened at the neck and their feet clothed in socks without any shoes. The dress of the islanders caused a certain amount of merriment among the visitors from the mainland, and even among the natives of Kilmurrage, who did not consider themselves peasants, and were eager to associate themselves with the people from the mainland, and the islanders who looked on were irritated and threatened the visitors with their blackthorn sticks, while the visitors jeered them.

Then the revolver shot rang out and the race started. The six men shot forward with heads bent low. The two men from Kilmurrage ran according to the rules of running, as prescribed by the GAA, with their arms doubled, their heads low, with their fists clenched tightly together, moving only from the shoulders downwards, swinging their arms from front to rear, like soldiers on a parade-ground. The peasants ran according to no studied rules. They swung their arms in all conceivable directions. They changed the positions of their heads, so often that it appeared that their heads were a heavy burden of which they were eager to dispose in their flight. They spat out now and again, as if to relieve their insides of extra ballast. One of them wore a cap, and several times he put up his hand to change the angle at which it rested on his forehead. Another tightened his belt several times with a fleeting movement, and all the while the spectators kept up a perfect din of entreaty and encouragement, waving their sticks and their hats in the air and urging on their favourites, as eagerly as punters at a race meeting. At half-way three of the runners were left far in the rear, two of the peasants and one of the men from Kilmurrage. Far in front, running as fleet as a deer, with his arms swinging like windmills in wild circular strokes, bounding off the ground like a ball at each stride, with the end of the red scarf that he wore around his waist floating in the breeze, ran Paud O'Donnell from Rooruck. Close behind him panted the Kilmurrage man, running straight as an arrow, making up by training what O'Donnell gained by pure natural speed. While out on the very edge of the course ran John Walsh, of Coill Namhan, as big and bulky as a bull, with teeth gritted, swaying his head from side to side between his massive shoulders as if he were gnawing a way through the atmosphere.

The excitement rose to a violent pitch. They had only fifty yards to go. 'Rooruck! Rooruck Abu!' cried the backers of O'Donnell, waving their sticks. 'Coill Namhan! Coill Namhan!' roared the backers of Walsh, while the natives of Kilmurrage, disdaining such barbaric localism, shouted 'Give it 'em, Matt!' Thirty yards to go, and Rooruck seemed to have victory in its grasp. O'Donnell was as fresh as ever. His chest was rising and falling distinctly and evenly. Nothing moved about him but his long arms and his subtle legs. The Kilmurrage man and Walsh were now running neck to neck, showing in their disordered breathing and the violent efforts they made that their powers of endurance were diminishing.

And just then, when O'Donnell was about to let loose his reserve of strength, in order to fly past the winning-post like an arrow, O'Donnell's mother, forgetting herself in her excitement and becoming hysterical with fear, called out in a shrill voice of terror, 'Paud, Paud, ye divil ye, look behind ye, they're comin' up on ye.' And Paud looked for an instant, tripped, tried to keep his feet, stumbled again, and fell head over heels within ten yards of the tape and victory.

A roar of anguish went up from the people of Rooruck. Curses were hurled at the unfortunate woman who had robbed them of their victory, but only for an instant. The next instant they had united with Coill Namhan in order to present a united front to the common enemy, Kilmurrage. The volume of support for Walsh doubled, and Walsh, roused by the danger to the prestige of the peasantry of Inverara, seemed to swell to twice his size. In spite of the heavy garments that he wore and that clogged his progress, he hurled himself forward and shot past his opponent. Five yards from the tape. 'Coill Namhan Abu!' 'Walsh has won!' 'No, he hasn't. Go it, Matt!' The Kilmurrage man was almost level; he was level, he was in front; and then Walsh, exerting himself again, spread out his hands and took a headlong plunge, carrying the tape before his breast and rolling on to the ground with the impetus of a bull being floored in a slaughter-house, and the judge cried, 'Walsh has won!'

The people crowded around Walsh to congratulate him and to beg of him to come to Mulligan's to have a drink, but Paud O'Donnell, smarting under the misfortune that had befallen him owing to his mother's untimely warning, declared in a loud voice that the race was not valid, and that he was prepared to run any man in Inverara, or in Ireland for that matter, any distance from five yards to a mile, or to fight them if they so preferred; and Walsh, being eager to prove himself a man equal to the occasion, refused the offers of drinks, and, going over to O'Donnell, offered to take up the challenge of personal combat. He was, however, restrained by his supporters, who clung to his body, declaring that it was ridiculous for him to want to fight such a skimpy fellow as O'Donnell, who might be able to run, but could not surely be expected to fight such a powerful man as Walsh. Then O'Donnell's supporters took umbrage at this suggestion of lack of prowess in their hero, and declared truculently that there was never a man bred in Coill Namhan who could equal a Rooruck man at any pastime, so that a free-fight seemed imminent between the rival villages, when the secretary of the County Board pacified them by promising that both parties would have an opportunity of settling their differences and of testing their merits in the 'one hundred yards open' half an hour later; and O'Donnell and Walsh, gladly accepting this solution of the question, shook hands and retired together to get a drink in Mulligan's and forget their enmity. [...]

The dancing competition, next to the boat-race, was the most important event of the day, for the islanders looked upon dancing as a great art, an art which they cultivated on all possible occasions, and particularly when they had a liberal supply of potheen consumed. There were three events – the jig, the reel, and the hornpipe – and the number of competitors was so great that they had to perform in threes. There were three judges, and of the three Pat Conneally and Pat Coleman were the more important, for the reason that they knew nothing about dancing and might therefore be expected to give an unprejudiced judgment. The third judge was from the mainland and a professor of Irish Dancing. He was a man who was interested in the Gaelic Revival, and had therefore consented to give his services as judge at half the usual rates. Three fiddlers sat on the rear of the platform, tuning up their instruments, each casting a doleful look at the audience, in silent protest at the stupidity of the other two.

At last the musicians started in harmony and the first three dancers took up their position on the platform, facing the judges, ready to commence the jig. [...]

The dancers were now patting the platform with nimble feet, turning around and around in the treble, jumping half their own height, clapping their hands together between their thighs in mid-air, crossing their feet in a series of interminable twists and turns, and then miraculously disentangling them and coming deftly to a normal position at the end of the bar, holding their hands on their hips with their heads erect, looking straight in front of them, moving from the hips downwards without a muscle moving above the hips, moving continually and rhythmically without losing a stroke, up and down the platform, across the platform, circling on the platform and then facing the judges at the end of the bar, changing places, back again, forming figures of eight, triangles and parallelograms, advancing forward, rippling with their feet like the patter of a machine-gun, retiring again on their heels with their toes in the air, and with their toes touching and touching like drum-sticks, and then suddenly raising both feet in the air, they clicked their heels and stamped on the platform, all three together, just as the bar finished. They bowed to the judges and a roar of applause greeted their finish.

The musicians wiped their brows and took a drink from the can of porter that stood beside each. The judge from the mainland ran his pencil over the notes he had taken, sucked his pencil, scratched his head with it, and then turned to his two fellow judges. The two fellow judges were sitting, quite calmly smoking their pipes, having decided beforehand who was the winner, since they knew each of the three competitors, and it was common knowledge in Inverara that Dan Brosnan was the best dancer of that three. But the judge from the mainland had different views and maintained that another of the competitors had won that heat, since he had danced more in accordance with the dancing rules prescribed by the legitimate Gaelic Revival. Pat Coleman and Pat Conneally smiled scornfully at him.

153

'Excuse me, sir,' said Coleman, 'but people who are supposed to know say that Dan Brosnan is the best, so that's enough.'

The judge from the mainland shrugged his shoulders and had to agree, for the affair was not of sufficient importance to warrant him giving a minority report, in keeping with the rules of the Gaelic Revival in matters of that sort, when there was an anglicized element present, and the next three dancers mounted the platform. [...]

When the curate reached the platform, the final heat in the dancing competition was about to commence. The struggle for mastery was between Dan Brosnan and Michael Corbett, Michael Corbett the wastrel and beggar. The people, showing that their love of art placed them above such paltry considerations as dress or character, were cheering lustily for Corbett, in this way showing themselves superior to more civilized people, who cheer a prima donna merely because of the jewels she wears and her reputation among the nobility. And the appearance of Corbett would prejudice his chances in any other audience assuredly, unless he were acting the rôle of a clown. Never clean, he surpassed himself that day in the general decay of his clothes, the unkemptness of his beard and the debauched look in his features, for he had spent the previous night in Brannigan's shebeen in Kilmillick, drinking potheen at the expense of visitors from the mainland. He was wearing shoes of raw cow-hide, and the cow-hair on the shoes was very long and of several colours, so that Corbett had the appearance of a satyr, dressed in the skins of wild beasts, with his tangled beard and his eyes grinning devilishly beneath his bushy eyebrows.

But when the fiddlers struck up a tune and the dancers got in motion, everybody forgot Corbett's appearance or the incongruity of his dress. Corbett disappeared as Michael Corbett the drunken beggar. In his place, a lithe figure skipped around the platform, tapping the platform with his feet as an angel might tap it and with the sharp biting sound of hailstones pattering on flat rocks. His arms were swinging and gesticulating in the air, outwards, upwards, circling around his body, one moment on the hips, another moment clasped behind his head. And then his feet and hands would get intermingled and Corbett would present the appearance of an acrobat turning somersaults on a stage, and then again he would stand erect, with his beard standing out straight in front of his mouth as if it had suddenly been transformed into stiff bristles. And then he would utter a wild yell and treble until his feet were lost from sight in a crazy whirlwind of cow-hair, going round and round with dazzling rapidity.

The crowd forgot to cheer, watching Corbett. Even Pat Coleman and Pat Conneally, the judges, took their pipes from their mouths and watched Corbett, while Dan Brosnan hammered away with determination, doing the steps with a manly precision, and watched only by the judge from the mainland, who even in that moment of excitement was not forgetful of his duties as a judge and the responsibility he owed to the rules of dancing as prescribed by the Revived Gaelic Movement.

The fiddlers fiddled until their fiddles vibrated with the power of a brass band, and when one of them paused to wet his lips at the can of porter beside him, the crowd yelled at him to get on with his work, 'and be damned to him', or they would have his life. And thus for half an hour Michael Corbett held the vast concourse of people enthralled with his exhibition, until at last Dan Brosnan, his rival, dropped with exhaustion to the platform, and then Corbett with a yell gave a few more flourishes, a few more trebles, then a wild whoop and a whirl in the air. He brought his two feet together in the air, touching the soles together so that the dried raw leather resounded like the crack of a whip, and finally he hit the platform, with one foot stretched forward in front of the other and his body bent forward in a graceful bow.

'Is le Corbett a buadh,' yelled the peasants furiously. 'Corbett wins,' cried the natives of Kilmurrage. Even the visitors from the mainland, who were not concerned with 'the soul of the nation', applauded vigorously, crying, 'Well done, Corbett.' But the supporters of the Gaelic revival in art, literature, manufactures, and military prowess dissented. They favoured Brosnan, because they regarded Corbett as the stage Irishman, a man who should be put down and banished with a strong hand, a drunken waster whose kind had disgraced the country since the English invasion, an insult to the morality and sobriety and steady robust self-respect of the revived Gael. In agreement with their prejudices they opposed Corbett and shouted for Brosnan, claiming that he had won, since he had danced more in accordance with the rules of dancing prescribed by the Gaelic Revival. So that the professor of dancing from the mainland, being himself a Revived Gael, and eager to curry favour with the Revived Gaels in the audience, suggested to Coleman and Conneally that Brosnan had won.

Coleman and Conneally immediately rose to their feet and looked to the supporters of Corbett in the audience, at the same time casting a deprecatory look in the direction of the dancing master. And then Coleman, taking upon himself the rôle of presiding judge, announced in his most professional voice that Corbett had won. There was a roar of applause that drowned the voices of protest from the Revived Gaels, and Corbett was carried off to Mulligan's, while the secretary of the County Board announced through a megaphone that there would be an hour's recess for lunch and that the boat-race would commence sharply at two o'clock.

SUMMER

Inverara lay in the bosom of the sea, like a maiden sleeping in the arms of her lover. As the sun rose each morning, the night mists rolled away before it to the West in pale blue columns. They rolled up the steep slope of Coillnamhan Fort, and then banked along the high ridge that runs athwart Inverara from south to north between Rooruck and Coillnamhan. They lay there at dawn, a pale blue wall dividing the east from the west. Then the sun rose clear above the Head of Crom, and they vanished into space as it shone through them.

A million rays then danced on every crag. The tall clover grass in the fields beneath the crags sparkled, each blade an emerald. The roof of the old church at Coillnamhan could be seen for miles, a pool of light lit up by the sun. The trees behind O'Daly's cottage were in bloom, an oasis in a treeless desert. Each tilled field was big with crops. The dark green potato stalks were covered with pink and white and red blossoms, and tall poppies and sunflowers waved above the stalks, scattered here and there like soldiers on sentry. Each glen along the south of Inverara was a flower garden. Sheltered by the ivy-covered hills where the sparrows chirped, the valleys were covered with pure simple little flowers, primroses, bluebells, daisies and buttercups. On the cliff-tops over the sea, where the salt air smelt like an elixir from a fairy-land, other flowers grew, whose names nobody knew. They were tender little flowers; they grew in a night and died in a day. They were as delicate to the touch as a butterfly's wing, and as multi-coloured as a rockbird's egg. Down in the crevices among the crags, where the wind never came and where the sun was only reflected by slanting dim shadows, the maidenhair ferns grew from the black earth. Their roots were moistened by water from the very heart of Inverara. Their green heads stood silent and beautiful like living poems.

All over Inverara the air was heavy with sweet smells. The wind, making slow sensuous music as it drifted slowly in from the calm sea, mixed all the smells together. It blew so tenderly that the bluebells hardly waved their heads under its caress.

Around Inverara the sea lay calm and vast like a great thought. The waves rolled slowly in on the sands at Coillnamhan. They rolled sleepily, playfully making deep channels in the sand. Then they crept back again, murmuring, 'Summer, summer, summer.' There was not one speck of seaweed along the whole stretch of sand. It was clean and spotlessly white, like the seagulls that strutted about it, with their heads stuck low on their shoulders, or scratching their breasts with their beaks. The sea stretched around Inverara, its back silvered by the sun, the waves so small that they seemed to be strokes drawn by a child's finger. Beneath the cliffs on the south there was never a wave at all. The sea there was a mirror reflecting the colours of the cliffs, yellow and black and grey. Round rocks stuck from its bosom near the cliffs, and shoals of birds scurried around in it, teaching their young how to catch fish.

The sweet languorous odour of summer permeated every living thing in Inverara. The cows standing knee-deep in the brackish pools in the meadows above the beach at Coillnamhan, chewed their cud with half-closed eyes, their tails whisking at the gadflies. Horses stood in the shade of the fences, their tails to the sun, their heads drooping and a hind leg limp, dozing through the day. The men watched their crops growing. Lying in the shade, they stretched themselves languidly and said, 'Laziness is a devilish thing.'

*

Skerrett

On a wild day in February 1887, the hooker *Carra Lass* brought David Skerrett and his wife from Galway to the island of Nara. They left the town at dawn and then tacked down the bay, through ice-cold rain and hail and lurching seas that rode white-maned across the hooker's bow. It was already noon when they came abreast of the Black Head, lying close inshore for shelter.

Then as the boat lay upon the heaving water like a brown-winged fly, beneath the towering, black mountain, along whose rain-bright upper slopes great shreds of cloud were driven by the wind, the sky grew sudden clear and the sun came forth. Up rose the island to the view, ten miles to the south-west, a black speck upon the horizon, a dismal sea-lashed rock, lying across the harbour mouth from land to land, except where two foaming channels east and west made roadways to the ocean. Through the eastern channel the ocean's fury swept into the bay, so that when the hooker tacked west into the wind, she bounded like a ball. The wind-filled bellies of her sails near touched the waves and she seemed like to founder with each careening plunge.

Amidships in the shallow hold, her passengers lay crouched among their cargoes, all island men and women. The women, with their red petticoats and many-coloured cashmere shawls lashed about their bodies, moaned in a great agony of fear and sickness. The men, though neither sick nor afraid through use of seafaring, had until now lain sombre and silent. When the sun came out and the ocean became dazzling in its light, they sat up, stretched themselves and began to chatter in loud voices.

Attracted by the sudden speech, Skerrett crawled up the hatchway of the fo'c'stle, where he had been waiting on his sea-sick wife since leaving port. The islanders in the hold examined him with interest, he being a stranger. They saw a man in the prime of life, tall, of heavy build, with a brown beard that masked the almost brutal coarseness of his countenance. His thick, moist lips curved outwards and his nose was like that of a prize-fighter, being short, thick and flattened at the end. His brown eyes were bold and sullen. A loose oilskin coat covered him from head to foot.

'When do we reach the island?' he called out to the people in the hold.

They looked at one another and whispered in Irish. As he had spoken in English they did not understand him. Then a man with a crooked leg came forward and spoke in English, though with a foreign accent.

'By night-fall, sir,' said this man, 'or a little sooner. There is Nara out there.'

Skerrett looked, blinking, at the distant rock, that seemed to rise suddenly from the ocean and then disappear once more, as the hooker plunged from crest to trough of the waves. His forehead became furrowed as he looked. Then he shaded his eyes with his arm and glanced all round, at the white-ridged sea, at the black mountain falling fast astern, at the low dun line of mainland going west upon the north. All looked dismal, cold and savage to him, though there

From *Skerrett* (1932).

was beauty in the sunlit, foam-capped sea and vigour in the strong perfume of its brine, carried on the wind.

'It looks a lonely and a wild place,' he said gloomily.

'It is faith,' said the man with the crooked leg. 'Though it's old and honoured in the history of man. The island of saints and scholars it's called in the story books. It's how in the early Christian times it was inhabited by saints that near covered it with churches and monasteries. But the marauding Danes and then the robber English came and destroyed everything. They burned the saints in boiling oil and now there's only poor people on the island, except a few protestants that are put there by the government to tyrannize.'

The man spoke with great energy.

'Do you live on the island?' said Skerrett.

'I do faith,' said the man. 'I'm Pat Coonan, the rate collector. I live at Ardglas, where we are going to land. It's the most important place on the island. It will soon be a town. You are Mr Skerrett, the new schoolmaster at Ballincarrig. I heard you were coming. You were pointed out to me yesterday in the main street of Galway.'

Skerrett nodded his head without looking at Coonan. His eyes were still fixed on the rock and his face was gloomy.

'Have you no word of Irish at all?' continued Coonan.

Skerrett turned to him angrily. Coonan was a tall, lean man, with a brown skinny face and peering eyes like a small bird. Though only about forty years of age, five years older than Skerrett, his body had already shrivelled, through scanty nourishment, hardship and exposure to the wildness of the island climate. Skerrett seemed to be of quite another race, heavy, well-fleshed, placid, slow of movement, dominant.

'I know no Irish,' he said. 'I'm from the county Limerick. They have no Irish there.'

'It's a pity, then,' said Coonan, 'for without Irish you'll have a hard job of it in Ballincarrig. Around Ardglas, where I live, the people speak English. God knows, it's a poor sort of English we have, but we get along with it. It's how we get in the habit of speaking it to the coastguards and the police and the government people that do be coming and going. In the west of the island, the people speak no English at all. Only an odd person understands it.'

He looked behind him towards the islanders in the hold and then said in a fawning fashion:

'The place you're going to, they're half savages. They have no word of English at all.'

Skerrett looked at him arrogantly, stroked his beard, threw back his powerful shoulders with a jerk and then said in a booming voice:

'I'll soon make them learn it.'

'God bless you, sir,' said Coonan. 'I hope you will. The school there is not long open, only five years. But you know that yourself, I suppose. There was only one regular teacher there before you. Up to that, the young people used to come into Ardglas to school and it was only an odd person that came. But Mr Scanlon was there in Ballincarrig for five years and faith it was little good he did.'

'Huh!' said Skerrett contemptuously. 'Why was that? What sort of man was he?'

'It's like this,' said Coonan. 'He was a quiet sort of Christian man at first and he lay a great compliment on what he did and said. But sure they made a show of him and then he took a conceit to the place altogether, as he was able to teach them nothing and only an odd person came near his school at all. So he began to drink, until in the end he had to be sent to the madhouse.'

'Huh!' said Skerrett again.

'Yes, sir,' said Coonan. 'Sure enough it's a wild place, but faith we are making great changes in it. We have a great priest there now, Father Harry Moclair. He's like a king over us. Before he's done with the island, we'll be as rich there as in the fine fat county you came from. God bless you, sir.'

Skerrett looked gloomily at the distant rock that now began to lengthen in the sea. Then he shrugged his shoulders and crawled down the hatchway into the fo'c'stle, where a woman's moaning could be heard. Coonan walked, bow-legged, back to the shallow hold. There the islanders gathered around him, asking questions about the new master.

Coonan treated them as he himself had been treated by Skerrett as a social inferior. They all wore the native costume of the island, rawhide shoes, blue frieze drawers held with a belt, hand-knitted, of coloured threads, a sleeveless frieze waistcoat, blue in front and white at the back, dark blue frieze shirt with white bone buttons from throat to breast, wide-brimmed black felt hat. Coonan wore shop clothes, a swallow-tailed coat, trousers, boots and a cravat. Although, at birth, his condition had been identical with theirs, he had begun the slow ascent towards the bourgeoisie by virtue of his position as rate-collector; a type of Irish middle class man in the infancy of that class, when it began to detach itself from the peasant stem. He affected difficulty in pro-nouncing the Irish words when he spoke to them and in almost every sentence he inserted an English word or phrase; just like a slightly educated African negro posing before his fellow tribesmen on his return to the bush from a Christian settlement. Indeed he filled his pipe and began to smoke before he condescended to answer their questions. Then he said:

'He seems to be a tough man, this new schoolmaster. A proud and uncivil sort of man.'

'What did he say?' said an islander with buck teeth, squatting on his heels and pulling at the stump of a clay pipe.

'He said he was going to make the Ballincarrig people learn English within a month or dance on the guts of their dead bodies,' answered Coonan.

'Huh!' said a handsome young man, who lay on his back with his cap over his eyes. 'He'll soon find himself stretched flat with a broken skull if he isn't careful.'

'We don't want any English,' said another. 'The language our ancestors spoke since God made the world is good enough for us.'

'Hold your whist and don't talk nonsense,' said Coonan indignantly.

'Sure without English ye'll remain in misery and poverty and ignorance, same as ye always were. How can ye go to America without English? How can any of ye get a job like I have without English? It's English gave me bacon of a Sunday morning for my breakfast and gives me tea twice a day, while ye all are living on Indian meal porridge and potatoes and salt fish.'

There was general agreement with this statement.

'Faith,' said one, 'you're becoming a sort of little half-sized buck, Pat Coonan. It's true for you.'

'Of course, it's true for me,' said Coonan. 'This man'll be the makings of ye over there in the west of the island, for he's a tough man to handle.'

He looked furtively towards the fo'c'stle and lowered his voice.

'I heard the whole story of how he was driven out of his last school from a man in Galway,' he said. 'He beat a scholar and the lad's father came to complain. Begob, Skerrett laid out the father with a blow of a fist and the poor man's jaw was broke. There was a rumpus in the place so the parish priest had to ask him to resign. So then Father Moclair took pity on him and gave him this school in Ballincarrig.'

'So that's the class of a man he is,' said the islander with buck teeth.

'That's the class of man he is,' said Coonan. 'He's a proud and saucy man, but maybe he'll get tamed and go away with his tail beneath his belly from this place that he despises. So I say and I know a thing or two.'

Later the wind changed and blew upon the hooker's stern and she raced south-west at a great pace. The island grew distinct, until the people could see the boats riding at anchor in the roadstead of Ardglas. The rocky land rose high to a great ridge of cliffs that stretched from end to end of the island facing the southern ocean.

As the boat entered the harbour, Skerrett came out of the fo'c'stle, supporting his wife. She was a little round woman, big with child, wearing a black cloak and a feathered bonnet. Her face was yellow with sickness. He pointed to the island and said fiercely:

'That's where you brought me to live. Look at it.'

She looked in wonder at the rocky place that was like a chess-board with an immense multitude of stone walls encasing stony fields. She shuddered and clung to her husband's arm.

'It's like a wild desert, David,' she said.

'And to think,' he growled, 'that only for you, I'd be on my way to America now, instead of coming to live on this bloody rock.'

He frowned upon the island and in his sensual face anger blazed against the fate that had driven him hither. In the light of the setting sun the island rock was radiant with a gaunt and fearsome loveliness, but the cloudy eye of this unhappy man saw only its stark and lonely nakedness.

*

AUTUMN

They were opening the bowels of Inverara. The potato stalks, once green, flower-decked and beautiful, were withered. They crackled as the women tore them from the ridges. The men rooted up the earth avariciously with their spades to gather the fruit that had matured in its womb during the heat of summer. Rain-bleached potatoes lay in rows on the flattened ridges. There were only bristles left in the ryefields. Inverara was being stripped naked.

The horses, carrying home the crops, no longer galloped as they did in spring. They moved slowly with downcast heads, their baskets creaking on the canvas of their straddles. There was a melancholy silence in Inverara, broken only by the bleak whine of the autumn wind, chanting the death song of the year. Cattle were driven southwards each day from the parched plains to the long hill grass in the valley between the crags. The flowers were dead. And the blackberries had ripened, the enchanted fruit that were eaten by the black devils that rode on the storm of winter.

Inverara was like an old man groaning with his years and talking of death. Rain fell each day, drowning summer. The air was damp, and heavy mists hung by day and by night over the ridge of Coillnamhan. Sometimes the mists shut out the sea, and only its sad murmur could be heard, coming through the fog like the wheezing of an old man sick with pleurisy. The shore at Rooruck was strewn with offal, rotting timber, torn seaweed, heads of dogfishes, worthless refuse after the joyous debauch of summer. The broad grey crag of Rooruck shone sombrely, washed by the ceaseless rain mist. And water gushed from the crevices in the faces of the cliffs, falling with sad sounds in zigzag courses down the cliffs to the sea, as though autumn were washing Inverara. The sun shone dimly through the dun clouds on Rooruck, dimly as if it perpetually frowned. Hosts of shadows continually flitted along the Jagged Reef southwards towards the cliffs, like spirits shielding something that fled. The men working in the harvest fields often stood erect, caressing their sore backs and cursing the laggard sun, for work that was joyous in spring was now painful, and the time dragged slowly, like a dying man's breath. For time is a measure of pain.

*

Máirtín Ó Direáin

'Árainn 1947'

Feadaíl san oíche
Mar dhíon ar uaigneas
Mar fhál idir croí is aigne
Ar bhuairt seal,
Ag giorrú an bhealaigh
Abhaile ó chuartaíocht.
An tráth seo thiar
    Níor chualas.

Amhrán aerach,
Scaradh oíche is lae,
Ó ghroífhear súgach,
Gaisce ard is goití dúshláin
Is gach uaill mhaíte
Ag scoilteadh clár an chiúnais,
Tráth a mbíodh gníomha gaile a shinsear
Á n-aithris do dhúile an uaignis,
An tráth seo thiar
    Níor chualas.

Liú áthais ná aitis
Ó chroí na hóige
Ag caitheamh 'cloch neart'
Mar ba dhual tráthnóna Domhnaigh,
Nó ag cur liathróid san aer
Le fuinneamh an bhuailte.
An tráth seo thiar
    Níor chualas.

Ní don óige feasta
An sceirdoileán cúng úd.

From *Dánta 1939–1979* (1980).

Máirtín Ó Direáin

'Aran 1947'

Whistling at night
As a defence against the eeriness,
A barrier between heart and brain
In a time of disquiet,
Shortening the road
Home from late visiting,
This time in the West
   I heard not.

A lively song,
When day left night behind,
From a tipsy stalwart,
Loud boasts and defiant gestures
And many an arrogant yell
Splitting the length of the silence
While the brave deeds of their forefathers
Were named to the spirits of solitude,
This time in the West
   I heard not.

A shout of joy or pleasure
From the heart of the young
As they tossed the great stone,
Their Sunday evening custom,
Or shot a ball in the air
With force behind the stroke,
This time in the West
   I heard not.

Not for the young any more,
That narrow windswept island.

Transl. Tomás Mac Síomóin and Douglas Sealy in *Tacar Dánta/Selected Poems* (1984).

Pat Mullen

The Prince of Liars

There dwelt an old queen in Erin long ago, who had been wife to King Ladair More, King of the Western Lakes. They had an only son, Ladair Beug, but the King died when the boy was ten.

At the time we see them, Ladair Beug was talking to his mother. 'I am twenty-one to-day,' he was saying, 'and I have made up my mind to go out into the world and bring home a wife with me, after some wandering and adventures.'

'I have been expecting this,' answered the Queen Mother, 'because your father before you did the same thing. But have you any notion what part of the world you are going to see, and where you expect to find the maid you wish to marry?'

'I am going to the Kingdom of the Lonely Isles, because the King there has promised to give his daughter to any prince who brings him a bag of gold and who can make him say, "You are a liar" three times, by telling him bigger lies than he tells himself.'

'My son, that is a thing which cannot be done,' replied the Queen. 'That King is the greatest liar who has lived in any world since the beginning of time. If you go there, your head, like that of many another ardent young prince who was foolish enough to go seeking his daughter's hand, will adorn a spear-head on his castle wall.'

'I would agree with what you say maybe,' answered Ladair Beug, 'if I had not been much in the company of Shauneen, our servant man. He is a born liar, and I have learned how to tell lies very well, so I am setting out to-morrow.'

'There is no use in trying to stop your father's son,' said the Queen, wiping away her tears. 'I hope good luck goes with you on your journey.'

On his way to the stables, the young King met the servant man of whom he had spoken to his mother. 'Shauneen,' he said, 'I am going away to see the world and bring a Princess home with me as my bride. I am going to visit the Kingdom of the Lonely Isles.'

'It is a fine thing to see the world, King,' agreed Shauneen, 'but I should advise you to take me with you as a body-guard. I have heard tell of the Lonely

From *Irish Tales* (1940).

Isles, and you need a man like me with you to give good counsel.'

Ladair Beug looked at Shauneen and laughed. It was no wonder, because this servant had three names and was covered from head to foot with ashes, having hardly ever left his seat in the chimney-corner. He was called Shauneen of the Ashes, Shauneen of the Lies, and because of his continual sitting down, which made him spread out crossways, Shauneen Broadbeam.

'Do take me with you,' urged Shauneen again. 'I have heard tell of the many young princes' heads that are stuck up over the castle walls of this bloodthirsty King. All he wants is gold and blood, and his talk of giving his daughter to any prince that can lie better than he, is only a trap.'

'Come with me then,' replied Ladair Beug. 'That is, if you think you will have washed yourself clean enough by evening, to be fit for my company. Get a couple of men to scrub and wash you.'

'All right, I will,' cried Shauneen with delight, and he hurried away to the wash tubs.

Two men began to scrub him, but it was not until the ninth tub of hot water that Shauneen was clean at last. Leaving him to dry for awhile in the sun, the scrubbers took Shauneen's clothes into a near-by rocky field, where they began to slap and sweep the ashes out of them. A cloud of dust rose in the air that darkened the sky overhead. The wind blew it away somewhat, and as it was settling down, it covered a great bare crag, seven acres wide, to a depth of several inches, and it is well known that for long years after, the soil of this crag produced the best grain in the King's realm.

'I think they look as good as new,' said Shauneen when he put on the clothes again. 'They will do for the journey.'

Ladair Beug cried out with pleasure when he saw the clean, manly, broadbeamed appearance of his servant.

Shauneen was equally pleased with his King's clothing, for he was dressed in gold-embroidered silk with a shimmering green cloak thrown across his shoulders. Golden buckled shoes were on his feet, a peacock plume waved from his hat with every step he took, and he had his sword of flame gripped in his hand.

Sea and wind favoured them, and their way was clear, so that it was not long before they arrived at the Kingdom of the Lonely Isles, where they asked the way to the King's castle.

Outside the castle gate on a mound stood a huge battle-gong. The sight of a battle-gong of such heroic size stirred Ladair Beug's blood, and he leaped towards it to deliver his challenge. He crashed his fist down upon it with such force that its ringing shook the castle, and went echoing through the hills and valleys for a full score miles and more. Again and again he hit the gong, until frightened faces began to look over the castle wall, and the wicked King himself, startled by the uproar and the wild war-cries high over all other sounds, sent out a runner to bring in news of who this mighty warrior might be. The King also sent a hurried message to his old man of wisdom.

'What do these fierce cries of war mean outside my gates?' he questioned anxiously.

The wise man listened. 'Ha!' he cried, 'I make them out. The challenger outside has come from Erin. He is of fierce, fighting breed. Ha!' he cried again, as they heard the rattling of splinters when Ladair Beug smashed the battle-gong to pieces with a last furious blow. 'He is shouting out, "For Ladair More and the Kingdom of the West, I challenge ten thousand men before me, five thousand behind me, one thousand on each side of me, and twice as many more when I have killed all these."'

The runner came to the young King and tremblingly asked what message he was to carry to his King.

'Tell him', commanded Ladair Beug, 'to send out warriors to back my challenge, and that when I have conquered these I shall demand his daughter for my bride. Be quick and carry my will to your King,' and Ladair Beug kicked what was left of the battle-gong over the castle wall into the courtyard.

The King had gathered his councillors around him when the runner returned with his message. 'We have never had to do with such a terrible warrior,' said they, 'and it would be well to act with caution.'

'Yes,' agreed the King, 'it is better to receive him with hospitality, and then trick him in the way we have tricked the others.'

So the runner was again sent out to Ladair Beug. 'You are to be received in friendship,' he said. 'The King of this Lonely Kingdom longs for news from distant lands. Enter, Prince of the West.'

Shauneen, carrying the bag of gold, followed his master, and they were conducted into the presence of the King and his councillors. Ladair Beug took but little interest in the latter, but looked directly at the King, who was a stoop-shouldered man with leering eyes, a nose like the beak of a bird of prey, and a cruel, thin slash of a mouth.

'Welcome, Prince of the West,' he greeted. 'I can see by your bearing that you come of a kingly race. What news do you bring from over the sea?'

'I bring none,' replied Ladair Beug sternly, for the sight of the countless heads covered in pitch that adorned the spear-heads on the castle walls had not put him in the humour for talk. 'Shauneen,' he went on, 'throw the bag of gold to the King.'

Shauneen threw it at the King's feet, and the sound of the coins jingling brought a greedy look to the King's eyes. 'Ha!' thought Ladair Beug to himself, "tis the money the rogue is after.' Aloud he said:

'I have come to bring your daughter back with me to Erin. I have heard of the conditions to which a prince must agree before you allow her from under your castle roof. I am ready to begin answering questions, but I'd rather far fight for her than win her by outlying you,' and he glared round furiously with his hand on the hilt of his sword.

'We are for peace,' answered the King craftily, 'and you must stay with us for at least three days. I shall ask you a question every day.'

Ladair Beug agreed to this, and he was conducted through several long, dark halls, with Shauneen at his heels, till they reached the room where he was to sleep. Asked whether Shauneen should remain, Ladair Beug insisted that his servant should stay with him.

'Here is the clothing you must wear,' said the servant who had come with them.

Ladair Beug examined the clothes. They were made of cloth of gold, and were as soft to the touch as a maiden's cheek, and each time he looked at them as he moved about the room, they seemed of a different colour. He dressed himself in these clothes, but what made Ladair Beug look a fitting son for a King of Erin, was the pair of buckled, speckled shoes, which Shauneen had brought from Erin for him to wear. They were laced with golden thread, and on them were written the proud words which the kings of his line had always shouted when entering upon war: 'Here is the man who has the valour to kill tens of thousands of men.'

The King of the Lonely Isles looked at Ladair Beug as they were about to sit down to supper, and a thrill of fear ran through him when he saw and read what was written on the shoes.

It was a great feast, for Ladair Beug insisted that Shauneen had princely blood in him wherever he got it, and was therefore good enough to eat in any company.

The table groaned under its load of food. There were heads of wild boars and legs of rabbits, otters' pads and eggs of wild birds, and every kind of fowl and joint. They ate their fill of all these delicious dishes and washed them down with drinks of mead.

'To-morrow morning,' said the crafty King, 'I shall show you some of the sights of my island realm. Now go to your bed. May your sleep be untroubled by gloomy dreams.'

He leered as he spoke, and Ladair Beug knew that the King was imagining his head on the point of a spear. But before he fell asleep the young King suddenly sat up in bed as a disturbing thought came to his mind, for he felt all at once that it was the desire for adventure that had brought him so far from home, and that he had given less thought to the King's daughter than to how he could lie and outmatch the King himself.

'By all the gods,' he said to himself, 'what shall I do if when I win the Princess I find her as ugly as an old hen who has lost her feathers, and cold and dead as the bottom of the sea? And how can I ever face back to Erin, where all the maidens are fair to see, and each of them as graceful as a gull winging its flight along the edge of a gale? But a bargain is a bargain and being of the kingly blood of my race I shall not attempt to break it.' At last, despite his gloomy thoughts he fell asleep.

It seemed to the young man that he had only been asleep for the space of a breath, when he was awakened by a voice singing. He threw his cloak across his shoulders and went to the window. What he saw struck him dumb with astonishment and pleasure, for it was the Princess herself who was singing.

She stood barefooted beside one of the many fountains in the garden. A flowing orange and green cloak covered her slender figure; it hung from her shoulders almost to the ground, and over it her dark hair, long and curling, fell like a cloud. Ladair Beug could only gasp and look, and look and gasp at the sight of so much beauty. The mist from the fountain had formed dewdrops in her hair, and they glistened golden round her head and shoulders seen against the rising sun; while about her waist, outlined as she was against red and white flowers, they shone red as blood and white as snow. And in the lower lengths of this fairy creature's hair the dewdrops trembled greenly with every beautiful note, as she poured out her soul in song.

Ladair Beug was so overcome that his breath failed him entirely. He fell against the opening, and his slipping feet sent his buckled shoes sliding across the floor.

The Princess turned her head quickly at the sound and looked at him. Her hair swung as she moved, causing thousands of rainbow drops to spray all around her.

Ladair Beug found his voice. ''Tis herself that's in it,' he whispered. Then with his eyes fixed with adoration on this vision of glory, he fell to the floor unconscious with joy and love.

After Shauneen had helped him to recover, the vision still stayed with Ladair Beug. When he sat down to breakfast he was in good humour, having made up his mind to bring the beautiful Princess back to Erin at any cost.

'Come,' said the King, 'till I show you some of the riches of my kingdom.'

Ladair Beug agreed, eager for the great battle of wits in which he felt he was soon to be engaged, and they left the castle accompanied by Shauneen.

They walked through three fields of rich pasture. As they stood on a hill, Ladair Beug saw a greener field below them; it was very high in the middle and sloped away towards its edges, which were bordered by sparse, stunted trees.

'A grand-looking field,' said the young King aloud, 'what grows within it?'

'You shall soon see,' replied the old King.

When they had come closer, Ladair Beug saw that it was a cabbage field. But such heads of cabbage he had never seen or heard of before. By the border, they grew to a height the length of forty steps and slanted outward, being pressed out by the giant head, which grew pyramid-like in the centre of the field and was fully three hundred paces in height. Though marvelling much Ladair Beug hid his surprise and said calmly: 'These are fair-sized little heads of cabbage that you have growing here.'

'They are indeed,' answered the King, his voice tinged with a touch of just pride. A flock of goats disturbed by their voices, leaped up from a hollow in a leaf and bounded away.

'Well, my Prince from the West, did you ever see a head of cabbage as big as that which grows in the middle of that field?' the King asked carelessly.

'Ha!' thought Ladair Beug, 'he has begun. Now I am in for it.' But he said aloud, 'Why, it is not such a big cabbage. I remember once in Erin when war was on my father's kingdom. Big armies had to be put in the field. The weather was bad and there were great rainstorms. One day an army of ours, one hundred thousand men, were marching to the fray across a level plain, when a terrific rainstorm swept down upon them. Their commander looked around for shelter for his men until the storm blew over, knowing well that dry clad men fight much better than those with wet, sodden clothes clinging cold to their skin. He spied a garden with one cabbage growing in the middle of it. He ordered

168

his men to take shelter under its leaves. They did, but there was no need of them spreading out, for one leaf gave shelter to them all. And everything would have been all right if a hungry insect, of the family of flying ants, that lives entirely on cabbages, had not come under this same leaf. Its appetite got the better of its prudence, and though it had come under the leaf for shelter, it soon began to eat a hole in it through which poured such a flood of water from the lake that had gathered in the hollow of the leaf overhead, that fifty thousand warriors and the insect with them were drowned before they could get away from under it. That head of cabbage there is very small in comparison.'

The King of the Lonely Isles took on a lonely look and had opened his mouth to reply, when Shauneen stepped sideways from behind his master, and with a sneering grin on his face which greatly annoyed the King, interrupted his unspoken words.

'O King,' he said, 'are you talking about that head of cabbage under which the men were drowned?'

'I am, Shauneen,' agreed Ladair Beug.

'I know more about that head of cabbage than you,' returned Shauneen, and with another grin at the old King he went on: 'That was a head of cabbage indeed, and when it grew so big that it covered too many leagues of your father's kingdom, I was the man he ordered to collect men to cut it down. I got together seven times seven hundred men and gave each of them an axe, and it took them seven years to cut through the stalk, and during that time none of them were within the sound of each other's axes or within the sound of each other's speech,' and still standing a pace behind his master, he stuck out his tongue at the King.

This angered the King still more and he burst out, 'You liar! Your master is one,' he cried, looking at Ladair Beug, but again turning on Shauneen, 'You are a bigger liar.' He raged and stamped the ground until he suddenly grew aware what he had said. Yes, this Prince from the West had won the first battle of the three.

'You have won to-day,' he growled in anger, 'but beware of the next time.'

Shauneen and Ladair Beug were overjoyed and they ate heartily that night, but they did not make the mistake of rating lightly what lay before them.

Next morning, the young King was awakened by the Princess's singing, but this time he did not faint, and she smiled at him as she went her way beyond his sight.

After a wonderful breakfast, with every bite tasting of honey, the old King as on the previous day proposed a walk so that Ladair Beug could see some of the riches of his kingdom.

They had walked for some time along a broad, winding road when they saw a huge shed in the distance. Ladair Beug estimated its size as about half a league in length, the same in width, and about thirty paces in height. The old King led them towards this building. The young King's curiosity was aroused by the actions of many thousands of men busy in striking the ground with sticks, and of others furiously digging trenches, while still others were just as furiously filling in trenches that must have been dug shortly before. As they drew closer to these men, Ladair Beug and Shauneen, and indeed the King himself, had much ado to keep from trampling on the hordes of mice which now scurried along the ground all around them. On getting still nearer to the frantically working men, Ladair Beug saw that a deep trench wound its way for leagues over the plain, till it circled the huge shed. Countless millions of mice were rushing headlong into this trench, filling it up rapidly. Along the trench, as it became filled with the bodies of the mice, men were working, covering them over with soil; while others were digging a new trench to trap other millions of the pests. A narrow bridge led across the trench at the end of the road, and this was protected by a great storm door, lifted up and let down by ropes run through blocks that were fastened to two oak-trees, growing one on each side of the entrance. Men hauled on the ropes, and hoisted the door till the three men passed through. There was a scurrying of the mouse horde after them, but the thousands that succeeded in passing the door were at once slaughtered by men waiting inside with flat-headed clubs to finish them.

'What is the reason for all this activity on the part of these mice and men?' inquired Ladair Beug.

'Oh, the mice are trying to get at a piece of cheese in that shed over there, and the men are preventing them from reaching it,' replied the King with a brave show of carelessness.

'All the cheese in the world must be stored in that shed,' thought Ladair Beug to himself. But he kept his own counsel, and it was just as well he did, for he soon saw that his thoughts were not far from being right. The roof and the walls of the vast storehouse were cracked and bulging in many places, and through the cracks he saw cheese. Everywhere cheese. One solid block of it filled the storehouse from end to end, the doors had burst wide open, and even Shauneen's eyes opened wide when he saw this mountain of cheese.

The King still attempted carelessness. 'Did you ever see a piece of cheese as big as this?' he asked.

Ladair Beug collected his thoughts quickly. 'It is a middling-sized piece of cheese right enough,' he said, 'but it isn't anything in size compared to the valley of cheese which I saw in Erin. It happened once that there was a very dry summer, and most of the grain had failed. The people of our kingdom were in hard straits for food, and a neighbouring king having knowledge of this decided that it was a good time to wage war on us. My father was a great and far-seeing statesman. So he ordered all the cows of the kingdom to be driven into a deep valley. This valley was seven leagues long and three leagues wide. It was surrounded by cliffs seven thousand feet high. A wide hole had been cut through the mountain for cattle to go through for pasturage. When as many cows as had standing room had been driven into the valley, my father ordered the milkmaids to begin their milking, and when the cows were milked he ordered them to be driven out and others driven in to take their places. As the milk soured and grew thick, he ordered men with sharp tools to dig a hole in the bottom of the valley. "Dig it down to the Lower World," said he, "so that it will drain away the seepage from the milk." While this was done, plough-men drove in their horses, and week after week, they ploughed through the thickening valley of cheese, till it at length reached the level of the cliff tops. My father then ordered ten thousand spadesmen to station themselves there to be always ready to dig cheese to feed the army and all the people of the kingdom. The neighbouring king made war but his army was quickly defeated, for our warriors were strong and well fed on the cheese steadily being dug for them.'

Ladair Beug drew a deep breath, for it was not without effort that he had again beaten the King of the Lonely Isles, whose mouth had opened wide in wonder at the tale. He was wary, however, and uttered no word till Shauneen stepped sideways from behind his master, and with a horrible grimace in the old King's direction, he began:

'Master, you are talking about that valley of cheese that we had in Erin?'

'I am,' answered Ladair Beug.

'Well,' went on Shauneen, 'I'm the best man to tell about that, because I am the man whom your father ordered to direct the work of milking the cows and the ploughing of it, as well as digging it out to feed the people. What is not generally known about the amount of cheese in that valley, is that it fed the people of the Lower World as well as us. They had widened the passage that we had dug to let down the water and built a sloping road up under the cheese, and while we were eating it on top, they were hauling it down on horses' backs, and eating it at the bottom. It was by chance I found this out, because we went deeper in the digging in one spot and part of the cheese slid down into the hole. Two dappled grey colts which had raced up the road from the world underneath, jumped out and galloped away across the cheese. We caught them after some time. I broke them to harness, and they are the two beautiful animals that used to draw your father's chariot. And men have been busy ever since, digging cheese down into that hole, feeding the people of the Lower World, in case they might get restless and ascend, and attack us in the rear. A fine cheese that was surely,' ended Shauneen with a regretful sigh, as he looked squarely and innocently at the old King.

The latter was speechless. Then he gasped furiously, 'Liar! Liar! All lies, all liars, from master to servant.' Ladair Beug felt like smiling in his face, but he did not. Instead, he said calmly, 'King, it is plain that you do not know the men of Erin or their country. Queer things happen there.'

That night Ladair Beug and Shauneen ate well and slept well, but the avaricious King of the Lonely Isles slept very little, his mind torn between thoughts of losing his daughter who was the source of his great wealth, and thoughts of whether after all it were best if she married this king, who was such a fine young man, and above all, such a wonderful liar. His greedy nature won, however, and he made up his mind to have a spear-head specially sharpened the next day, ready for the youth's head.

The following morning Ladair Beug was awakened by the Princess's singing. He tiptoed to the window. She looked and saw him, then she walked forward till she stood beneath him.

'Princess,' he whispered, as she paused in her song, 'if I win to-day, will you come to Erin with me?'

'Ladair Beug, I will go with you. You must win. Keep your courage high. My name is Princess Shining Star.'

'I shall win to-day, for you shall shine by my side in Erin,' replied Ladair Beug earnestly.

Shining Star smiled encouragingly, as she glided away between the fountains. Rainbow colours played around her, as the sun shone on the dewdrops in her hair.

When the King, Ladair Beug and Shauneen had eaten a breakfast in which every mouthful had a special honey flavour, the King said, 'Come with me while I show you some more of the wonders of my kingdom.'

'What kind of honey was that which tasted so rich and sweet at breakfast?' asked the young King as they walked along the mossy bank of a river.

Level plains stretched away on each side of the stream, and thousands of fragrant flowers grew in the grass. Some of these flowers had stems twenty feet round and grew to an unbelievable height, taller than any tree. The smaller flowers were covered with swarms of bees, and the air was full of a sweet humming. But high in the air, Ladair Beug saw huge, bee-like creatures, with bodies big as bulls. They were flying in and out of the gigantic flowers that grew on the mighty stems, then they flew away to their hive. The ground trembled with the strength of their humming.

He stopped in amazement.

'I am beaten at last,' he thought. 'I can never think of any wondrous thing to beat this amazing sight before my eyes.' He did his best to hide his wonder but the watchful King noticed it, and smiled crookedly.

'The honey that we tasted this morning,' he said, 'came from those bees that fly high up on those big flowers. I will show you their hive shortly.'

They came to a cliff facing the sun. It was over a hundred feet in height with banks of long, brown moss growing thickly against its face. These banks of moss were honeycombed with huge apertures in and out of which the big bees crawled. Bee-men guarded these hives, which were filled to the brim with honey, as Ladair Beug soon saw, for at a signal from the King, three bee-men lifted up a part of the moss and he saw huge lumps of honey everywhere. A gigantic bee was just crawling to get into a comb, and a bee-man pushed it with a forked stick. This bee was surely bursting with honey, because it dropped a pail full of the shining stuff.

'What do you think of my beehives?' asked the King. 'Or did you ever see any bee giving as much honey as that?'

Ladair Beug groaned inwardly, but his quick mind was working swiftly.

'They are nice little honey-bees,' he answered, 'but you know little of Erin or you would never ask that question. Shortly before I came from there,' he went on, 'there was a great famine in my father's kingdom, and had it not been for the wonderful breed of honey-bees that we kept, the people would have starved to death. Even with the great supplies of honey they gave, we should still have starved, except that among them was one which gave more than all the rest. They gave bucketfuls at a time, but this bee had a never-ending supply, and every time she got a blow of a stick across her back she dropped a huge barrel of honey. Even the King of Alba heard about this bee, and asked my father to send her in a special ship that the wise men of his kingdom might study her and learn how to improve their breed of bees, to make them as good honey-givers as those of Erin.'

Ladair Beug stopped speaking and before he could continue, Shauneen had stepped from behind him. 'Is it talking about that bee your kingly father lent to the King of Alba you are?' he asked.

'It is,' replied his master.

'I should know more about that bee than anybody,' continued Shauneen, 'for it was in my charge. And that King of Alba was an ungrateful king, because he tried to keep the bee entirely when he found that all the people of his kingdom had to do was to grow flowers, and the bee would feed them with honey. So one day I had to go out into the courtyard and call her by blowing a blast on a horn. We heard afterward that at the first blast I blew, the bee shook herself and knocked down all the castles in Alba. At the second blast she spread her wings and darkened the land. At the third blast she rose from the ground, which trembled under the kick of her legs, and then she flew straight for home. The bee was much excited because it well knew that the third blast meant great need and hurry, so that in her excitement, she dropped a barrel of honey with every flap of her wings. They were falling from the sky in a straight line as she came flying. We were sorry to lose so much honey, to have it eaten by people who wouldn't maybe have wished us well. But we did not regret the loss when we heard that the bee, when over the castle of a king who had been making war on your father, gave two flaps of her wings in the same space of time as before she had only given one. Two barrels of honey fell from the air, straight down. The first one crashed its way through the roof of his castle. The King sat up in bed on hearing the noise, and the next barrel crashed down on top of his head. It flowed and stuck all over him, and though he tried to eat and suck his way through it, he failed. The honey shut off his wind and stuck his lips together. He was found dead in the middle of it, and there hasn't been any war against our kingdom since. That bee is wonderful and a great boon to Erin, because she keeps the peace between the kings of all the kingdoms, by flying from time to time over the land and enriching the people with barrels of honey.'

'By all the gods!' cried the King, 'if there are many more liars in Erin like you two, it is a land well worth visiting. Young King, you have won my daughter, and some day, if you do not mind, I shall visit your land and listen to your liars.'

Next morning, Ladair Beug found his way to the garden. Princess Shining Star ran to meet him and he clasped her in his arms. The next day Shauneen steered their ship back on her course for home. Ladair Beug and Shining Star were in the cabin, talking of love and the happy times they would have in Erin. Their hopes turned out true, for they all, Shauneen included, lived happily ever after.

Máirtín Ó Direáin

'Ómós do John Millington Synge'

An toisc a thug tú chun mo dhaoine
Ón gcéin mhéith don charraig gharbh
Ba chéile léi an chré bheo
Is an leid a scéith as léan is danaid.

Níor éistis scéal na gcloch
Bhí éacht i scéal an teallaigh,
Níor spéis leat leac ná cill,
Ní thig éamh as an gcré mharbh.

Do dhuinigh Deirdre romhat sa ród
Is curach Naoise do chas Ceann Gainimh
D'imigh Deirdre is Naoise leo
Is chaith Peigín le Seáinín aithis.

An leabhar ba ghnáth i do dhóid
As ar chuiris bréithre ar marthain;
Ghabh Deirdre, Naoise is Peigín cló
Is thug léim ghaisce de na leathanaigh.

Tá cleacht mo dhaoine ag meath,
Ní cabhair feasta an tonn mar fhalla,
Ach go dtaga Coill Chuain go hInis Meáin
Beidh na bréithre a chnuasaís tráth
Ar marthain fós i dteanga eachtrann.

From *Dánta 1939–1979* (1980).

Máirtín Ó Direáin

'Homage to John Millington Synge'

The impulse that brought you to my people
From the distant pasture to the harsh rock
Was partnered by the living clay
And the intimations of loss and sorrow.

You didn't listen to the tale of the stones,
Greatness lived in the tale of the hearth,
You paid no heed to tombstone or graveyard,
No whimper escapes the lifeless dust.

Deirdre appeared before you on the road
And Naoise's currach weathered Ceann Gainimh;
Deirdre and Naoise went to their death
And Pegeen flung abuse at Shawneen.

The book was always in your hand –
You brought the words in it to life;
Deirdre, Naoise and Pegeen took form
And leaped like heroes from the pages.

The ways of my people decay.
The sea no longer serves as a wall.
But till Coill Chuain comes to Inis Meáin
The words you gathered then
Will live on in an alien tongue.

Transl. Tomás Mac Síomóin and Douglas Sealy in *Tacar Dánta/Selected Poems* (1984).

Tom O'Flaherty

Coming Home

The next day we were to land in Galway. The great liner was thrashing her way through heavy seas and the severest storm she had met since leaving New York. Giant waves struck her with the force of ten thousand trip hammers, making her shudder from stem to stern. Deck seats were torn adrift and thrown here and there. Nobody slept. A rumour went the rounds that the captain would not bring the vessel to Galway with such a gale raging in from the west.

All night the big seas kept pounding away. Towards morning it calmed down considerably. Those of us who were to land in Galway were up before the dawn. The rumour of the night before was unfounded. The liner was making direct for the old City of the Tribes. She would pass to the south of the Aran Islands and of my native village Gort na gCapall which I had left twenty-one years ago and never visited since.

With the first streak of dawn a light glimmered in the distance. It was from the lighthouse on the most westerly of the two little rocks that lie outside Aran Mór. My grandfather on the mother's side, one Thomas Ganly, built it some eighty years ago.

My mother often told me interesting stories about him. He visited many countries building lighthouses and piers. His father was an Orangeman, who married a Catholic girl, and my grandfather and a sister of his followed the Catholic faith. My grandfather was as intolerant in religious matters as his father had been tolerant. It was often my mother told me of his fights for the faith in Orange strongholds. In one of those fights he had his skull cracked by a blow of a chair, wielded by an infuriated Orangeman who did not like my grandfather's attitude towards the glorious, pious and immortal William! How the Orangeman fared in the fight I never heard.

He came to Aran building lighthouses and piers. There he met my grandmother who was the descendant of a colourful character who went by the name of *Mícheál Riabhach* (Speckled Michael). Mícheál was a successful smuggler, and had picked out a nice grassy plot for himself in the village of Mainistir there to end his days when he got weary of smuggling. My grandfather liked Mainistir and decided to drop anchor there.

From *Aranmen All* (1934).

But he had not much interest in farming, and what little he had never resulted in profit. He could not tell his own sheep from a neighbour's and one day as he was passing by one of his fields he saw a number of sheep in it which he mistook for those of a villager for whose honesty he had little regard.

'Bad luck to that thieving Pat Mór,' he muttered, as he knocked down the gap and drove the sheep to the pound. Returning home he threatened to flog his son for not keeping an eye on his land. My grandmother wept and said he would send her to the poorhouse. He had to pay twopence each to get his own sheep out of the pound.

The lighthouse is there as solid as ever but the engineer who built it is dust. 'Many a thing is more lasting than a person,' the Aran islanders say.

I felt anything but cheerful approaching my island home, or what was once my home. My parents and many of my boyhood friends were in the graveyards of the island. Most of my other associates had gone to America to 'make their fortunes'. The sight of the lighthouse and the thoughts of my blood relationship with it had a galvanizing effect on me. After all I was closer to the things that mattered in this barren island than I was in the materially richer country whence I came. The liner sped on and now we could see the outline of Aran Mór like a flat green cloud on the horizon. I stood as if glued to the rail, recollections chasing each other through my mind.

Brannock Island can be seen now. Then across a narrow channel the village of Bungowla with its little bay protected from the Atlantic swells by the Black Rock of Woe which takes the strength out of the waves that dash unceasingly against its jagged crest.

At Bungowla the island slopes down to the sea on every side. A fairly prosperous fishing village when there was a good demand for mackerel. Kelpmaking was also a source of wealth. Small fields could be seen here and there among the rocks. Almost every rood of cultivated land in Bungowla was made by the people. My one recollection of Bungowla is that I used to lie on the rocks with a friend when I was a boy to shoot at cormorants as they flew southwards to their homes in the tall cliffs. They flew low and close to the land at this point.

On goes the liner and we are now opposite Creig a Chéirín. The land rises sharply from Bungowla and from the shore on the Conamara side of the island and steeply to a height of two hundred and fifty feet on the south. The land here is even poorer than in Bungowla, though it seems impossible. The cow droppings are used as a substitute for peat, and but for the constant fertilizing of the land with seaweed it would in time produce neither grass nor vegetables. The island is peatless and almost treeless, and when the peasant fishermen have not enough money to buy turf from the Conamara men or when the weather is so bad that the turf boats cannot come in they are obliged to burn dry dung as fuel. In fact dry cow dung makes a bright clean fire, and the more thrifty of the islanders never allow a bit of it to go to waste. Experts in cow dung fuel could tell you what kind of cattle feed produces the best substitute for turf.

In the tall cliff to the south of Creig a Chéirín is the Piper's Castle and the secret underground path that runs from the Atlantic to the Red Lake on the bay side of the island. Here an outlaw piper from Conamara hid from the minions of the law, and never appeared to the eye of man again. The natives did not inquire into the nature of his crime. It was enough for them to know that he was hunted by the British Government. Food and shelter they gave him, and then he vanished. Legend has it that he still plays mournful tunes on his pipes, but nobody wants to hear the music for it is believed that the person hearing it will before long be called to the Piper's Castle from which there is no returning.

In those cliffs, wild birds nest on the ledges that run for miles along the face of them. Indentations are made in the gravel seams between the layers of rock by wind and water. Here guillemot and cormorant, seagull and *crosán* (puffin) lay their eggs and hatch out their young.

In my youth, expert cliffmen had themselves lowered down in the evening to those ledges and they lay around them all night killing birds and gathering eggs in the season. In the morning they would have the birds hauled up to the top of the cliff. Sometimes they scaled the cliffs alone and unaided. The most famous of the cliffmen is now too old to climb, but he cannot resist the temptation to stand on the verge of a narrow slab of stone that juts out from the top of the cliff at Creig a Chéirín and look down.

Every rock and cranny along those cliffs has an appropriate name and I recollected the thrill I got from looking for pieces of wreckage among the giant boulders at the foot of those cliffs when I was a boy. And when I found a barrel, or a piece of board with the name of a foreign country on it I and other boys of the village used to wonder what this strange country was like or if its people were like ourselves.

We pass Creig a Chéirín. The cliffs grow taller. We are opposite Eoghanacht, the site of one of the four forts in Aran Mór. Archaeologists are in doubt about the origin of those fortresses, when they were built or by whom. But I came to the conclusion that the builders had a keen appreciation of the value of land, for this and the other forts in the island command the choicest pieces of land in Aran Mór. From the tall cliffs on the south of Eoghanacht to the sloping beach on the north there is a fairly decent pasturage, water is abundant, there are some large fields on which the soil is from four to six inches deep while the shore on the Conamara side is one of the best in the island for seaweed.

This stretch of land once belonged to the peasantry of Eoghanacht, but a namesake of mine took a fancy to it and gave the tenants the choice of accepting their transportation to America or being thrown out on the road without any compensation. Some of them went to America and others stayed at home. Many things have happened in Ireland since then, but the descendants of those tenants are still landless. The landgrabber's heirs lost Eoghanacht as well as another section that was acquired in a somewhat like manner. My father who was the chief leader of the Land League movement in Aran was one of those responsible for the landgrabber's tribulations, yet it came to pass that a sister of mine married the man who purchased this estate ...

I am now looking at the level field with the short sweet grass on top of the cliff where she and I often stood of a fine day looking out at the Brandon mountains; I telling her that some day I would be going out that way to foreign countries, Australia maybe, perhaps the United States, or even to the Argentine, and she listening and hoping I would stay at home and amuse her with my fanciful stories, settle down in the old homestead and get married, die in my dotage and be buried with my ancestors.

People would say that nobody could have luck with land that was grabbed from the peasantry. People 'say more than their prayers' for if this were so the 'best people' in Ireland would not have any luck for they have inherited their broad acres from plunderers. My brother-in-law paid for this farm with money he earned in the United States, and there was no odium attached to his acquisition of it. My sister never saw me off to the United States. She died long before I fled the parental nest. My brother-in-law died. The *Teach Mór* (Big House) he built is untenanted.

I am glad when I see the noble fort of Dún Aonghus, cresting the tallest cliff in the island, three hundred feet from sea level. It awakens more pleasant memories.

The fort comprises three rings of horseshoe-shaped walls overlooking Port Murvey and the best land in Aran. This is where the landgrabber's cattle were walked blind-folded over the cliff during the stirring days of the Land League. But for the Land League the whole island might have been his by grace of the landlord. Near Port Murvey on the bay side is the village of Killmurvey. The villagers were allowed to live on the land the grabber thought not worth taking. For generations they have been hauling sand from the seashore, mixing it with seaweed and silt from the roads and turning bare rocks into tillage land. Someone has written that 'angels from heaven must have poured down blessings on the bare flags of Aran' otherwise the land could not produce the finest cattle and sheep in Ireland, and excellent crops of potatoes.

It is quite possible that the angels took a friendly interest in the island, if for no other reason than because of the number of saints who settled there and built monasteries, but it must be admitted that the angels were ably assisted by the hard-working peasants who broke rocks with sledges, levelled out the area about to be 'made', carried precious soil in creels on their backs and oftentimes fought fierce battles with rivals to gain possession of the loam to mix with the loose sand and yellow clay. The Gaedhealtacht peasant is oftentimes charged with laziness by superior persons from other parts of Ireland who themselves failed to make a living out of good tillage and pasture land, but if any one of these critics had to rear a family of from ten to fourteen children on sixteen or twenty-four acres of Aran Mór or the other two islands in the chain he would have a different story.

We pass Dún Aonghus. The landscape now becomes even more familiar. There is the Cliff of the Swan and the Blind Sound, where the steep descent of the land from Dún Aonghus stops. Underneath the cliff at this spot the sea has bored a deep hole. For centuries the ocean has waged a winning battle against the rock. It aims to cut the island in two. Time is on its side and the sea is patient. I see the Yellow Rock where I caught my first bollach and the Worm

Hole, that remarkable oblong hole, like a Roman bath, carved out of the limestone flag. It ebbs and flows through an underground passage. There should be a legend about the Worm Hole, but if there is I never heard it. It is about time one should be invented.

Now we are opposite the Port of the Fort's Mouth and the village of Gort na gCapall. An ancestor of mine by the name of Bartholomew founded Gort na gCapall. I am sorry he did not pick a choicer location.

There is a story they tell in Aran about a wealthy Englishman who suddenly became aware of his conscience and wanted to go to some remote and desolate spot to live the simple life and do penance for his sins. He travelled the world and selected Gort na gCapall, as being in his opinion the most desolate place on the map. He offered the villagers a large sum of money for the townland, but they laughed his offer to scorn and went on braving the wild seas off the Port of the Fort's Mouth in their curachs searching for fish, carrying seaweed on their backs up steep cliffs, making land out of rock, filling fissures in the crags with stones for fear the cattle might break their legs in them, making kelp, fighting landlords and tax gatherers and living rather happily in the place a wealthy Englishman had selected for his Purgatory.

Bartholomew's descendants still live in Gort na gCapall, and work with the primitive implements Bartholomew and the men of his time used. Bartholomew built his house upon a rock, not for reasons of security or because he considered the rock symbolical of continuity, but because he did not want to waste a piece of good pasture or tillage land under a house.

Directly opposite Gort na gCapall is the village of Oatquarter, where in the old schoolhouse, now a ruin, David O'Callaghan taught me to read and write my native language thirty odd years ago.

My most treasured recollection of Oatquarter national school is the memory of Roger Casement, tall and thin, his black beard accentuating the pallor of his countenance. I believe he was British Consul at Lisbon at the time. He visited the school house and told the teacher he would like to know if he had a pupil who could grind his way through Eoghan Ó Neachtain's column in the *Cork Examiner*. The teacher fondled his luxuriant brown beard and smiled. 'Indeed I have,' he said. I was called to the front and came out of the test with drums beating. Sir Roger gave me half-a-crown, and afterwards sent me three books: *The Story of Ireland,* by A. M. Sullivan; *Séadna*, by Father O'Leary; and *Fairies at Work*, by William P. Ryan, then the editor of the *Irish Peasant*. The two latter books were in Gaelic. Later Sir Roger planned to send me to Summerhill College, Sligo, but fate intervened and the project fell through.

Mr O'Callaghan had no word of Irish when he came to Aran. He learned the old tongue and after he had mastered it he impressed upon the islanders the importance of preserving it and taught them to pride themselves on its possession.

In those days the islands were being rapidly Anglicized. Policemen, tax collectors, and the native shopkeeping shoneens were at work hammering a sense of inferiority into the people. 'English is the language that'll stand by you when you go to America,' was the maxim. Children were reared for export to the American labour market.

Mr O'Callaghan did great work. He was no cheap Jingo nationalist of the type who froths at the mouth at the mention of an Englishman; but he hated British imperialism with all its works and pomps. He was the first *Sinn Féiner* in the island, and had no difficulty in making one of me. My father threw in his lot with us, when he learned that there were not more than four hundred *Sinn Féiners* in all Ireland. He was a strong believer in minorities and was always ready to side with the underdog.

As the liner sneaked along in the now smooth sea I wondered where my old schoolteacher was, if he were still alive, and if he recollected the many tricks I played on him for which he thrashed me with violence and with demoniacal fury. He was a fine man. How many workers like O'Callaghan are forgotten when the ideals for which they struggled are realized in whole or in part, while the blatant politicians and the gentlemen who always manage to pick the winning side are honoured?

The cliffs are rising steadily again since we left the Port of the Fort's Mouth, the only beach on the south side of the island. The next village is Comhrac, which means conflict. The English post-office name for the hamlet is meaningless, like the phonetic atrocities that go for names of places all over Ireland. Comhrac is distinguished for having the best seaweed shore in Aran Mór, and for being the site of the church of the Four Beautiful Saints, set in a sheltered plot where the grass grows long and green all the year round.

Next comes the village of Baile na Creige which is, as the name implies, unusually rocky. Here lives the famous cliffman, cobbler, dog-fancier, and amateur archaeologist, Michaleen son of Sarah. He claims to have discovered diamonds in the boulders by the seashore. Baile na Creige, like all the other villages in Aran Mór, cannot be seen from the south. The island rises in tiers from the bay and most of the hamlets are sheltered by low cliffs from the storms that come from the west.

The next townland is Eochaill, the site of one of the two Catholic churches in the island, a fort and an old disused lighthouse. The chapel is on the sloping lawn over the road overlooking the bay. Here I served Mass when a boy, and when I had outgrown the soutane my brother Liam took my place and my soutane!

How I used to envy the men and the young boys of my own age who lay on the grass outside the church before Mass, talking and laughing while I and my associate altar-boy stood in the sacristy waiting for the arrival of the priest. And how great used to be my satisfaction in ringing the bell and seeing the idlers on the lawn jump to their feet and make a rush for a seat in the gallery.

And when the people were all gathered in church I carried the pail of holy water for the priest and the sprinkler made out of straw, and sometimes when a large face with all the earmarks of piety got an extra splash of holy water, I chuckled inwardly and glanced at the priest's face to see if his generosity was intentional.

I remember one curate who doubted the sincerity of those who ostenta-tiously manifested their piety by loud groans and moans during Mass, and he often expressed himself frankly on this subject in his sermons ...

The steamer is streaking her way rapidly over the smooth sea, but she is not moving more rapidly than my thoughts. One moment I am in Aran, the next in Boston, New York, Chicago, Montana, London, Paris, Berlin, Moscow. From Aran with its primitive economy to America, the last word in industrial efficiency. From Aran where nobody got rich or even wished for riches, to America where some made fabulous fortunes and almost everybody hoped his turn would come! Leaving Aran when the world was peaceful and full of hope, with only a black speck here and there on the political horizon to keep the pessimists in good mood. Returning when the world is black with despair, the bubble of prosperity burst, wars and civil strife the order of the day, and world war rumours in the air!

Leaving Aran twenty-one years ago with the Union Jack flying over police barrack and coastguard station. Returning to see the tricolour of a Free State of twenty-six of our thirty-two counties flying in its place – a tricolour designed to be the flag of an All-Ireland Republic. Intervening years of civil war and bloodshed. Millions of human lives sacrificed to human greed. The noble Casement whose great heart went out to all suffering humanity, to the slaves of the notorious King Leopold of Belgium in the Congo, and the unfortunate chattels of the rubber exploiters in the Putumayo, South America, as well as to the Irish people who chafed under British rule – Casement dies on the gallows, killed by the Government that knighted him for his humanitarian work in the Congo. Did the British capitalists covet King Leopold's rubber? Did they hanker for his slave-gotten loot? Connolly, Pearse ... The liner speeds on.

We are now opposite the little village of Mainistir, snuggling unseen by me under the hills overlooking a small bay. The village that was more home to me than my native Gort na gCapall. It was my mother's birthplace. And I liked the emotional, soft, witty, story-telling Ganlys better than the harsh, quarrelsome, haughty, 'ferocious O'Flaherties'. Only one Ganly left in Aran: a cousin of mine. She married an O'Flaherty. All my Ganly aunts and uncles dead. Father William died in Melbourne. A fine Gaelic scholar, melancholy and joyous in turns. My uncle Thomas who took a shot at a bailiff during the Land League days and went to America, after being released from prison, where he was held as a 'suspect' with my father – he died in Boston. My uncle Pat, carefree and irresponsible who inherited the family estate – he took the landlord's eviction notices and other essential documents out of the courthouse during the Land League days. A great rebel, the best story-teller in Aran, and my favourite relative. My Aunt Kate who died with a witticism on her lips. Aran would be cold without them! The little green fields of Mainistir, the little ruined temple under the ivy-clad hill, the little well where I used to go with my cousins to get water for the tea, the low cliff outside the door of the house on which my uncle used to stand and tease the men working in the garden – they would revive old memories. Well –

Dún Dubh Chathair strikes the eye. It's the last of the forts in Aran Mór. We are now in line with Kilronan, the largest village on the island. Next comes Killeany, a fishing village of landless peasants forced to depend entirely on the sea for their existence. They were robbed of their land by Aran's greatest landgrabber. When the seas were rough, they could not fish, so they sat on the walls or lay on the limestone flags. Superior persons said they were very poor because they were very lazy. They were very poor because they had been robbed.

Beyond Killeany – called after Aran's greatest saint, Enda – is the graveyard. On the sandy mound over a long strand. Here is where the bones of my people rest.

We pass Iar Árainn, the most easterly village and sand-swept. We sight the lighthouse on Straw Island at the entrance to Kilronan. We pass Gregory's Sound, Inismaan, the Foul Sound, and then Inisheer. Now we are heading for the great Bay of Galway.

NETTING GUILLEMOTS

Of all the birds that haunted the tall cliffs at the south side of the island, the guillemot was the only one sought after by the islanders for its flesh and its feathers. The cormorant's flesh was tough, and he was an ill-smelling bird anyhow. The puffin resembled the rock-bird, but he was not found in large numbers. The sea-gull was worthless, and the gannets that shot down out of the sky after fish did not inhabit the cliffs. Where they went to at night nobody knew. Some said they slept on the sea with their heads sheltered under their wings. Others believed that they went off to some island on the coast of Kerry.

Hundreds of thousands of guillemots visited the cliffs every year about the end of May to clean out the ledges on which they laid their eggs. This house-cleaning job accomplished they went off and returned early in June to lay their eggs and hatch them. This was the time selected by the islanders to catch them. There was a law which made it an offence to catch guillemots in the nesting season, but the islanders were able to evade the law as the coast-guards could be seen coming at a distance, and there were plenty of sgailps and clefts to hide the birds in until the guards were gone.

There were thirty men in the village able to take a hand in catching guillemots. One half the number would be stationed on top of the cliff and the other half in canoes at the bottom, or on the shore, when the tide went out.

This year I was fishing bream with Colm of the Shaggy Beard and Patsy Holland, and though they hailed from a neighbouring village we allowed them to come rock-birding with us. They had what was known as a 'fishing relationship' with the people of Portadun.

I went home to waken my father. My mother got up and made tea. As we were embarking on a dangerous mission she was worried, and not only did she make the sign of the cross on my forehead with a drop of holy water, but she saw that I had my little statue of Saint Anthony with me.

My father and I went to the corcair where the men of the village were

From *Cliffmen of the West* (1935).

gathered. They greeted each other joyously and offered felicitations on the loveliness of the morning. There was a community spirit among them that morning which contrasted so favourably with the spirit of greedy rivalry that prevailed when each one tried to gain an advantage over the other gathering seaweed on the shore. When Little Jimmy announced they were going to the Cliff of the Font there was a murmur of disapproval, but it was quelled by a few words from my father, who was supported by my uncle and by Colm of the Shaggy Beard and Patsy Holland.

'Little Jimmy is the leading cliffman in Portadun,' my father ruled, 'and where he says we'll go that's where we go. Anybody who's afraid of Paddy the Climber's ghost doesn't care much for guillemots.'

'It's not afraid of the ghost some of us are as much as of the sharp snout that juts out from the cliff under the ledge where the guillemots are,' said Shawneen O'Neill. 'And you know the net is likely to get caught there. Also there is a rotten spot in the cliff and it may fall down at any moment.'

'I'll take care of any entanglement of the net in the cliff,' said little Jimmy, 'and if the cliff falls it will make a big noise, and there is no music sweeter than large rocks falling down to the bottom. Heh, heh!'

'Not if they fall on the people in the curraghs,' said Shawneen.

'We have eyes in our heads, haven't we?' my father snorted.

'Let's be going in the name of God,' said Jimmy, and off we went.

Our equipment was an old mackerel net, several strong ropes and a pair of old trousers attached to a line.

Five men went into each canoe, three on the oars and two as passengers. Most of them would go ashore to man the ropes. The net was placed in my father's canoe. He was the look-out man, the leading man at the bottom of the cliff. He had charge of the curragh fleet.

We rowed eastwards along the foot of the cliff. The spring tide had barely gone into the sea and there was an early ebb. The wind was to the north-west and here under the shelter of the cliffs there was hardly a puff. The water was perfectly calm. Here, where the waves rose mountains high in stormy weather, there was hardly a ripple. Only a gentle murmur where the water danced lazily around the rocks. We rowed slowly, letting our oars fall heavily into the water. No sound came from our canoes except the rumble of the sticks on the thole-pins and the splash as the oars fell. We passed by the Cliff of the Fish, and now the view was unhindered by jutting rock as far as the Cliff of the Font.

'How long since Paddy the Climber lost his life at the Cliff of the Death Grip?' Colm of the Shaggy Beard asked Patsy Holland.

'It is twenty years if it is a day,' Patsy answered.

'God between us and harm,' said Colm, 'wasn't it a terrible death?'

'It was, indeed. It was a long time afterwards when his bones were found on the rocks below. Nobody knew where he had gone. And it was a week after he was last seen in Cragmore that people went looking for him. It seems he was trying to pass through the Grip of Death and his head got caught. He would be in that position only a minute when his head would swell, and unless somebody was behind to pull him back he was gone. So he stayed there until the scavenger birds picked the flesh off his body and nothing was left of him on the Cleft of the Grip of Death except a piece of his skull that remained stuck to the rock above as if it was glued to it. May the Lord have mercy on his soul!'

'Amen, musha,' Colm encored.

We arrived in the semi-circular bay at the Cliff of the Font. The top cliffmen had not yet arrived. Here the cliff was about one hundred fifty feet high, and the ledge on which the birds nested was seventy-five feet from the sea-level. We backed into the rock and put three men ashore. Other canoes did likewise. I stayed in the curragh with Colm. We paddled about, pulling lightly on our oars. The men who went ashore were stretching the net along the bottom of the cliff. They made as little noise as possible lest they might frighten the birds.

Soon the men who were to man the ropes from the top appeared. Little Jimmy guided their efforts from a narrow plank of rock that went out about two feet from the face of the cliff. He could see the men below as well as the men on top. He was signalling to my father at the bottom. My father was on the first stand in his canoe. He was using his hat to signal. The top men let down three ropes, one for each end of the net and one in between. The latter would be attached to the trousers at the bottom. It would be hauled up when the net was in place in front of the ledge. Then a man above and below would pull on it and it would flap against the cliff and frighten the birds off their eggs. They would dash madly out and go right into the net.

Everything went according to schedule. The net was hauled up and the trousers began to flap against the rocks. The birds scampered out screaming and into the net. My father signalled to Jimmy to warn the men against the impact of the birds against the net. I could see their heads, one behind the other, as they sat on the ground with their heels against pieces of rock.

The net bellied out with its load of birds and my father signalled to lower. Some of the birds managed to escape, but most of them were hopelessly entangled. They screamed and bit at one another in a mad frenzy. I uttered an expression of pity for the poor things, but Colm said gruffly:

'They were made to be plucked and eaten, and we might as well pluck and eat them as any others. Where would the people get feather beds to give their daughters when they get married only for the rock-birds?'

There was sense to this talk, but still I did not get as much fun out of the catching of the birds as I expected to. In a moment, however, something happened that lifted my thoughts off the humane plane on which they were ruminating. One of the side ropes slid into a narrow slit that ran down the face of the cliff right by the Grip of Death, and the bottom horizontal rope of the net got caught on a chin of rock.

My father waved his hat horizontally and Little Jimmy gave the signal to the top men to hold fast. He also waved to the men at the foot of the cliff to clear east and west to safety. Stray rocks might fall or, worse still, a whole section of rotting cliff might break loose and mangle them into pulp beneath its crushing weight.

The men hauled on the rope and I thought I noticed a tremor on a bulge of cliff around the rope that was in the slit. For a moment the men were undecided what to do. Then Little Jimmy signalled that he was going to descend.

Soon he appeared over the edge with his back to the sea. There was a rope around his hips and he held on to it with one hand while he gripped jagged pieces of rock with the other as he came down. He landed on a platform which communicated with the ledge on which the birds nested. Taking off the rope he started on his hands and knees towards the Grip of Death. I noticed for the first time that he carried a boat-hook in his hand. He often used this when fighting off the Great Raven at the Gable of the Big Mountain in the western end of the island.

'He'll have to go through the Grip to unloosen the net off the rock,' I said to Colm. 'He should have gone down on the other side.'

'He knows his business,' said Colm. 'The cliff may fall any minute, and if it does he'll have the shelter of the awning over his head. And his head is small enough to let him through the Grip of Death.'

'I hope so!' I prayed, burning with anxiety.

There was a hush over the cliffs, broken only by the whirring of birds' wings flying around the enemy and an occasional scream from the captured guillemots in the net. The men at the bottom had taken to the canoes for safety. They watched little Jimmy almost breathlessly. He was now flattened on the rock at the narrowest spot on the ledge, his head turned to one side. Soon he appeared on the other side.

'By the strength of the Book, he's out,' came the simultaneous shout from the men below.

'May God not weaken you!' Colm shouted.

Stretching himself alongside the edge, Little Jimmy lowered his boat-hook. He inserted it in the horizontal rope and gave it a sharp jerk. He lifted the rope off the ledge, and when he did the weight of the net and the birds pulled the handle out of his hand. At the same moment my father shouted to the men on top to let go the ropes. He waved his hat frantically with a downward motion. I saw the bulging cliff around the perpendicular rope tremble. Before I had time to shout dust flew from the cliff, and in an instant down came tons of rock and dirt with an awful roar carrying net and birds with it. Little Jimmy was safe under his limestone roof.

After we satisfied ourselves that the fall was over, we put our men ashore and they proceeded to disentangle the rope from the rocks. Fortunately only a small part of the end got caught in the cascade of stone. We were so interested in the work that we had forgotten Little Jimmy. The men were busily engaged wringing the birds' necks and tossing them into the canoes when somebody shouted:

'Jimmy is entangled!'

'Oh, God of Glory!' my uncle shouted.

He waved his hat to the men on top to lower a rope. It came down instantly. Patsy Holland wanted to climb, but my uncle was at the rope ahead of him. Up he went like a fly, steering himself with one hand while he held on to the rope with the other. Shortly he was at the ledge where Little Jimmy was caught. My father signalled to the top men to stop pulling. In a moment Little Jimmy was released. His face was bleeding. My uncle ruthlessly pulled him back by the legs, tearing the skin off the side of his face.

'It was the only thing to do,' Colm explained.

Jimmy climbed up to the top on the rope and my uncle came down.

'It's a wonderful day,' was his only comment. We did not count the birds but we guessed there were about a thousand in the net. The top ropes were unloosed and hauled up. We took the net into one of the canoes and rowed west to the Big Byre. There we took two hauls without untoward incident, and when we had the three canoes almost filled we started back to the Port of the Fort's Mouth.

The women and old men and children of the village were there before us with baskets. There was great rejoicing when we began to throw out the birds on the rock. Married women were making the young girls blush by saying that there was the makings of many a marriage-bed of feathers in the three canoes.

The birds were divided into thirty lots, a share for each man who was engaged in catching them. We counted out one hundred twenty birds into each lot. That meant two hundred forty for our house.

After we got the guillemots home and had tea we set about washing the dirt and salt off them. Then we stuck their beaks in the gables of our houses and let them dry in the sun. It was a pretty sight.

'The coast-guards are coming!' came the warning from a young lad who was sitting on the comb of the highest house on the village.

Immediately the villagers took the birds out of the gables and hid them in various clefts. Some took them to Eireamon's Cave which went a long distance under a low cliff near the village. We threw our birds in a hole near the house, which was used for hiding rifles during the land war.

My father was at the gap leading to our house when the coast-guards came up the corcair. The officer in command greeted him cordially.

'Fine day, Manus!' he said.

'It is, indeed,' my father replied.

'It should make a fine day for catching guillemots,' the officer followed.

'It would, but unfortunately it's a closed season on guillemots.'

'I understand the villagers are very fond of guillemots, and I am afraid that the efforts of the British government to protect the birds are not always effective.'

'I believe the people of Portadun are every bit as fond of guillemots as the British government,' my father said, with a twinkle in his eye.

'I am glad to hear that,' said the officer. 'It is my duty to see that His Majesty's laws are obeyed.'

'It would be a queer person who would blame a man for doing his duty as he sees it,' my father observed.

The officer looked round suspiciously, but there were no birds in sight.

'I am glad everything is in order,' he laughed, as he turned on his heel.

'This is an orderly village,' my father countered, also turning on his heel.

Soon the birds appeared in their gables and the business of plucking followed. Then a sharp stick was inserted into the gullet of each bird and the guillemots were turned over a blazing fire to remove the down. After this was done they were split and gutted, salted and packed in barrels. Later on they would be put out on the flags to dry and eaten every day of the week except Friday.

Máirtín Ó Direáin

'Stoite'

Ár n-aithreacha bhíodh,
Is a n-aithreacha siúd,
In achrann leis an saol
Ag coraíocht leis an gcarraig loim.

Aiteas orthu bhíodh
Tráth ab eol dóibh
Féile chaoin na húire,
Is díocas orthu bhíodh
Ag baint ceart
De neart na ndúl.

Thóg an fear seo teach
Is an fear úd
Claí nó fál
A mhair ina dhiaidh
Is a choinnigh a chuimhne buan.

Sinne a gclann,
Is clann a gclainne,
Dúinn is éigean
Cónaí a dhéanamh
In árais ó dhaoine
A leagfadh cíos
Ar an mbraon anuas.

Beidh cuimhne orainn go fóill:
Beidh carnán trodán
Faoi ualach deannaigh
Inár ndiaidh in Oifig Stáit.

From *Dánta 1939–1979* (1980).

Máirtín Ó Direáin

'Uprooted'

Our fathers
And their fathers before them
Were at grips with life
And wrestled with the naked rock.

They were happy
When the seasons revealed to them
Earth's kindly abundance
And they were eager
To hold their own
Against the force of the elements.

One man built a house
And another
A dyke or a wall
Which outlived him
And kept his name alive.

We, their children,
And their children's children,
Are compelled
To make our homes
In apartments whose owners
Would levy rent
On the drip from the ceiling.

We will be remembered yet:
A stack of files
Weighed down with dust
Will survive in a government office.

Transl. Tomás Mac Síomóin and Douglas Sealy in *Tacar Dánta/Selected Poems* (1984).

Máirtín Ó Direáin

Two Blind Men in Inis Mór

We had two blind men. One lived in the village to the east and the other in the village to the west and neither of them had a good word for the other. Not since the day they collided and had a tremendous session of abuse. Both of them had sharp tongues but the man to the east was master of the man to the west when it came to sarcasm, repartee, wit and all other manners of speech.

A woman in our village sold fish, when fish was scarce. One day the blind man to the east came to buy a certain fish. He took it and fingered it carefully as blind men do.

'How much is this, little sister?' he said.

She told him. 'Well, little sister,' he said, 'Put it back until it grows a bit.'

People were afraid of this blind man. They believed he had power and that if he was annoyed and cursed someone the curse would certainly fall. Another of his feats, it was said, was to have hatched a clutch of chickens in his bosom when the hen stopped clocking.

It was also said that his brother, who was in Connemara, heard him calling him to his dinner one calm day. The blind man didn't know his brother had gone to Connemara. He thought he was down in the garden. In those days, people were in the habit of going to Connemara all of a sudden, on calm days, when they felt the urge.

The blind man to the west was most concerned by holiness. He spent a lot of time with priests who came on holidays and they told him a lot of pious stories. He had them all off by heart. One of my oldest memories is of him visiting our house one day when the man from the house with the flat roof had called to see my father. I think my father had just fallen ill. The other man was also in poor health. Indeed, I think both of them died that very year. The blind man was talking about the day of judgement. 'What will happen to the land that people are so greedy for?' someone said. The blind man lashed the hearthstone with his stick.

'Embers,' he said. 'It will all be reduced to embers.'

'It's futile to expect people to have sense in that case,' said my mother.

Then the blind man turned to my father and the other visitor.

From *Feamainn Bhealtaine* (1961).

191

'We should all be in under that cliff above there,' he said, 'Fasting and praying.'

'Ah, what about the cold droplets,' they said.

'Night will fall on you,' I said boldly late in the evening.

Everyone in the house laughed, but none so heartily as the blind man himself.

'With me it's always night-time, little brother,' he said.

I blushed when I realised what I had said. There was a dwarf in another village further west. I never heard him called that name. I never even heard that word. If it was in use at all it was unknown to me. I never heard him called anything but 'little Coilmeen'. I never saw anyone so tidy as the same Coilmeen. He wore a blue shirt, little trousers and a pair of boots. His clothes were always neat and clean. He used to come to the shop in our village after getting the pension and carried a load home such as a woman with a houseful of children would not have, although he lived alone.

I noticed that the women came to the doors to gaze after him in wonder although they saw him frequently.

'Upon my soul,' one of them would say to a young girl, 'that fellow was married to a great big blonde lady from Connemara, but she left him there and went off to America. My God, but she was a fine woman.'

'Musha! By the souls of all belonging to you,' the young girl would say.

'On my solemn oath,' the woman would say, 'they lived in that outhouse that belongs to Micil Shorcha now.'

'Will you look at him going down,' they would say, 'isn't he beautifully wrapped up. His little trousers, his little vest, his little boots.'

'Hasn't he the neat and proper go to him.'

'On my solemn oath, but he's the cocky fellow.' I'm afraid the children were much more mischievous than the women. They often drove the poor man to distraction with their teasing. It seems that Coilmeen had no curse or if he had that it wouldn't fall on anyone.

What I now recollect is my father's dignity when he was laid out. I would probably have been aware of it at the time had such a thought entered my mind; if I possessed the word dignity, if I understood its meaning. The corpse has much more dignity than the living people who surround it. As long as there is life in a person he is capable of doing or saying something which would make him a laughing stock, something that doesn't apply to the dead. There were two people in the room where my father was laid out, my mother and the man who had shaved him.

'He had wonderful bones,' said the man, 'and he didn't fail all that much either.'

'Ah! brother he did,' said my mother. 'He failed terribly, God help us.' I found such talk very strange.

I can now see the tall, strong man beginning to fail. We children could not understand why he was so cranky, shouting at us to clear out of the house when we were playing with our cousins. Children are selfish; cruel and shameless at times. A child is capable of carrying out an act so terrible that its memory will haunt him for the rest of his life. If only he could undo what he had done! Searing regret frequently follows the act, but the child finds it difficult to articulate his regret or ask an adult to forgive him.

I remember a tranquil, sleepy evening. The sort of evening that finds it difficult to submit to night. My father was walking down the yard to the garden near the shore. Not that he was capable of doing much at that stage, but peevishness was driving him out of the house. I called him a few names and threw some little pebbles at him. I think he burst into tears. 'Now do you see what you've done to your father?' said my mother. Sick as he was he should have given me a thrashing. I went around the gable end of the house and was overcome by emotion. It was a mixture of shame, contrition and disgust. In the end I began to cry.

What a malicious, contrary little animal a child is, although his behaviour can change completely in the blinking of an eye. I deeply regret what I did that evening. I wish its memory did not haunt and hurt me.

I remember him going down to the hospital a couple of times and that it did him little good. But above every other abiding memory is my recollection of the night he died. I saw my mother putting on her coat and going out to my uncle's house and I shuddered. At that early stage of my life I understood the meaning of the words 'cold' and 'fear'. I was cold and fearful that night.

I knew I was in the presence of death but for all that I fell asleep again shortly afterwards. And now they were speaking of him while he was incapable of speaking for himself and a seven-year-old orphan listened. My memory of that day and the following two days is very fragmented. That's the way of it. Our memories of childhood happenings are like the trailer for a film. That which precedes and follows a certain scene is hidden from us, and that may be for the better at times.

I know that women in shawls were there and they killed me entirely. They would discuss something and you would think it had nothing to do with sadness or death, and then, as if responding to a message from eternity itself, every one of them would move her shawl an inch or two further forward on her head and the hard, piercing keening would commence. Keening that would tear at your vitals, but which also had a certain beauty. Ancient, mysterious beauty.

I wandered into the little garden down behind the house. Men were making my father's coffin. They were laughing and telling stories. I found this strange. I thought that no one should laugh on such a day.

Before he was coffined we were all sent into the room to the bed to take his hand and bid him farewell. I refused to bid him farewell although I was the oldest of the children. I could not take his hand.

It was said that if you bade farewell to the dead you would not fear them afterwards. I was very fearful for a long time, but I think it would have been the same for me even if I had taken his hand for the last time.

Máirtín Ó Direáin

'Ó Mórna'

A ródai fáin as tír isteach
A dhearcann tuama thuas ar aill,
A dhearcann armas is mana,
A dhearcann scríbhinn is leac,
Ná fág an reilig cois cuain
Gan tuairisc an fhir a bheith leat.

Cathal Mór Mac Rónáin an fear,
Mhic Choinn Mhic Chonáin Uí Mhórna,
Ná bí i dtaobh le comhrá cáich,
Ná le fíor na croise á ghearradh
Ar bhaithis chaillí mar theist an fhir
A chuaigh in uaigh sa gcill sin.

Ná daor an marbh d'eis cogar ban,
D'éis lide a thit idir uille
Is glúin ar theallach na sean,
Gan a phór is a chró do mheas,
A chéim, a réim, an t-am do mhair,
Is guais a shóirt ar an uaigneas.

Meas fós dúchas an mhairbh féin
D'eascair ó Mhórna mór na n-éacht,
Meabhraigh a gcuala, a bhfaca sé,
Ar a chuairt nuair a d'éist go géar,
Meabhraigh fós nár ceileadh duais air,
Ach gur ghabh chuige gach ní de cheart.

From *Dánta 1939–1979* (1980).

Máirtín Ó Direáin

'Ó Mórna'

Traveller straying in from the mainland,
You who gaze at a tomb on a cliff-top,
Who gaze at a coat of arms and a slogan,
Who gaze at inscription and flagstone,
Do not leave the graveyard by the bay
Before you know the dead man's story.

The man was Cathal Mór the son of Rónán,
Son of Conn son of Conán Ó Mórna,
But don't rely on common hearsay
Nor crone signing the cross on her forehead
To give you a true report of the man
Who entered the grave in that churchyard.

Don't condemn the dead man because of women's whispers,
Following a hint let fall between elbow
And knee by the old people's hearth,
Before you consider his blood and lineage,
His station, his power, the age he lived in,
And the snares that loneliness sets for his sort.

Consider also the dead man's heredity,
How he sprang from the line of great Ó Mórna,
Think of all he heard, all he saw,
As he went around he listened intently,
Remember also no prize was denied him
But all that he took was taken by right.

Transl. Tomás Mac Síomóin and Douglas Sealy in *Tacar Dánta/Selected Poems* (1984).

Chonaic níochán is ramhrú dá éis,
Chonaic mná ag úradh bréidín,
Gach cos nocht ó ghlúin go sáil
Ina slis ag tuargain an éadaigh,
Bean ar aghaidh mná eile thall
Ina suí suas san umar bréige.

Chonaic is bhreathnaigh gach slis ghléigeal
Chonaic na hógmhná dá fhéachaint
Dá mheas, dá mheá, dá chrá in éineacht.
D'fhreagair fuil an fhireannaigh thréitheach,
Shiúil sí a chorp, las a éadan,
Bhrostaigh é go mear chun éilimh.

'Teann isteach leo mar a dhéanfadh fear,
Geallaimse dhuit go dteannfar leat,
Feasach iad cheana ar aon nós,
Nach cadar falamh gan géim tú,
Ach fear ded' chéim, ded' réim cheart.'
Pádhraicín báille a chan an méid sin.
Briolla gan rath! mairg a ghéill dó.

Iar ndul in éag don triath ceart
Rónán Mac Choinn Mhic Chonáin,
Ghabh Cathal chuige a chleacht,
A thriúcha is a chumhachta,
A mhaoir, a bháillí go dleathach,
A theideal do ghabh, is a ghlac.

An t-eolas a fuair sna botháin
Nuair a thaithigh iad roimh theacht i seilbh,
Mheabhraigh gach blúire riamh de,
Choigil is choinnigh é go beacht,
Chuaigh chun tairbhe dó ina dhiaidh sin
Nuair a leag ar na daoine a reacht.

Mheabhraigh sé an té bhí uallach,
Nach ngéillfeadh go réidh dá bheart,
Mheabhraigh sé an té bhí cachtúil,
An té shléachtfadh dó go ceart,
Mheabhraigh fós gach duais iníonda
Dár shantaigh a mhian ainsrianta.

He saw the washing and then the thickening,
Saw the women scouring frieze,
Each naked leg from knee to heel .
Like a wash-staff pounding the cloth,
Woman sitting opposite woman
Along the sides of the makeshift trough,

Saw and noted each white wash-staff,
Saw the young women gazing at him,
Sizing him up and tantalizing him.
The blood of the robust male responded,
Traversed his body, suffused his face
And urged him on to swift demand.

'Press in there close to them like a man,
I warrant you'll feel an answering pressure,
Sure they know already
You're no empty spunkless cod
But a man of your rank and direct ancestry.'
Pádhraicín the bailiff spoke those words.
A worthless rascal! You should have ignored him.

After the death of the titular lord,
Rónán the son of Conn the son of Conán,
The young Cathal took over his prerogative,
His lands and his jurisdictions,
His stewards and bailiffs as the law appointed,
He took his title and his power.

The knowledge gained in the cabins
Frequented before his accession,
He'd remembered every least bit of it,
Saved it up and treasured each detail;
He used it later for his own advantage
When he laid his law on the people.

He thought of the one who'd been stiffnecked,
Who wouldn't readily comply with his schemes,
He thought of the one who'd been obsequious,
The one who'd truly grovel before him,
He thought long of each virginal prize
For which he hankered with unbridled passion.

Mhair ár dtriath ag cian dá thuargain,
Ba fánach é ar oileán uaigneach,
Cara cáis thar achar mara
B'annamh a thagadh dá fhuascailt,
Is théadh ag fiach ar na craga
Ag tnúth le foras is fuaradh.

Comhairlíodh dó an pósadh a dhéanamh
Le bean a bhéarfadh dó mar oidhre
Fireannach dlisteanach céimeach
Ar phór Uí Mhórna na haibhse,
Seach bheith dá lua le Nuala an Leanna,
Peig na hAirde is Cáit an Ghleanna.

An bhean nuair a fuair Ó Mórna í
Níor rug aon mhac, aon oidhre ceart;
Níor luigh Ó Mórna léi ach seal,
Ba fuar leis í mar nuachair;
Ina cuilt shuain ní bhfuair a cheart,
É pósta is céasta go beacht.

Imíonn Ó Mórna arís le fuadar,
Thar chríocha dleathacha ag ruathradh,
Ag cartadh báin, ag cartadh loirg,
Ag treabhadh faoi dheabhadh le fórsa,
Ag réabadh comhlan na hóghachta,
Ag dul thar teorainn an phósta.

Ag réabadh móide is focail
Ag réabadh aithne is mionna,
A shúil thar a chuid gan chuibheas,
Ag éisteacht cogar na tola
A mhéadaigh fothram na fola,
Ina rabharta borb gan foras.

Ceasach mar mheasadh den chré lábúrtha
Leanadh Ó Mórna cleacht a dhúchais,
Thógadh paor thar chríocha aithnid,
Go críocha méithe, go críocha fairsing,
Dhéanadh lá saoire don subhachas
Dhéanadh lá saoire don rúpacht.

Our chief lived prey to melancholy's assaults,
Odd man out on a remote island,
An understanding friend from across the sound
Seldom came to his rescue
And he hunted on across the crags
Yearning for ease and alleviation.

He was advised to take in marriage
A woman who would bear him as heir
A legitimate and noble male-child
To continue the line of mighty Ó Mórna,
Instead of consorting with Alehouse Nuala,
Peg of Ard and Kate of Glen.

The wife, after Ó Mórna found her,
Bore him no son, no proper heir;
Ó Mórna lay with her only a while,
His newfound bride made a frigid mate;
In her drowsy bed his right was denied,
His marriage was nothing but torture.

Ó Mórna departs once more in haste,
Rampaging beyond the legal limits,
Digging the fallow land, digging the furrowed,
Ploughing with headlong violence,
Forcing the gate of virginity,
Crossing the bounds of marriage.

Breaking pledge and word,
Breaking commandment and vow,
Prompted by his greed's excess,
Listening to the whisper of desire
Increasing the clamour of his blood
In its rich and restless springtide.

Sated, they said, of base-born flesh,
Ó Mórna followed the ways of his forebears,
Used to take jaunts from known domains
To lush domains, to vast domains,
Abandoning all for the sake of pleasure,
Abandoning all for the harlot's embrace.

Maoir is báillí dó ag fónamh
Ag riaradh a thriúcha thar a cheann,
Ag comhalladh a gcumhachta níor shéimh,
Ag agairt danaide ar a lán,
An t-úll go léir acu dóibh féin
Is an cadhal ag gach truán.

Sloinnte na maor a bheirim díbh,
Wiggins, Robinson, Thomson, agus Ede,
Ceathrar cluanach nár choigil an mhísc,
A thóg an cíos, a dhíbir daoine,
A chuir an dílleacht as cró ar fán,
A d'fhag na táinte gan talamh gan trá.

Níor thúisce Ó Mórna ar ais
Ar an talamh dúchais tamall
Ná chleacht go mear gach beart
Dár tharraing míchlú cheana air:
Threabhadh arís an chré lábúrtha,
Bheireadh dúshlán cléir is tuata.

Tháinig lá ar mhuin a chapaill
Ar meisce faoi ualach óil.
Stad in aice trá Chill Cholmáin
Gur scaip ladhar den ór le spórt,
Truáin ag sciobadh gach sabhrain
Dár scaoil an triath ina dtreo.

Do gháir Ó Mórna is do bhéic,
Mairbh a fhualais sa reilig thuas
Ní foláir nó chuala an bhéic:
Dhearbhaigh fós le draothadh aithise
Go gcuirfeadh sabhran gan mhairg
In aghaidh gach míol ina n-ascaill.

Labhair an sagart air Dé Domhnaigh,
Bhagair is d'agair na cumhachta,
D'agair réabadh na hóghachta air,
Scannal a thréada d'agair le fórsa,
Ach ghluais Ó Mórna ina chóiste
De shodar sotail thar cill.

Stewards and bailiffs were at his disposal,
Administering his territories on his behalf,
Cruelly carrying out his instructions,
Causing grievous loss to many;
They had the whole of the apple to themselves,
Each starveling had the peel.

I give you the names of the stewards,
Wiggins, Robinson, Thomson and Ede,
Four crafty men who shunned no evil,
Who collected rents, who evicted tenants,
Who drove the orphan away from his hovel,
Who left hundreds without field or strand.

No sooner had Ó Mórna been back
On his native ground for a while
Than he quickly got up to the same tricks
Which had already gained him disrepute;
He ploughed again the base-born flesh
In open defiance of priest and layman.

One day he came on horseback,
Laden to the gills with drink,
Stopped beside the strand of Kilcolman
To scatter a handful of gold for sport;
The starvelings snatched at each sovereign
The lord tossed at their feet.

Ó Mórna roared and gave a shout,
The dead of his kin in the graveyard above
Must have heard that shout;
He declared as well with a sneer of contempt
That he could easily put up a sovereign
To match each louse in their arm-pits.

The priest named him on Sunday,
Threatened to use the powers against him,
Denounced him for profaning virginity,
Vehemently denounced the scandal to his flock,
But Ó Mórna set off in his coach
At an arrogant trot past the church.

D'agair gach aon a dhíth is a fhoghail air,
D'agair an ógbhean díth a hóghachta air,
D'agair an mháthair fán a háil air,
D'agair an t-athair talamh is trá air,
D'agair an t-ógfhear éigean a ghrá air,
D'agair an fear éigean a mhná air.

Bhí gach lá ag tabhairt a lae leis,
Gach bliain ag tabhairt a leithéid féin léi,
Ó Mórna ag tarraingt chun boilg chun léithe
Chun cantail is seirbhe trína mheisce,
Ag roinnt an tsotail ar na maoir
Ach an chruimh ina chom níor chloígh.

Nuair a rug na blianta ar Ó Mórna,
Tháinig na pianta ar áit na mianta:
Luigh sé seal i dteach Chill Cholmáin,
Teach a shean i lár na coille,
Teach nár scairt na grásta air,
Teach go mb'annamh gáire ann.

Trí fichid do bhí is bliain le cois,
Nuair a cuireadh síos é i gCill na Manach
D'éis ola aithrí, paidir is Aifreann;
I measc a shean i gCill na Manach
I dteannta líon a fhualais,
Ar an tuama armas is mana.

An chruimh a chreim istigh san uaigh tú,
A Uí Mhórna mhóir, a thriath Chill Cholmáin,
Níorbh í cruimh do chumais ná cruimh d'uabhair
Ach cruimh gur cuma léi íseal ná uasal.
Go mba sámh do shuan sa tuama anocht
A Chathail Mhic Rónáin Mhic Choinn.

Denounced by all for raiding and rapine,
Denounced by the girl for taking her maidenhead,
Denounced by the mother for her family scattered,
Denounced by the father for field and strand,
Denounced by the youth for raping his sweetheart,
Denounced by the husband for raping his wife.

Each day that passed meant one day less,
Each year that passed meant another gone,
Ó Mórna was falling to flesh and greyness,
More sour and petulant in his drunken bouts,
Venting his spleen on the stewards
But the worm in his flesh he could not defeat.

When the years caught up with Ó Mórna
The aches of desire were replaced by pain,
He lay for a while in the house of Kilcolman,
His ancestral house in the heart of the wood,
A house that grace had never shone on,
A house where laughter seldom sounded.

Threescore he was and a year besides
When he was buried in Cill na Manach
After Unction, Penance, prayer and Mass;
Among his ancestors in Cill na Manach
Along with the tally of his kin,
On the tomb a coat of arms and a slogan.

The worm that gnawed you in the grave,
Great Ó Mórna, lord of Kilcolman,
Was not the worm of your vigour nor of your hauteur
But a worm that heeds not birth nor blood.
Calm be your slumber in the tomb tonight,
Cathal son of Rónán son of Conn.

V

Man of Aran

*R*obert Flaherty came to Inis Mór at the end of 1931 and was taken on a tour of the island by Pat Mullen. He returned the following year and hired Pat as the local contact man for a film he had planned to make on the life of the island community. Filming took place over a two-year period and Man of Aran was released in 1934 to a mixed reception from the critics. Most praised its striking visual qualities, but many, especially those with left-wing political views, accused it of glorifying primitivism.

In Ireland it was almost universally praised. The then Taoiseach, Éamon de Valera, and the entire Cabinet attended the Irish première in the Grafton cinema on 6 May 1934. The film had an extended run, playing to packed houses. It was seen as confirming those values of self-reliance and frugal material comfort which the government espoused. It also seemed to confirm the officially sanctioned view that the West was the residual repository of all that was best in Irish life, a pure and untarnished bastion of Gaelic civilization.

One of the most severe criticisms came from Graham Greene: 'photography by itself cannot make poetic cinema. By itself it can only make arty cinema. Man of Aran was a glaring example of this: how wearisome were those figures against the skyline, how meaningless that magnificent photography of storm after storm. Man of Aran did not attempt to describe truthfully a way of life. The inhabitants had to be taught shark-hunting in order to supply Mr Flaherty with a dramatic sequence.'

Though it has long been assured of its place in film history and is often accorded classic status, Man of Aran continues to provoke disagreement among film critics and historians of film. Leslie Halliwell thinks it is 'highly impressive scene for scene, but tedious as a whole', while Pauline Kael says it 'achieves a true epic quality', being 'a truly exalted work – the greatest film tribute to man's struggle against hostile nature'.

In his book Man of Aran, Pat Mullen gives a first-hand account of how this strange but enduring film was made: the choosing of the cast, the difficulties Flaherty had in filming the shark-hunting sequence and his fear of losing a whole currach crew while filming a landing in really dangerous seas off the western tip of Inis Mór.

Flaherty decided to structure his film around a family. The Man, Colm 'Tiger' King, a blacksmith from Fearann an Choirce; the Woman, Maggie Dirrane, a housewife with a young family from Eoghnacht; and the Boy, Michaeleen Dillane from Cill Éinne.

Graham Greene's accusation that Flaherty did not attempt to describe truthfully a way of life is accurate but, of course, that was not what Flaherty set out to achieve. He filmed a world that never existed by deliberately avoiding all traces of community life and social customs – villages, churches, schools, contacts with the mainland and much more.

To add drama to the scene where the Woman carries a basket of seaweed on her back under a beetling cliff, with the sea breaking over her, Flaherty had to take seaweed from one side of the island (where it was harvested) to the other (where it was not). It is but one example of many such falsifications.

In a television interview given some years before his death, Tiger King was asked *about some of these scenes and how he felt about taking part in them. 'Ara, bhí fhios againne go maith gur bullshit a bhí ann ach ba chuma linn,' he said ('Yerra, we knew well it was bullshit but what did we care'). For all that, the film has taken its place among the acknowledged classics of the 'thirties and its success is a triumph for photography.*

The principal actors, chosen by Flaherty and Pat Mullen, never made another film. Maggie Dirrane returned to the island, reared her family and lived to be a great age. Tiger King went to England, worked as a farrier and on building sites and did not return to Inis Mór until his remains were brought home for burial in Cill Éinne. The Boy, Michaeleen Dillane, was sent to boarding-school in Galway but left to join first the Irish and then the British army. He was reputedly wounded at Dunkirk but he vanished without trace in the war's aftermath and is now but a hazy memory among the oldest islanders.

Pat Mullen also returned to the island and is buried in Cill Éinne cemetery.

Robert J. Flaherty

Man of Aran

Nearly three years ago, I was on my way across the Atlantic, in the *Berengaria* on my way from New York to Germany. I had just returned from the South Seas, where I had made my film *Moana*, and had no very definite plans for the future.

I met an Irish motor-engineer aboard the liner. He was travelling from America to the Co. Cork works of a great motor-car firm, and in the course of many conversations we had, this man told me something of the wild magnificence of the Aran Islands, and of the ceaseless struggle for the bare necessities of life carried on by the islanders. When the boat docked, I lost sight of him. I have never seen him since; I do not even know his name. But it was this chance-met Irishman who first gave me the idea of making a film in Aran. Had it not been for our shipboard talks, there would be no *Man of Aran* to-day.

I spent five months in Germany, and then, with my unknown friend's stories of the Aran Islands in mind, suggested to Mr Michael Balcon, of Gaumont-British Picture Corporation, that I should go to Aran and spy out the land.

I travelled to Aran, and there, only fifteen hours from London, this is what I found. A bare rock, nine miles long and three wide at its broadest point. There is no shade and no shelter, for there are no trees; there are no trees *because there is no soil*. Tremendous seas, rolling in from the Atlantic, pound the island, sending their spray over the 500-feet-high cliffs, and sometimes blowing clean across the island, borne on savage gusts of wind. The island has no natural resources; the thirty-mile passage to Galway City is fraught with danger, a terror to sailors. Yet on this barren slab of rock nearly 1,200 souls have their existence.

The first islander I took care to find was Pat Mullin. Pat has had an adventurous life, travelling in America and other parts of the world, but now lives once again in his native Aran, and drives a jaunting-car on the island. I asked him how many people lived in the little seaport-village of Kilronan, for Pat knows everything and everybody on the island. He thought for a long time, and he answered, 'Two hundred and thirty.' He had been counting the inhabitants, cottage by cottage, in his head!

Film press release, 1934.

When a little while later, I returned with my three hand-cranked cameras and equipment, it was Pat who became my major-domo and casting-manager. He found me my headquarters, near the only spring which would supply enough fresh water for our needs, and we settled here, in a six-roomed cottage belonging to an English-woman, in Kilmurvey, in the western part of the island. We converted an old stone lean-to shed into our laboratory, and installed a tiny petrol-engine, which developed enough electricity for the house-lighting, our film-lamps, and for the drying-machine and portable projector. I fancy that ours was the first 'foreign location' to do its own printing, developing and even cutting, on the spot.

Work started soon on the building of a small Irish cottage which I needed for interior-scenes, and it was while we had workmen engaged in clearing the ground, levelling and building that I was able to study 'types' and make my first contacts with the islanders.

There was Old Patch Ruadh, who, as his Irish name implies, sports a huge red beard. There was little Michael Dillane, whom I first saw at an Irish dance in the village one night. He was only twelve years old, and Pat had the devil and all of a job to persuade Michael's parents to let the boy come and act for me. Maggie Dirrane, the 'Madonna' character of the film, came and worked in our house, so that we had plenty of opportunity to study her and get to know her. She was glad to act in the film, for it gave her the chance to earn a little extra money. This was precious to Maggie, for her husband had been crippled gathering seaweed in a storm, and was unable to work.

You will see this process of seaweed-gathering in the film. The islanders collect it in baskets. Then they scrape up what little grains of soft earth they can find hidden in crannies in the rock, mix it with boulders crushed to powder with blows from the heavy sledge-hammer, and perhaps add a little imported earth. They spread this compost in thin strips on the bare rock, manure it with seaweed, and in it plant their potatoes. A few yards treated in this way constitute a kitchen-garden; a quarter-acre is a farm! Potatoes, fish and bread are the islanders' main food. There is no other produce, except a few cattle, kept in artificially grassed pounds surrounded by stone walls. A man will, maybe, sell one yearling at Galway Market in a year, and that will pay his rent and rates. An old man is rich if he draws the 10s. a week old age pension.

For the big storm-scenes in the picture, we had the services of Big Patcheen Conneely, Pat McDonough and Stephen Dirrane, the three most expert boatmen on the island. They took their frail curraghs – canoes made of tarred skins stretched over a wicker frame – to sea in weather in which you would have thought no boat could live. No man, indeed, but these three, knew the treacherous currents and narrow channels sufficiently to survive the storms they braved, and even so, the three canoemen went in peril of their lives for my storm-scenes.

These are terrible seas. They have snatched men from the very cliff-tops and dashed them to death on the rocks below. They have pounded the cottages themselves and laid them in ruins. One day we were shooting Maggie from above, as she gathered seaweed on a ledge fifty feet above the water. The sea was quite calm yet suddenly a great lazy swell loafed in from the ocean, and burst in a spatter of stones and spray which reached Maggie's ledge, and threw her down, bruised and battered, on the rock's edge. And I was told stories of how eight men in one family were 'taken by the sea' in one winter, and of curraghs, coming from Galway, reaching the island only to be driven by the furious waves clear back to Galway City again.

We spent nearly two years on the island, making our Gainsborough Picture, and the party was sad enough when we finally left. You cannot live two years with fine folk like the Aran Islanders without growing to love and know them, and we had worked with them, played with them in the evenings at billiards, at dancing; we had sat at their hearthsides, drinking potheen and telling tales. Great times we had had, and the women were weeping when we went down to the sea to go away back to England.

Later, nine of my Aran Island friends came to London. They had never been to England before; and, though they moved among wonders, they were calm and philosophical about it all. 'London's a great place, a fine place,' they said, 'but not for us. We must go back to our Island.'

And I hope that when you see *Man of Aran* and recognize the thrill of the islanders' age-long battle with the rock, the sea and the storm, you will understand why.

GAUMONT-BRITISH PICTURE CORPORATION, LTD,

presents

"MAN OF ARAN"

A GAINSBOROUGH PICTURE

Directed by **ROBERT FLAHERTY**

Collaborators : John Goldman and Frances H. Flaherty   Assistant Director : Pat Mullin (John) of Arran

Field Laboratory : John Taylor   Recordist : H. Hand

Editor and Scenarist : John Goldman

Specially composed score based on the original Irish Folk Songs of the Aran Islands

Musical Score by JOHN GREENWOOD

Under the direction of LOUIS LEVY

CHARACTERS

COLMAN (" TIGER ") KING - - - - -	A Man of Aran
MAGGIE DIRRANE - - - - - -	His Wife
MICHAEL DILLANE - - - - - -	Their Son

Pat Mullin - - - - - - -	
Patch Ruadh (Red Beard) - - -	Shark Hunting Crew
Patcheen Faherty - - - - -	
Tommy O'Rourke - - - - -	

" Big Patcheen " Conneely of the West - - -	
Stephen Dirrane - - - - - -	Canoe Men
Pat McDonough - - - - - -	

The Arran Islands lie off Western Ireland. All three are small, wastes of rock, without trees, without soil.

In winter storms they are almost smothered by the sea, which, because of the peculiar shelving of the coast, piles up into one of the most gigantic seas in the world.

In this desperate environment the Man of Aran, because of his independence is the most precious privilege he can win from life, fights for his existence, bare though it may be.

It is a fight from which he will have no respite until the end of his indomitable days—or until he meets his master—the sea.

Recorded on British Acoustic Film, New Process Full Range.

at Gainsborough Studio, Islington

Controlled throughout the United Kingdom

and Irish Free State by

Gaumont-British Distributors, Ltd.

Pat Mullen

Man of Aran

I

One day, late in the year '31, I drove to the pier and met a man named Mr Jaques, an English man. I drove him around. He was staying a week. He was very fond of fishing, so I got two other chaps with myself to row him out into the bay. He fixed up his own lines and killed, during the few days, a good share of mackerel and pollock. At night we used to adjourn to Daly's pub, have a few drinks, and talk over the sport of the day. I liked Jaques very much. He went away with a promise of coming again soon. He came back in a few weeks. It was about the end of November. He was on the bridge of the *Dun Aengus* as she came alongside the pier, and I waved my hand to him. When the steamer was moored, I jumped on board and we shook hands.

'Where is your bag?' I asked him.

'In a minute, Pat,' he says. 'First I want you to meet this gentleman, Mr Flaherty,' and he introduced us.

I shook hands with Mr Flaherty who was a great giant-bodied man, white-haired and blue-eyed. He in turn introduced me to his wife and three very beautiful daughters. 'Drive us all up to Ganly's,' said Mr Jaques.

I did, and when we got there Mr Flaherty said he'd be staying over until the next boat day, and asked me if in the meantime I'd drive his family and him around the Island and show them all the interesting places that were to be seen.

'I shall be glad to,' said I, 'because driving tourists around and showing them all the places of interest is part of my way of living.'

That night they invited me to have supper with them in Ganly's. Mr Flaherty talked, and talked well. Most of the time he kept asking me questions about the Island and the people, enquiring as to how they lived on it, asking if the sea ever washed away any of the little gardens we had made by the shore. We all, including Mr Jaques, passed a very enjoyable evening.

Next day I drove the Flahertys around to see the duns, the cloughans, and the churches. They were interested in what I pointed out to them, but not nearly as much, so I thought, as other tourists that I had taken to these places before. But as I drove along the road Mr Flaherty kept stopping me while Mrs

From *Man of Aran* (1935).

Flaherty took shots, as they called them, with a camera which she held up to her eye and clicked. However, I passed a very enjoyable day, for I like meeting interesting people, and the Flahertys were all of that. The girls Barbara, Frances and Monica were very jolly and friendly. Next day the three of them insisted on paying me a visit at my house. I refused at first, because a house like mine that had been for years without the touch of a woman's hand was no house to bring anyone into, especially when I had to be out of it night and day myself trying to earn a living. I had made several efforts to straighten it out, but it seems that to some people, as old age comes on, old memories freshen; and what I used to throw out of the house as useless, my father would, with tears in his eyes, bring back again, saying that this thing belonged to one of his boys or that to his wife, Mary. Anyhow, the girls won me over, and with a promise of helping me to clean the house they got in. They did help, and with a piece of cloth that I got for each of them they sent the dirt and cobwebs flying, and we all together puffed and spat till we made a fairly good job of it. Then we sat down for a while and had a chat, they talked about school and fishing, about Samoa in the South Seas where they had learned to swim, and they talked of New Mexico through which they had travelled and where they had spent some little time. They expressed a wish to go out fishing in a curragh, and though there was no sign of any fish in the bay, still, to please them, I got a couple of herring nets, put them into the canoe, and out we went. When we got out to where there used to be a good berth for catching herrings, we shot the nets, tying a buoy on the end, and then we came back home. Next morning I took two of the girls in a punt or small boat. The two chaps who were with me when we took Mr Jaques fishing went in the canoe, and Mr Jaques and Monica went with them. We rowed out to where the nets were moored and there wasn't a fish to be seen as far as we could see down through the water, but as they began to haul the nets into the canoe we saw that the bottoms of the nets were full of herrings. We had a grand catch, about eighteen hundred in all. We staged a kind of race coming in, but it wasn't a fair one. We were ahead in the small boat and we kept blocking the canoe every time she tried to pass us. I sold the herrings to a shopkeeper – I took Monica with me and tipped her off to help me with the sale, because in Aran as elsewhere you will find that the shopkeepers buy cheap and sell dear. This particular shopkeeper tried to bargain with me in Irish. It was one shilling and sixpence a hundred; but I would have none of his Irish; I kept answering him in English so that Monica could understand. I also kept asking her her opinion and she got excited.

'Why,' she says, 'Mr Dolan, you don't mean a word of it. One and six for such beautiful fish. I never heard of such a thing. The least you can give the poor man is three shillings a hundred!'

We kept on at him – she did, anyway – and finally we got our three shillings.

Next day they prepared to leave Aran. Mr Flaherty called me aside and said:

'Pat, I'm sending in a report on the conditions here, and don't be surprised a bit if you see me back here again making a film.'

'I hope you do come back,' I said, and with that we all shook hands and they sailed away.

That same evening I asked Mr Jaques what he thought of Mr Flaherty.

'He seems to me to be a very fine man. Indeed I think they are a very fine family,' he replied.

'The family are all right,' said I, impatiently, 'anybody can see that, but there is something in Mr Flaherty that I can't fathom.'

'Do you think so, Pat?' said Mr Jaques, 'I didn't notice anything.'

'There is something,' I said, 'I can see it by the look and the colour of his eye, but for the life of me I can't make out what it is. I can't lay my finger on it. Mr Flaherty has a heart as big as a house,' I added, 'but yet – '

And I may as well say here that later events proved that I was right. Mr Flaherty came back, and what I didn't know at first I was soon to find out. It was this: that Mr Flaherty was a man who was bound to be leader in any game where he played a hand, and I felt that, should we ever meet in any deal, there were bound to be some clashes, because I never had much use for leaders of men who believed that every man was as good as another; besides my nature always rebelled at taking orders from anybody. As things turned out we did have clashes. I have often since thought that there were times when he was right; but to be honest, there have been times when I felt sure he wasn't.

The time came for Mr Jaques's departure. He sailed away with a promise to return on his lips, but he never came to Aran again. He had grown tired, that I knew, but I hadn't realized how tired. I would have prevented his going away from Aran had I known, and I know that he would have stayed had I asked him. Shortly afterwards came the news that he had deliberately crossed the Big Divide, and I was saddened because he was a true friend.

A few days before the New Year Mr Flaherty sent me word that he was coming back, and now I knew that I would have to leave my kelpmaking and other work behind and start on an entirely new line of endeavour. I had heard and read a little about film making, but in actual fact I knew almost nothing.

I had been able to make ends meet more easily of late years. I had become fairly expert at patching my clothes, and I had become a middling good cook when I had time enough to do it. Baking bread was hard to learn, and I pretty nearly gave it up after my first try. I kneaded the stuff together and put it into a big oven, and put a nice fire underneath it and a lot of red coals on the lid. After a while I fancied I smelt something burning. It was my bread. The fire was too big and the bread was burned black on top and had stuck to the bottom of the oven. I had to cut it into pieces with a knife in order to get it out. The bottom had also been burned black, but the middle of it was as soft and as sticky as ever; I threw the whole thing out in the garden, and sat down to think things over. Speed, my dog, came along and gobbled the whole mess up. It nearly killed him. It must have made a lump in his stomach, for he went around for the rest of the day with a sorry look on his face, and every once in a while he rolled himself on the ground trying to soften it!

My father, who was on his own hook at this time, made one try, and one only, at making bread. I came in one day and when I saw what he was up to I nearly died laughing. He had taken a large bowl, filled it with flour and water, and was mixing it up. It was too soft, and when I came in he had his two hands held out and was looking at them. The dough was dripping from his hands on to the floor. He was weeping at his sad fate and mourning all his relations that had died as far back as his memory went! I got a handful of flour and managed to get the dough off. He never tried again.

Mr and Mrs Flaherty arrived back, and with them a fine looking boy who would soon be a grown man. I was thinking about the film and forgot that Mr Flaherty had no son, and I absent-mindedly called this young man Flaherty. His name was, however, John Taylor. He had come to assist Mr Flaherty with camera work and also to develop the film in the laboratory. I drove them to Mrs Ganly's again, and soon they began to talk about a cast for the film, also about the making of land and storm scenes, evictions and shipwrecks. They were indeed very keen about their work. After a week they decided to settle in Mrs Sharman's house at Kilmurvy. It was near the sea and was in a central position on the Island. They began to get ready for making the *Man of Aran* film, as it was to be called. I was hired, and I was to be what is known as a contact man between Mr Flaherty and my own people. Carpenters were put to work turning a fishing shed into a laboratory – part of the work was the putting in of developing and drying rooms. I knew nothing about this kind of work, and I never cared much about learning it. The fact is I never had the time, and even if I had, I believe I wouldn't have had the inclination.

An Irish cottage had to be built for the inside scenes, and Mr Flaherty left this job to me. This was work I liked, and I took great interest in it. I searched the three most westerly villages of the Island for a gang of picked men, men who I knew were good at handling stone; then I searched through the different villages for a tumbled-down old house that had in it an arch over the fireplace suitable for our cottage. A friend of mine in Gortnagapple village owned one, and like the fine man he is, he tore down the walls of the old house, took out all the stones that formed the arch, put them on his own cart, brought them to where we were building the cottage, and made us a present of them. While this work was bustling along, I spent some days driving Mr and Mrs Flaherty around. We met and spoke to many people here and there along the road. Mr Flaherty looked these people over very carefully with an eye to finding suitable people for his cast. We also visited people in their homes and chatted with them partly to become on sociable terms with them and partly with the idea to find out if they would be suitable for the film. Both reasons were important. One night there was a little bit of a dance in Killeany village. The Flahertys expressed a desire to go, so that they could get a chance to look the young people over. They did go, and there they saw little Michael Dillane. His appearance struck them so favourably that Mr Flaherty was eager to get some shots of him. A few days later he did, but he had to take shots of Mikeleen's brother as well. The shots of Mikeleen came out very well, and though he took shots of many other boys, Mr Flaherty never took any that he felt sure would fit as well as Mike's; so Mr and Mrs Flaherty then and there decided that Mike was the boy they wanted for the film. So they asked me to go to Killeany and speak to his parents about letting him come to Kilmurvy to go to work on the film. His father was away fishing, but a few days later when he came home I asked him about it, and I painted Mikeleen's future in glowing colours.

'Well now, Pat,' said he, 'you know yourself that it is the woman who gets the most trouble from the children, so whatever she says herself I will be satisfied with it.' I went to see Mrs Dillane, and I went many times. What questions she asked, questions which to me were absolutely senseless and time-worn, but which to her as to the majority of the people of the Island were questions of more than life and death, because they involved the hereafter and eternity.

The Great Famine and its aftermath had left the Irish people frightfully poor and broken-spirited, and it was unfortunate that at this time some Protestant proselytizers attempted to change the faith of the poorest of them by setting up soup kitchens. In these places they endeavoured to make the Irish people alter their faith in exchange for soup and a smattering of education! I'm not a bit interested myself whether a man professes any form of religion or not, because I believe God is so good that there is hope for us all. The incident I quote above was unfortunate because to this day amongst backward communities the fear of having their faith taken away from them by strangers, under the form of one line of endeavour or another, is a real fear. I can well believe of course that those proselytizers were sincere in their belief that they were rescuing the poor Irish from hell's fire, but that does not help the matter at all.

I do wish all such people would let us Irish go to hell or to Heaven in our own way, just as we feel inclined. Hell, yes, I'd rather go there just for devilment than to be pushed up to Heaven in spite of me. However, this idea has been handed down to us, and a few of the old people still remember those evil days.

Aran people were looking sideways at Mr Flaherty and his talk of making a film; some of them believing at the back of their minds that his talk of a film was only a blind, and that once he had got a foothold and a grip on things the same old story would begin again but in a new way. Mrs Dillane asked:

'What does Mr Flaherty do, Pat, when no one is looking at him? Do you think he says his prayers? Some people say that he is a queer kind of a man. Do you think if I send Mikeleen over to him my son will lose his religion? Will they try to take it away from him?'

'Musha, don't you know, ma'am,' said I, 'that there is no fear of that happening. Those days are gone forever. These days everyone has enough to do to make a living and they haven't time to care or think about what religion anybody else has. Besides,' I added, 'Mikeleen is a relation of mine through the Dillanes, and sure you know well enough I wouldn't be where anything like that would be tried on him.'

She smiled faintly and said: 'I believe that indeed, but if you want to know it, lots of people say that the divil a much you have of it yourself any more than Flaherty.'

I laughed and kept on with my coaxing, and finally, after many attempts, she consented to come with me to the Sergeant of the Civic Guards in Kilronan village. Mikeleen was only twelve years old and she would have to give her consent before the sergeant in order to allow Mike to go to work on the film. It had to do with the school regulations. All signs pointed towards a favourable ending at last to the objections of Mikeleen's mother. We appeared before the sergeant, and he asked her if she were willing to allow her boy to go to Kilmurvy for film work. The question was, I thought, put to her a bit abruptly. Anyhow, she suddenly got excited and frightened looking and said:

'Isn't it all right to send him there? What will they do to him? Do you think they will try to take his religion away from him?'

'My dear woman,' said the sergeant, 'that has nothing to do with me. Are you willing, or are you not, to let your son go to work for Mr Flaherty?' She got still more excited and rushed out waving her arms, crying: 'No! No! I will never give them my little boy without knowing what they are going to do with him.'

And away she went home, and left me feeling very crestfallen after all my wasted efforts.

Rumours were rife that Mr Flaherty was a Socialist. Not many on Aran know what Socialism means. To the great majority it means an organization backed by the devil. Other rumours said that the cottage we had now nearly built was to be used as a 'Birds' Nest'. 'Birds' Nests' were buildings or homes that were put up in Ireland during the famine years, and there destitute Catholic children were clothed and fed and brought up in the Protestant religion. So after all it was rather hard perhaps to place much blame on Mikeleen's mother. However, after some months we managed to get her consent. Mikeleen came to Kilmurvy, but for many weeks he did nothing but fool around the place, doing whatever he liked, except when once in a while I placed a little check upon him. The rest of the cast had to be found before Mikeleen could be used.

Amongst the men who had built the cottage was Patch Ruadh, a fine honest old man with red whiskers. Mr Flaherty had noticed him and said to me: 'Who is he, Pat?' I said he was known as Patch Ruadh or Red Pat, but that his right name was Patch Mullen.

'I must get some tests of him,' said Mr Flaherty, 'he looks very dramatic.'

I couldn't see where there was anything very dramatic about Patch, but I was no great judge, and I didn't voice my private opinion to Mr Flaherty. I said instead:

'Test him any time you like. He is a friend of mine and anything I say to him goes.'

Patch was tested and sure enough he came through with flying colours. Now I knew of course that he must be dramatic, even though I couldn't see where it was in him. I spoke to him in Irish, for he knows very little English, unless you put the words in his mouth and pull them out again, but having a quick mind he can do it that way. I asked him how he'd like to work on the film.

'Indeed, brother,' he said, 'if there is no harm in it, I will, and I'm glad to get the work. But I don't see the reason why I'm wanted when there are lots of finer men around.'

'Well,' I said, 'Mr Flaherty says your face is dramatic, and it seems that kind of thing suits the picture.'

'What kind of a thing is it?' says Patch.

'Don't ask me, because I know nothing about it,' said I, 'but you have it a plenty whatever it is, and you are surely a lucky man. But if I was to give you my honest opinion,' I added, 'I'd say 'tis in your whiskers you have it!'

'Well, then, a thousand thanks to God that I have it in my whiskers or some place else. But anyhow, I may as well look after them now you say that 'tis in them it is,' said Patch.

He knew from then on that his work would last until the film was finished. Days passed by and we were still trying to find the rest of the cast. Patch was doing jobs around the house, milking the cow that Mr Flaherty had rented, and doing any other little things that turned up.

One never knew when a call would come for one of us, but there were times when Patch was called for and there was no sign of him. I soon noticed that always between nine and ten o'clock in the morning he disappeared for half an hour or so; so without saying anything, I set myself to find out where he went, though by the looks of things I had a pretty good idea. I watched out next morning and saw Patch, after giving a look around, disappear behind a huge boulder down near the shore. I slipped down the beach and peered around the corner of the boulder, and there was Patch, with a piece of a comb and a broken cracked piece of a looking glass, lovingly combing his whiskers. I made my way back silently. I explained to Mr Flaherty about Patch's absence, and it was agreed between us that nothing should be said about it. Patch all through the making of the film kept his whiskers in order, and now that he believes they are so valuable, I think he will keep up the good work as long as he lives. [...]

II

Next morning, although the sky was clear the weather was unsettled, so we could not tell what fortune the day was going to bring to us as regards sunshine. Everything else looked favourable, for a strong gale blew from the west and a terrific sea was running. This was surely the day for us to get our final storm scene. It was important that we should, because Mr Flaherty had got word that he must hurry to England with the *Man of Aran* film.

So getting everything ready, we made for Bungowla. A little to the south of it is the cove where we intended to take the storm scene and the landing. It was the place I have referred to before, when mentioning Big Patcheen's father and his barrel of oil; the place where a landing could be made at low tide provided that one could get through the breakers outside. It seemed doubtful on this day, for when we got there and surveyed it the breakers were coming clear across the entrance, and it was only at long intervals that a chance could be taken of running the passage.

219

I had a long earnest talk with Big Patcheen and his men, and explained to them that this was the day of all days when the work must be done, because any day now this annual week of rough weather would be over, and no more storm scenes could then be taken, as Mr Flaherty had to leave Aran soon.

They agreed with me, and said that they would do their best, but they went on to say that the day looked very threatening, and if the wind veered out to the south-west later on, which it looked like doing, we were sure to have showers of rain with squalls.

That I knew, of course, but looking Big Patcheen in the eye, I said: 'We will finish the picture to-day, rain or shine, by hook or by crook.'

He was much stirred, and he smiled. 'Mullen,' he said, 'if I can get out there I am not coming in till you give the signal, that is, if there is a chance of a bit of sun at all.'

In about an hour's time the tide would be at its lowest ebb. We had some further talk and decided that the safest way was to leave Bungowla shore, dodge the seas there by rowing down around the north side of Brannagh Island, then out through the Sound between it and Rock Island, turn south east and come up into the wind outside the breakers in the mouth of the cove, there to wait till they got the signal from me to make a try for the passage. The long row around we deemed safest; we didn't like the idea of having the curragh run the breakers twice, going out from as well as coming into the cove. As they tightened their crisses securely, Big Patcheen was all fire and energy, Steve Dirrane was calm and steady, believing always that when with Patcheen nothing could ever happen to him, and McDonough's blue eyes were lit up with indomitable courage and resolution.

We carried down the curragh and, while some other men held her, Patcheen and his crew jumped in, caught their oars and, after a final prayer and wish of 'God strengthen your arms this day' from us on shore, Big Patcheen gave the word, the curragh was shoved off and they were away. These words from McDonough and Patcheen came back to me over the water:

'Don't be afraid for us, Mullen!'

Then they began to battle their way through the seas and soon gained deep water. They swung around the north point of Brannagh Island and disappeared from our sight. We hurried out to the Cove, and there Mr Flaherty set up his camera. David Flaherty set up the other.

After about three-quarters of an hour we sighted the curragh to the south of Brannagh Island. She was already having heavy weather, and I began to get uneasy. Cloud banks had begun to appear low down in the south-western sky, and the wind gradually began to haul out there – it had begun to strengthen if anything – and I could see that our hopes of continuous sunshine for the day were shattered, and that we would be very lucky if we managed to get our storm scene without any serious accident occurring. Finally, the curragh came into position outside the breakers.

It was now low tide, and the right time for our landing scene because the canoe had the best chance of running the breakers and coming ashore before the turn of the tide. At dead low water the tide is at its slackest; even the great waves seem to rest a bit before beginning their onslaught anew; at low tide this cove was somewhat sheltered and once a curragh was inside the breakers she was safe, but after the first half hour of flood tide it began to get dangerous, because Brannagh Island Sound breaks across and into it in two places. Great sharp rocks are piled up here and there in between these two channels, so that as the flood tide gets higher, the sea runs into the cove from the south-east, and also from the south-west and north, and on a stormy day for ten hours. During the last five hours of the flood and the first five hours of the ebb tide, the cove becomes a veritable whirlpool of clashing seas; three different lines of breakers meeting together in its centre, only to be thrown back again and caught by the next oncoming seas. Sometimes all three breakers, after dashing, seem to recede each into its own respective channel, at other times the breakers from Brannagh Sound overpower the others, beat them down and rush over them out into the deep towards the south-east.

Amidst all this turmoil of water, the sharp-pointed rocks become exposed for an instant as a breaker rushes over them; then they are submerged again, and woe betide a curragh if one of those treacherous rocks grips her bottom: her whole framework is ripped to pieces as easily as one would tear a sheet of paper. Nor would there be much hope for the crew. The currents run so strongly that even a good swimmer would be helpless, assuredly being swept out to sea and dragged under. So that a landing is practically impossible unless done at the last hour of the ebb or the first hour of the flood tide.

'It will be an in and out day, Pat,' said Mr Flaherty, as heavy dark clouds were driven over the face of the sun. 'We are lucky if we can do anything. I don't like it. That curragh out there is standing up against heavy weather enough as it is, yet we can't do anything without sunshine.'

'The sun will soon be out again,' said I hopefully, but to tell the truth I was becoming more and more uneasy. The clouds were banking more heavily and, though the sun shone brightly in flashes, it wasn't staying out long enough for Mr Flaherty to get his camera going.

Suddenly Mr Flaherty would shout: 'All ready, Pat. Will we signal her to come in?'

But before anything could be done the clouds had covered the sun again, and another spell of waiting took place.

I had the signal flag ready in my hand. When I raised it on high it meant that we were ready for the canoe to make a try for the passage, but it was understood between us that Big Patcheen was to use his own judgment absolutely in the running of the breakers. Time was passing and Mrs Flaherty became very anxious.

'When is the turn of the tide, Pat?' she asked.

A heavy rain squall swept in from the sea and we had to seek shelter behind a high boulder.

'The tide has turned long ago, ma'am,' I answered, adding: 'I know the men out there are in a bad position, but they are the pick of the best men, and with God's help the day may clear yet, so that Mr Flaherty may finish his picture.'

'Oh, Pat, I don't know,' said she. 'Not for the world, as I have told you many a time before, would we have anything happen to anybody engaged in working for us. At the same time, of course, you know more about those men and what they are able to do than I, so if you think the sun will come out and that there is not much danger as yet, then do as you think best. But just the same,' she went on, 'it looks simply awful out there to me.'

Still Big Patcheen and his crew kept their curragh's bows to the sea, waiting and watching for the sun and the flag. At about half past one a rift appeared in the clouds and we knew the sun would break through.

'All ready!' said Mr Flaherty.

'A few seconds more,' said I, 'and we might as well venture it. You might get something done before the clouds come again.' As the last wisp of flying cloud was passing over the sun, I raised the flag, and the curragh headed for the passage; and being eager to get some good work done while the sun shone, they came on bravely. Glancing ahead, and on each side at the lines of breakers, Big Patcheen thought he would chance the run through. Half a dozen more strokes, eager though watchful as a hawk, he saw on the western reef a great sea rise up in a monstrous menacing black wall; a moment it towered, then it broke and raced towards them. Quick as a flash of light, síx oars dipped as one. The curragh was turned out; a few strong stretching strokes and she was clear again.

The breaker tore across the passage with a roar as if of rage at being cheated of its prey. The curragh went farther out on the deep.

'Was there danger then, Pat?' asked Mrs Flaherty.

'Plenty of it,' I answered. 'Any other men in that boat would never get through.'

She looked at me with one of those strange looks she sometimes gave me, as if trying to find out whether I had not become quite heartless and cared not a jot whether men lost their lives or whether they didn't, provided the film was finished. I do admit that at this time I did have very strange thoughts, and like Mrs Flaherty I too have sometimes wondered. But indeed the making of *Man of Aran* was enough to make any man think strangely.

We had another long spell of waiting, and Mr Flaherty spoke many times of signalling the curragh to come in, sun or no sun. The narrow channel inside the passage had by this time become a hell of tossing tumbling seas, coming from all directions at once. Now there was no landing possible, at least there was none such as we had ever seen a curragh make before.

When Mr Flaherty spoke about getting the curragh in without the sun shining, disappointment was written so largely over his face that I knew that even he was hoping against hope that the curragh might be able to hold out for a while longer, so that after all these long months of waiting this scene that was to finish the film might be completed. There came another rain squall but as I gazed anxiously into the south-western sky, I spied a patch of blue.

'All ready after the shower,' I shouted. 'The sun will be out when the rain passes.'

The curraghmen were also watching. The rain passed, and as the last shadow sailed past the sun I hoisted my flag. The curragh came in closer, but now the great seas broke clean across the passage, the rush through could not be made, and the blue patch of sky was being pushed away hurriedly by heavy black clouds. It seemed to be an entirely hopeless situation, and yet if those breakers just lowered for only a few minutes, Big Patcheen might make a try for it.

'Ready! Ready!' I shouted, as I saw the oars snap forward. On the reef the breakers still reared high, but not so high it seemed as they did a few seconds before. Yes, they were trying, these great picked men of the west. On they came through those mighty seas, rowing strongly, yet finding it difficult to make much headway because of the terrific undertow. They disappeared down into the trough of the sea. My heart stood still, and through our minds on shore the same thoughts flashed: will she ever be seen again, will she win through? Yes, we see her again, and the superb skill shown in her handling by Big Patcheen and his men bring wild cries of admiration from Shauneen Tom and some other men who had by this time gathered on the shore.

A great wall of water lifted its length on the reef. It was the first of three great breakers. Higher it rose as it gathered its strength for destruction, and from the men on shore the cry arose: 'Ah, God! Give them strength, it is coming! It is down on top of them. They are lost!'

But they weren't lost. The curragh had come through the worst of the passage and now as this monster sea came raging towards them there was a chance to fight it, and this Patcheen and his men, with superhuman effort, prepared to do. I shall never forget the thrill it gave me, when I saw Big Patcheen with a left-hand stroke, his men timing their strokes instinctively with his, get ready to meet the crest of the wave, and how McDonough flashed up his right-hand oar to let the cap of the sea go by.

A dozen more strokes and they were inside and in safety, that is they would have been safe had the sun been shining continuously all day. The delay caused by having to wait for the clouds and rain to pass had now made a landing frightfully dangerous. It was blowing hard, and the sea had been getting up since the first of the flood tide. Through the three channels the great seas came breaching, storm-tossed and angry, smashing each against the other. Channels and passage were now in one continuous turmoil, while here and there as the seas drove in or receded, sharp-spiked treacherous rocks hid their heads, only to lift them up cruelly through the waters, as if waiting and watching to deliver a death blow to the gallant little craft that was now fighting for its life.

It was not a question with us on shore now as to whether the sun shone or not. To have the curragh land as quickly as possible was the first thought in our minds. Mike and Maggie were on the shore; I had pointed out to them the place where the curragh must land – that is if it ever landed – and all through the curragh's battling with the waves they shouted and signalled to the crew, pointing to the only spot where as a last chance a curragh might make a run for it.

Mrs Flaherty hurried to where I stood, and looking at me beseechingly, said: 'Oh, Pat, Pat, can they ever land?'

'I will tell you something, Mrs Flaherty,' I answered. 'They cannot land, that is come ashore in any way that a curragh ever landed before, as far as *I* know. The day has turned out so terribly bad that they cannot go back out again through the passage, and I'm afraid after another hour and a half the curragh will be lost in this channel because the high tide will come breaching over that ledge of rock. That is the only protection they now have from the whole force of the western ocean.'

As the curragh topped a gigantic wave, and then disappeared out of sight, Mrs Flaherty cried out: 'Oh, my God!' She turned away and covered her eyes with her hands. 'What shall we ever do if anything happens to those brave men?'

'I wouldn't take on as bad as that,' I said, 'because there is still hope. Patcheen believes he will never be drowned, and when a man believes that and knows his business besides, 'tis hard to lose him!' I told her some more about how I had impressed on his mind the dire necessity of doing the work this day, and what it meant to Aran and to the Flaherty family.

She looked at me very reproachfully, and said: 'May God forgive you.'

Now and again a spot of blue appeared, but Mr Flaherty was working his camera in sunshine and in cloud, all the time shouting: 'Can they make it, Pat? Can they make it?'

Such work as these peerless curraghmen were doing could never be done again. Time and time again they tried to make a landing when the great seas were not coming through all three channels at once, but they were driven out again and again to continue fighting what now seemed to be a losing battle.

Shauneen Tom turned on me, his face white and his eyes blazing, saying: 'Oh, you ruffian! You have the men lost! There is no blame coming to the Flahertys, but *you* know what kind of a sea ran here with a high tide and a storm.'

'You are right, Shauneen,' I answered, 'but even so, I have hopes yet that Patcheen will make one big try and he will either live or die in the doing of it.'

'I know', said Shauneen wildly, 'that they are three as good men as ever caught an oar. But there is no curragh that was ever laid on sea can last there much longer.'

By this time other men had appeared, some coming from their gardens, while others had run from Bungowla shore and village on hearing that Big Patcheen was out on the south side on this wild and stormy day, trying to run the passage of the breakers there.

These men kept shouting to one another and to the curraghmen, though of course the latter couldn't hear them. They were wild with excitement, as they asked God to give strength and help to the men in the canoe. Still Big Patcheen, with his chances lessening more and more because of the rising tide, watched all three channels with eagle eyes. This was the biggest moment in his life, and he meant to combine brain, skill and muscle into a final effort – do or die!

Once again they had to row out. A heavy sea had broken on the reef, and rushing in against the ledge to the west, it was thrown back and caused such a dangerous cross sea that Patcheen for the first time put into execution the most difficult, muscle-straining stroke of a master curraghman, and only used on occasions of desperate need. Ordinarily, when a curragh is to be brought about, the three oars on one side make a forward stroke, the other three are held with ends resting in the water, or at most with a light backward pressure. But in Big Patcheen's case this couldn't be done. They had the curragh's bows facing out as they rowed, when suddenly this sea broke on the ledge and was thrown back on them in a second, leaping, as it seemed, in its fury to reach the curragh and take her unawares before her bows could be brought on to it. It was on her, she was doomed – so it looked to us on shore, and we all yelled wildly:

'Ah! Bring her up to it, Patcheen, or you are lost! You are lost!'

Patcheen and his men in a flash saw their danger. It was a matter of only a couple of seconds in which to save their curragh. But look at him – this man of iron strength and reckless courage! The curragh could not go forward, as the sea was coming so swiftly on her. She had to face it without moving ahead one inch. Quick as thought Patcheen's right hand went forward for a powerful stroke, while his left hand came back for a backward drive. Thus one side of the man was exerting every muscle for a forward pull, while the other side was tensed for a backward push. Lower he bent, straining, lower still till his head almost reached as low as the curragh's gunwale.

The sea struck her. But Patcheen had won. His two men had helped all they could, but we on shore knew that it was that great stroke of Patcheen's that had really saved her, and we drew deep breaths of relief when we saw that once more she had come clear, out from the jaws of death.

The curragh was now being tossed and buffeted here and there by the force of the seas, Patcheen and his men trying fiercely to hold her in a favourable position so that if the chance came they might be able to run for the shore. Three times we could see they almost fancied that their chance had come, but with lightning strokes they had driven their curragh out again. Great monster seas tore through the Brannagh Sound channels. This last time, that they rowed out, there came in front of them a giant wave, bellowing in through the south passage, and, though we on shore had thought that it was from the seas in the Brannagh Sound channels that Big Patcheen had expected the danger to come, we soon saw that this was not so, for by far and away the biggest sea of all that had come up to this time came rushing in through the south passage. This was where the real danger lay. It might have caught and driven the curragh against the Brannagh Sound breakers, and, had such a thing happened, nothing could have saved either men or curragh.

We didn't know that when Patcheen saw this giant wave coming that at last he had sensed his opportunity, and he prepared to take advantage of it. He rowed out to meet this wave before it broke. The curragh topped its crest and disappeared from sight down the other side. The great sea broke and came raging into and through the channel and on to meet the other breakers racing in from Brannagh Sound.

We looked and could hardly believe our eyes, for the curragh had turned in after it had let the great wave pass, and now here they were rowing with all their power for the shore, putting into their work the last atom of their strength. Patcheen had taken the slender and only chance of the giant wave being able to overpower and hold in check the seas from Brannagh Sound long enough to enable him to reach the shore. It was a long chance but it was the only one, and he was taking it. Would they come through? They should now be able to hear our shouts of encouragement, but our shouting suddenly turned to cries of dismay, because farther in and directly in front of them, sometimes clear of the foaming water, sometimes hidden under it, were those treacherous rocks.

I shouted through the megaphone, telling Patcheen to beware, especially of one that was in the centre of the channel. My voice grew hoarse with excitement, but still the canoe came on, seemingly paying no heed to any warning; her crew were glancing swiftly on every side as they rowed, and now for the first time real fear for their safety struck my heart. If they failed to judge to the inch the position of the submerged rocks and should the receding sea suddenly leave the fangs exposed, then Patcheen and his men would be seen no more, except for the few seconds before they would be sucked under by the current and swept away.

Though the great wave had smashed the force of the other breakers, they still struggled onward on their course towards the curragh. The rocks were now entirely submerged. The curragh is amongst them – she has now almost passed the spot where we knew the most dangerous one to be.

'Run her in, Patcheen! Run her in!' was shouted from the shore; but it was almost impossible to drive the canoe against the current, and before Patcheen could head the curragh for the straight short run to the shore, another sea came roaring in from the South Channel, and he had to swing his curragh's bows to meet it. The current dragged her relentlessly toward where death lay lurking. As the curragh swung around, those rocky fangs came up dripping white and seemed to reach out for her, but death missed Patcheen and his crew by a foot; with superhuman strength and uncanny skill they had managed to hold the curragh about a foot from the cruel toothed rock as she met the next sea bows on, while the next breakers came foaming in; she was turned in again in the flash of an eye, and was now running straight for the shore.

Shauneen Tom and some others were for rushing down, but I cursed them back, for here was the chance to finish the film, as Mr Flaherty had planned, and I now depended on Big Patcheen and his men being able to save themselves without any assistance from us.

As the canoe was driven up on the rocks, Patcheen and his men leaped out of her. A great sea was rushing in, and after one glance at it, to judge its power, they ran up over the rocks to safety. The oncoming sea caught the curragh, dragged it out and smashed it to pieces, and this last sea finished the *Man of Aran*.

Patcheen and his men were drenched with sweat and brine, but their blue eyes were lit up with fire, and a great thrill of wild pride shot through me as I looked at them, for here had been a trial of some of the old, old stock, and the blood still ran true.

Frances Hubbard Flaherty

The Odyssey of a Film-Maker

From then on Bob's filming became catch-as-catch-can. It was eight years before he had another film of his own to do. The hope of one more film like *Moana* did flare up, not from the great foundations, not from the arts and sciences, or government or big business – but from Hollywood again, another Hollywood company willing to take a chance, this time in our own Southwest, with our Southwest Indians, the vanishing cultures in our own land. And you who know that country and its breathtaking landscape, and the Indians, those people whose whole life, and the wholeness of it, is the living poetry and religion of that landscape, will understand how we felt when, after a year, the film was called off.

We took a ship for Europe. We might find opportunity there. On the way over, Bob fell into conversation with an Irishman. They talked about the Depression in America. 'You should see', said the Irishman, 'how the people in my country, the Aran Islanders, live. They even have to make their soil.'

When, a year later in England, Michael (now Sir Michael) Balcon, of Gainsborough Studios, wanted to make a low-budget film somewhere in the British Isles, Bob told him the remarkable story he had heard about the Aran Islanders. Sir Michael found this story remarkable too, and we went to have a look at the Aran Islands. Well I remember the day we first saw those grey, barren, three-hundred-foot cliffs rising up out of the sea, – a day in November. The air was fresh, the water sparkling; dolphins were playing in it and beyond them the Twelve Bens of Connemara rose snow-capped into the clear blue of the sky. Clinging from generation to generation to these sea-swept rocks, the Aran Islander has met the challenge of the sea and come to terms with it. There is always a special feeling about a place where people have taken root. I remember how, as I dabbled abstractedly in the shining water lapping at my feet, there came over me a deep contentment, a sense of well-being that was like an enchantment. We could make a film here, somehow we knew.

We settled on Aranmore, the largest and farthest seaward of the three islands, midway on its lee shore beside a cove as round and shining as a silver dollar. We overlooked the white-capped bay and the fleets of little turf boats

From *The Odyssey of a Film-Maker* (1960).

bobbing over from the mainland, their slanting sails looking like gulls, and hardly bigger than gulls, as they brought turf to this island without fuel. They would unload on the pier in our cove beside the fish-shed we had converted into a laboratory.

It was a never-ending delight to sit on the wharf-edge over the water and peer down into clear depths watching perhaps for a conger eel to show. One day two monsters came into the cove, two basking sharks. We saw them first as twin sail-like fins cutting the surface. Beneath the surface, their huge bodies thirty feet long, with white jaws open as they fed on plankton, we could reach down and touch with our hands as the curragh passed over them. This was an Aran wonder of which we had never been told. But now we heard the whole story of the Aranman's fight for the oil for his lamps in years not so long ago, harpooning these monsters from the prows of their pookawns as whales are harpooned, and often being towed far out to sea, sometimes not to be heard of again. The tales of the hunting of the basking shark, the largest fish in the world, had become legendary, for the great migrations had for some years ceased. Now here they were again! Old harpoons were still to be found in the rafters of Aran cottages, and there was an old man in Galway who as a boy had been taken out harpooning himself. Bob made a trip to Galway to see this old man, this source of vital information. He left no stone unturned. For the hunting of the basking shark had become for him, as had the hunting of the bear for *Nanook*, an obsession. He sent for books about the creature; he wrote to museums; he studied the medicinal properties of fish-liver oils. He had an old friend of his Hudson Bay days who had been a whaler. From his home in Dundee we called him, chartered a boat for him, rigged it for whaling, and when the next year one of the greatest shark migrations ever seen (announced by the look-outs we had set to watch for it) came into Galway harbor, we were ready for it.

But in the meantime, and first of all, we had to find our cast, gather together our Aran family. At first the people were shy of us and suspicious. They still remembered Cromwellian days when the Protestants coming from England had tried to make 'soupers' of them, offering them soup to save them from starvation if they would change their religion. We were Protestants. Our name was Flaherty, to be sure, but how did they know we hadn't assumed it on purpose? It was rumoured that in his pocket Bob carried a phial of a liquid which, if thrown upon any of them, would turn him into a Protestant like ourselves.

Who were those who finally became our family? There was old Brigid. I am not sure she wasn't the first to come. For her old bones were very creaky; she was always feeling poorly, very poorly. But in our hallway by the kitchen door we always kept a keg of porter, and this for Brigid was the finest medicine in the world. Steadfastly every day she came and sat in our kitchen, for one day we would surely see that she was just right for our film.

The next to come was Maggie, the Woman of Aran, with her madonna face framed in her black shawl. Perhaps she came readily because she was poor and had a crippled husband and four children to provide for. Her husband having broken his back carrying a load of kelp without a donkey to help him, it was Maggie who now had to carry these heavy loads. It was the fairies who broke her husband's back, said Maggie; they threw him off a cliff, that's how it was. The fairies also steal children – not girls, but little boys. Maggie dressed her boy in skirts to outwit the fairies.

Maggie was one of the blessings of this blessed isle. She taught me about potatoes, the way – when I saw potatoes actually come as if by magic out of a layer of soil no thicker than a rug laid on the limestone – she cupped them in her hands and crooned over them, 'Ah, the beautiful praties!' She had no cow for milk for the children. But when Christmas came and we gave her a cow, this only confused her – for what if the children got used to milk and then the cow might die? We had a Christmas tree, and set it up on the cement floor of our cottage. Christmas morning when she saw the tree there, Maggie crossed herself – she thought it had grown through the floor in the night.

As you can see in the film, we almost drowned Maggie. But that was not the only time a wave caught her. There was another time, much worse. Maggie's back was bent under a heavy load of kelp. She was staggering under it, making to climb up a ledge from the sea. Bob and I had already had our own experience of those ledges. We had climbed from a lower to a higher one barely in time to look down and see the ledge we had left overwhelmed to a depth of six feet by a sudden swell of the sea. It is told on the Island how thirty men were fishing along the cliff edge one calm summer day when a wave rose up and picked them off, every one. We watched Maggie anxiously; we were too far for her to hear us, for any warning cry. We saw the wave coming. I think I shut my eyes. There was an awful moment; then Bob by my side gently said, 'It's all right. She's safe.' And I opened my eyes and saw her flattened on the ledge under her load of kelp, like a wrack of seaweed herself, half drowned. She had managed to cling to some part of the rock and resist the backward surge of the great wave as it left her.

An important member of our family was its major-domo, Pat Mullen, our go-between between the Islanders and ourselves, and coach for our cast. After the film was over Pat took pen in hand for the first time in his life and wrote a book about it, *Man of Aran.* It is the classic account of making the film; it is the feeling of the people about it; it is his feeling about it; a portrait of Bob; and there is the sweep of the Irish imagination in it and a tang of the sea.

Evenings when we sat before our big Aran fireplace with the little peat fire glowing there, listening to an Aran story-teller tell old tales of Ireland, usually in Gaelic, it was Pat who would translate them for us. These tales, as everyone knows, are of queens and kings, of giants whose heads reach the stars, and 'between their legs you can see the wide world', and there is a great stirring in them of great deeds. This oral literature, this poetry, repeated over again, always marvellous, is for these people a spiritual food.

For our boy of Aran we chose Michael Dillane. Michaeleen's mother wanted him to become a priest, and this truck with Protestants was for her a very worrisome thing. I had to drink several cups of tea with Mrs Dillane, and Michael became the proud possessor of a bicycle, the finest Bob could buy.

Michael was a 'broth of a boy', a daredevil and a bit of a show-off.

Tiger King, the Man of Aran, was our most difficult catch. A great tall figure with dark, curly hair like a Spaniard, he looked something like a gypsy and had a fey air about him. Aranmen ride their horses bareback, sitting far back on the horse's rump like a circus rider, sideways. We would hear a great galloping along the road; it would be Tiger King lashing his horse as he approached our cottage, passing it at high speed and looking the other way. One day there was a wedding, a time of celebration, of tea and biscuits for the women in the kitchen; but for the men there was poteen, a potent potion. Tiger was practically unconscious when at last Pat brought him to us, and Bob got out his camera and we made a screen test of our hero.

Last but not least, there was Patch Ruah, Red Patch, Patch of the red beard. Patch was our animal man; he had a great way with our turkeys, pigs, donkey, and two little kids. Patch's beard was magnificent, long, red, and silky. One day we got old Patch into a curragh and put him into the film. Patch was beyond himself. 'Now why', said he to Pat, 'would they be wanting me in the film?'

'Well, I dunno, Patch,' said Pat, 'but perhaps it's because you have in you some of that drama they are always talking about.'

'Drammer?' said Patch. 'And where would I be having it in me?'

Pat thought a while, looking Patch over. 'Well now, Patch, maybe,' said he, 'it could be it's in your beard you have it.'

From then on there were times we would lose Patch; he would disappear, we couldn't find him. One day as we were shooting, Pat, with his fingers to his lips, motioned me to come over. He was standing beside a big boulder. I looked behind the boulder. There was old Patch sitting there, with a bit of cracked mirror in one hand and a bit of broken comb in the other, carefully, lovingly, combing his beard.

We had two main sequences to do, a land sequence and a sea, or storm, sequence. First the land sequence: how could we express the feeling of the people for their little plots of land they make with so much labor, first breaking the rock, sledging it to make a bed, then laying on it soil and sand – handfuls of soil wherever they can find it on the island between its rock crevices – then laying over that seaweed, one load after another of the heavy, wet kelp they have to bring up steep rocky slopes from the sea? In my mind I see again the raging figure of a man against the sky, standing on a hilltop, looming like a giant as he cursed and threatened the life of a neighbor who he believed had taken from his little plot a handful of its soil.

Three times we shot the land sequence, shot the whole sequence through on three different locations. Twice we failed; the camera gave us nothing. We put the sequence aside and went ahead with other scenes. Finally, when the film was almost finished, we tried the land sequence a third time. The people were the same, the action was the same; there was nothing we could think of to do but simply try another location. This time – what it was I don't know, whether it was the light that day, or the location, whether it was the way the figures moved, their relations to each other and to the land – or something else

— whatever it was, it was a mystery, there was nothing we could explain about it, but at last it was there, we had it, the camera had found it. Often we would come back from a day's shooting happy and excited, sure that we had shot some wonderful stuff. Perhaps as we neared home Bob would take a pot shot at something, anything at all, just to use up the tag-end of film in his camera. Like as not the stuff we had thought would be so wonderful turned out to be nothing at all, while the pot shot, so casually taken, would turn out to be a revelation.

It was the same with the storm sequence, which Pat in his book has described so magnificently. Aran villages dot the shoreline of the Island at those points where there is a launching and a landing place for curraghs. And each village has its picked crew who pull the oars together. With each storm that came we took our cameras and our long lenses to one of these villages. Each village and each crew had its chance to show us what it could do. Perhaps one would be better for the camera than another.

'He [Bob] would see a spot in the distance', says Pat, 'where he would figure he should put up his camera. Well, nothing could stop him getting there. He made a direct line, and he'd bolt through a field of briars, you know, that would hold a bull – that sort of way. He had that fire in him, you see – say nothing, but do it if it costs you your life.' We worked and the men worked, returning time and time again to bend to their oars and prove their skill in the Aranman's never ending contest with the sea.

And as we shot, we developed and projected. And after the intense excitement of a day with the men and the great seas, at night in the projection room we would see it all again on the screen and our spirits would sag. As Pat put it, 'Though it passed all right, it didn't look half as thrilling to me as it was when I was in the curragh doing the work. I don't know how Mr Flaherty felt, but I was thoroughly discouraged. We even tried the other islands (there were three of them), and couldn't get anything done that was worth while – anything, that is, with this elusive dramatic quality which seems so necessary for the making of a good film, that finishing touch, the touch that goes between a good piece of work and the work of a master ... That evening he called me into the Big Room. I went in and sat down. He was drinking his black coffee as usual. He looked at me with an unspoken question in his eyes. I said, "Yes, it must be Bungowla and Big Patcheen Conneely!"'

Now, Bungowla is a shore on the western side of the Islands where the Atlantic swells roll in free and unbroken from the farthest reaches of that ocean. They roll up against cliffs three to four hundred feet sheer. At the base of these cliffs is a shelf of rock jutting out beneath the surface. By this shelf the waves against cliffs are borne upward in great walls of water and spray and spume that top the cliffs and fall in a drifting curtain of mist beyond them. It makes one of the most spectacular seascapes in the world. Here along these reaches is the village of Bungowla, primitive, isolated, one of the last strongholds of a pure Gaelic people.

In Bungowla in time of storm, curraghs are laid up, face down on the cobbles, lashed down against the fury of the wind. We had shied away from the thought of Bungowla. 'I dread the thought of it,' said Bob. 'I don't want any lives lost.'

But here in Bungowla was Big Patcheen Conneely, master curraghman of them all, and the crew who rowed with him, had always rowed with him; knew the ground, knew each other, knew the curragh under them, knew the currents, the tides and eddies, the hidden rocks, knew the sound of the wind and the feel of the sea, and knew them as one man together.

And so one day with our cameras we stood on Bungowla shore where it steps down from cliff to ledge to giant boulder. Here we had a pick of vantages from which to get with our long lenses that 'elusive, dramatic quality', the 'finishing touch' for this scene.

The sky was black, the wind rising and the seas mounting, as we waited for the critical moment when the men could launch the curragh. 'None of them could swim,' says Pat, 'but I praised their blood and I praised their generation before them, and I stirred them to it ... It was splendid to see the canoe take the breakers. A huge sea broke over Patcheen's head and the big canoe almost stood straight up on her stern as she leaped over to fight another sea. Big Patcheen shook the water from his eyes, and as he bent to the oars for a powerful stroke he threw a quick glance toward the shore. I was laughing for sheer joy and pride of how well the canoe was being handled and how I had picked the right man for the bow. He saw me laughing and, strange as it may seem, as he drove the canoe up the next great sea, and in spite of the great risk he was taking, he laughed back at me.'

This was film, spirit like this! Bob loved it, and his love gave that spirit even more of a lift. Those three men in the curragh fighting through the storm became a little bit bigger than life size. They became characters out of one of their own heroic legends, a saga of themselves.

As finally the canoe crashed on shore and the men jumped free, 'A great thrill of pride shot through me,' writes Pat. 'For here had been a trial of the old, old stock, and the blood still ran true.'

There was a great opening of the film in London. The cast were there. They got a great ovation. There they were in the theatre and there they were on the screen, and they themselves had done it. It was their film, they had made it; it was a film to tell the world what kind of people they were. As hard as ever they worked at kelp-making they had worked at making this film. They stood up in their seats, beaming with happiness. And Pat Mullen sitting beside me, I heard him say, 'And God knows tonight I am glad they are happy.'

Derek Mahon

'Epitaph for Robert Flaherty'
(after reading *The Innocent Eye*, by Arthur
Calder-Marshall, in Montreal, Canada)

The relief to be out of the sun,
To have come north once more
To my islands of dark ore
Where winter is so long
Only a little light
Gets through, and that perfect.

From *Poems 1962–1978* (1979).

VI

'To possess Aran ...'

*A*ran today is a very different place from that described by nineteenth-century visitors. In some ways it has lost much of what made it so distinct in times gone by. Electricity, telephones, cars, factories, a modern fishing industry and a regular air service – all have combined to reduce the differences between the islands and the mainland. Even the Irish language, while still as strong (or stronger) on Aran as anywhere else in the country, is showing definite signs of decline.

At the same time, Aran remains a place apart. Every year thousands upon thousands of people travel there, drawn by its past reputation as well as the continuing air of calm and isolation. The enigma of Dún Aonghasa exercises its fascination still for Etienne Rynne as it once did for George Petrie. In 1953 Brendan Behan spent some time on Inis Mór, writing an occasional column for The Irish Press. Here, too, he wrote part of his spoof thriller, The Scarperea, which was published serially in The Irish Times under the pseudonym 'Emmet Street'. Leo Daly has used Inis Mór as the backdrop for his unique and memorable novel, The Rock Garden. He, Shevawn Lynam, Ria Mooney, and the poets here for whom Aran was an inspiration are among many who have gone away from the islands enriched by the experience.

Richard Power lived for several months on the islands and also went to London to work with the islanders on English building sites. His novel Land of Youth (1964) is based on his knowledge of the islands, but better-known is his first work, Úll i mBarr an Ghéagáin (published 1959 and translated in 1980 as Apple in the Treetop), a vivid, affectionate account of island life.

Perhaps the only recent work of comparable insight and intimacy with the life and history of the islands is Tim Robinson's magnificent Stones of Aran. A Yorkshireman, he was first attracted to Inis Mór by Robert Flaherty's film in 1972 and published a beautifully detailed map of the islands in 1980 before the first volume of Stones of Aran appeared in 1986. In that work, he lovingly combines history, geography, folklore, archaeology, geology, linguistics, philosophy and almost every other branch of human learning to give a portrait of the island that will never be superseded.

In quite a different vein indeed is John Messenger's anthropological study of Inis Oírr. Based on visits by himself and his wife between 1959 and 1966, it was published in 1969 under the title Inis Beag, one of the first such studies on an area of Ireland to appear. As with so many subsequent visiting anthropologists who fondly imagine that using initials instead of names and spelling place-names backwards will conceal their sources and areas of study, Messenger's work caused much talk and, indeed, embarrassment when it appeared. It should be said in his defence that he exhibited far more sympathy for and identification with the community he studied than did many of his successors, and there is much in his book that is informative and revealing. But in some areas, especially in his study of island sexual practices and attitudes (also published as a separate article), one has to question the extent and accuracy of his information, neglecting as he does to mention anywhere his total lack of fluency in Irish. In the introduction to Inis Beag, Messenger remarks – without irony – how islanders would often jokingly misinform outsiders about island life.

As we end our look at Aran as it has appeared over the centuries to both islanders

237

and outsiders, we are struck by many things: the variety of interests to which the islands appealed; the extraordinary and abiding potency of the images created by Synge and Robert Flaherty; and, above all, the sheer numbers of those who have thought, dreamt and written about Aran. To them, to the islanders, and to the islands themselves, 'those three limestone rocks in the Atlantic', this book is dedicated.

Ria Mooney

Autobiography

It was during this holiday at home in 1930, that I first visited the Aran Islands. I have always boasted that the Islands' Parish Priest, the Captain, a journalist from a Dublin newspaper and I were the only people aboard the good ship *Dun Aengus* that day, who weren't as sick as the proverbial dog. I had remembered the advice of my 'doctor' friend on the *Laurentic*, and having acted on it, was one of the four people still on their feet when that sturdy boat steamed into Kilronan Harbour. It had been such a rough crossing that we'd thought we'd never make it, and it seemed extraordinary to me that strong men who earned their bread by fishing from tiny frail currachs, often risking their lives in gales, should be seasick in the comparative comfort of the steamship. The reason probably was that they had gone to the cabin below, which was hot and steamy, with a nauseating smell from the engines. I, however, remembered the advice to stay in the fresh air, and walked off as fit as when I had walked on, while sailors and passengers who had been stretched out in misery below, staggered off with their belongings.

After finding my guest house, I had a fine meal, and fell into a comfortable bed at about 10 p.m., only to wake again about 1 a.m., so sick I wanted to die. The bed rolled and pitched beneath me! There was no bell, of course, and the walls were as thick as in any old castle, so that I wouldn't have been heard even if I had plucked up enough courage to cry out. It was dawn before I fell asleep again, but I awoke after a few hours, none the worse for my uncomfortable night. When, over a fine breakfast of bacon, eggs and home-made brown and white bread, I related my experience, I was told that many people were affected similarly after a rough crossing. They weren't seasick until after they had been to bed for some time.

After breakfast, a cheery voice was heard on the road outside the cottage. It was the voice of Tom Casement, whose brother Roger had been one of our earliest 1916 patriots, and about whose reputation we are still wrangling with England. Tom was staying at Kilmurvey with the Robert Flahertys, who were making a film about life on the Aran Islands. Flaherty had already come into prominence with his film *Nanook of the North*, but in those days documentary

From George Spelvin's *Theatre Book* (Summer 1978).

films were little known to most of us in Ireland. Tom told me that the Flahertys wanted me to stay with them; that they had a big comfortable cottage, plenty of help, and that they loved company. When I agreed to go, I was put on a sidecar and driven to their place in Kilmurvey.

I was greeted warmly by a tall, handsome man in bainin jacket, pampooties and homespuns. At first I thought this was Flaherty himself welcoming me to his home, but Tom told me he was an islander named Pat Mullen who acted as the equivalent of one of our modern PRO men to Flaherty.

Mrs Flaherty was a superb cook and had trained a girl from the island to help her. When I arrived, she was in her garden picking herbs which she had grown herself, there being none to be found on the island. She greeted me with quiet sincerity, and introduced me to their other house guest, Dr Robin Flower of the British Museum. We three were chatting happily when Flaherty himself arrived with his brother and the camera-man, John Taylor. (John afterwards married Pat Mullen's daughter, Barbara, who has become a popular star on British TV.)

We afterwards met Tiger King and Maggie Dirrane, a handsome island pair who were playing the leads in the film. Everyone seemed to dress in the same way: the men wore the white collarless bainin jacket over their hand-knitted jerseys, pampooties, footwear – made from oblong pieces of unplucked cowhide – on their feet, and a *crios* (a belt woven from coloured wools) around the waist of their trousers. On their heads, they wore the Bobailin cap or the large, sombrero-like felt hat. The large hats, however, seemed to be dying out, as only the older men wore them, and I doubt if they could be bought in Ireland after the early years of the century. The Bobailin cap was very attractive. It was round, crocheted in thick white wool, with a large tassel at the top. It has become fashionable now for children or teenagers to wear one with an 'Aran' sweater or lumber-jacket. At that time, the children of Aran would wear their sweaters to Mass on Sundays – each family having its own traditional indi-vidual design, and all in spotless, gleaming white. The girls wore mostly red woollen skirts which they called petticoats. Married women and widows had begun to wear black, but the majority wore the skirts that were made from the homespun wool they had dyed with the juice of red berries.

The effect of these traditional clothes, and the simple good taste of the people who had remained on their island, was marred by the cheap American clothes which some of the girls wore on Sundays, proclaiming the fact that they had relatives or friends who had emigrated to the States. Some of the older women wore fawn-coloured shawls which had been bought in Galway, and others were very proud when on Sundays they could show off one of the newfangled machine-knitted garments called 'cardigans'. The men's trousers were made from cloth woven from the wool of the black sheep – bainin was made from the wool of the white sheep.

Already, in 1930, because of the publicity being given to the islands from Flaherty's work, and the many visitors, forerunners of the tourist trade, the old ways were changing. To some extent, these changes were a blessing in disguise for the islanders whose lives had been so hard, as J. M. Synge has depicted so magnificently in *Riders to the Sea* and in his book *The Aran Islands*. For my own part, I am glad I saw something of the old customs before they disappeared altogether. Pat Mullen told me that in his youth, before he had emigrated – to stay only a few years – to America, the women were even more colourful in their dress. White, red, blue, purple and striped petticoats were worn. Their newest, which they wore on Sundays, was turned up in front, and caught in folds to form a kind of bustle at the back, when they were performing any tasks at which their new petticoats might get splashed or spotted. But even at the time of my visit it was a picture for the mind to store away to see those women, with their red skirts spread out, sitting on the sloping golden sands of Inisheer in the evening, their back supported by a green bank, waiting for their men to come home with currachs full of supplies brought in on the *Dun Aengus* from Galway.

I cannot imagine a more instructive or sympathetic companion for a tramp across the island of Inishmór than Robin Flower. This big, plain, companionable Yorkshireman was a mine of information on the habits and the folklore of the islands. I often wish I'd made notes when I came back to the Kilmurvey house, but I never have been one for notes or diary-keeping. Dr Flower's first loves among the islands were the Blaskets off the west Kerry coast. There, he was known as 'Bláithín' – in English, 'Little Flower' – which title amused him greatly. He loved those islanders, who came to know him almost as intimately as he knew them, and his affection was deep and true, without sentimentality. He poured it all into that beautiful book, *The Western Islands*. It was joy for me that summer to walk through Inishmór with him. Even if I've forgotten the facts, I can live again the peace and relaxation I knew in that land of stones and wild flowers, while I listened to stories of the ancient ones who sojourned there, who loved and fought on that rocky ground.

I have a clear picture in my mind of crossing to one of the islands with one of the Flaherty brothers, accompanied by an islandman with his dog, to look for a Gaelic story-teller whom Flaherty wanted to film for the Irish government. These storytellers, or seanachies as they were called, were gradually dying out, and an effort was being made to put them on record for future generations. I remember that it had been a wild and windy day, but now on this June evening, the sea was like glass, reflecting sky and cloud formation, with the background of the Clare and Connemara hills. I longed for the ability to paint the colour above and about me. As we moved into the strip of sea between Kilmurvey and the mainland, the sun began to tip towards the west. A band of crimson made a wide path across an indigo ocean towards our boat, and tipped the cloudbanks above our heads with rose. To our right, the rain clouds had gathered in a heavy dark mass above the Clare coast. Against their sombre background, gulls were flying, silver in the light. Silver and black were the colours on our right, pink and blue above our heads, crimson and gold on our left. Perhaps there are other countries that could give such sudden and unexpected glory, but I haven't visited them.

When we arrived at Rossaveel, Flaherty and his brother went off to interview the storyteller. The rest of us made for the tiny building that was the local pub. I remember only two buildings on this lonely, rocky coast – the cottage where the Flahertys were going to visit, up the road, and this tiny shebeen. Our set for Synge's *The Playboy of the Western World*, on the Abbey's small stage, seemed enormous when compared with this or any other public house I had been in on Inishmór. Here, in Connemara, with a real Pegeen Mike behind the counter, there was room for only two people to sit or stand on either side of the door, and the bar-counter was not as big as a kitchen table. The girl behind it was a country girl of medium height, handsome but not pretty. She had strength and vitality in her appearance – a perfect Pegeen Mike who could be brought to vivid life by the 'poetry talk' of a wandering playboy.

Tom Casement, who seemed to worship the memory of his executed and much-maligned brother, Roger, would not talk about him unless asked directly. He was to have left Inishmór the day after I arrived, but stayed on and on and refused to leave until I did. I left regretfully after two weeks, refusing Flaherty's suggestion that I give Tom the slip in Galway, and return to Rossaveel, where they would pick me up. We were not on a corridor train to Dublin, as far as I remember, so I found myself alone with Tom in the railway carriage from Galway.

He had been threatening to commit suicide, and join his beloved brother. I had gradually come to believe he really meant it, so before I left, I wrote to a very great and good friend of his, telling her my fears. She wrote back, saying I was to pay no heed to him; that he had been threatening to commit suicide ever since Roger was executed in 1916, and that he was merely trying to draw attention to himself, and had no intention of taking his own life. Therefore, when during the train journey to Dublin, he went to open the carriage door, telling me he was going to jump out, I simply sat in the corner seat and looked the boredom I felt. Again he repeated his threat to jump, and this time I said, 'Jump, for God's sake, and have done with it!' At this he drew back, sat down silently in his corner, and sulked all the rest of the way to Dublin. My unsympathetic approach must have been the right one!

However, between my next term in New York and return visit to Dublin about two years later, I heard that his body had been found in the Grand Canal near Baggot Street Bridge, clad only in his dressing-gown and pyjamas. (Had he walked in his sleep and slipped off that wooden pedestrian's bridge that crossed the canal at that point? Or had he carried out his threat? No one will ever know.) My last memory of him is seeing him rise from his seat in the front row of the Abbey stalls, to place a large bottle of whiskey in the footlights for Paddy Carolan, who was playing the part of a drunken man, the unwanted father of the principal girl character. Paddy came reeling across the stage, demanding whiskey. This was too much for drunken, generous, kindly Tom, so he offered Paddy his own, crying out, 'Poor Paddy! Here, have mine!' I'm sure he was very hurt when Eileen Crowe, without missing a line, walked down to the footlights, took the bottle, placed it in the wings, and finished her scene.

Richard Power

Apple in the Treetop

There was fog in the morning, without a puff of wind. About midday the wind sneaked in, an invisible invader that gradually gathered strength. The dark storm clouds threatened to the west. The sun shed its thin, wavering light down on the water. The clouds pushed east to drown out the sun. You noticed drops of water in the breeze that was gaining force, knocking a bar of music out of the telegraph lines. The night arrived early, mixing its darkness with the fog, like ink mixing with soup.

Two Spanish boats in the twilight sailed into the bay making for Kilronan. Tall, ghostly trawlers they were, their lights flickering, ploughing the majestic waves, twisting left and right. They reached the sheltered coast at last and dropped anchor. The throbbing engines died down. The wind ripped over the empty quay, screeching through the abandoned rigging. You'd see the great waves moving past the mouth of the harbour, the thin-edged white crests poised like unsheathed swords.

Only in this kind of weather you'd meet a Spaniard in Kilronan. They're the harbinger of storms. They come ashore and walk the street in wooden clogs. Occasionally they make an effort to get to know a shopkeeper but, normally, they don't bother with the natives except to salute them solemnly. And the locals receive them like they'd receive a fairy wind crossing the road.

Some of them are prisoners, silent, hardy men who will never return to their native lands until they are freed. It is said they are better off than the normal prisoners at home. If that's the case, I'd just as well not be a normal prisoner. Although they are able to earn a share of money, they have a desperate life on the ocean in the black frost of the year, twenty crammed into one boat, labouring, changing watches with each other, with no stop or respite. It is said that they hug blocks of ice to their chests for heat in the winter when they're cleaning fish.

When they came to this coast in the years after the war, the locals weren't too happy at first. It was the English who fished there previously. Bulky comfortable boats they had and every modern device to kill the fish. The islanders liked the English. They were fond of drink, fun loving and rich.

From *Apple in the Treetop* (1980).

When they'd encounter the fishermen in curraghs out to sea, more than likely they'd heave to and fill the curragh with a fine cargo of fish. Sometimes they'd provide a good meal, bacon, beans and canned fruits, to the curragh crew on board the trawler. Indeed, there'd often be found a man from the islands among the crew members of the trawler.

But the Englishmen grew tired of fishing this area. They began to roam further west, and eventually, they were seen no more. Frenchmen, particularly Bretons, took their place.

They were uncouth, drinking, fighting men bent on creating disturbances day and night. They had no moderation at all, especially when they'd play football, a dangerous game they played without stockings or boots. They'd steal cabbage and potatoes from the stony patches, and it was a sturdy man who'd go against them. They were a strange tribe. It was said the sea salt was in their veins, that they had no regard for any kind of death except drowning. In the height of a gale they'd put into the bay and often they'd do their best to stay out to sea altogether. Often one of their boats would be lost. The other crews would accept the story of the loss philosophically. It was only what fate had destined for them.

A Breton captain arrived one time who was after buying a new boat. One day, he lay docked at the quayside, on his maiden voyage, and he was like a child with a new toy. He was reluctant to leave it even to step ashore. He'd stroke the rails. He'd track his fingers on the polished bulwarks. He'd run his hands around the helm like he'd fondle a woman. He got some mystic pleasure from it, and exhilaration from the smell of paint and scrubbed wood.

His boat was not seen in the harbour when the next gale roared this way. It was said that he wasn't willing to make for land and that he sailed straight into the gale without a dog's regard for god or demon. No one knew where he was lost. Maybe he's out there still, too full of *hubris* and pride of possession to direct his beautiful boat to the safety of the harbour. At any rate that is what the Bretons like to theorize and, perhaps, the Aran Islanders too.

The Bretons drifted west, gradually, and the poor Spaniards came to scoop into their nets whatever was left on the coast. Dirty old boats they have and very little money. If a curragh meets with them, the islanders don't expect even the gift of a pollock from them. They come ashore and walk the streets – in their black ganseys and oily britches, adorned with large patches. They don't go into public houses at all, but take to the country, casually, looking over the houses and the vegetable patches.

Although the islanders are convinced that they're a strange solemn bunch, they had another opinion of them one time. When the first fleet of them sailed in years ago, the islanders became greatly agitated. In a pitch darkness they arrived when the wind was howling. They'd lost their way and the boats hove to in Galway Bay waiting for a pilot. It was their bad luck that it was opposite Aran Beg, the Land of Youth of the islands, that they clustered. It was immediately concluded that the mythical underwater cities had drifted to the surface, that the prophecy was fulfilled, and the Day of Judgement had arrived. But it was clear, after a while, that the lights emanated from boats, and a curragh put out to guide them to land.

They weren't over the worst yet, however. They had an even greater obstacle to surmount, the hurdle of morality. Perhaps it was the bad example of the Bretons was responsible for it, but the impressionable people on the island feared that their moral sensibilities would be'ruptured if these barbarians were permitted to come ashore. Probably their women would be seduced by winning words and exotic manners. ...

The Spaniards no doubt were taken aback when they heard this prediction ... but it was nothing compared to the disgust that the women felt when they caught sight of the strangers at close quarters. Repulsive little yellow men! How could anybody think their virtue might be assailed by their falling for such specimens! They are kinder to the unfortunate Mediterranean visitors now, but there is still no foundation for the concern of the island's holy water hens.

The Spaniards are probably not as subdued by nature as people think. They have their own pursuits, especially when they have a *gitano* in their midst. They are inclined to be tuneful and sensitive, however poor they may be as sailors. Often one hears the strum of a guitar in Kilronan Bay and the clicking of a flamenco dance. It's an eerie feeling to hear the sound curdling towards you on a dark wintry sea, between the slate grey cloud and the black wet rocks.

No wonder there is a haunting echo in the Spanish melody.

They have fun and jokes too, whenever a lively crew are on board. A trawler arrived from Southern Spain one time, from Puerto Santa Maria, a town which exports wine. They had a small Barbary ape on board, which they dressed up in sailor's clothes to put the fear of God in the locals. They gave the ape a cigarette and let it loose on the streets. The crew was almost thrown out of the village entirely by residents who thought it sacrilegious to dress up an animal in this way to make a mock of people. And in a way, you could hardly blame them.

When the Spaniards came to church on Sunday you'd often hear them chatter and whisper like schoolchildren. They'd sit just inside the porch in a body. Sometime, during the sermon, they'd take out old newspaper clippings and pass them from one to the other, looking at the pictures of *toros* and *fotbal*. Occasionally, one of them would get up and clatter out of the church in his wooden shoes to make sure the boat was still moored and that nobody had attempted to make away with it.

Toros and *fotbal* are the topics which absorb them. But that's not fulfilment enough, of course. I remember an islander who came from Galway in a Spanish boat one time describe the jampacked cabin deep in the boat. Some of the crew were asleep in their hammocks, some of them talking quietly on the floor, playing dominoes or plucking lonely chords on the guitar. One of them had pasted a picture of Rita 'Ayvort' on the wall above his bed so that he could see her from any point no matter how much the boat would sway or toss. The figure of a woman was drawn by somebody else on the wall. ... 'Every act but a bodily one.'

They had one delicious pastime however when they came ashore, and that was selling brandy. Any time that the wind gains strength over the islands, the local constabulary become very vigilant. They spend sleepless nights for as long as the boats are anchored in the harbour. Standing in the shelter of the quay they keep a wary eye out to sea, their ears attuned like radar for the sound of oars. But, in spite of their best efforts, many is the bottle of cognac that is run ashore, not only under the cover of darkness but in the light of midday too. Some brandy is even smuggled to the other islands so long as the price is right. Often, you'd spot a tea chest or a soap box being carried ashore from the steamer. Each onlooker keeps his eyes glued to it, his mouth working with the nervousness that it might slip into the sea. And it's not a shortage of tea or soap that's causing the anxiety!

One gusty evening we sailed past the boat furthest out. A middle aged Spaniard was standing at the rails. He gave a shout, and the next minute the whole crew joined him in observing us. They stood at the rail, silent, their dark eyes brooding down at us.

'Cognac?' asked someone in the back of our curragh. There was not the slightest motion out of them. My companion raised his two hands and displayed eight fingers.

'Ocho,' he said.

They looked at him as if they didn't know what he was talking about.

Then the middle aged man shook his grey head.

'Pound,' he said curtly.

'The devil,' said our man. 'You think a lot of yourself.' He showed both hands, thumbs and all. 'Ten,' he said. 'Diez.'

'Kiss my arse, yeh whoor,' said our man grabbing hold of the oars.

'Pound,' repeated the Spaniard.

'Let's go, lads,' said the curragh owner. 'Let them go fuck themselves.'

There wasn't a gug out of the Spaniard as we departed, nor from his shipmates either. The dark eyes continued to gaze at us soulfully. Expecting they'd burst out laughing I was, or at least that they'd talk to us, or even attack us.

But they remained there, motionless, until one by one they disappeared. They knew very well that the curragh would return and that a bargain would eventually be struck. They could afford to wait.

A civic guard was waiting for us as we went ashore. He nodded to us, inspecting us closely. But it must have been clear to him from the look on our faces that our journey had been fruitless. But the guards seek other people besides the purchasers of cognac.

I heard of a dispute between a guard and a Spanish captain, one autumn evening. A couple of days before that, a Spaniard was seen fishing close to the cliffs, inside the fishing limits. The guard had binoculars and was able to read the number of the boat, which he wrote down in his notebook. He was delighted when the force of the gale blew the very same boat into the harbour straight to him.

He strolled majestically down the quay. He asked the Spanish boy to summon the captain immediately. He came up. He shot open the wheelhouse window and stuck his head out. He was a formidable man. He couldn't have

246

been more than five feet tall, but the same measurement would have encompassed his stocky shoulders, which had the lineaments of a bullock's. The long black hair on his bare chest, and indeed on his forehead, would remind you too of a bullock, especially with the smouldering eyes under the ribs of hair glaring out at you.

To complete his fearsome appearance, there gleamed the scar of some ancient battle on his upper cheek, not the clean, surgical line of a knife wound but a jagged cavity such as a broken bottle might inflict. He gazed fixedly at the guard, without a word out of him.

The guard enumerated the crime to him as if he were reading out of his black book; that he had observed the vessel within the territorial limit of three miles; that he intended to enforce the law strictly on him and impound the nets; that he was required to give his name and the name of his port of registry; that he would note down everything he said which might be used in evidence against him. ...

'No entiendo,' said the captain.

The guard repeated the summons to him. The black eyes fixedly locked in on his, without blinking.

'Well,' concluded the guard, 'tell me. Your name and port.'

'No entiendo.'

The guard began again. The captain placed his two hands on the window ledge, then folded them slowly. It was clear he was giving the speech a lot of attention. But when the tide of talk had receded, he had nothing to say but 'No entiendo.'

The story flew around the village. The layabouts pushed forward in the hope that something might happen, straining, as they leaned forward to listen. They upset the guard, whose voice came and went in gusts. But it was all in vain.

He turned about suddenly and marched away down the quay, furious. There wasn't a stir out of the captain; he remained exactly where he was, his eyes still focused on the spot where the guard had stood. The layabouts remained, their eyes fastened on the captain in the chance he might do something else newsworthy, that he might let a triumphal roar out of him, say, or offer some other comment besides 'No entiendo.' But he did nothing. Their patience gave way eventually and they headed back for the hill to await the next bit of diversion.

'The creatures,' I heard the woman of the house say. 'Aren't they an odd crowd, them Spaniards!' They had a right to be; their lives forever suspended on the top of waves, and the prospect of a sudden death before them always. A couple of years ago, there was a fleet of trawlers returning to Vigo after spending a long tour at sea. They were only a short distance from the Bay of Biscay when the sea erupted and a gale smashed them. Five of the boats sank. It was said that the city of Vigo was in mourning for a week, the flags lowered, black crepe on the front doors, the women and children heart-broken, but the businessmen and politicians busy trying to balance their accounts. If you didn't understand such a strange life, you would hardly understand the meaning of the old man who once came ashore at Kilronan. A storm was lashing the island, the violent swells breaking on the rocks, the houses crouched in the shadow of the cliffs with the seafoam blowing over them. A withered old man he was, a thin beard on him, his skin burnt by the sun and the wind. You'd hardly take him for a man at all, or surmise he had any of life's common cares. He was too akin to the spirit of the storm, a seagull shrieking past him, his scraggy, grey hair tossing about with the bursting tempests like some reptilian, accursed nest.

An islander encountered him.

'Mal tiempo,' he said as he might say 'Bad day.'

The old man looked at him. When he spoke, his voice was like a deep echo from hollow lungs. There was despair in every syllable he uttered, despair at this savage life that had no sense nor reason in it.

'Sempre mal tiempo,' he said. 'Every day is a bad day.'

Seamus Heaney

'Lovers on Aran'

The timeless waves, bright sifting, broken glass,
Came dazzling around, into the rocks,
Came glinting, sifting from the Americas

To possess Aran. Or did Aran rush
To throw wide arms of rock around a tide
That yielded with an ebb, with a soft crash?

Did sea define the land or land the sea?
Each drew new meaning from the waves' collision.
Sea broke on land to full identity.

From *Death of a Naturalist* (1966).

John Messenger

The Supernatural and the Esthetic

Because of the writings of Nativists, most visitors to Inis Beag believe that the Catholicism of the folk embodies an ideal unattained even on the mainland, where the faith is thought to set an example for all of Christendom. In fact, however, the worship of the islanders is obsessively oriented toward salvation in the next world with a corresponding preoccupation with sin in this world; there is a marked tendency toward polytheism in the manner in which they relate to the Blessed Virgin and certain Irish saints; rituals and sacred artifacts, Christian as well as pagan, often are employed by them to serve magical ends; and, finally, many observances that they hold to be orthodox Catholic are in reality idiosyncratic to Inis Beag or to Ireland. Christian morality in its outward manifestations, as we have seen, is realised to a remarkable degree, but it is less a product of the emphasis placed on good works as a means of gaining salvation than of the techniques of social control exercised by the priests and an overwhelming fear of damnation. [...]

The islanders know little of the church dogma and the purport of rituals and feast days. What knowledge they do possess often is distorted, and they seldom read the Bible or manuals of instruction or engage in doctrinal discussions among themselves. I discovered by consulting priests and church histories, dictionaries, and exegeses – both before and during my stay in Inis Beag – that I came to know far more about the faith than any of the folk, and sometimes imparted what I had learned to the curious in homes and even in the pubs. Instruction is welcomed by the islanders, but they dislike criticism from any quarter of their idiosyncratic Catholic observances, pagan retentions and reinterpretations, and non-Christian behaviour. They also dislike being told, especially by returned emigrants, that 'Catholic culture' in Ireland is quite unlike that in other parts of the world and arouses dismay and even incredulity in many foreign Catholics who visit Ireland.

From *Inis Beag* (1969).

The paths to salvation, according to the islanders, are threefold: obeying the curate, performing the rituals of the church diligently and punctiliously, and conforming to the moral laws of Christianity. Being saved, however, is to them much more a matter of escaping Hell than of achieving Purgatory and eventually Heaven, and they experience more anxiety about failing to conform to the moral laws than pride in conforming to them. Furthermore, it is sins of thought rather than sins of deed which preoccupy them. While they boast of their morality as expressed in behaviour, they labour under a heavy burden of guilt arising out of repressed sexual desires, jealousy and envy of their neighbours, and anti-clerical sentiment, among other attitudes. It is difficult for most of them to confess these to the priest, and thus their feelings of guilt and fear of damnation are compounded. Many times in Inis Beag I heard a 'good Catholic' defined as one who 'thinks mostly of death, Judgment, Heaven, and Hell' and guides his conduct accordingly. Life on earth is regarded as merely a brief prelude to the 'eternity stretching beyond the grave', to be lived only in preparation for the Day of Judgment and borne patiently in all its 'pain and suffering'. Priests and nuns are envied for many reasons, among them the fact that they can 'spend most of their time preparing for death' and thus are in a better position to achieve salvation.

It is apparent to outside observers and to the folk alike that women are more pious than men. They attend church more regularly, are more serious of mien at mass and during other religious observances, and are more prone to talk of religious matters than men. Many women go to mass daily, and it is said that all of the women of the island, but only ten men, have evaded going to Hell magically by attending mass nine Fridays in succession after Ash Wednesday (or, according to some, the first Friday in each month for nine successive months, or the first Friday after Ash Wednesday for nine years in succession). The reasons for this are several, but the most important are that women are less contented than men and thus have a greater need for the solace that religion affords, and they are more restricted socially than men and by fulfilling various church obligations can escape household confinement and interact with other women. Some islanders are thought to be overly pious – 'wear their religion on their sleeves' – and are subjects of amusement and derision; those who use piety to cloak avarice and other Christian vices are detested and are likely to become the butt of satirical anecdotes and ballads.

In many primitive and peasant societies, in which Christianity has dispossessed polytheistic religions, it has been observed that polytheism has left a legacy whereby the Virgin Mary and various angels and saints are worshipped as dispensers of personal power in their own right. This has been extended to the Trinity among the Anang of Nigeria, who believe that God provided independent power for his human son, Jesus, with which to convert the world to Christianity, and for the Holy Spirit (who has joined the indigenous pantheon of spirits) to act for mankind as healer, prognosticator, forgiver of sins, and protector against ghosts, witches, and sorcerers. Most Inis Beag folk regard God and the Devil, among Christian supernatural beings, as the only possessors of personal power. But some think that power emanating from the deity is manipulated by the Blessed Virgin and particular saints, and they as well as he must be propitiated for best results. When asked why she prayed to St Enda rather than to other saints, an old woman said that this saint is 'nearer to God' and therefore able to capture more of his power than others. A few islanders hold that these intermediary entities possess power not emanating from the deity, and thus may be approached individually through prayer and sacrifice for their favour. The saints most often appeased are St Patrick, St Brigid, St Enda, and the patron saint of the island.

The Devil is thought to command power for evil as great as or greater than that of the Virgin Mary and the saints for good. Some believe that he controls malevolent pagan beings as well as his own minions from Hell, and he both tempts Christians to sin and attacks them bodily causing sickness, injury, and other misfortunes. He is abroad at all times, although his power is amplified on such occasions as Allhallows' Eve, and sometimes he can be seen by human eyes – as a huge, dark, indistinct figure standing at a distance, usually after nightfall or when it is raining heavily. One evening during a severe storm, I visited without advance notice a man milking his cow at the back of the island, and he would not approach me as I stood atop a fence wearing oilskin and sou'wester until I called out to him and established the fact that I was not the 'big fellow' come to do him harm. Animals are especially sensitive to the presence of Satan, and asses which run about braying loudly are believed to have seen him. [...]

Twice a year, Inis Beag is visited for a day by the parish priest and a curate, who join the local curate to celebrate special masses, called 'the stations' ('the confessions' in Irish), in two homes and in the church. Homes are chosen in such a manner that each of the four villages is represented every year, and each home in the island is so honoured every sixteen to twenty-two years. For weeks in advance of the stations, both families are hard at work cleaning, painting, and repairing their houses and surrounding streets, fences, and outbuildings in preparation for the event. Confessions are heard by the three priests the night before, and holy water is sprinkled by them in the streets and on the out-buildings near the two houses as a blessing prior to the masses at nine o'clock in the morning. Stations in the homes are conducted by the visiting clerics and in the chapel by the Inis Beag curate, and the folk are free to attend any one of the three services. Following the masses, the priests and the three local teachers are entertained at breakfast in the chosen homes, after which the sacrament is carried to those who are confined. The families involved look forward eagerly to the event, for the stations are believed to bring them luck and 'to drive out the "big fellow" for a long time'. It also forces them to put their property in a state of good repair, which, in retrospect, is regarded as a benefit, however much they might have complained of the labour involved during the previous weeks.

The sacred well, probably appropriated from the Druids fifteen centuries ago, still attracts the folk and occasionally pilgrims from Inis Thiar and other islands. On the mainland, patterns often were associated with holy wells named after saints, but this does not seem to have been the case in Inis Beag. It was customary until about ten years ago for those who came to pray here to attach bits of cloth, rosaries, or sacred objects obtained from holy places of pilgrimage on the mainland and abroad, but this practice was halted by the clergy as smacking of paganism. Now it is visited for religious purposes mostly by small groups on Sunday afternoon, and by persons about to emigrate and their families who come to pray for the good fortune of the soon departed. The water in the spring is not considered holy, but capable of 'bringing the grace of God and the saints', and if it is drunk during prayer, it is believed to be especially efficacious for curing sterility, among other afflictions. In this century, a partially blind islander is believed to have regained his sight after paying nine visits to the well on successive Sundays, and other miraculous cures from earlier times are reported. Those who come to the spring always seek a tiny fish or eel in the water, which, if observed, is merely a good omen to some but an assurance of reaching Heaven to others. Attaching rags to the well and seeking cures and omens there are all examples of reinterpretation. The spring also is used as a source of water by farmers who pasture stock in nearby fields and by thirsting passersby. [...]

RELIGION AND PERSONALITY

It is appropriate here to assess the basic personality structure of Inis Beag islanders, since traits such as sexual puritanism, hypochondria, depression, masochism, and conformism, and ambivalence toward authority are linked causally with religion in a very direct manner. Other personality characteristics, already or yet to be considered, which are more peripheral to religion include secretiveness, envy and jealousy, dogmatism, indolence, feelings of inferiority, and verbal skill.

Probably the most prominent trait of Inis Beag (and Irish) personality is sexual puritanism. Its etiology is complex and much debated, but appears to embrace most significantly historical (such as the influence of ascetic monasticism and Jansenism), sociocultural (such as the Oedipus complex and male solidarity), and psychological (such as masochism) variables. How long it has been a major component of Irish national character is conjectural, for it is impossible to appraise with accuracy Irish society, culture, and personality prior to the nineteenth century. Sexual attitudes and behaviour in Celtic, medieval, and early modern times can be surmised only from tangential and questionable sources; depending on which sources are quoted, as good a case can be made for sexual puritanism as its opposite before 1800.

The inculcation of sexual puritanism in Inis Beag must be examined in three contexts: informal social controls of the curate and those imposed by the islanders on themselves, the influence of visiting 'missions', and enculturation in the home. The first of these has been taken up at length in the last chapter. Suffice it to say here, some folk (especially certain youths who consider themselves 'worldly') resent the intrusions of priests and neighbours into their sexual lives. They ask what right have young, virginal, inexperienced, and sexually unknowledgeable curates to give advice and pass judgments in this sphere. Equally resented are those persons who hide themselves in the darkness or behind fences to overhear the conversations of passersby, which may pertain to sexual matters, and those who maintain close scrutiny of visitors during the summer, both day and night, in order to discover them in 'compromising' situations. Sexual rumours run rife in the island, such as those concerning the 'nude' sunbathing of mainland girls (bared shoulders and lower thighs) and the 'attacks' on them at night by boys and young men (attempts to hold their hands or kiss them, while under the influence of stout). Over a dozen efforts on the part of my wife and me to determine the truth behind the most pernicious rumours of this genre revealed sexual fantasy at their core in every case.

Church influence also is exerted through missions which come to Inis Beag every three to five years. On these momentous occasions, two Redemptorist priests (usually, but also Franciscans, Dominicans, and Passionists) spend a week in the island, where they conduct mass each morning and preach long sermons in the chapel every afternoon or early evening. Everyone – even old people and mothers with newborn infants – is urged to attend to receive the 'blessings of the mission'; to some this means gaining time out of Purgatory for themselves or a deceased kinsman, while to others absence carries with it the penalty of damnation. A mission usually has a theme whose variations are explored with high emotion and eloquence by the visiting priests in their exhortations. The most common theme is 'controlling one's passions', but abstaining from intoxicating drink and maintaining the faith as an emigrant also are addressed. Collections are made by children to support the endeavour, and a list of contributors and their donations is displayed publicly. It is said that a mission creates an emotionally charged atmosphere in the island which continues for weeks after the departure of the clerics.

The seeds of repression are planted early in infancy by parents through instruction supplemented by rewards and punishments, conscious imitation, and unconscious internalisation. Although mothers bestow considerable attention and affection on their offspring, particularly on their sons, physical love as manifested in intimate fondling and kissing is rare in Inis Beag. Verbal affection comes to supplant contact affection by the time that the child can walk. Any forms of direct or indirect sexual expression – masturbation, mutual exploration of bodies, use of either standard or slang words relating to sex, and open urination and defecation – are punished severely by word and deed. Care is taken to cover the bodies of infants in the presence of their siblings and outsiders, and sex never is discussed before children of any age. Separation of the sexes starts within the family among siblings in early childhood, and is augmented by separation in almost all segments of adolescent and adult activity. Brothers come to associate mostly with brothers, and sisters with sisters, at play in and near the cottage, travelling to and from school, and in the chapel. Boys and girls are separated to some extent in classrooms and completely in play at recess. During the church services, there is a further separation of adult men and women, as well as boys and girls, and each of the four groups leaves the chapel in its turn. Even on the strand during summer months, male tourists and vacationing emigrants tend to bathe at one end and women at the other; some swimmers change into bathing suits there, under towels and dresses 'daringly' – a custom practised elsewhere in Ireland which bespeaks of sexual catharsis.

Parents and their school age offspring read the popular religious journals found in most homes, and many of the articles therein deal with sexual morality of the Irish Catholic variety. Several times my wife inadvertently inquired as to whether or not certain women were pregnant, using that word before children, only to be 'hushed' or to have the conversations postponed until the young people could be herded outside; even then the adults were so embarrassed by the term that they found it difficult to communicate with her. One steamer day she aroused stupefaction among a group of men on the strand when she tried – unsuccessfully – to identify the gender of a bullock about to be shipped off.

Lack of sexual knowledge and the prevalence of misconceptions about sex combine to brand Inis Beag one of the most sexually naive of the world's societies. Only three mothers admitted giving sexual instructions, briefly and incompletely, to their daughters. It is said that boys are better advised than girls, but that the former learn about sex informally from older boys and men, and from observing animals covertly. Most islanders who were questioned about how sexual knowledge is imparted to youths expressed the belief that 'after marriage, nature takes its course', thus negating the need for anxiety creating confrontations of parents and offspring. I was unable to discover any cases of childlessness in Inis Beag based on sexual ignorance of spouses, as have been reported from other regions of peasant Ireland.

Menstruation and menopause arouse profound misgivings among women of the island, because few of them comprehend their physiological significance. My wife was called on by perplexed women to explain these processes more than any other phenomena related to sex. When they reach puberty, most girls are unprepared for the first menstrual flow and find the experience a traumatic one, especially when their mothers are unwilling or unable to explain it satisfactorily. It is commonly believed that the menopause can induce insanity; in order to ward it off, some women have retired from life in their mid-forties and, in at least three contemporary cases, have confined themselves to bed until death years later. Yet the harbingers of 'madness' are simply the physical symptoms announcing the menopause, which in Inis Beag include migraine headaches, hot flashes, faintness in crowds and enclosed places, and severe anxiety. Sometimes women who have not yet reached the menopause or have passed it and who fear becoming mentally ill from other causes will experience these symptoms in the anticipatory role playing.

As to sexual misconceptions, the folk share with most Western peoples the belief that men by nature are far more sexually disposed than women. The latter are informed by the curate and in the home that sexual relations with their husbands are a 'duty' which must be 'endured', for to refuse coitus is a mortal sin. Women frequently affix the guilt for male libidinal strivings on the enormous intake of potatoes by their spouses (among the Anang of Nigeria, men fear the excessive sexual demands of their wives and place the blame on clitoridectomy). Asked to compare the sexual proclivities of Inis Beag men and women, one woman said, 'Men can wait a long time for "it", but we can wait a lot longer.' There is much evidence to indicate that the female orgasm is unknown or not experienced (or considered a deviant response not to be divulged). A middle-aged bachelor, who considers himself wise in the ways of the outside world and has a reputation for making love to willing tourists during the summer, described the violent bodily reactions of a girl to his fondling and asked for an explanation; when told the 'facts of life', he admitted not knowing that women also could achieve climax, although he was aware that some of them apparently enjoyed lovemaking. Inis Beag men feel that sexual intercourse is debilitating, and they will desist from it the night before they are to perform tasks which will require the expenditure of great energy. Women are approached sexually neither during menstruation nor for at least six months after childbirth, for they are considered 'dangerous' to the male at these times. Returned Yanks have been denounced from the pulpit for describing American sexual mores to local youths, and such 'pornographic' magazines as *Time* and *Life,* mailed home by relatives from abroad, have aroused curates to spirited sermon and instruction.

Male masturbation seems to be common in Inis Beag (sometimes called the major 'escape valve' for frustration in Ireland), but premarital coitus is unknown and marital copulation is limited as to foreplay and the manner of consummation. Elders proudly insist that premarital sexual activities of any sort do not occur in the island, but male youths admit to it in rumour. The claims of young men focus on 'petting' with tourists and a few local girls, whom the bolder of them kiss and handle outside of their clothing. Inis Beag girls, it is held by their lovers, do not confess these sins because they fail to experience pleasure from the contact; the male perpetrators also shun the confessional because of their fear of the curate. Absolute privacy at night is sought by married couples when they copulate, and foreplay is limited to kissing and rough fondling of the lower body of the woman, especially her buttocks. Sexual activity invariably is initiated by the husband, and the wife is usually totally passive. Only the male superior position is employed, and intercourse takes place with underclothes not fully removed; orgasm for the man is achieved quickly, after which he falls asleep almost immediately. Whenever I talked with males of sexual practices other than those just described, my remarks were met with disbelief, or I was accused of 'codding' my listeners.

Many kinds of behaviour disassociated from sex in other societies, such as nudity and physiological evacuation, are considered sexual in Inis Beag. We have noted elsewhere the fear of nudity – which precludes washing the body and bathing in the sea – and the secrecy surrounding the acts of urination and defecation and the use of human manure as fertiliser and cow dung as fuel. The sexual symbolism of nudity not only has resulted in the drowning of seamen who might have saved themselves had they been able to swim, but in the death of men who were unwilling to face the nurse when ill, because it might mean baring their bodies to her, and thus were beyond help when finally treated. An island nurse confided to me that she was physically assaulted by the mother of a young man for diagnosing his illness in the mother's absence and bathing his chest as the woman entered his bedroom. Even the nudity of household pets can arouse anxiety, especially when they are sexually aroused during time of heat. In some cottages dogs are whipped for licking their genitals and soon learn to indulge in this behaviour outside when unobserved.

Hypochondria and depression in Inis Beag are inextricably linked, in that the former composes part of the syndrome of the latter; and just as sexual puritanism is undergirded by masochism, so are these two traits. Little more need be said about the causes of depression among the folk, other than to bring together factors which have been discussed earlier: the extent to which their lives are circumscribed by the will of the priest and other figures of authority; their poverty and the never ending toil needed to maintain present subsistence standards; the spying and malicious gossiping of their fellows and the ubiquity of jealousy and envy; the isolation of the island, particularly during winter months; numbing boredom and the dearth of social activities; for women, the lack of freedom and of attention and affection from their spouses, as well as the necessity of enduring sexual relations; and, as stated above, hypochondria. Much has been written about isolation and its depressive effects on the islanders, and the folk themselves constantly complain of being shut off from the world and prey to wind, rain, fog, and raging sea. But isolation need not lead inevitably to depression, for my wife and I conducted research in another island of Ireland – far distant from and even more inaccessible than Inis Beag – where the inhabitants do not feel isolated and are not depressed.

I have expanded the clinical usage of the term hypochondria to include fears of the spirit as well as fears of the body, for ill health can as often be induced by supernatural forces, and death – whether by disease, injury, or ageing – is the ultimate fear with its threat of eternal damnation. Colds, influenza, dyspepsia, migraine headaches, teeth decay, the crippling effects of joint and muscle ailments, hypermetrophy, and mental illness are paramount among health concerns. 'Flu' epidemics are frequent in the island and are a chief cause of death among people who have become weakened by old age. As the folk advance in years, they come to spend more time in bed and by the turf fire and venture out less during the winter and when it rains. Drafts are avoided whenever possible, and clothes dampened by seas which wash the canoes or by rain are changed for dry ones at the first opportunity. Colds, flu, indigestion, and headaches more than any other afflictions send the islanders to the nurse for drugs and to their own folk remedies for relief. Dyspepsia is known as 'wind' and is thought to result from diet, but the nurses say that most cases of indigestion are the result of tension – 'nervous stomach'. Nine cases of migraine were reported in Inis Beag during 1959, but many other islanders, most of whom are women, suffer from 'nervous headache' which can approach migraine in intensity of pain. Neither my wife nor I were ill during the winter of 1959 and 1960, even though we were abroad in all sorts of inclement weather against the advice of our neighbours; when we began picking wild garlic to season our food, it was reasoned that the condiment afforded us protection against the flu, which reached almost epidemic proportions that year, and as a result this folk medicine was used more widely and consistently than usual.

Nativists and primitivists praise the health and hardiness of the folk and boast of the absence of rheumatism and allied infirmities among them and the sharpness of their sight. But, just as most adults past thirty years of age suffer from decay and loss of teeth, they also suffer from muscle and joint ailments, caused by the 'damp and cold', and from farsightedness. It is not known how many folk wear glasses in the privacy of their homes, but only two persons, both men, wear them publicly – and self-consciously when they do. Most glasses are not prescription made but are purchased in mainland shops after many pairs displayed on the counters have been tested, and often a single pair will serve the needs of all the elders of a household. The islanders among themselves constantly complain of these and other ailments, although some will praise the health and hardiness of the local population in the presence of strangers, to conform to the nativistic and primitivistic stereotype. Probably the most robust of the two dozen islanders past the age of seventy years believes that he will live to be a hundred years old, because he continues to be active physically and doesn't 'worry about the health'; he accuses his fellows of 'worrying themselves into the grave' over matters of body and soul.

The etiology of mental illness as conceived by the islanders is varied and embraces both natural and spiritual realms. 'Insanity' stigmatises the victim and his family, often for many generations, no matter what its cause, and as many psychotics are treated at home – hidden from the probing eyes of strangers – as are incarcerated in the mental institution serving the region of which Inis Beag is a part. Statistics on mental disorders are hard to come by because of the opprobrium attached to insanity, but at least eight of the folk were institutionalised for various periods between 1940 and 1965. Only one of these is a woman, and none was violent prior to admission. Inheritance, inbreeding, and the menopause are the natural causes most widely accepted by the islanders, but some claim that heavy blows to the head, acute alcoholism, and even prolonged emotional tension – or 'nerves' – can induce insanity. In explaining why a former Inis Beag curate was committed to a mental institution, an old man revealed what is probably the most significant cause of mental illness in Ireland, when he said that the constant association of the priest with a pretty housekeeper 'drove him mad from frustration'; he advocated that only elderly, plain-appearing women (who will not 'gab' everything that they know to 'our man') be hired for the task.

Supernatural forces are believed capable of causing not only mental illness, but most other maladies and injuries as well. Pagan dispensers of ill health are vengeful or capricious fairies, ghosts, and witches of the evil eye; while Catholicism provides an unpredictable Devil, a deity who punishes sinful thoughts and deeds in this world as well as in the next, and priests who in Inis Beag often have interpreted the boundaries of sin according to Irish and personal criteria. In the case of certain folk stricken with mental disorders, I have heard specific causes put forth to account for their condition: parents who are second cousins, the evil eye of a neighbour, punishment by God for a particular misdeed, and a priest's curse. A man who mistreated his aged bachelor uncle before his recent death now is haunted with the spectre of being struck down from the grave with sickness, injury, or madness by the shade of the uncle seeking revenge. His despair and erratic behaviour arouse little sympathy from his fellows, who await the day of reckoning. The stigma of mental illness arises from its designation as inheritable or a sign of the deity's displeasure, both of which may doom those of generations to come. There is a strong suspicion among the folk that other maladies which are deforming or leave physical aftereffects once cured can be transmitted through inheritance. In this category are two mongoloids, one dwarf, one epileptic, one person with goitre, one with a cleft palate, and one who has just recovered from poliomyelitis. These disabilities also can stigmatise a family.

Probably the most infamous custom associated with the Irish is their excessive intake of intoxicating drink, and certainly Inis Beag islanders are no exception to the stereotype. Men drink far more than women, but even though the latter widely condemn the practice many are known to send their children to the pubs to procure stout and brandy (ostensibly a general purpose medicine in this case) in disguised containers to be consumed at home. The drinking of the men takes place, for the most part, in the pubs and at parties, and seldom is indulged in to the extent that the imbibers become physically incapacitated. There were no cases of alcoholism in Inis Beag during 1959, according to the nurse. Although drinking obviously is done to combat depression and boredom, dissolve feelings of shyness and inferiority, alleviate the sense of sin and guilt and overcome secretiveness which limits extroversion, the folk defend the practice by claiming that it makes them more articulate and convivial and thus better able to sing, dance, converse with one another, and tell stories. The often used phrases 'to give us courage' and 'great gas' connote just these benefits. In Ireland today, there are nearly half a million members of the Pioneer Total Abstinence Society – founded in that country 125 years ago – who have 'taken the pledge' not to drink spirits in any form; they wear a small badge shaped like a shield which bears the emblem of the Sacred Heart. Twelve 'Pioneers' in Inis Beag have taken a lifetime pledge and about thirty others a two year pledge not to imbibe. Most of these persons are old men, women, and boys. Young and middle-aged men who are members of the society are the objects of a good deal of indirect ridicule and direct jesting.

Etienne Rynne

Dún Aengus – Fortress or Temple?

Dún Aengus, the large stone fortress on the edge of Inis More, the Aran Islands, is one of the most impressive and best-known ancient monuments in Ireland. Everyone recognises the site, even if they have never been there, as there have been so many photographs of it published and, furthermore, because it has such a distinctive appearance. First of all, there is a huge, strong, semi-circular rampart, built of stone on the top of a vertical cliff rising almost a hundred metres above the Atlantic; secondly there are two other fine stone ramparts, lower and weaker, around the main citadel, and thirdly there is a *chevaux-de-frise* (i.e. a band of sharp slabs stuck into ground, like spikes) between those two outer ramparts. The inner and central ramparts have terraces, giving them a stepped appearance from within. Generally forgotten in most plans and descriptions, however, is a natural rectangular rock platform sited on the cliff edge in the centre of the whole monument.

But what is the purpose of this huge and complex monument? The general opinion is that it is a fortress, built for defensive military purposes, but this is now being seriously questioned. In many ways the monument is highly unsuitable for such a military purpose: it has no running or other source of fresh water, and its terraces (apart from the highest one) are not suitable for looking outwards over the rampart for defensive or other such purposes. Anyway, the ancient Irish did not normally engage in siege warfare and would not, therefore, have had a good reason for such a fortress.

There are four main reasons why any monument should be built, namely for burial, habitation, military or ceremonial purposes. Straight away the first two can be eliminated, and despite its apparent attractiveness the third seems unlikely – which leaves the fourth. Is Dún Aengus, therefore, to be regarded as a ceremonial centre or temple?

Dún Aengus must be included with other such well-known Irish monuments as the Grianán of Aileach and O'Boyle's Fort (on Lough Doon, near Portnoo), both in Co. Donegal, as Caher Ballykinvarga, Cahercommaun and Caherdooneerish, in the Burren, Co. Clare, as Staigue, Cahergal and others in Co. Kerry, as the other six huge 'forts' on the Aran Islands, and, perhaps surprisingly, as the stone 'fort' enclosing the Early Christian monastery on Inishmurray, Co. Sligo. All are clearly related and can be confidently dated to the Pagan Celtic Early Iron Age, that is to within a couple of centuries on either side of the birth of Christ. By the same process of elimination, all can be interpreted as having been built for ceremonial purposes, purposes such as inauguration ceremonies, or for the annual or seasonal *aonach* of the *tuath*, where and when payment of tribute, making of treaties, important marriages, ritual games, passing of laws, etc., would take place.

When one examines these sites with such purposes in mind one readily appreciates their suitability. They are all most impressive, one might even say majestic, structures, just as are all ancient temples and contemporary cathedrals, ranging from the parthenon in Athens to St Peter's in Rome – even to Galway's new Cathedral of Our Lady Assumed into Heaven and St Nicholas! They are also sited in positions which immediately command attention and respect, generally in prominent places overlooking vast areas and eminently suitable as places of assembly for the people of the surrounding regions. Furthermore, their stepped and terraced walls are much more suitable for looking inwards than for looking outwards, suggesting that these monuments should be regarded as amphitheatres rather than as forts – nobody ever thinks of Rome's Colosseum as a fort nor considers the terraced sports stadia from Olympia to Croke Park as places for defensive warfare!

Nor are there annalistic records of any of these sites ever having been used in war or battle. Indeed, the only historical associations any of them have are with ritual or ceremonial functions. The very fact that the massive stone enclosure of this type on Inishmurray was used secondarily as the enclosure of an Early Christian monastery surely supports a ritual use for it originally – Christian monasteries are more likely to succeed and replace pagan sanctuaries than military forts, cf. Armagh Cathedral built on Ard Mhacha, a proven pagan ritually enclosed hilltop. The Grianán of Aileach, furthermore, still served until the twelfth century, at least, as the royal seat and assembly place of the Cinél Chonaill, rulers of the Uí Néill kingdom of Aileach.

But there are several other good reasons why Dún Aengus can best be regarded as a monument specifically built for ceremonial purposes. The natural platform centrally placed within it on the cliff's edge would serve as a perfect focal point for ceremonies, while the *chevaux-de-frise* is so totally unnecessary on Aran as a defensive feature that it can best be considered as having been erected for prestige reasons, to give the place a sense of awe (just as are the battlements, crenellations and turrets on nineteenth-century 'castles' such as Ashford and Dromoland – or even on University College, Galway!). That Dún Aengus is one, albeit the most impressive, of seven such sites on the Aran Islands also supports a ceremonial or prestige interpretation for it. Each of them is to be found within a different townland, townlands which are topographically distinct and which may owe their origins to earlier Celtic *tuatha*; each Aran 'fort' should be looked upon as the temple of the local *tuath*, just as each parish nowadays has its own church and each political entity (town, city, county, state) its own meeting-place (town hall, mansion house, county buildings, parliament). These massive 'forts' of the West of Ireland ought to be regarded as the stone-built equivalents of such well-known and acceptably pagan ceremonial centres in the east and middle of Ireland, as Emain Macha near Armagh, Ráth na Rí on the Hill of Tara, and Dún Ailinne in Co. Kildare, not to mention lots of other less well-known examples throughout Ireland (e.g. the one at Grannagh in south Galway excavated some years ago).

Next time, therefore, when visiting Dún Aengus, the visitor should not think of it as a place where desperate men held out against ferociously attacking enemies, men prepared to jump almost three hundred feet to certain death in the Atlantic waves below rather than to surrender. Dún Aengus was no Masada. Instead, the visitor should conjure up an image of druids, ollavs, bards, kings and nobles all processing formally through the Dún's impressive entrance, some to perform rituals on the stage-like platform, some to assist in the enclosed area, and others to stand on the surrounding terraced wall chanting incantations or singing sacred songs while viewing the solemn proceedings taking place against the dramatic backdrop of the wild Atlantic Ocean whose waves sonorously thunder against the rock-face out of sight below.

Leo Daly

The Rock Garden

The first leg of the home journey was uneventful. John Michael showed no reaction to the throbbing engines as the plane, gathering speed, raced down the runway and took off. Anxiously watching from her seat opposite, Peig saw his chest heave as he sighed and then, when he rested his head against the vibrating window, she thought she saw a trace of a smile relax the strained face.

She watched, aware that his mind was out there somewhere, wandering. Disappointed, she turned to the window beside her, resigning herself to her own dreams. Down below was the sea, masquerading as usual, coaxing her surrender to past memories, the salty tang of yesterdays, visions of the pier in the cold grey early light of that morning as she prepared for her first trip in the small boat. Her first trip with John Michael, the sea reminded her, as she wondered if the silent man at the other window was also on the cold quayside, her hand in his, setting out on their legendary journey.

Coley was already there when she appeared with John Michael, but too busy sorting out nets and tackle and throwing rubbish overboard to acknowledge their arrival. John Michael hailed him, and he manoeuvred the boat close to the worn steps, holding it steady. Hesitating, she looked at the boat far below and counted the twelve grimy footholds leading down to water level, but John Michael took her firmly in hand, guiding her faltering descent on the slippery granite slabs. Coley modestly averted his gaze as she floundered once, spread-eagled, but when she came within distance he grabbed her searching feet and guided her down.

Then both of them had a hand on her, and she was passed grudgingly from one to the other finally finding herself breathless in Coley's arms as he swept her to the safety of the bobbing boat. Already she was aware that a skirt was hardly the dress for a journey like this; for everyone's comfort she should have worn trousers.

Nervously, she sat on the wooden seat, wondering what was to come. With great care her bags were stowed away safely under canvas and the area around her cleared to allow her a little leg room. She gripped tightly on the seat and the gunwale, afraid of the rocking craft, as the men got ready for the journey.

From *The Rock Garden* (1985).

John Michael fuelled the engine from a large oil drum which was stored under the stern seat and they cast off. Coley rowed the boat with easy strokes until they were clear of the pier wall and then John Michael lowered the engine into the water. A creaking thole-pin was treated to a dash of seawater and John Michael gave his first pull on the starting-cord of the outboard engine. He pulled again and again, and then impatiently he gave a mighty pull which shook the boat. The engine spluttered, started and died. Making some adjustments and ignoring advice from Coley he pulled once more. This time the engine fired, spluttered, then roared to life. There was no mistaking the jibe as Coley quipped:

– Third time's lucky, but often it takes more.

Nor the sarcasm in John Michael's reply.

–It's like yourself, hard to start but easy enough to stop. Aye, but it's a grand morning anyhow.

They all joined in a good-humoured laugh. It was a fine start, and, as if in salute, John Michael angled his cap to a rakish slant, opened the throttle gently till almost full, and they were away, leaving a tumbling wake of foam fanning out from the stern. Through the calm water in the sheltered harbour the boat behaved with assuring smoothness, but on nearing the lighthouse island the rolling started and Peig, much to the amusement of the men, held on tightly to the gunwale.

She was beginning to feel the first qualms in her stomach when the engine was suddenly cut, and Coley took the oars. Alarmed, thinking a break-down or something unforeseen had arisen, she looked to the men, and John Michael explained that they were dropping a net. He untangled lines and floats, constantly searching out landmarks as he worked. Occasionally, his eyes found hers and he gave her one of his smiles.

Her own gaze travelled over the great panorama of sand which formed the headland of the island. Fog was taking the sharp outline off visible landmarks, softening the whole scene with a silver mist. She clutched her jacket tightly around her thinking unashamedly of the warm bed she had left.

The net seemed never-ending; finally it was floating in position but invisible as the boat drifted away from it. Another uneasy moment as the engine failed at the first pull and gave a spluttering start at the second, then Coley took in the oars and they were off again.

John Michael was bolder with his smiling eyes as they resumed the journey, and Peig, feeling that he was taking advantage of the situation, swung her legs over the seat and sat facing Coley. He was crouched, kneeling in the prow, and at first she thought he was praying, but then she saw the flash of the knife and the fish in the basket at his side. A large pollock, a bream, a few mackerel and a dog fish were being shaped into tasty cutlets as bait for the lobster pots.

Coley, somehow aware of her interest, turned towards her and explained his work to her in detail, naming the fish and holding the pieces aloft for her to see. Behind them, John Michael was enjoying the lesson as he repeated Coley's remarks, sometimes in ridicule, but they ignored his interruptions.

Coley, she noticed, was so different from John Michael, red-haired and freckled, with powerful arms and shoulders topping his stocky body, and yet he was almost as tall as John Michael, but did not look it. His hands fascinated her; she had never seen such strength displayed as when he gripped the oars, his arms taking the weight of the pull. The canoe shot forward under Coley's strength and as the rhythm gained full momentum, she wondered at that grip which could crush an ordinary hand. And yet he seemed the gentlest of men, shy, considerate and with an impish sense of humour. You could look him in the eyes without unease or embarrassment. Not like John Michael, who seemed to demand a return stare as bold as his own. Yes, Red Coley was straightforward and uncomplicated, the type of man a stranger to the islands would feel attracted to, especially if the stranger were a lonely woman, groping in the uncertainty of her own world, searching for the comfort of a guiding hand.

Turning awkwardly on her seat, she was greeted by John Michael's smile, but gave no return. Then he spoke, as if to annoy her:

– Lovely morning now. We'll make a fisherman of you yet!

Again she turned her back on him and faced Coley. The swell was now taking the boat to itself and the spray splashed, making her settle deeper into her jacket to avoid a drenching. She had never anticipated the journey would be like this. Surely there was some other way of travelling where she would be spared the misery of the sea. And yet, even now, the sea was teaching her some lessons as if the great waste of water was conscious of her personal misgivings and was willing to help. Out here there were no bosses, no underlings. The sea was master. That was the first lesson, and there were others to follow.

Once she had believed that her personal insecurity was the only faithful companion she had always at her side, never deserting her. Often she had been accused of hiding her cards up her sleeve, but the cards she hid were no better than the ones on display. Such tags as loving, kind, unselfish and forgiving to a point of foolishness, had been hers, but she had her doubts, and would have welcomed an opportunity of putting herself to the test, especially in matters she had so far avoided. That was the main reason she had accepted the challenge of the islands.

Her senses swam in the confusion of beauty, misery, and the ever-present warnings of sickness as the boat rolled, but suddenly there was something else, an approaching danger telegraphed in the alertness of the crew. The boat was edging slowly towards the massive cliff-line, and the increasing swell rocked the small craft like a cork. Under the towering cliffs great dark boulder-sentinels showed like teeth, foaming defiance as the tossing seas crashed on them in fury. The rising and falling of the boat was terrifying, and the gaping rocks seemed preparing to devour them.

She watched, sick now with fear, and sought Coley's eyes for assurance. But there she saw alarm as great as her own, and in anticipation of sudden disaster she swung suddenly on her seat and confronted John Michael. The boat lurched and she was severely reprimanded.

– You'll drown us if you don't stay easy. Where do you think you are at all?

Their whole attention was on the sea as they sat, alert, balanced, moving in unison with the boat. After some fumbling behind her she heard the oars creak under the strength of Coley's hands and arms, and was comforted, but panicked again as the motor was suddenly cut. She held on, watching the giddy cliff-line dancing before her eyes while the boat swayed desperately, praying silently for deliverance for all.

John Michael pulled on a pair of yellow oilskin trousers and having secured them grabbed a long-handled hook from under the seats. Like a harpoonist about to strike he stood poised, then hooking a float which had appeared bobbing beside the boat he grasped the rope laced through it. Dropping the hook, he pulled hard on the rope, and yard by yard he hauled until a lobster-pot, up from the depths of the sea, was safely astride the gunwale. Coley shouted first:

– Didn't I tell you it was our lucky day?

A fine crayfish was trapped inside the basket, to Peig the most terrifying of God's creatures, but to the fishermen the most beautiful sight in the world. She gazed fascinated at the snapping claws and twitching pods, their dreadful clicking noises emanating as if from some monstrous machine.

John Michael was jubilant, and lifting the twitching body, offered it to Peig for closer scrutiny. She screamed and he dropped the fish at her feet. She screamed again, kicking it away, but he was enjoying her panic. She noticed as she tried to avoid the claws that the men's excitement at the catch lessened their sense of danger; even Coley was gloating over their good luck and her discomfort. Her fear and annoyance grew as he shouted, waving the crayfish and rocking the boat in his victory:

– Isn't he lovely?

The pot was rebaited and dumped over the side, causing a drenching splash which caught her unawares. The shock of the icy water forced a gasp from her as she wiped the blinding salt from her eyes. Furious and humiliated, she waited for an apology.

– You'll get used to it soon. We don't mind it at all.

She ignored John Michael's laugh and tried to catch her breath as another pot was being pulled. Not caring any further about the fishing or the fishermen, she turned away, and took silent pleasure in hearing John Michael swear at the empty pot. With much greater venom than before, the freshly baited pot was dashed back to the depths. She suffered another baptism of brine, but gritting her teeth and lowering her head, she refused to complain. Silently she cursed the crew and the lobsters and the islands.

Six pots were pulled, only four lobsters aboard, and then they headed for South Island. Six more pots there, less luck than before, but everywhere the tumbling splashing sea and the drowning spray. There was no escape, and gradually she accepted the misery as part of the trip.

She was also uncomfortably aware that she was sitting in a pool of water and wondered if the crew knew of her predicament.

A fine pair of primitives, of course they knew; they were probably enjoying their knowledge. Never again would she travel with them. Never!

And then the miracle happened as the sun shone through the early morning mist. Everything was transformed when sullen island shadows gave way to the light. The sea glistened and sparkled delightfully and the crew came to life in the first heat of the day.

— When it gets a bit warmer you can hang out your drying.

Just as she expected, and even Coley had his say:

— You'll get your death sitting there before we get to South.

She couldn't hold the retort which escaped from her salt-caked lips:

— If you were gentlemen you would jump overboard and let me change, but I suppose it's more fun just watching me?

Her jibe was in bad taste. She knew they lived in terror of the sea and never joked about its dangers, expecting others to show the same respect. They were aware of her ability as a swimmer; they had watched in wonder with the rest as she dived off the pierhead, and had accompanied her in the boat as she achieved the impossible by swimming to the lighthouse island.

But out here under the cliffs it was different; if you got into trouble in the water 'twas easier to drown and be finished with it. Nobody swam out here.

She was punished by being ignored as they headed in silence for her landing-place, but as the small pier came in sight, the silence was broken.

— We won't make our fortunes today!

There was a tinge of bitterness in John Michael's forecast, but none in Coley's reply:

— Fortune? Did you hear that Miss? If a woman had half his money she'd have enough fortunes for half a dozen husbands.

It seemed to her that she was forgiven, but she hadn't really forgiven them, not yet.

— What would any woman want with six husbands might I ask?

— Aye indeed, or even one? It's men the women want, not husbands. Isn't that right Coley?

— Well you know what Brid Timmy said to the curate? ...

With a jerk which knocked Peig off her seat and sent the men sprawling, the boat reared and stopped. John Michael in panic cut the threshing engine as Coley grabbed the oars. They were aground on a sandbank west of the pier, a hazard to any boat at low water. Then the cursing started, John Michael blaming Red Coley for the disaster:

— I told you many a time to keep an eye out for that bank. It's not the first time it happened, and anytime you mention that Brid Timmy we're not far from shipwreck. The sea is no place at all for women, and nobody only a fool would come in here at low water even if they were all dying on South!

She could have cheered at their distress, but discreetly kept her silence.

After some minutes of swearing, pulling and tugging, in a vocabulary of special disaster words which shocked her, the boat was afloat and Coley rowed it to the pier. Because of the low water, the wall was high above them, and to Peig it looked far out of reach. But the tall stretch of John Michael's arms aided by a lift from Coley's folded hands reached the parapet and soon he was standing on the pier, the boat secured.

Peig looked up at the waiting hands and smiling face of John Michael who was lying flat on his belly, reaching down for her. Coley stood at her side, an uneasy grin on his face as he noticed her bewilderment. It was no time for nonsense, she thought.

— Have I to get up there?

John Michael laughed loud as Coley answered dryly:

— It looks that way now unless you wait for high water.

— But how? I could never reach that high.

From above came John Michael's encouragement:

— It's no bother at all if you try. Just stretch up your arms over your head and Coley will do the rest.

She looked at Coley, wondering if he would reassure her but he said nothing. She faced the pier wall, doing as she was bid, her arms raised, waiting.

— Up you go lass. Just keep stretching until he grips you.

And before she could object to the hands that fumbled on her hips before gripping her thighs and pushing firmly on her bottom, she was hoisted up and jammed against the rough stones of the wall in case she slid down. As she struggled to grasp John Michael's hands, she became very conscious of the water from her saturated clothing trickling down her legs, and of Coley's complaint from below:

— For God's sake pull her up quick or she'll have me drowned top and under.

She was completely at their mercy and they were making the most of it. Her humiliation was, she felt, part of the game, and they loved it.

— Grab her quick, man, or I'll have to drop her in the tide.

— Lift her a bit higher can't you? She doesn't mind you putting a hand on her, she's getting used to it man!

A final push from Coley squeezed the breath from her and again forced her tightly against the pier wall, enabling John Michael to grab her wrists. But Coley still held her feet and when the boat floated from the wall she was the only means of pulling it back.

— For God's sake let me out, I'm dragged asunder.

She screamed while the powerful hands used her as a life-line. Then Coley let go, but John Michael held on, trying to stand and lift her clear. Her feet scrambled frantically for purchase on the rough wall, relieving the weight on her arms as he finally hauled her to safety. He made a fuss of encircling her with his arms as she was pulled clear, and lifting her to his own height he held her close before putting her down. She was beyond objecting and lay limp in his clutches. Coley watched from below, aware of John Michael playing his own special game and his helpless bundle.

— She's not dead, is she? You'd think it was a child you were handling. Put her down, man, and give her a chance of a breath.

John Michael released her and left her standing alone, hands dropped to the sides, a picture of misery. Her luggage was unceremoniously thrown up and landed beside her, and no word was spoken until the boat with the crew was moving off. With all the sarcasm she was capable of she bade them farewell:

— Thanks very much, gentlemen. I must say you offer a very good service, especially at low water!

They moved off without answering and she sat on the wall watching them steer past the sandbank before starting the motor. A great loneliness possessed her and she waved frantically after the departing boat. They waved back, once, and then no more. She watched until they were out in the sound, then she turned and clambered up the rise to the shore road, still conscious of her clinging soaked clothes, but enjoying the comfort of the morning sun.

The journey had been miserable, yet strangely exhilarating, the sea showing its tantrums and power. The trip had brought her very close to the men in the boat, their intimate presence at times uncomfortable, and yet she had felt isolated. John Michael, she thought, was younger than her own twenty-five years but older than his boyish smile might suggest. Red Coley was older and had an indefinable quality of maturity lacking in the other man.

She looked out to sea and gave a final wave of her hand, but there was no response from the small boat already nosing into the breakers. They were returning to their beloved lobster-pots buried deep in the white sand of the ocean floor, guarded by treacherous towering cliffs. She was forgotten; they were well rid of her and she of them, she reflected, as opening her sack she stood in the shade of a boulder, preparing for a quick change of her wet skirt and underwear.

Nearby, from a crag of rock, three squawking cormorants eyed her intrusion in alarm as inquisitive gulls hovered above, adding their protest. Then, in her nakedness, she panicked at a fluttering of wings from across the road announcing, perhaps, the approach of an islander. Alone, however, an exaltation of larks rose nearby in a flurry of greeting. Banking, swooping, and then soaring, their song shrilled in the early morning as if greeting the undressed stranger.

She listened and watched, fascinated, no longer self-conscious, and then dressed leisurely as the songsters soared higher until almost out of sight.

It was time to go, but she lingered, stretching flat on the boulder, luxuriating in the heat seeping into her body. Then overtaken by the urgency of her mission and feeling much revived, she walked on, enjoying the increasing warmth of the sun and the beauty of the morning. The misery of the sea and the discomforts of the past few hours were forgotten as she surrendered to the enchantments of South Island. The next time it would be different, but even now, although slightly sick still from the ordeal, she wondered if she would ever relive the joys of that first trip.

Before her on the road a man appeared. He must have been sitting under the short shore wall watching the boat's approach. His dress was primitive, even to the raw-hide shoes, his face grey and exhausted. The shock of his sudden arrival was followed by the realization that he may have had her under observation as she changed her clothes, and had been a witness as she had stood naked behind the boulder. But his harsh voice when he spoke drove all such thoughts from her mind:

— The nurse?

The dreadful anxiety of his tone was as plain as if he had made a speech.

– Yes, I'm the nurse.

The day seemed to lose some of its allure as she committed herself to the unknown.

– You'd better hurry; she's bad all night. They're ringing for the doctor and the lifeboat; she's bad all the time.

She chased after the islander, stumbling at times in her efforts to keep up with him, and hopping on one foot for relief when she twisted her ankle. He kept his distance of a dozen steps ahead of her, dodging light-footed through the rocky fields, never once looking back to see if she was following. She wanted to stop and rest, but there was no stopping. He disappeared over a stile ahead, and when she saw him waiting to help her down on the other side, she knew they had arrived.

Ahead at the gable of the low thatched cottage a crowd was gathered. Immediately they complained of her long delay in arriving and the sorry condition of the patient inside waiting all night for help. They muttered about the neglect they suffered, no doctor, nor nurse, and even the priest having to answer another call and desert them when he should have stayed to give comfort. They were suffering all the time so they were, but nobody cared.

Having groped her way into the dark kitchen, she was guided with haste to the sick-room, where the drone of prayers from a group gathered around the bed faltered and ceased on her appearance. She read the hostility in their eyes, and would always remember this initiation.

Reluctantly, the women rose from their knees and silently left the room. All except one young woman who remained at the bedside, her eyes unflinching as they answered Peig's unasked questions. Obviously they did not trust her, not until she had proven herself, and this was her first great trial. A life was in her hands, and the South Island people demanded that it be restored safely.

Peig Flaherty awoke as the plane was circling the island airstrip for a landing, the pain in her ankle the only tangible reminder of her dream. John Michael seemed still absorbed in the view from the window, but if he had been her companion on the boat journey to South Island, he was betraying no enjoyment of those halcyon hours. For him, it seemed, they were lost forever.

–We are home John Michael, home at last!

But there was no response, no recognition of the familiar welcoming faces which surrounded him, and she felt a bitter disappointment and embarrassment as she helped him into the taxi which would take them to the village.

– Welcome home, John Michael; 'tis well he's looking Mrs Flaherty. A few months now back among his own and you won't know him from the man he was.

Barney Gill, the driver, had made this journey with them more times than he could count, but John Michael had no word for him now. Barney understood.

— Don't worry, Mam; give him a little time. It's no joke, I'm telling you, up in them aeroplanes; you wouldn't know whether you were coming or going; anytime I go up there I forget what year it is, never mind the day. I'm back in my second childhood, lost!

Peig smiled. The taxi bumped on, taking them home.

Derek Mahon

'Aran'

(for Tom Mac Intyre)

He is earthed to his girl, one hand fastened
In hers, and with his free hand listens,
An earphone, to his own rendition,
Singing the darkness into the light.
I close the pub door gently and step out
Into the yard, and the song goes out,
And a gull creaks off from the tin roof
Of an outhouse, planing over the ocean,
Circling now with a hoarse inchoate
Screaming the boned fields of its vision.
God, that was the way to do it,
Hand-clasping, echo-prolonging poet!

Scorched with a fearful admiration
Walking over the nacreous sand,
I dream myself to that tradition,
Fifty winters off the land –
One hand to an ear for the vibration,
The far wires, the reverberation
Down light-years of the imagination
And, in the other hand, your hand.

The long glow springs from the dark soil, however –
No marsh-light holds a candle to this.
Unearthly still in its white weather
A crack-voiced rock-marauder, scavenger, fierce
Friend to no slant fields or the sea either,
Folds back over the forming waters.

From *Selected Poems* (1991).

Shevawn Lynam

A Change of Outlook

'Enough is as good as a feast' is a proverb I was always hearing as a child, but I don't think I had the faintest notion what it really meant until recently. I'd decided I needed a change – not just a change of air and scene, but a change of outlook – and the place I'd selected to seek it was Inishere. It's the smallest of the three Aran Islands, which stand like sentinels across the mouth of Galway Bay in the west of Ireland.

'Aran's the poorest place this side of Hell,' a Dublin friend said when he heard where I was going. At first it might seem so: a rock five miles in circumference, without a tree, a road, a wheeled vehicle, a telephone, a daily paper, a doctor, a policeman, or even a slip on which to land the islanders' currachs.

On a hot day you could imagine you were in the South Seas, with crystal-clear sapphire water, a long strand of pale sand dropping sheer into it, a haze hanging over the whitewashed cottages, and Anne, the old woman with whom I lived, exclaiming all day, 'I'm roasted alive with the heat!'

That was how I first saw it – but the next day the whole landscape had turned to grey, and the island seemed to heel over in the wind. The western doors into the cottages were sealed against the gale and the eastern ones were opened, donkeys and cattle huddled together to leeward of the high stone walls, and I began learning how to lean on the wind as I walked, a habit it took me months back on the mainland to lose.

It was on one of these tempestuous evenings, after I'd been an islander for almost seven months, that I discovered how close I'd got to the change of outlook I was seeking. I was just getting into bed when I heard a tap on my windowpane and voices calling me to come out. A large trawler had been sighted about three miles offshore, sheltering between the island and the mainland from the storm raging in the open Atlantic. One of Anne's sons and two of his friends had decided to go out to get some deep-sea fish from the trawler, but they'd guessed she must be foreign and were afraid not to be able to make themselves understood.

Within a few seconds I was running down the dark strand, still struggling into my clothes. Life on the island was always like that – tinged with

From *Accent on Living* (1955).

expectancy. One was always scanning the horizon for the sails of a turf boat from Connemara, or for the weekly steamer from Galway, thirty miles away, or simply for a sign that there would be a sufficiently long lull in the storm for one to get to the next island or to the coast. There was always the possibility of sighting some timber from a wreck, or a trawler with deep-sea fish, and then the boys would run to put out their boats and race for the prize.

Anne would frequently talk of the sea being 'mountains high'. That night it was mountains high. Every time the bow of the little canvas boat plopped into the water on the far side of a massive wave, I assumed we were about to capsize. But gradually, as we continued somehow to survive from wave to wave, I grew curiously elated with the sensation of galloping a bucking horse across the ocean.

As we approached the trawler a searchlight began playing on us, and as we came alongside I could read the name of the port – Vigo – painted across the bows. I tried then to shout up to them in Spanish against the wind, while I was being pushed and hauled up a rope ladder which almost swung me into the water at each lurch of the boat.

Once aboard, we were handed pint mugs of Cadiz brandy and taken over the ship. Then, installed in the captain's cabin, the moment arrived for me, as the official interpreter, to state the purpose of our mission. The islanders, I explained, could not go out after deep-sea fish, such as plaice, in their small curraghs, and they wondered if the Spaniards had any to spare. But when the captain, with typical Spanish generosity, offered a few baskets of whiting, the Aranmen pulled faces and instructed me to explain that whiting was no good for salting down – and salting the fish they've caught in the season to sell on the mainland in the autumn is the islanders' main industry.

The ship was rolling and pitching. The brandy was leaping out of our mugs and making little puddles on the floor, and the chairs and tables were jazzing crazily to and fro across the cabin. The captain stared out of the porthole at the black outline of the island, which looked like some archaic monster crouching on the horizon, and he asked how many houses there were on it. I replied that there were eighty.

The captain then became pensive, as if he were working out a complicated sum. He reached for the bottle and began to refill the mugs and to soak the floor alternately, sometimes pirouetting gracefully or suddenly running at full speed across the tilted room to keep his balance. And all the time, he was calculating under his breath.

At last he said, 'Well, if each house contributed an equal share, the island could buy a trawler like this one, on a coöperative basis, and they could go out to fish wherever and whatever they liked.'

I conveyed all this to the islanders. They stood six foot one, two, and four, each as spare as a spruce, with chiselled features, curiously fine little hands and feet, and the manners of mandarins. They murmured together in Irish, and then one of them smilingly explained: 'We'd rather each to be going out on his own hook.'

The captain's jolly, fat face dropped in astonishment and I found that subconsciously I'd been hardening against mainlanders; they obviously couldn't understand us. It seemed hardly worth explaining that the islanders grow their own clothes on their own sheep's backs and that the island weaver weaves them: or that they make their shoes – pampooties, they're called – from their own cows' hides: or that they make their land with their own hands – they spread sand on the rock, fertilize it with seaweed, and produce some of the best potatoes in the world. They don't really care how the world outside does things – they do everything for themselves.

The captain had meanwhile been consulting his companions, and he came back to the charge. 'Maybe they don't understand,' he said persuasively. 'Explain to them that they'd make much more money this way.'

But the islandmen only smiled gently and replied: 'Haven't we enough the ways we are?'

Well, we left the captain flabbergasted, and in the end we took the whiting. The journey back was little different from the journey out until we reached the shore. But there we found enormous breakers hurling themselves at the strand which they'd turned into a high shelf, and as they recoiled, the shingle withdrawing with them rumbled like thunder. Our little boat seemed like an animal at bay as we prowled up and down, manoeuvring to attempt a landing. We even thought of returning the three miles to the trawler, but the storm was growing worse. At last, almost in desperation, we swung the curragh around to face inland, and suddenly the wave we were trying to race rushed snarling after us and flung us onto the strand – capsized, but on land and smothered in whiting.

The next day, as so often happens, the sun was shining; the wind had swung around and we could hear the ocean humming gently on the far side of the island, like some giant machine that kept the whole life of the place turning.

I found Anne sitting in her rocking chair in front of the cottage, knitting; her only comment on the night's adventure was her disgust at hearing that the Spaniards spoke no English. After all, she explained, the islanders were Irish, but they spoke English as well as Irish. The Spaniards must be very uneducated people, like most foreigners, she felt – and for her that included mainlanders.

'Aren't they forever composing lies at us about the places they're from?' she said, clicking her tongue disparagingly. 'An island woman'd be out of her latitude entirely in thim places.' I knew well she wouldn't change the island life for any other.

I can still see her sitting there, as neat as a pin in her long, red tweed skirt and velvet-trimmed bodice, as she rambled on in her picturesque English, translated literally from the Irish: 'Musha, I'd ever my fair share of trouble, Shevawn asthore. And if I had itself, hadn't I ever my enough, too? And would you believe this, now – and there's no more lie in this than if I was going down to the grave today – I never was wance without my breakfast, never wance. Wasn't that the great thing, now? Musha, God was good, surely.'

I think that's what I remember most vividly about the island. As an islander myself, I'd grown to think of it as one of the richest places on earth.

Aidan Higgins

Balcony of Europe

Mogens Stenicke stood once more in the house where, half a century before, he had first seen the light of day, Danish day in Woody Humlebaek. He had been through the war, all the time confident of his immunity to German lead, as confident as Baamonde, at the other end of Europe behind the Pyrenees, had been confident that he was immune to Republican lead. Three years he spent in an English monastery looking for an austerity that was not there.

I was not three minutes in the place, he told me, when I knew it wasn't right for me.

And you came out again, I asked, after three minutes?

No, Mogens said, I stayed in three years.

Then he spent eight years in the Star of the Sea church on the Dublin quays. There by Butt Bridge the Liffey stank of ammonia, old men, lost hopes, diarrhoea. Life there was hard enough, looking after the needs of the destitute. He left, searching for a barer existence, landed on Aran with little money and no trade, slept under curraghs on Inishere, watched the island-women weaving on hand-looms, took eels from the black lake by night and sold the catch in Galway, ate little, listening to Wagner on his pick-up, the *Liebestod*: Isolde hampered by her veils, the yellowish obsession of the fevered. Then he set up two looms on his own and became as accomplished a weaver as the best of the women. He lived in a small cottage near the beach, did without fire or help, staring at the formations of cloud rising over the Clare coast. He made a living where a less resolute man would have starved, lived alone, thinking little of his fellow-men and nothing at all of his fellow-women.

You don't need a fire in winter, he said, observing me with washed-out blue eyes. The limestone retains the heat of the sun.

What sun? I said.

Mogens Stenicke loved to study the clouds, never the same at any hour of the day over the coast. He told Olivia that he knew where he was going to die. She had met him before I did. He spoke reluctantly, not mixing with the islanders, but when he opened up to Olivia in the bar one night, his tongue loosened by pints of black draught Guinness, he could not be stopped. He told

From *Balcony of Europe* (1972).

276

her where he was going to die. It was a place called Humlebaek outside Copenhagen. If he never left Aran, would he not be immortal, live forever, watching the generations come and go, playing Wagner? Where better could he take refuge? Where better?

You cannot break wind on the island, he told me, but they know of it.

We walked around Inishere one afternoon, by the lake, the tall lighthouse, the long rusted hulk gone aground on the rocks (a cargo of Vat 69). Kelp, rocks, wreck, a rabbit or two, gulls: all progress, all human history, was reduced to that. Olivia told me what Mogens Stenicke had confided to her on the previous night in the bar. It was my third visit to the islands spread over twenty years; my first time with Olivia on Inishere, the smallest of the group. We followed the path leading to the ruined tower of the O'Briens, the wind was blowing in off the sea, like scarves, coming in over the prospective harbour (island dreams of affluence). Children in knickerbockers, Gaelic-speakers, straggled ahead of us on the path to school, an illustration from an old *Strand Magazine*. The yard of the school was silted up to the windows in sand, fine and persistent as snow. I thought of my mother at Salt Hill, that most forlorn of seaside resorts, photographed on a public bench, squinting into the camera lens. She had sat there watching the old *Dun Aengus* ploughing out to the islands, and wrote a postcard to me in remotest Canada. Dear Dan. My sweet dead mother.

Fish were drying on the roofs of the cottages, as on Neolithic lakeside dwellings of the Lower Danube, in the uplands of Anatalia, in Karanova in Bulgaria, Barkaer in Denmark. New Grange in the Boyne Valley. A passive civilization of scattered huts and villages. Homes of the 5th millennium B.C. The smoke that gathers blue and sinks, stench of burning fur. Our precarious beginnings.

In a small walled field at the back of the island I had re-read *Gulliver's Travels*. The ground I lay on was the nearest landfall to America, the Yahoos. A trawler moved between Inishere and Inishman, only its masts visible in a white press of gulls. Above their cries I heard the panting of the engine and saw sandy beaches and paths on Inishman where on the day of our arrival a young girl had drowned. The islanders rarely undressed or swam in the sea; the men seldom seen in the daytime and the females never at night. A shy fringe of Celtic society perpetuated there, hardly exposing their bodies to the air. The sea ended in a sad blueness beyond time.

What does it mean when a girl runs three times around the island? Once, on St John's Night, I had seen them dancing about a bonfire. Pretty colleens I'd never laid eyes on in the daytime; and pin-points of the fires all along the Clare coast. *Beltane*, or was it later? the summer solstice when the sun is farthest from the equator and appears to pause before returning. Rites of the earth. Peasants of the Vendée play the violin and accordian and the donkeys get erections and mount the she-asses. Wild-eyed island beauties dancing in red petticoats about the fires. In Andalusia, hidden away in dark little rooms, sewing-girls using up their youth and patience waiting for a *novia*. Plaza de los Martires.

Why are excrements, children and lice works of art? When a girl jumps three times backwards and forwards over a fire, they say she will soon be married, be happy and have a great many children. But when a young man and woman jump together over the fire without being touched by the smoke, they say she will not be a mother during the year, for the flames have neither touched her nor made her fertile. In other words, she has shown that she has the skill to play with fire without being burnt.

Fire festivals of India: songs and gestures, licentious to the point of indecency. On the day of the solstice the Estonians go in for debauchery. August. My night. The flames in the dark and the wind blowing sparks along the shore. Where are the red petticoats jumping in the darkness?

Martin O'Donnell had told me of the kind Dr Beck, the German who loved the islands and the islanders and had landed in a helicopter with provisions when Aran was cut off from the mainland in a storm. For twenty years he had been coming on research. Then there was another man, also called Beck but no relation. He had gone back to Germany. The older Beck lived in Dublin. The Dane had not got on too well with the good doctor, so they informed me on Inishere. I had never met either of the Becks, then or later. Mogens Stenicke showed me his paintings and brass rubbings from the old church up to its headstones in sand but when I was tactless enough to bring up the name of Beck, he cut me short.

I believe you didn't get on too well with the old one, I ventured to say.

The young one was worse, the Dane said, closing the subject.

Mogens Stenicke was stout, had white hair, wore a kris. His manner was evasive. He had met Behan on the island. We drank at night with the Dane in the bar near the slip. The other bar was run by a portly publican who had the manners of a Bishop.

The aired sheets smelled of lavender, stronger than the odour of horses or courage. The bedroom was bare and clean as a shell scoured by the sea. It was early and Olivia not yet stirring, sleeping with her arms by her side. In the outside jax I used pages of the *Irish Independent* for what it was intended and 'flushed' with sand. I stood in the cabbage garden. There was an abundance of hen shit on the low wall. I went down to the beach. Martin O'Donnell was there. We pushed the curragh out, while he pulled I waited to put out the lures for mackerel. There was a slick of their oil on the surface. Rings appeared on the water where the oars dipped and the curragh sped over the surface of the sea. It was one of those coral and pearl days that you get on the Atlantic in autumn. Dolphins jump, or sometimes roll. You see them in herds in the sea.

At the end of my first visit to Inishere, the two O'Donnells had not rowed me out to where the *Dun Aengus* rode at anchor, no, but a relative of theirs, McHale. When the old steamship began to draw away from the anchorage, blowing off steam, the two Martins rowed after her. They rowed with their profile to me keeping on a course two hundred yards astern, pulling hard while the steamship drew away. Then they stopped rowing, and sat there with the oars in their hands, staring after the ship, but at such a remove that I could not see their expressions. Young Martin's peaked cap with the clip button gone, the old man's white hair. The son waved to me, the old man just sat and stared, wrapped in his own thoughts, like Hudson marooned by his own crew in the bay that would bear his name. Was that shyness or island reserve? I had got on well with the old man, reading the *Irish Times* there in the inglenook.

The men were out fishing for mackerel under the cliffs of Moher, the seven-hundred feet drop into which 'Pinkey' Domenech had fallen or been pushed wearing only American black panties. The body had drifted up among the rocks on Doolin beach in County Clare. Romolo Imundi of the homicide squad and woman detective Julia McNamara drew back and the Irish police closed the Domenech file. The mother had been murdered about the same time, four thousand miles away in her New York flat. And the escort of the twenty-eight-year-old American beauty queen swallowed an overdose of barbiturates in a Florida motel. Elsewhere 'Bubbles' Schroder the high-priced Montreal whore had been choked performing fellation with a Jewish businessman, her last customer. So many rings on the water.

Hidden in the walled fields where the skinning Atlantic winds had left no trees, the men were spraying the potato crop with hand-manipulated German pumps slung on their backs, the copper gone the colour of duck eggs or the dome of the Four Courts. And masturbating with mute melancholy lust in the Neolithic trenches, their minds a riot of obscene images. The sun shone on the meadows, the walled paddocks, a land worked by men; nothing much had changed there since I had first visited the island, three visits past, a third of a lifetime away. I thought of the time in Spain: those transient friends which events bring and events take away.

Tim Robinson

Stones of Aran

THE WORM AND THE ROOT

If as an artist I wanted to find a sculptural form for my intuition of the Aran landscape, I would not think in terms of circles. Aran's circles of stone, the great inland cashels and lesser ring-forts, the ancient hunchback huts, Long's evanescent inscriptions, can be read as fearful withdrawals from these bare spaces or as egocentric stances within them, habits of thought born elsewhere and merely sojourning here, not deeply rooted in the specificity of Aran. In other landscapes the rounded might be equated with the natural and the right angle with the human contribution. Here, though, it is as if the ground itself brings forth right angles. Because of the limestone's natural partings along its vertical fissures and horizontal stratifications, the oblong and the cuboid are the first-fruits of the rock. These are the forms that coerce one's footsteps in this terrain, and hence have directed the evolution of the chief human stratum of the landscape, the mosaic of fields and the paths that side-step between them. These too are the forms that come to hand in picking up a loose stone to build a wall – and so the field-patterns rhyme with the patterns of the stones in their walls. On the largest scale the rectilinear skylines and stepped flanks of Aran remember their origins in the nature of the rock.

A block, then, would best embody the essence of Aran's landforms – or, since I am dealing in abstractions and have undergone the metamorphoses of contemporary art, the absence of a block, a rectangular void to stand for all blocks. And since the sea is the most decisive sculptor among the various erosive agents that disengage Aran's form from its substance, let this void be filled by water, reversing the relationship of sea and island. Site it on one of the great stages of rock below the cliffs; do it on a prodigious scale, a spectacle rather than a gallery-piece; let the ocean dance in it, and the cliffs above step back in wide balconies to accommodate the thousands who will come to marvel at this kinetic-conceptualist, megalominimalist, unrepeatable and ever-re-peated, sublime and absurd show of the Atlantic's extraction of Aran's square root!

From *Stones of Aran* (1986).

What I have imagined, exists. An exactly rectangular block over a hundred feet long has somehow been excerpted from the floor of a bay in the cliffs, a few hundred yards west of Port Bhéal an Dúin, and the sea fills the void from below. This is Poll na bPéist, the hole of the worms, or The Worm-Hole as it is called for English-speaking visitors; the word *péist*, like the English 'worm' in its older acceptances, covers everything from sea-monsters to the grubs that pullulate in rotten seaweed, and nobody knows what sort of creeping thing was originally in question here. It is impossible to see how deep the hole is, and I do not know if the missing block lies in fragments in a sea-cave below or whether it was blasted upwards by the surges and washed off the terrace. On a calm day and at low tide one can reach the spot by following the lowest level of the shore under cliffs that rise westwards from Port Bhéal an Dúin. The rock underfoot here is inhabited by countless purple sea-urchins, each of which has excavated a hole an inch or two deep for itself, and the population is so dense that the rock-surface is reduced to a layer of fantastically fretted, brittle spikes. The gap between the line of surf and the foot of the cliff narrows as one goes westwards; sometimes a seal raises its head from the waves close by to watch as one negotiates the shrinking passage. Then the cliff turns at right angles inland, and on following it one finds oneself on the stage of a natural theatre, with the oblong abyss at one's feet. On such days the water in it is usually still and dark, sunken into itself, leaving the sheer sides too deep to climb. It measures about thirty-six by thirteen slippery paces, and looks like a grim and sinister swimming-pool, the work of some morose civil engineer. However, despite its dank walls and impenetrable depths, the idea of swimming in it is not quite out of the question. Members of a sub-aqua club from Belfast have explored it, and swum out to the open sea through the cave below. And once I met an amiable fantasist here who told me how he had swum in it by moonlight with a beautiful girl forty years ago; it was, he said, one of those holiday affairs: he never even asked her name, and they never met again. ...

If, while one has been peering into the dark waters or exchanging amorous reminiscences with strangers, the tide has crept on and cut off retreat at the outer angle of the bay, one's best chance is to scramble up the rock-wall, deeply canopied in places and perfectly sheer in others, that shadows the broad pavements around the pool; a climb of sixteen or twenty feet brings one onto a wide terrace, above which another forty feet of rock completes the height of the cliff. This intermediate level is immediately recognizable from its amoeboid rock-pools as the 'mamillated surface', and here it is very evident that it once underlay a clay band, for erosion of the softer material has opened up a horizontal slot all along the base of the cliff above it, four to eight feet high and in places up to forty feet in depth; one can walk into this dripping cellarage, with its wavy floor and low, fossil-studded flat ceiling, and see that its rear wall is of clay, all glistening in the dark with seeping ground-water.

At high tide or in stormy weather these terraces are out of the question, and to see Poll na bPéist one has to struggle along the spray-blown clifftops and hold onto stones of the boulder beach up there to avoid being hurled over by the violent gusts. On such days the gladiatorial display in the arena below features primaeval chaos pitted against fundamental geometry. Each breaker floods the lower terrace and pours in torrents of froth down the sides of the shaft to meet the turbulence bursting up into it from below; the water's surface comes roaring up between the polished walls, alive with the snaking trains of bubbles that perhaps suggested the name of the place, swills its excess over the brink into the fleeing wreckage of the wave now retreating from the terrace, then sags and falls back with dizzying speed into the spray-clouded depths of the vault. Throughout the tumult the rock itself conducts a rigorous demonstration of its own theorem, like a deaf mathematics lecturer oblivious of his rowdy students; through the pelting spitballs of foam one can see that, for instance, the eastern wall of the hole lies in exactly the same place as the east-facing wall of the upper terrace just to seaward of it, both having been determined by the same joint, which is visible as a finely drawn line crossing the rock-floor between them.

One of the most curious features of this, Aran's most striking natural curiosity, is that there is no legend attached to it. The writer Tom O'Flaherty pointed this out fifty years ago, and if there had been any traditional tale about the place he would certainly have known it, as a native of Gort na gCapall. He adds that it is time someone invented a story, but I am not sure that I agree. These encircling, overhanging terraces cruelly intent upon the entrance to the tomb or dungeon below suggest frightful rites; Ariosto has an episode of a maiden sacrificed to a sea-monster on the coast of Ireland, and one could toy with the idea that it happened here. But since it seems that even the most voluble of folk traditions has been left speechless by the place, perhaps it is fitting that this void, this abstract exemplification of Aran's elements, should remain an emptiness without an explanation.

WRITING ON THE BEACH

Because the bay of Port Mhuirbhigh curves so deeply into the flank of the island its waters are undisturbed by the currents that sweep along the coast, and so have deposited a beach of fine sand. Onshore winds have carried the sand inland to build dunes, now grassed over. The whole area around the bay is a *muirbheach*, a sea-plain of sandy pasturage; hence the name Port Mhuirbhigh, the bay of the *muirbheach*. There was once a little burial ground or *cill*, perhaps an ancient church site, close to the head of the bay, which in turn has been buried by the dunes so that its only memorial is the name of the nearby village and the surrounding townland, Cill Mhuirbhigh, anglicized as Kilmurvey. The Kilmurvey House farm, which almost monopolizes this *muirbheach*, is the best holding in the three islands.

Sand, then, sets the tone here. A beach the colour of the moon waxes from a poor crescent to a good half and wanes again twice a day. Behind it is another crescent, a pale and ragged area of marram-grass hillocks between a foreshore path and the road going by to the village. Sometimes young visitors set up their tents in the snug hollows of this field, which for some reason is called The Vinegar, and the currachs of the Cill Mhuirbhigh men are kept on their stone stocks in the shelter of its walls. All around are the vivid green and unbroken acres grazed by the cattle of the 'Big House'; in contrast, the background of hill-slopes to the south-east and south-west is grey and lined with walls.

All the roads and tracks of this area run to or loiter by the beach. The stony coastline itself seems to holiday here and unwind from its severities. Sun-bathers and sandcastle-builders dispel the old equation of the shore with labour and its new one with loneliness, at least for those short and radiant times in which the angle of a gull's white wing against the unstable Atlantic blue defines high summer in Aran. At such hours even the pulse of the breaking waves, the universal constant of all shores, never quite still, becomes a whisper, a merely subliminal reminiscence of storm, of winter.

Winter is defined by a bird here too, a solitary great northern diver that comes with falling temperatures from the far north to haunt the bay, and lives for months out there on the heaving waters, rising and falling in time to the crash of waves on the beach, a dark, secretive thing that keeps its distances and refuses one a view, slipping silently under the surface if one approaches the water's edge and reappearing after a long interval farther off, half lost in the poor light. One gives up peering, identifying, and wanders along the heavy ever-repeated landfall of the sea. At this season the resistant depths of colour on land, sea and sky slow down the pace of perception to that of contemplation. If a gleam from the low sun comes across to catch the countless overlapping marks on the sand, then idleness and the absence of humankind can tempt one into the error of thinking: 'Signatures of all things I am here to read.' Each fallen wave, for instance, rushes up the strand with a million urgently typing fingers, and then at the moment between writing and erasing subscribes itself in a negligent cursive across the whole breadth of the page. Signatures and counter-signatures accumulate, confuse, obliterate. Seabirds put down their names in cuneiform, lugworms excrete their humble marks. And then come my boots to add the stamp of authenticity, not of the endless process of the beach which needs no authentification from anybody, but of my witnessing of it.

Is this an image of the work I have dreamed of, that book – with which the present book has a certain flirtatious but respectful relationship – preliminary to the taking of an all-encompassing stride? A muddled draft of it perhaps, or more usefully a demonstration of its impossibility; for the multitudinous, encyclopaedic inscription of all passing reality upon a yard of ground is ultimately self-effacing. But no; for if the book like the beach lies open to all that befalls it, welcomes whatever heterogeneous material is washed up or blown in, then must begin the magic transubstantiation of all this intractable stuff into the person fit to make the step. A work of many generations, I wonder? Let a few almost frivolous examples of the countless marks that have been impressed temporarily on this particular beach and more lastingly upon myself demonstrate how nearly overwhelming is even my limited and ill-defined project.

In the spring of 1975 almost the entire area of sand between high water mark and the foot of the dunes rather suddenly filled up with low clumps of a silvery-leaved plant never recorded in Árainn before, the frosted orache. This is in general rare on Ireland's western coasts, though commoner on the east, but I heard later that it had turned up at Roundstone in Connemara the previous year, and perhaps a drift of its seeds had come across the channel from there. This insemination has probably not added permanently to the Aran flora, for year by year since then its summer growth has been thinner and thinner, and now it is difficult to find a single specimen. In my capacity as self-appointed resident scientific busybody I kept the botanical authorities informed, and now I read in D. A. Webb's almost-but-of-course-not-quite definitive *Flora of the Aran Islands*, published in 1980:

> *Atriplex laciniata* ... observed in 1975 on Kilmurvey beach, where (*fide* Robinson) it has since much decreased.

The Latinism was new to me; I am tempted to adopt it as a motto.

Similarly, on the 27th August 1977, I witnessed the presence of a small bird running to and fro and pecking at the margins of retreating waves, a slim, stilt-legged, long-beaked wader very like a common sandpiper but with a reddish underside. Unlike the other shorebirds that feed in mixed flocks here from the autumn onwards, and which take flight as one approaches, circle round over the sea and re-alight behind one, this elegant little oddity stayed there, busy and preoccupied, until it was almost under my feet. Later the reference books told me it was a buff-breasted sandpiper, a vagrant from America recorded less than a dozen times in Ireland, and well known as an unusually tame bird – though 'tame' is hardly the word for a creature to whom human beings are of no more concern than any other solid obstacle in its way. I referred this observation to higher authorities too, and was informed that a body called the Rare Birds Committee was 'sitting on it' and might well accept it as an authentic record, but I never heard the outcome of their incubations. In fact I would say to them '*Diffide* Robinson!', for my certainty about the identification is of the sort oddly called a 'moral certainty', which seems to be inferior to a factual one. (For instance, Professor Webb once found on Inis Oírr a certain plant, a little stonecrop called *Sedum dasyphyllum*; at least, that is what the specimen he brought away with him turned out to be. The discovery was unusual enough to demand confirmation, but although he, his acolytes and rivals have like myself diligently searched the place, that particular stonecrop has not been refound. And although he is still 'morally certain' about it, he has excluded it from his Aran *Flora*.)

What else? The dolphins, forty or fifty of them, did indeed dance in the bay one year, just as I described to the lightkeeper who saw them praying on the beach. I am told that their splashy leapings are more practical than expressive, and that they were probably rounding up a shoal of fish; also that they were of the species known prosaically as the bottle-nosed dolphin, from the elongated snouts. Aran does not distinguish between the various dolphins and the smaller porpoises, lumping them all together as *muca mara*, sea-pigs, a libellous name for such lithe hydrobats. The expanding ring-waves made by that circus troupe can hardly have shifted a grain of sand on the shore, and I can include dolphins in this catalogue of beach-marks only on the strength of those fanciful, prayerful, kneeprints.

A last impression: a stumpy-legged dog, white with brown blotches, mainly gundog but 'with a bit of a seal in him' according to his owner; our adopted pet, Oscar, dearly loved and sadly missed as the death-notices put it. I used to throw a ball for him on the strand, a game that almost killed the neglected creature with delight. If I stood forgetful with the ball in my hand, lost in my musings over the riddles propounded by the sea to the sand, he would wait patiently at my feet, looking up, and very delicately place a paw on my toe to recall me. Then I would glance down and catch him saying, 'There are just two ways, or perhaps three, in which you can hope to give supreme pleasure to another living being. You can go home and make love to her who loves you, or you can throw that ball for your dog. This is the time for the second alternative, for the third is to go on trying to perfect your book, which I do not believe you have it in you to do.'

No, dogs do not speak. The sea does not riddle, dolphins do not pray, the vagrant bird neither trusts nor distrusts Robinson, waves never sign anything; what I myself witness is my own forgery. One should forego these overluxuriant metaphors that covertly impute a desire of communication to non-human reality. We ourselves are the only source of meaning, at least on this little beach of the Universe. These inscriptions that we insist on finding on every stone, every sand-grain, are in our own hand. People who write letters to themselves are generally regarded as pathetic, but such is the human condition. We are writing a work so vast, so multivocal, so driven asunder by its project of becoming coextensive with reality, that when we come across scattered phrases of it we fail to recognize them as our own.

LOOKING INTO OTHER LIVES

The next bay to the west of Port Chorrúch is Port Eochla, so called as pertaining to the village of Eochaill. But between Corrúch and Eochaill is Baile na Creige, the village of the crag. (All three are in fact rather arbitrary segments of a scattering of houses along the main road, half a mile inland, and no stranger could tell where each begins or ends.) Baile na Creige is the smallest village of the island, and its territory is an irregular strip just three or four hundred yards wide, running right across the island from the north coast to the south. Its northern shore is an unemphatic stretch of the low headland between the two bays named above, a few minutes of rough walking and enervating nullity that has never revealed itself to me in any memorable way, about which I have collected no lore, upon which I have met neither native nor stranger – and which by the logic of Aran's land-divisions corresponds to one of the most dramatic parts of the southern coast, the cathedral-like peninsula called An Bhinn Bhuí, and the vast cauldron of An Cró on its west. So the man who owns that amazing field on the peninsula, with one wall of stone and three of wind and vertigo and the cry of gulls, also owns a couple of fields, hardly better than damp bramble-patches, down by this shore, while the rest of his holding is in a dozen or so little parcels strung out like beads along the two miles between these extremes.

This northern coastline of Baile na Creige represents a failure in the terms of this book, as I can report scarcely a word from my several walkings of it (except – now it comes back to me – that of a heron I disturbed here one dreary day; a deathly, hoarse *khaaa*, exhaled as it lumbered on grey wings into a grey sky). Therefore I prefer now to retrace my steps from the stone boat, and linger around the 'lake of the white-headed cow' for a while before cutting across the headland by the coast road to Port Eochla – all the more so as Loch Phort Chorrúch and its surrounds compose one of Aran's frankest and most engaging landscapes.

On the west of the lake is the great rampart of shingle separating it from Port Chorrúch itself (allowing some seepage of the tide through fissures below, it seems, for the lake has a taste of salt and is not now, if it ever was, a 'pool of sweet water' as in the legend, and yellow-green *Enteromorpha* weed grows in it and is gathered to keep the rain off stacks of more useful seaweeds drying on the back of the shinglebank). There are reedbeds along the foot of this shingle shoreline of the lake and around its northern perimeter. The eastern shore is of little fields, that make green capes and promontories, kept trim by grazing cattle; sometimes after rainy weeks the lake reaches across a boreen that runs back to the shore through these fields, and borrows a few more of them for a while. The road goes by close to the southern bank, and there are secretive little steps down from it to a freshwater spring that feeds the lake, opposite an islet upon which the waterfowl pursue their private lives oblivious to the woman filling a pail for her cow there.

One March morning I noticed that this islet appeared to have been paved with large pebbles, and it was only when one of them showed twinges of restless life that I identified them as knots, a species of wader, moderately sized, moderately long-beaked and long-legged, of a nondescript grey, and to my amateur eye at least, chiefly distinguished from the dozens of other waders by its lack of distinguishing features. This whole area, bay and lake, is especially vivified by birds in the winter. All the dark members of the crow family including the raven and the chough, and a few rooks that fly in from the mainland at that season, come to forage on the great bank of rotting weed amassed by the gales on the outer face of the shingle. Countless waders work the rock-pools, following the tide down the shore; one needs binoculars to resolve all these fidgety brown-grey scraps into so many highly distinctive species, and I have never learned to discriminate the half of their individual parts in the web of vibrant calls stretched like taut nerves over the shore. The dunlins, ringed plovers and turnstones all run mingled together, a few redshanks and the occasional greenshank hold aloof, half-a-dozen bar-tailed godwits keep to themselves. The sanderlings, diminutive clowns of this winter circus, amuse us by forming a wavering line across any patch of sand and running down it after each receding wave, picking morsels out of its rim, and then all turning together and running up again before the next wave catches them, matchstick legs whirring under their fat little bellies, keeping just ahead of the spreading foam as if afraid to get their feet wet.

In winter too there are often thirty or forty whooper swans on the lake, together with half-a-dozen mute swans. Occasionally the whoopers all take off with long splashing runs over the water, huge wings labouring, and come sailing low over the shinglebank, necks outstretched, emitting that strange breathy hoot in time to the hiss of their wingstrokes, and land on the waters of the bay, where they rest for an hour or two with heads under their wings before returning to the lake. Sometimes in the depths of winter there comes an isolated day of summer (a pet day, *peata lae*, as they say here) that holds a lens of stillness and clarity over all this life of the shore; each feather, each rustle of a feather, is as incisive as diamond in the memory – at least one feels it so at the moment, but then the day passes and one's impressions of it merge into a dazzled nostalgia.

With spring the gatherings disperse. The whooper swans fly north to their nesting grounds in Iceland and beyond, while the mute swans fight balletic wars until just one pair holds the lake for its territory. I know where some of the shore-birds go, for we find the ringed plovers nesting in the dunes at Cill Éinne, and I remember from my childhood on the Yorkshire moors how the curlews would arrive there in time for my birthday (as I put it, with a child's egotism) in late March (and having so long ago learned their horizon-circling, sky-probing call as the annunciation of spring, to hear it now on their return to the shore in August as the thin premonitory trumpet of autumn gives me a sense in the marrow of my bones of the Earth's curvature and my ageing).

After the curlews have gone in the early spring, the very similar but smaller whimbrel breaks its northward migration here, so picking up (and leaving behind) its local name of *crotach Bhealtaine*, May curlew. And then throughout the summer there are more birds on the lake than on the seashore. Dabchicks and waterhens nest in the reeds, so does a pair of herons, and invariably the mute swans convoy a flotilla of six or eight grey cygnets in and out of their harbour in the recesses of the reedbeds farthest from the road.

The lake is curiously open and indifferent to observation; a few islanders come wildfowling here but not so often as to dispel its trust. The human routes around it – the high walkway of shingle used only by a few men preoccupied with seaweed, the open road that carries sometimes a couple of tourists on bicycles and sometimes a man driving cattle into Cill Rónáin, the boreen sidling through the fields that give covert views of the water through gaps in the reedbeds – at once present the lake to the eye and half avert themselves from it; and the lake-dwellers know and care as little of them as do the figures in a painting of the title on its frame.

I remember that for some reason one spring (it was in 1978) a single whooper swan stayed behind when all the rest had flown, and spent the entire summer pottering about the banks, because whenever it tried to put a foot into the water one of the resident pair of mute swans would come sailing towards it with wings half-raised and head poised on its elegant stalk above a chaos of white plumes – a ruffled rococo beau with a duellist's eye – and the whooper, gauche and gooselike with its stiff straight neck and bland face, would turn away resignedly. Witnessing a little defeat like this almost every time I passed the lake used to make me uncomfortable. Un-swanlike in practical life, having to assume a finely feathered style before trusting myself even to the eyes of the future, I would prefer for my own ego the unflappable self-possession of a heron I watched here once. It had caught a large eel and had just swallowed its head when I saw it, with the rest hanging from its beak. A passing crow had seen it too and alighted nearby hoping to profit in some way. The heron ignored the crow and concentrated on gulping down a little more of the eel. The crow rose into the air and called up its mate, and the pair of them set up an intimidating racket, one on either side of the heron, which merely threw back another few inches of eel. The crows tried making little hopping, flopping flights from one side of the heron to the other, only just clearing its head; but the heron calmly raised both broad wings into a canopy for itself, and after a pause for breath downed the rest of the eel in one violent convulsion. Then it cleaned its beak, eyed the ground narrowly as if to ensure that not a single scale was left for the crows, and took itself off with leisurely flaps.

Enviable bird, gorging on the moment, contemptuous of dark forethought and afterthought! Whereas even as I stand here noting every detail of the scene I can imagine some islander pausing from spadework on the hillside above and shaking his head over my wandering and staring about this island; and as I write up the incident wonder if those haunting eyes, the reader's, which the writer must exorcize if he is to inhabit his work, will read me as I intend myself, or unimaginably otherwise. Perhaps what will last will be nothing of my writing, my thought self, but some chance observation of me, marginal to an anecdote about a bird, or a fiction prompted by my alien name in an old census return, resurrecting me in a body and mind I would not recognize. At this very spot I have done the same to a fellow alien, as I will tell:

The little field to the south-east of the lake, where the boreen around it meets the road, is called Garraí Wilson; a *garraí* is a 'garden', which in Aran means a potato- or a vegetable-plot (I remember being puzzled when we were new here by an islander telling me he had a little garden down by the shore; the idea seemed charming, impractical, and absolutely un-Aranish). As for Wilson, nobody remembers who he was, but in the census of 1821 I found:

Robert Wilson, half-pay Lieutenant; Royal
      Marines, age 36, Head Lightkeeper
Ann, his wife, age 30
Robert, his son, age 5
Ann, his daughter, age 3
Eliza, his daughter, age 1

In those days the only lighthouse was above Eochaill on the highest point of the island, whence its ruins still look down towards the lake. Wilson must have leased this garden to grow vegetables for himself and that young family living up there on the windy skyline in the disused signal tower by the lighthouse. Why was he retired on half-pay? Perhaps he had a stiff knee which he allowed it to be understood had a Napoleonic bullet lodged in it, but which in fact he broke by tripping over a bollard in Plymouth docks while turning round to look after a passing shop-girl, Ann. I picture him in this field, paunchy, grunting, puzzling ineffectually with his spade of unfamiliar design at the shallow stony soil of Aran. He straightens up, putting his knuckles to his spine, and sees through the reeds a heron swallowing an eel. He stands there open-mouthed, long-dead Lieutenant Wilson, keeper of the long-extinguished light, never suspecting that we are watching him through words, those chinks in Time.

THE BAY OF DOUBT

Cill Rónáin's waterfront comes to a dead end to the south, after the old quay, the crafts shop and one or two fishermen's storehouses, and sometimes it is my pleasure to jump over the low sea-wall onto the rocky foreshore and sneak out of town behind the backs of the houses instead of going up through the busy parts, for after some months of life in Fearann an Choirce even Cill Rónáin seems to buzz with illicit distractions and tiresome obligations.

Once over the wall, the moody sea reasserts itself even while the town is still lagging alongside. The first point of rock beyond the end of the waterfront is Spur Cháit, but of the woman Cáit I can learn only that she had a little cottage on it and was perforce at home to high spring tides. Such anomalies are not tolerated now; the town keeps well back from high water mark, and even where the road running around the bay towards Cill Éinne follows the curve of the shore closely, it is separated from it by a concrete wall the waves slop across only when a spring tide coincides with a northerly gale. Nevertheless a very high tide is psychologically disturbing to those who live nearby, especially when it comes in stillness and silence. I remember a young woman coming out to stand in the doorway of her shop in the part of Cill Rónáin that looks out this way, and murmuring more to herself than to me, 'The tide's very high today' – and there at the end of the street was the bay, much nearer than one had remembered, brimming, gleaming, pressing on some nerve in the town's subconscious.

But then the waters withdraw so far across the shallows here, exposing the luminous acres of sand called Cockle Strand, that this vast neighbouring mutability seems purely benignant towards the town, giving it a pleasure-ground for half a day at a time. The old Cill Rónáin people tell me how when they were children they would look for the tiny plump cowrie-shells they call 'pigs' here, for let's-pretend farms, and an almost salivary gleam comes into their eyes when they speak of the delicious cockles from which the strand is named. Far out on it among the rocks near low water lies a rusty boiler from some forgotten wreck, which children used to put bait in to catch the occasional foolish lobster that couldn't find the way out of it. The young lads of the town still sometimes go hunting razorfish here, the molluscs with long curved shells like old-fashioned barbers' razors, which can dig themselves deep into the sand very quickly and have to be prodded for with long skewers or made to come out of their burrows with a pinch of salt.

Cockle Strand is the delight of summer visitors, who come here to bathe or paddle, or to sunbathe on the rocky steps and slopes along the roadside. For me, though, when I walk or cycle by, there is usually an inkling of unease about the place, a rawness of the adjustment between its vaguely open oval of unemphatic naturalness and its patchily socialized rim, which I think ante-dates the new houses so crudely sited above scarps to the south of the road. The sun-cultists sprawled on their awkward rocks look uncomfortable, and even the vegetation of this shoreline is somehow dispiriting. At the Cill Rónáin end of the curve there is almost a low hedge along the concrete wall of an odd conjunction of species, both with coarse and ragged leaves and flowering in a barbarous dissonance of colours, the creamy yellow of sea-radish and the pinkish purple of common mallow; while at the other end of the beach where broad sheets of rock interrupt the sand, the principal growth is a four-inch forest of glasswort, like a miniature translucent cactus, and seablite, a dull rubbery-green dwarf. The slight tedium I feel sometimes along this shore has been replaced on occasion by a more positively disquieting atmosphere. About half a mile from the town there is a little cabbage-plot on the shore side of the road called Garraí na Taoille, the garden of the tide, because a high enough tide makes a little promontory of it. I remember watching the still waters come creeping up around this garden one stifling day when there were muttering fog-banks offshore and lighting punching down into the sea; the mullet, big grey fish that visit muddy shallows in summer, were making sudden rushes to and fro, ripping the glassy surface. It was a sinister hour, that dispersed with the turning of the tide.

Sometimes I like to go and poke about a small lake over the road from the shore a little farther on, although it is not now a peaceful spot, as the generators supplying our electricity grumble and throb in a slovenly enclosure nearby; nor is it attractive at the first glance, for the waters are often covered by a green slime and seem to lie inertly among grey sheets of limestone pavement. One of these expanses of unfissured rock is so broad and smooth that it has been made into the floor of a handball alley, little used nowadays, the great blank wall of which (built, it used to be said, with the money from some nineteenth-century relief scheme) seems to mirror the ambience of dereliction. This sullen water is Loch an tSáile, the lake of the brine (for although it is a hundred yards from high tide mark the sea infects it through fissures running under the road), and its name, anglicized as Lough Atalia, recurs in many of the botanical reports on the island written by generation after generation of visiting scientists. Its fascination is primarily the extraordinary interpenetration of diverse habitats around its margins, giving rise to a species list that might make one think a botanist had muddled together field-notes taken in a variety of different places, and secondarily, the anomalies in some of those botanical reports, which successive investigators come here hoping to resolve, so generating further reports and making for a self-perpetuating cult of Lough Atalia.

For instance, the earliest attempt at a comprehensive listing of the Aran flora was made by Dr E. P. Wright, Professor of Zoology in Trinity College, Dublin, in 1866, and he includes among his finds at Lough Atalia *Ranunculus lingua*, the greater spearwort, a large and rather uncommon buttercup of fens and marshes, not to be expected in Aran. The next important investigator was H. C. Hart in 1869; he searched the lake and found the lesser spearwort, which is common, but not the greater. He also noted here a rare horsetail, *Equisetum variagatum*; Robert Lloyd Praeger, most ubiquitous and comprehensive of Irish naturalists, confirmed this find in 1895, but since then nobody else has been able to do so. During the intensive combing of the islands and the critical re-examination of old records undertaken in the preparation of the most recent and definitive work on the subject, Professor D. A. Webb's article, 'The Flora of the Aran Islands', of 1980, the lake was closely scrutinized by amateurs and experts, but neither of the missing plants was found. The conclusion was that Wright must have mistaken a particularly hearty specimen of the lesser spearwort for the greater (after all, he did describe his sufferings in the Atlantic Hotel, working at his specimens in the evenings, when the only choice of light was between 'a farthing dip of the worst description – i.e. with the thickest possible wick and the smallest amount of tallow – and a slender cotton thread lying in a saucer of fish-oil'). The rare horsetail is accepted as a reality, however, and may yet turn up in the anomalous margins of Loch an tSáile.

Coming on the scene after these illustrious discomfitures, it would give me a slightly improper pleasure to find either of these plants, and so I turn off the road here now and again and make a circuit of the lake, trying to tune out of my mind the buzz of the generator, the egoistic discovery-ethic, and other frag-menting influences on the consciousness. Laying aside the search for rarities, it is marvellous to see how a single crevice running into the surrounding rock from the edge of the lake contains a summary of Aran's flora, from the seaweeds of the middle shore like *Ascophyllum* (the knotted wrack, which only grows in the inmost parts of Cill Éinne bay, as it needs quiet water), and those of the upper shore like channelled wrack and spiral wrack; then the flowers of shinglebanks and rocky foreshores like thrift, sea campion, pellitory, and the sea spleenwort fern that one finds in fissures on the clifftops; and only a few feet away from them all of the usual crag-plants, wall-pepper, hemp agrimony, thyme, and dozens of others; while a muddy hollow nearby will hold a miniature saltmarsh of glasswort and seablite, then sea aster, and farther back where the freshwater springs feeding the lake from under the scarp south of it make themselves felt, the plants of Aran's turloughs such as marsh pennywort, loosestrife, watermint, bog pimpernel, etcetera. These ecological sentences (all multicoloured punctuation and no sense) lead me back to the seductive tangles of the scarp itself, with its sweet-smelling hawthorns and dog roses sheltering rank garlic mustard, delicate wood sorrel and hidden gardens of violets and primroses in spring, and thence to the open hillside above, luring me away from the puzzles of the shore, to which I must now return.

Beyond the lake and the ball alley the road climbs the scarp and leaves the coast, which here stretches out a low headland into the bay, dividing it into two lobes. This flat area of crag, thicket, little fields of rough grazing and low stony shore, has a name that remains indeterminate however often I hear it: Carraig an Bhanbháin, Carraig an Mharbháin, the rock of the something-or-other; its consonants seem to hesitate between *b*'s and *v*'s and *w*'s, *r*'s and *n*'s, and everyone is ready to make wildly various senses of it: the rock of the little piglet, of the corpse, of the white woman, of the sultry weather. ... I record another of these guesses out of respect for deathbed testimony, for an old man of the locality who died a few years ago used one of his last breaths, no one knows why, to explain to those around his bedside that this shore is really Carraig na Mara Báine, the rock of the white sea. Unlikely, I am afraid; but it does make me think of a night I have heard of when the sea was white with foam along this normally sheltered shore. It was on the evening of the 28th of December, 1899, and a number of fishermen were sleeping in their boats moored offshore in readiness for an early start the next morning, when a storm struck suddenly into the bay. One man was by himself in a nobbie and managed to lower the mainmast single-handed, reducing the wind's purchase and saving the anchor from dragging. Five other boats were driven against the rocky shore and three of them were utterly smashed. The seas were so fierce that those on land could do nothing to help; four men were drowned, and the corpse of one of them never recovered. It was a terrible blow for Aran's new fishing-fleet. Synge heard of the tragedy when he visited Inis Meáin the next summer:

'Ah!' said the man that told me the story, 'I'm thinking it will be a long time before men will go out again on a holy day. That was the only storm that reached into the harbour the whole winter, and I'm thinking there was something in it.'

The name of the headland, like this event, remains uninterpretable for now, but the low rockface the boats were smashed on is Aill na mBád, the cliff of the boats, and it was baptized by this disaster.

There are slight traces of a ruinous stone quay there, for the blocks used in the building of Cill Rónáin pier in the 1850s were quarried close by and rafted across the bay from this point. Later on, the stone for Kilmurvey House came from here too, and there is a big block with a curved face lying not far away which looks as if it had been intended for one of the lighthouses. A field near the old quay is still called Garraí na Craeneach, the garden of the crane, from the winch used in loading the blocks. Evidently these massive pieces of stone were split out of the bedrock by tapping wedges into rectangular slots, for rows of these slots can be seen here and there in what remains of the original limestone pavement surface. The interior of this headland always seems to promise archaeological discoveries, in the way the lake nearby promises botanical rarities, which do not materialize, for it is a neglected corner of the island and very overgrown, but the intriguing hummocks of stone half-hidden in brambles all derive from nineteenth-century quarrying, so far as I can tell.

Disappointed, I return to Aill na mBád, the site of the disaster. What exactly did Synge's islander think was 'in it'? What significance did he see in its happening on a holy day? And what art have I been exercising on this bay through the epithets I have associated with it (moody, disturbing, uneasy, raw, dispiriting, tedious, ominous, sinister, slovenly, derelict, anomalous, indeterminate, uninterpretable, disappointing)? I become anxiously aware of a convergence between these two questions as I walk on towards the turn of the headland, mentally reviewing what I have written. (And what a peculiar shore this is, beyond Aill na mBád, confirming me in my choice of adjectives: dreary rock-flats patched with an extraordinary black-and-white strand made up of limpet-shells and wave-worn lumps of coke, perhaps from the same wreck as the rusty boiler stuck out there in the tide.) The islander did not have in mind any such comparatively modern and well-formulated concept as that of a jealous Old-Testament God snatching up a storm to smite those who slight his feasts. Similarly I would not impute to this bay a devious recalcitrant, inconsistent personality, nor indeed a human characteristic of any kind. The islander's thought moves in a vague and ancient terrain around a craggy idol only half-worked into a human face: Luck. On the one hand luck is merely the interplay of the random; on the other it is a force influencing the outcome, if not absolutely fixing the game then at least improving the odds. Observing the feast-days, whether they be Christian in origin or Celtic or even neolithic, is lucky; skimping their observance is unlucky. I worship Art, another half-humanized boulder lying on unprofitable ground. Calling Nature names is only my way of claiming a relationship deeper than blood. Observe the rites and obey; observe the facts and describe; otherwise, it is hard to know what to do for the best, for survival in this improbable, probabilistic world. We are not all as hard-headed as that other native of Inis Meáin who told Synge, 'A man who is not afraid of the sea will soon be drownded, for he will be going out on a day he shouldn't. But we do be afraid of the sea, and we do only be drownded now and again.' Under the fey charm worked by Irish grammar on English speech, this is a classic statement of the facts of life in a chancy universe, in which anything can happen at any moment. ...

But at this moment I hear strange voices from beyond the turn of the headland; it sounds like a row. I leave my puzzling and hurry on, full of curiosity.

Michael Longley

'Leaving Inishmore'

Rain and sunlight and the boat between them
Shifted whole hillsides through the afternoon –
Quiet variations on an urgent theme
Reminding me now that we left too soon
The island awash in wave and anthem.

Miles from the brimming enclave of the bay
I hear again the Atlantic's voices,
The gulls above us as we pulled away –
So munificent their final noises
These are the broadcasts from our holiday.

Oh, the crooked walkers on that tilting floor!
And the girls singing on the upper deck
Whose hair took the light like a downpour –
Interim nor change of scene shall shipwreck
Those folk on the move between shore and shore.

Summer and solstice as the seasons turn
Anchor our boat in a perfect standstill,
The harbour wall of Inishmore astern
Where the Atlantic waters overspill –
I shall name this the point of no return

Lest that excursion out of light and heat
Take on a January idiom –
Our ocean icebound when the year is hurt,
Wintertime past cure – the curriculum
Vitae of sailors and the sick at heart.

From *Poems 1963–1983* (1985).

Notes on Contributors

MARY BANIM (*c.*1850–90). Born and reared in Kilkenny where her father was a postmaster and businessman. She was one of three daughters of Michael Banim (1796–1874) who, with his brother John (1798–1842), wrote novels; they became known to the world as the 'Banim brothers'. Mary wrote a series of articles for the *Weekly Freeman*, which appeared in book form under the title *Here and There Through Ireland*, published by *The Freeman's Journal* in 1892. Her gentle yet vivid portrayal of individuals and talent for description – of scenery and historical remains – complemented by her sister Matilda's line-drawings, anticipated Synge's *The Aran Islands*.

CHARLES ROBERT BROWNE. An elected member of the Royal Irish Academy; in 1892 he published extensively in the Academy's *Proceedings* on the ethnography of many areas of Ireland, including Inisbofin, Inishturk, Inishshark, Garumna and the Aran Islands. He also worked with such scholars as Thomas Westropp and Alfred Haddon in the study of archaeology and craniology.

GIRALDUS CAMBRENSIS (*c.*1147–*c.*1223). Born in Wales, he studied in Paris and became archdeacon of Brecknock. He visited Ireland in 1183 and again in 1185 with Prince John. His best-known works are the *Topographia Hiberniae* (The Topography of Ireland) and the *Expugnatio Hiberniae* (The Conquest of Ireland), both invaluable sources for the history of twelfth-century Ireland despite their inaccuracies and bias.

ETHNA CARBERY (1866–1911). Pseudonym of Anna MacManus *née* Johnston. Born in Ballymena, Co. Antrim, she founded a monthly paper, *The Irish Patriot*, and contributed poetry to *The Nation* and *United Ireland*. She married the writer Seamus MacManus. Her books include *The Four Winds of Eirinn* (1902), *The Passionate Hearts* (1903) and *In the Celtic Past* (1904).

NATHANIEL COLGAN (1851–1919). Born in Dublin, he spent his life working in the Dublin Metropolitan Police Court. Contributed to many literary journals, but his chief interest was in botany and zoology, both in Ireland and in Europe. He was elected member of the Royal Irish Academy in 1894 and became President of the Dublin Field Club in 1913.

LEO DALY (1920–). Born in Dublin, he was educated and lives in Mullingar, Co. Westmeath. A qualified psychiatric nurse, broadcaster, photographer and journalist, he has published one novel, set in the Aran Islands, *The Rock Garden* (1984), as well as a guide-book to the islands, *Oileáin Árainn* (1975).

ALICE DEASE (1875–?). Born in Co. Westmeath, she wrote romantic, patriotic novels and stories before the First World War, including *Good Men of Erin* (1910) and *Down West & Other Sketches of Irish Life* (1914). In the war she served with the French Red Cross.

FRANCES HUBBARD FLAHERTY (1883–1973). Born Frances J. Hubbard, she married Robert Flaherty in 1914 and travelled extensively with him during his film-making. She played an important role in his films as editor, production assistant and stills photographer. She wrote an account of her husband's life, *The Odyssey of a Film-Maker*, in 1960.

ROBERT FLAHERTY (1884–1951). Born in Michigan, USA, he is considered by many to be the father of the modern documentary. His first film, *Nanook of the North* (1922), about the lifestyle of the Eskimos, was a great success and secured studio funding, but the failure of his second feature, *Moana* (1926), meant he had to struggle for further finance. Among his later films were *Man of Aran* (1934), *Elephant Boy* (1937) and *Louisiana Story* (1948). His work attracted controversy, with critics frequently questioning its accuracy.

LADY AUGUSTA GREGORY (1852–1932). Born in Co. Galway, she married Sir William Gregory in 1880 and was widowed in 1892. She played a leading role in the Irish Literary Revival, helping to found the Irish Literary Theatre in 1898. This became the Abbey Theatre Company in 1904. A close friend of W.B. Yeats and Edward Martyn, she collected large amounts of folklore around her native area and further afield, including the Aran Islands. She devoted most of her energies to the theatre, writing 27 plays and supporting playwrights like Synge and O'Casey. Her many published works include *Poets and Dreamers* (1907), *Cuchulainn of Muirthemne* (1907), *Our Irish Theatre* (1914) and *Visions and Beliefs in the West of Ireland* (1920).

ALFRED CORT HADDON (1855–1940). Anthropologist and craniologist, he began a brilliant academic career in Cambridge in 1875. He was appointed Professor of Zoology in Dublin in 1880 and was elected to life membership of the Royal Irish Academy in 1884. He moved to Cambridge in 1893 and raised anthropology to proper academic status.

SEAMUS HEANEY (1939–). Born in Co. Derry, he was educated at St Columb's College, Derry, and Queen's University, Belfast and worked as a teacher, lecturer and broadcaster before moving to Dublin in 1972. Arguably Ireland's foremost modern poet, he has published many collections from his first *Eleven Poems* (1965) to *Seeing Things* (1991). He has won numerous awards and is Boylston Professor of Rhetoric and Oratory at Harvard University. He was elected Professor of Poetry at Oxford in 1989.

B. N. HEDDERMAN. Born in Kilkee, Co. Clare, she arrived on the Aran Islands in spring 1902 as District Nurse for Inis Oírr and Inis Meáin, a post she occupied for many years. In 1917 she published a first volume of her reminiscences; the second volume never appeared.

AIDAN HIGGINS (1927–). Born in Celbridge, Co. Kildare, educated at Clongowes Wood, and worked in England and South Africa. Playwright, and broadcaster and author of travel and short-story collections and several novels of distinction, including *Langrishe Go Down* (1966), *Balcony of Europe* (1972) and *Bornholm Night-Ferry* (1983).

JAMES JOYCE (1882–1941). Ireland's greatest writer was born in Rathgar, Dublin and left the country in 1902 after attending Clongowes, Belvedere and University College, Dublin. He met a Galway girl, Nora Barnacle, in 1904 who went to Trieste, Zürich and Paris with him. He married her in 1931. He returned to Ireland in 1912 to arrange the publication of his first book, *Dubliners*, and visited the Aran Islands at this time. *Dubliners* (1914) was followed by *A Portrait of the Artist as a Young Man* (1916), *Ulysses* (1922) and *Finnegans Wake* (1939).

MICHAEL LONGLEY (1939–). Born in Belfast, and educated at the Inst. and Trinity College, Dublin, he taught from 1962 to 1969 before joining the Arts Council of Northern Ireland in 1970. He has published several collections of poetry, from *No Continuing City* (1969) to *Gorse Fires* (1991).

SHEVAWN LYNAM (19–). Born in Dublin, raised in Co. Galway and educated in Madrid, she worked in the Paris headquarters of NATO and with Bord Fáilte from 1963 to 1971. Novelist and broadcaster, she has published many books and articles on a wide range of topics, including a celebrated biography of *Humanity Dick Martin, 'King of Connemara' 1754-1834* (1975/89).

DEREK MAHON (1941–). Born in Belfast, and educated at the Inst. and Trinity College, Dublin, he travelled widely through North America and moved to London in 1970. His first poetry collection, *Night-Crossing* (1969), was followed by many more, culminating in his most recent *Selected Poems* (1991). He has also adapted many Irish and French works for television and stage, and is a noted translator of Jaccottet, the French-Swiss poet.

VIOLET MARTIN (1861–1915). Born in Ross, Co. Galway, she wrote under the name Martin Ross with her cousin Edith Somerville. She also wrote two volumes of autobiography. She never completely recovered from a serious hunting accident in 1898 and died in 1915.

THOMAS HOLMES MASON (1877–1958). Born in Dublin, educated at Wesley College, a noted antiquarian, naturalist and optician, he was best known for his book *The Islands of Ireland* (1936), and his huge collection of photographs. He was active in organizations such as An Taisce (President 1951), the Dublin Naturalist Field Club and the Bird Protection Society. One of the few non-university members of the Royal Irish Academy.

JOHN C. MESSENGER (19–). Professor in the Department of Anthropology at Indiana University, he conducted fieldwork among various communities around the world, including the Anang of south-west Nigeria and the Montserrat Islanders of the West Indies. His study of Inis Oírr was published in 1969 under the title *Inis Beag*. He is currently engaged in a study of the Anglo-Irish.

RIA MOONEY (1904–73). Born in Dublin, she studied in the Metropolitan College of Art, joined the Abbey Theatre Company in 1924 and was chosen by Seán O'Casey to play Rosie Redmond in the first production of *The Plough and the Stars*. She toured Britain and the USA and became Director of the Gaiety School of Acting in 1944. She was also the first woman producer in the Abbey Theatre.

PAT MULLEN (1883–1972). Born on Inis Mór, he emigrated to the USA at the age of nineteen and returned in 1921. He acted as Robert Flaherty's chief assistant during the making of the film *Man of Aran* and wrote a book of the same title giving an account of his experiences (1935). He also wrote a novel set in the Aran Islands, *Hero Breed* (1936), and a collection of folktales collected in Inis Mór, *Irish Tales* (1940).

MÁIRTÍN Ó DIREÁIN (1910–88). Born on Inis Mór, he joined the postal service in Galway in 1928 and played a prominent role in the Taibhdhearc Theatre, 1928–37. He moved to Dublin and spent the war years as a postal censor. He published many collections of verse, of which *Ó Mórna agus Dánta Eile* (1957) is arguably the best. A selection of his poems has been translated into English in *Máirtín Ó Direáin: Selected Poems* (1984). In addition, he published a collection of autobiographical essays, *Feamainn Bhealtaine* (1961). He was awarded an Honorary D. Litt. by the National University of Ireland in 1977.

LIAM O'FLAHERTY (1897–1984). Born on Inis Mór he was educated in Rockwell College, Blackrock and University College, Dublin, studied very briefly for the priesthood and in 1917 joined the Irish Guards under his mother's name of Ganly. Invalided out of the British army after fighting at the Somme, he became involved in the Irish war of independence and civil war. He went to London in 1923 and his first novel, *Thy Neighbour's Wife*, appeared that year. It was followed by *The Black Soul* in 1924 and, possibly his most famous work, *The Informer* in 1925. More novels and short story collections followed, including *Famine* (1935), *Skerrett* (1932) and *Dúil* (1953) – this last his only publication in Irish. Many of his works were banned in Ireland.

RODERICK O'FLAHERTY (1629–1718). Born in Moycullen, Co. Galway, where his family lost Moycullen Castle and its estates in the Cromwellian confiscation, though he later recovered a small portion of them. A noted scholar and historian, he published the *Ogygia*, a history of Ireland in Latin, in 1685. *A Description of West or H-Iar Connaught* was written to help Sir William Petty in his survey and first published in 1846, edited by James Hardiman. Famously described by writer and physician Thomas Molyneaux (1704 Letter, TCD MS. 883). His later years were spent in increasing poverty.

Tom O'Flaherty (1891–1936). Born on Inis Mór, he was an older brother of Liam O'Flaherty's. He emigrated to Boston in 1910 and worked for the *Boston Globe* but left to write and edit various left-wing periodicals for the American Communist Party. He became a Trotskyist when the Party split but returned to Ireland because of bad health. He wrote many articles in both Irish and English for *An tÉireannach* and *The Irish Press*, as well as two books about the Aran Islands, *Aranmen All* (1934) and *Cliffmen of the West* (1935).

Patrick Henry Pearse (1879–1916). A poet and revolutionary, he attended the Royal University and was called to the Bar. He was always deeply interested in the Irish language and devoted most of his energies to promoting it, joining the Gaelic League, editing its newspaper, *An Claidheamh Soluis*, and setting up St Enda's, a bilingual school for boys, in 1908. He spent long periods at his cottage in Ros Muc (in the Connemara Gaeltacht). He joined the Irish Republican Brotherhood, a secret revolutionary organization, in 1913 and was central to the planning of the Easter Rising of 1916. During the Rising he was Commander-in-Chief of the forces of the Irish Republic and President of the Provisional Government. He was courtmartialled and executed on 3 May 1916.

George Petrie (1790–1866). Born in Dublin, he was best known as an artist and antiquary. He exhibited at the Royal Hibernian Academy in 1828, was elected a member the same year and became President in 1857. He contributed hundreds of illustrations to guide-books and he wrote many articles on aspects of Irish history and archaeology. His prize-winning *Essay on the Round Towers of Ireland* appeared in 1833 and *The Ecclesiastical Architecture of Ireland* in 1845. He also collected a large amount of music on his travels, published in 1855 as *The Ancient Music of Ireland*.

Richard Power (Risteard de Paor) (1928–70). Born in Dublin, he was educated in Trinity College, Dublin, and joined the civil service, taking leave of absence in 1959 to study writing at the University of Iowa. Two plays in Irish, *Saoirse* (1955) and *Oidhreacht* (1957), were followed by his description of life in the Aran Islands, *Úll i mBarr an Ghéagáin* (1959), translated in 1980 as *Apple in the Treetop*. He published two more novels, *The Land of Youth* (1964) and *The Hungry Grass* (1966), before his early death.

Tim Robinson (1935–). Born in Yorkshire, he studied mathematics at Cambridge and worked as a teacher and artist in Istanbul, Vienna and London. He moved to the Aran Islands in 1972 and produced maps of the islands in 1975 and 1980, which were followed by maps of the Burren in County Clare and of Connemara. In 1987 he received a prestigious European Conservation Award for his work. *Stones of Aran: Pilgrimage* appeared in 1986, and the second volume, *Labyrinth*, is in preparation.

Etienne Rynne (1932–). Born in Dublin, educated at Clongowes Wood and University College, Dublin, he worked at the National Museum of Ireland for ten years before becoming lecturer at University College, Galway in 1968 and Professor of Archaeology in 1980. Has excavated widely and published numerous papers on the Celtic Iron Age and other matters.

EDITH ŒNONE SOMERVILLE (1858–1949). Born in Corfu, she met her second cousin Violet Martin in 1886 and a literary partnership was born, Violet adopting the pseudonym Martin Ross. Their first work, *An Irish Cousin* (1889), was well received and encouraged them in their efforts. They are best known for *The Real Charlotte* (1894), *Some Experiences of an Irish R.M.* (1899), and *In Mr Knox's Country* (1915). They also wrote many pieces describing their travels around the country. When Violet Martin died in 1915, Edith continued to publish under both their names.

ARTHUR SYMONS (1865–1945). Born in England's West Country, he was a poet and editor of *The Savoy* (1896) but is best known for *The Symbolist Movement in Literature* (1899), an epochal literary survey. He was a close friend of Yeats, Moore and other figures in the Irish Literary Revival, and visited the Aran Islands with Yeats in 1896. After a mental breakdown in 1908 his work declined, although he continued to write for many years.

REVEREND ALEXANDER SYNGE (1821–72). A Protestant clergyman, as were so many of the Synge family, he arrived on Inis Mór in 1851 as first permanent representative of the Church of Ireland and was replaced in 1855 by the Reverend William Kilbride. He received two medals from the Royal Humane Society for saving the lives of sailors. He moved to a parish in Sussex, where he died.

JOHN MILLINGTON SYNGE (1871–1909). Born in Rathfarnham, Dublin, and educated at Trinity College, he travelled extensively throughout Ireland but especially in Wicklow and the Aran Islands. In Paris in 1899 Yeats advised him to set down his experiences of Aran, which led to his world-famous *The Aran Islands* (1907). Writing of Irish affairs for an Irish audience, he can be regarded as Ireland's first true dramatist: *The Shadow of the Glen* (1903), *Riders to the Sea* (1904), *The Well of the Saints* (1905), *The Tinker's Wedding* (1905) and *The Playboy of the Western World* (1907) were attacked and bitterly criticized when first performed in Dublin's Abbey Theatre.

THOMAS JOHNSON WESTROPP (1860–1922). Born in Co. Limerick, he was a noted illustrator and antiquary, becoming a member of the Royal Society of Antiquaries in Ireland in 1886 and President in 1916. A major contributor to the *Clare Island Survey* (1911–15), he wrote on a wide number of subjects in the scholarly journals of the period. His papers and sketches are in the Royal Irish Academy.

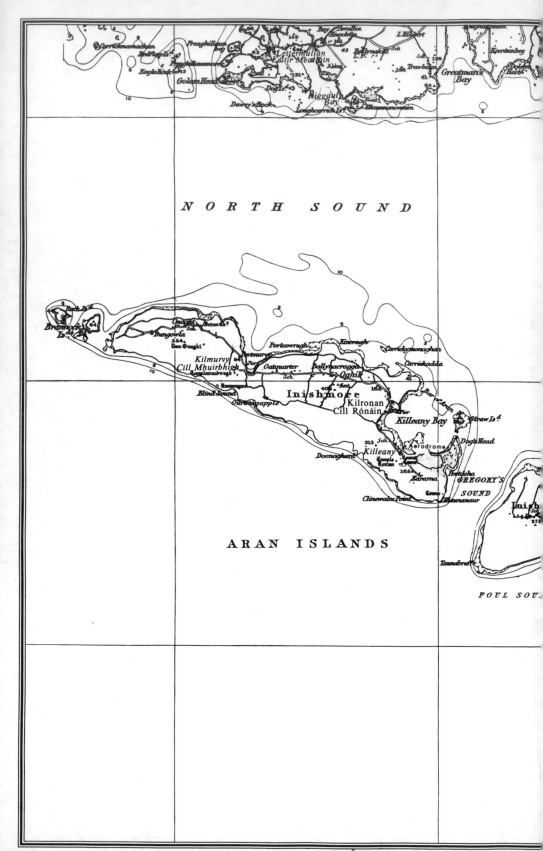

GALWAY BAY

SOUTH SOUND

Black Head

Murrooghtoo

Fanore

Craggagh

Ballyelly

Cloghaunlv

Derreen

Balliny

SLIEVE ELVA

Ailladie

Knockaunsmountain

Megalithic Tomb

Ballynahown

Poulsallagh

Oughtdarra

T H

Ballynalackan Ho.

Inisheer

Trawkeera Point

Aerodrome

Rushgara Point

Knockfin Cross Roads

Cahercoon

Doolin

Roadford

Aille R.

LISDOONVARNA
LIOS DÚIN BHEARNA

Mineral Springs

Spectacle

Crab Is.

Fisherstreet

Sch.

Toomullin

L.Goller

Doonagore Cas.

Ballyvoe

Luogh

Doonmacfelim

Knocknalarabana

Aillenasharragh

Carrownaff

Kilshanny

Inveran
Indreabhán

Loughathevnen

Cannusnagark

Naskannira

Cartronlakan

Ballinluggaun

Aille

Colaiste

Botoona

Spiddle
An Spideal

Banraghaun

Ballynahown
Baile na hAbhann

Blake's Lo.

Ballinteemore

Topletter

Loughaunbeg

Sch.

L.
Nagravin

Clogmore South

Castle Pt.